Rights Guide to Non-Means-Tested

17th edition — General Notes

Paid to carer

Premiums linked To benefits CP, ICA Note
Can apply premium if qualify for benefit icn
But not receiving under overlap Rule

**Richard Poynter
and Clive Martin**
eg qualify for ICA but Spouse
already claiming dep addition
only get one — & still use premium

SDP = Applied if Receiving Middle or higher rate of.
Care comp of DLA ✗ Note if Some-one
claims ICA — lose SDP eg Couple disabled
getting double SDP — lose one SDP if ICA
claimed Note SDP paid on top of DP.
See green book — 342.

SDA = DP.
IVB =

DLA = SDP
SDA = DP
IVB = .

Child Poverty Action Group

First edition 1977 by Richard Drabble
Second edition 1978 by Richard Drabble, Mark Rowland and Nicholas Warren
Third edition 1980 by Mark Rowland
Fourth edition 1981 by Mark Rowland
Fifth edition 1982 by Mark Rowland and Roger Smith
Sixth edition 1983 by Roger Smith
Seventh edition 1984 by Roger Smith and Mark Rowland
Eighth edition 1985 by Roger Smith and Mark Rowland
Ninth edition 1986 by Roger Smith and Mark Rowland
Tenth edition 1987 by Mark Rowland and Jan Luba
Eleventh edition 1988 by Mark Rowland
Twelfth edition 1989 by Mark Rowland, Campbell Kennedy and
    Jeremy McMullen
Thirteenth edition 1990 by Mark Rowland
Fourteenth edition 1991 by Mark Rowland
Fifteenth edition 1992 by Richard Poynter and Clive Martin
Sixteenth edition 1993 by Richard Poynter and Clive Martin
Seventeenth edition 1994 by Richard Poynter and Clive Martin

Published by CPAG Ltd, 1 – 5 Bath Street, London EC1V 9PY

© CPAG Ltd, 1994

A CIP record for this book is available from the British Library

ISBN 0-946744-60-2

Cover and design by Devious Designs, 0742 755634
Typeset by Boldface Typesetters, London EC1
Printed by Bath Press, Avon

The authors

Qualifying conditions pg 158

ICA = Care Comp of DLA or AA.

Richard Poynter is a solicitor. For the last eight years he has worked for Sinclair Taylor & Martin in North Kensington where he has specialised in helping advice workers and representing claimants in disputes with the DSS and local authorities. He has been involved in many test cases and lectures and writes extensively on social security and administrative law.

Clive Martin has worked as a rights adviser for Disability Alliance and as a hospital-based welfare rights officer in Manchester. Clive has been employed as a consultant with Ferret Information Systems Ltd in the development of benefits-related software. He currently works for Manchester city council's advice service.

Disability benefits

Incapable of work – SSP
IVB
SDA

look at Carers premium

Paid to Person.

Care / Mobility needs DLA – Care
– Mobility

AA – 65+.

ICA = goes to Carer. – looking at needs.

apable of work / Low income
isabled – DWA

Special Compensation Scheme.
Industrial Injuries Benefit
– Disablement Benefit
– Reduced earnings Allowance
– War Disablement pensions

Acknowledgements

As always, this year's *Guide* has benefited from readers' comments on previous editions and from new points which other advice workers have come across in practice, and shared with us. We are grateful to all those who have taken the trouble to write to us and make suggestions for improvements. In particular, the comments of Julian Barker, Martin Barnes, Dan Finn, Charles Fuller, Sean Price, David Thomas, Pauline Thompson and Penny Wood are acknowledged with thanks. Others who have provided advice, made useful suggestions and pointed out errors include Carlos Dabezies, Jim Dickson, Richard Drabble, Jane Field, Arnie James, Paul Lewis, Ros Raizada, Pat Strickland, Gary Vaux, Nick Wikeley and David Williams. If you have any comments on this edition, please write to us c/o the Citizens' Rights Office at CPAG, 1-5 Bath Street, London EC1V 9PY.

We would also like to thank our partners, Barbara Zolynski and Caroline Freedman, for putting up with us while the book was being written.

Many thanks to Renée Harris for editing and co-ordinating the production of the book, to June Taylor at Boldface Typesetters for the high quality of her work and to Kay Hart for her index. Thanks are also due to Mary Shirley for checking the notes, Peter Ridpath for promoting the book and to Debbie Haynes for ensuring its distribution far and wide.

Once again, we are extremely grateful to Nick Warren who, as in previous years, made time to read and comment on the whole of the *Guide* in draft, generously placing his knowledge and experience at our disposal under the pressures of a very tight schedule.

Finally, we would like to take this opportunity to congratulate Mark Rowland – the sole or main author of the *Guide* for many years – on his appointment as a social security commissioner. We still benefit from his groundwork on previous editions.

Contents

ABBREVIATIONS   ix

STANDARD RATES OF BENEFIT   x

PREFACE   xii

PART ONE – INTRODUCTION

CHAPTER 1:   **Introduction to the social security system**   2

1. Means-tested and non-means-tested benefits   3
2. Contributory and non-contributory benefits   4
3. Earnings replacement and other non-means-tested benefits   4
4. Short-term and long-term benefits   5

PART TWO – THE BENEFITS

CHAPTER 2: **Unemployment benefit**   8

1. Conditions of entitlement   8
2. Payment   9
3. How to claim   11
4. Availability for work   13
5. Actively seeking employment   20
6. Special rules if you work part-time   25
7. Payments from your previous job   30
8. Disqualifications   33
9. Special rules for people over pensionable age   43
10. Special rules for students   44
11. Other benefits   44
12. Tax   45
13. Future changes   45

CHAPTER 3: **Benefits for people incapable of work**   47

1. Incapacity for work   48
2. 'Invalidity cut-off' – disputes about your capacity for work   51
3. Statutory sick pay   64
4. Sickness benefit   73

5. Invalidity benefit   76
6. Severe disablement allowance   81
7. Future changes   86

CHAPTER 4: **Maternity pay and benefits**   88
1. Statutory maternity pay   88
2. Maternity allowance   95
3. Future changes   96

CHAPTER 5: **Widows' benefits**   97
1. Introduction   97
2. Widow's payment   104
3. Widowed mother's allowance   105
4. Widow's pension   106
5. Industrial death benefit for widows   108
6. Special rules for polygamous and invalid marriages   109

CHAPTER 6: **Retirement pensions**   112
1. Introduction   112
2. Category A retirement pension   116
3. Category B retirement pension for a married woman   119
4. Category B retirement pension for a widow   120
5. Category B retirement pension for a widower   122
6. Category D retirement pension   123
7. Graduated retirement benefit   124
8. Future changes   124

CHAPTER 7: **Benefits for severely disabled people**   126
1. Introduction   126
2. Disability living allowance mobility component   127
3. Disability living allowance care component   134
4. Attendance allowance   142
5. Matters common to disability living allowance and attendance
   allowance   144

CHAPTER 8: **Invalid care allowance**   158
1. Conditions of entitlement   158
2. How to claim   158
3. Amount of payment   159
4. Tax and other benefits   159
5. 'Regularly and substantially' caring   160
6. 'Gainfully employed'   160
7. 'Full-time education'   160
8. People over pensionable age   161

CHAPTER 9: **Industrial injuries benefits**   163
1. Introduction   163

2. Industrial accidents and diseases   164
3. Disablement benefit   175
4. Reduced earnings allowance   179
5. Retirement allowance   186
6. Industrial death benefit   186

CHAPTER 10: **Benefits for children**   188
1. Child benefit   188
2. One parent benefit   195
3. Guardian's allowance   196
4. Child's special allowance   198
5. Industrial death benefit for children   199

CHAPTER 11: **Increases for dependants**   201
1. Introduction   201
2. Extra money for your wife   202
3. Extra money for your husband   203
4. Extra money if you are not married   203
5. Extra money for your children   205
6. Residence and maintenance   206
7. The earnings rules   208
8. Trade disputes   210
9. Tax   211
10. Miscellaneous rules   211

PART THREE – GENERAL PROVISIONS

CHAPTER 12: **Contributions and earnings related pensions**   214
1. Introduction   214
2. Payment of contributions   217
3. Credits and home responsibilities protection   225
4. Contribution conditions for benefit   231
5. The State Earnings Related Pension Scheme (SERPS)   235
6. Future changes   239

CHAPTER 13: **Residence conditions and going abroad**   240
1. Introduction   240
2. Residence and presence conditions   241
3. Absence from Great Britain   245
4. Northern Ireland, the Isle of Man and the Channel Islands   247
5. The European Community and the European Economic Area   248
6. Reciprocal agreements   250

CHAPTER 14: **Other general provisions**   251
  1. Periods of interruption of employment   251
  2. Hospital in-patients   254
  3. People in legal custody   257
  4. Overlapping benefits   258
  5. Calculating earnings   261
  6. Christmas bonus   262
  7. Recovery of benefits from compensation payments   263
  8. Deductions from benefit   265
  9. Criminal offences   265
 10. Equal treatment for men and women   267

PART FOUR – ADMINISTRATION AND APPEALS

CHAPTER 15: **Administration**   276
  1. Claims   276
  2. Decisions   283
  3. Reviews   288
  4. Payments   294
  5. Recovery of overpayments   295
  6. Complaints   301

CHAPTER 16: **Appeals**   303
  1. Social security appeal tribunals   303
  2. Medical appeal tribunals   308
  3. Disability appeal tribunals   311
  4. Social security commissioners   313
  5. Late appeals   318
  6. How to prepare an appeal   323

APPENDICES
APPENDIX 1: Miscellaneous benefits for the disabled   331
APPENDIX 2: Prescribed degrees of disablement   338
APPENDIX 3: Prescribed industrial diseases   340
APPENDIX 4: Social security adjudication   350
APPENDIX 5: Books, leaflets and periodicals   352
APPENDIX 6: Legislation   355

NOTES   360
INDEX   382

Abbreviations used in the text

AO	Adjudication officer
CTB	Council tax benefit
DAT	Disability appeal tribunal
DLA	Disability living allowance
DWA	Disability working allowance
EC	European Community
EEA	European Economic Area
ECJ	European Court of Justice
EOC	Equal Opportunities Commission
FC	Family credit
HB	Housing benefit
ICA	Invalid care allowance
IS	Income support
MAT	Medical appeal tribunal
REA	Reduced earnings allowance
IVB	Invalidity benefit
SDA	Severe disablement allowance
SMP	Statutory maternity pay
SSAT	Social security appeal tribunal
SSP	Statutory sick pay
UB	Unemployment benefit

STANDARD RATES OF BENEFIT FROM 11 APRIL 1994

Earnings replacement benefits

	Claimant £pw	Adult dependant £pw	Child dependant £pw
Unemployment benefit			
under pensionable age	45.45	28.05	
of or over pensionable age	57.60	34.50	11.00*
Sickness benefit			
under pensionable age	43.45	26.90	
of or over pensionable age	55.25	33.10	11.00*
Invalidity pension	57.60	34.50	11.00*
Invalidity allowance			
higher rate	12.15		
middle rate	7.60		
lower rate	3.80		
Statutory sick pay			
higher rate	52.50		
lower rate	47.80		
Severe disablement allowance	34.80	20.70	11.00*
Age-related addition – higher rate	12.15		
middle rate	7.60		
lower rate	3.80		
Statutory maternity pay (lower rate)	48.80		
Maternity allowance	44.55	26.90	
Invalid care allowance	34.50	20.65	11.00*
Widowed mother's allowance	57.60		11.00*
Widow's pension	57.60		
Non-contributory widow's benefit	34.50		11.00*
Retirement pension			
Category A	57.60	34.50	11.00*
Category B for a married woman	34.50		11.00*
Category B for a widow	57.60		11.00*
Category B for a widower	57.60		11.00*
Category C for a person not a			
married woman	34.50	20.65	11.00*
Category C for a married woman	20.65		11.00*
Category D	34.50		

Benefits for the severely disabled   £pw

Attendance allowance		
higher rate		45.70
lower rate		30.55
Disability living allowance		
care component	higher rate	45.70
	middle rate	30.55
	lower rate	12.15
mobility component	higher rate	31.95
	lower rate	12.15

Industrial injuries benefits

Assessment of disablement		£pw	
		lower rate	higher rate
Disablement benefit			
	100 per cent	57.70	93.20
	90 per cent	51.39	83.88
	80 per cent	45.68	74.56
	70 per cent	39.97	65.24
	60 per cent	34.26	55.92
	50 per cent	28.55	46.60
	40 per cent	22.84	37.28
	30 per cent	17.13	27.96
	20 per cent	11.42	18.64

Constant attendance allowance	
higher maximum	74.80
lower maximum	37.40
Exceptionally severe disablement allowance	37.40
Reduced earnings allowance (maximum)	37.28
Retirement allowance (maximum)	9.32

Industrial death benefit   £pw

Widow	
higher permanent rate	57.60
lower permanent rate	17.28
Widower	57.60
Child	11.00*

Benefits for children   £pw

Child benefit	
for the only, elder or eldest child for whom benefit is being claimed	10.20
for other children	8.25
One parent benefit	6.15
Guardian's allowance	11.00*
Child's special allowance	11.00*

* These are reduced by £1.20 for any child for whom you receive the higher rate of child benefit.

Preface

Developments in the field of non-means-tested benefits over the past year have been few and generally of a technical nature, but the *Guide* has continued the trend – noted in earlier prefaces – to put on weight. This is because, following the *Guide*'s policy of concentrating on the areas of social security law which cause practical problems for claimants and their advisers, we have expanded and improved the coverage of a number of difficult areas.

The first of these is the section in Chapter 3 which deals with disputes about incapacity for work. This has been entirely rewritten to take account of the tightening of Benefits Agency procedures and to give clearer advice on the tactics which can be used to ensure that benefit is not stopped incorrectly. We hope that the increasing number of claimants who are facing the worry and stress of an 'invalidity cut-off' on top of their ill-health will find it easier to use.

Chapter 7 has also been revised. There is an expanded, more practical section on the special rules about entitlement to disability living allowance care component and attendance allowance in certain types of accommodation. There is also more detail on using the review process.

An entirely new section deals in greater detail with the European Community Directive which forbids sex discrimination in the rules for non-means-tested benefits (Chapter 14). Realistically, anyone whose own claim for benefit is referred to the European Court of Justice will need specialist legal help, but this section is designed to help claimants who may be affected by a European test case (and their advisers) to identify and understand the issues.

Another new section in Chapter 16 gives detailed tactical advice about the rules for late appeals and, in particular, what amounts to a 'special reason'. This has been included because of the widespread failure of 'late appeal' campaigns which have aimed to circumvent the 'anti-test-case rules' following the *Cottingham and Geary* case on occupational pensions and the dependant's earnings rule, and the *McSherry* decision on building insurance and income support. The moral of this failure unfortunately seems to be that more attention needs to be paid to the individual details of each case. There is almost always some sort of 'special reason' if you look hard enough for it but this does need to be identified and explained to the tribunal chair or commissioner. A *pro forma* letter simply asking for a late appeal to take advantage of a favourable test-case decision generally does not succeed.

Perhaps because of the increasing length of the queue in the Court of Appeal and for judicial reviews in the High Court, the year has also been short on court decisions. It is pleasant to be able to report a major success for claimants in the *Kitchen and Evans* case where the Court of Appeal held that the regulation which obliges medical appeal tribunals to give reasons for their decisions means what it says: we hope that the decision will have a knock-on effect for the decisions of other tribunals which have to consider medical issues. On the downside, the practical effect of the Court's decision in *Jones and Sharples* is to blur the distinction between a misrepresentation and a failure to disclose and seems likely to cause additional hardship for claimants who through no fault of their own have been overpaid benefit. The failure of the *McKiernon* appeal on the retrospective validation of the absolute time limits for those suffering from occupational deafness and occupational asthma to claim disablement benefit is also disappointing.

If few major changes to non-means-tested benefits have been implemented since the last edition of the *Guide*, announcements of future changes have come thick and fast as national insurance benefits suffer the brunt of the Government's cost-cutting offensive. The most important of these are the abolition of sickness and invalidity benefit next year, the abolition of unemployment benefit in 1996 and the increase in pensionable age for women to 65 with effect from 2010. Details of these announcements are contained in Chapters 2, 3, 6 and 13 and will be updated in CPAG's *Welfare Rights Bulletin* and in subsequent editions of this *Guide*.

However, the idea that social security spending is in crisis and can only be contained within what will be accepted by taxpayers by swingeing cuts in entitlement is itself highly questionable. The increase in the social security budget has been caused largely by circumstances outside the welfare system, most notably the large rise in unemployment. To respond to this by inflicting futher cuts on those who already have least is, quite simply, indefensible. For more information and a resounding refutation of the notion that non-means-tested benefits are badly targeted or could be replaced by self-insurance, readers should turn to Carey Oppenheim's excellent *The Welfare State: Putting The Record Straight*, available from CPAG (£4.95).

Richard Poynter and Clive Martin
March 1994

PART ONE

Introduction

CHAPTER ONE

Introduction to the social security system

This chapter covers:

1. Means-tested and non-means-tested-benefits (p3)
2. Contributory and non-contributory benefits (p4)
3. Earnings replacement and other non-means-tested benefits (p4)
4. Short-term and long-term benefits (p5)

The social security system is notoriously complex. This chapter provides a brief introduction to it and to this *Guide* by describing the various types of benefit which are available.

This *Guide* covers only benefits under the legislation of **Great Britain**, which consists of England, Wales and Scotland, but *not* Northern Ireland, the Isle of Man or the Channel Islands (see p247).

With one exception, the rules for each non-means-tested benefit are set out in Part Two. The exception is war pensions which are administered under a separate system within the Department of Social Security (DSS). A brief description of them and other forms of compensation and assistance not generally regarded as part of the social security system is contained in Appendix One.

Some rules are common to all or many of the benefits and to save space these have been set out once in Part Three rather than repeated for each of the benefits to which they apply. As well as the contribution and residence conditions and the overlapping benefits rules (see p258), Part Three deals with the special rules for people in hospital or in prison, what happens to your benefit if you go abroad, how earnings are calculated and what a 'period of interruption of employment' is. It also explains the European Community (EC) rules which, in most cases, prevent the DSS from treating men more favourably than women – and vice versa – and summarises the present state of the case law on which benefits may and may not be paid on a discriminatory basis.

Part Four deals with the rules about the administration of the social security system – ie, how and when to claim, what happens to your claim when you have made it and what to do if you are unhappy with the outcome.

The *Guide* tries to give answers to most of the problems which claimants meet in practice. But to answer a particular question, you may sometimes also have to look at the Acts of Parliament, regulations and decisions of the courts and social security commissioners which govern the social security system. The footnotes in each section are designed to tell you where to find the relevant legislation and cases, and a list of all the most important Acts and regulations is contained in Appendix Six. Appendix Five has a list of books and periodicals to which you can refer for help and the section on 'Checking the law' in Chapter 16 may give you tips for further research, even if your problem has not yet reached the stage where you are preparing an appeal.

1. MEANS-TESTED AND NON-MEANS-TESTED BENEFITS

Some benefits are paid only if you have limited income and capital. These benefits are known as **means-tested benefits** because there is an investigation into your means before you can be paid them. The most important are:

• income support if you *are not* in full-time work;
• family credit if you *are* in full-time work;
• disability working allowance if you *are* in full-time work; *and*
• housing benefit and council tax benefit whether or not you are in full-time work.

These benefits are *not* covered in this *Guide*. Instead, you should look at CPAG's *National Welfare Benefits Handbook* (24th edn, 1994 £7.95 post-free from CPAG Ltd).

This *Guide* is concerned with **non-means-tested benefits**, which do not involve a detailed investigation of your finances. You will be entitled if you satisfy certain basic conditions (called 'conditions of entitlement') such as being available for work, disabled or widowed. It may still be relevant to ask whether you have any earnings or an occupational pension, because many of the benefits are designed to compensate for your loss of earnings, but other types of income will not affect your entitlement. Similarly, you may be entitled to non-means-tested benefits even if you have savings or other capital.

2. CONTRIBUTORY AND NON-CONTRIBUTORY BENEFITS

The most important division of non-means-tested benefits is between those which are contributory and those which are not.

Contributory benefits	Non-contributory benefits
Unemployment benefit	Severe disablement allowance
Sickness benefit	Invalid care allowance
Invalidity benefit	Non-contributory widows' benefits
Maternity allowance	Category C & D retirement pension
Widow's payment	Disability living allowance
Widowed mother's allowance	Attendance allowance
Widow's pension	Industrial injuries benefits
Category A & B retirement	Child benefit
pensions	One parent benefit
Graduated Retirement Benefit	Guardian's allowance
	Child's special allowance

Contributory benefits are paid out of the National Insurance Fund. This is funded by social security contributions and one of the conditions of entitlement to contributory benefits is that you should, in the past, have made sufficient contributions to the Fund. These are known as 'contribution conditions' and are discussed in Chapter 12. However, unlike non-contributory benefits, there are no residence conditions (see below) for contributory benefits.

Non-contributory benefits are paid out of general taxation (except guardian's allowance which is paid out of the National Insurance Fund). It is a condition of entitlement to all of them that you must have lived in Great Britain (or, in some cases, in a member state of the European Community) for a period in the past. These are known as 'residence conditions'. Residence conditions are explained in detail in Chapter 13.

3. EARNINGS REPLACEMENT AND OTHER NON-MEANS-TESTED BENEFITS

Many benefits exist to compensate you for your inability to work through unemployment, sickness, pregnancy or old age. Others exist to meet particular needs because you are disabled or have children, irrespective of your ability to work.

[handwritten: can only receive one]

Earnings replacement and other non-means-tested benefits 5

Earnings replacement	Other benefits *[handwritten: Claim]*
Unemployment benefit *[handwritten: can only receive]*	*[handwritten: Those in italics]* Disability living allowance *[handwritten: but look]*
Sickness benefit	Attendance allowance *[handwritten: at qualifying]*
Invalidity benefit	Industrial injuries benefits *[handwritten: rules.]*
Severe disablement allowance	Child benefit *[handwritten: in addition]*
Maternity allowance	One parent benefit
Invalid care allowance	Guardian's allowance
Retirement pensions	Child's special allowance

The basic rule is that you may only receive one 'earnings replacement benefit' at a time. However, you may receive any number of the other benefits whether or not you also receive an earnings replacement benefit. These are known as the **'overlapping benefits'** rules (see Chapter 14).

Most earnings replacement benefits have **'earnings rules'** which limit the amount of earnings you may receive while remaining entitled to the benefit. Retirement pensions are an exception. The reason for this is that you (or your spouse) have earned your pension and ought not to lose out if you continue in employment. The decision to work or not is up to you.

Widows' benefits have not been included in the list above. They exist to replace the earnings of the widow's late husband and therefore her own earnings are ignored. The decision whether or not she should work is left to her, since her benefit was earned by her husband. Widows' benefits are not paid in addition to any other earnings replacement benefits which the widow may be entitled to in her own right. Special benefits are not usually paid to widowers – not even to those who were wholly financially dependent on their late wives. Widows' benefits are one of the few exceptions to the general rule of European Community law that social security benefits must not discriminate against men or women because of their sex (see p267).

Reduced earnings allowance and retirement allowance (both industrial injuries benefits and now being phased out) are payable on top of earnings replacement benefits.

4. SHORT-TERM AND LONG-TERM BENEFITS

This division applies only to earnings replacement benefits (including widows' benefits). As their names suggest, short-term benefits are paid for a limited period only whereas long-term benefits are paid for as long as the conditions of entitlement remain satisfied.

Short-term benefits	**Long-term benefits**
Unemployment benefit	Invalidity benefit
Sickness benefit	Severe disablement allowance
Maternity allowance	Invalid care allowance
Widow's payment	Widows' benefits (other than widow's payment)
	Retirement pensions (including graduated retirement benefit)

There are no non-contributory short-term benefits and, with the exception of widow's payment, the contributory short-term benefits all depend upon your having satisfied a contribution condition in the fairly recent past (unless you are over pensionable age). For widow's payment, the single contribution can have been satisfied in any year of the deceased husband's working life.

Short-term benefits are paid at a lower rate than contributory long-term benefits and, unlike long-term benefits, no increases are paid for dependent children unless the claimant is over pensionable age (see p113).

If you are receiving a contributory long-term benefit, you may also be entitled to an additional pension under the State Earnings Related Pension Scheme (SERPS). Details of this are given in Chapter 12.

PART TWO

The benefits

CHAPTER TWO

Unemployment benefit

This chapter covers:

1. Conditions of entitlement (see below)
2. Payment (p9)
3. How to claim (p11)
4. Availability for work (p13)
5. Actively seeking employment (p20)
6. Special rules if you work part-time (p25)
7. Payments from your previous job (p30)
8. Disqualifications (p33)
9. Special rules for people over pensionable age (p43)
10. Special rules for students (p44)
11. Other benefits (p44)
12. Tax (p45)
13. Future changes (p45)

I. CONDITIONS OF ENTITLEMENT[1]

- You claim within the time limit (see p280).
- You satisfy the contribution conditions (see p231) – these differ according to whether you are over or under pensionable age (see p43).
- For each day you receive benefit you are:
  – unemployed (but see p25); *and*
  – capable of, and available for, work (see p13).
- You are actively seeking employment (see p20).
- Each day for which you claim benefit falls within a 'period of interruption of employment' (see p251).

2. PAYMENT

Amount of payment[1]

	Claimant under pensionable age £pw	Claimant of, or over, pensionable age £pw
Claimant	45.45	57.60
Adult dependant	28.05	34.50
Child dependant	–	11.00

The daily rate is one-sixth of the weekly rate.[2] Payment is usually made fortnightly in arrears by girocheque.[3]

Pensionable age is 60 for a woman and 65 for a man (see p113).

Unemployment benefit (UB) is paid at a reduced rate if you are over pensionable age and only partially fulfil the contribution conditions for a Category A or (if you are a widow or widower), Category B retirement pension (see pp223-235). For other special rules for pensioners, see p43.

Duration

UB is not paid for the first three days of any 'period of interruption of employment'.[4] In practice this means that when you first claim UB you will not normally be paid for the first three days you are out of work. These are known as **'waiting days'**.

However, you do not have to wait a further three days if you become unemployed within eight weeks from when you last received UB, sickness benefit or invalidity benefit.

Example

You lose your job and are unemployed for two weeks. You then obtain temporary employment for a fortnight before becoming unemployed again. You will not receive UB for the first three days of the first spell of unemployment. However, you will be paid benefit from the very first day of your second claim.

You were employed on a temporary contract, but after you are injured in a car accident, your employer refuses to keep your job open for you. You receive sickness benefit while you are recovering, but when you become well enough to work again, you claim UB as you no longer have a job to go to. You will be paid benefit from the first day of your claim.

This is the 'linking rule'. In some circumstances, two periods of unemployment or illness are treated as part of the same 'period of interruption of employment'. For more details, see p253.

UB is a short-term benefit (see p5) and, once you have served the 'waiting days' (see above) it is paid for a maximum of a year (or, more precisely, 312 days – 52 six day weeks[5]) within any single period of interruption of employment (see p251). Once this period has expired you can only become entitled to UB again if you requalify for benefit (see below).

However, if you have not yet been paid benefit for the full 312 days, it may be possible for you to *break your claim* for benefit for at least eight *consecutive* weeks so that your old period of interruption of employment ends and, when you reclaim, a new one begins (see p254).

Requalifying for benefit[6]

To requalify for UB you must work for at least 16 hours a week for 13 weeks after the end of the last week during which you were entitled to UB. For this purpose a 'week' begins on a Sunday and ends the following Saturday.[7]

The 13 weeks need not be consecutive but they must normally be within the 26 weeks before the date of your claim or, if that would be more favourable to you, your first day of unemployment since you last worked.[8]

However, this rule will not apply to you if during any week of the 26-week period:[9]

- you did not work, or worked for less than 16 hours; *and*
- for at least one day in that week
  - you were entitled to statutory sick pay, sickness benefit, invalidity benefit, statutory maternity pay, maternity allowance, invalid care allowance or severe disablement allowance;[10] *or*
  - you were undergoing Training for Work and entitled to a 'training allowance'.[11]

If any of these exceptions applies to you, then any such weeks are ignored when calculating the 26-week period as long as the 13 weeks' work is still done within the 78 weeks before you claim or the first day on which you are unemployed since you last worked.[12]

When you requalify you will have to serve a further three waiting days.[13]

Breaking your claim

If you do not claim UB for eight consecutive weeks a new 'period of interruption of employment' (see p251) will begin when you reclaim benefit. After you have served a further three waiting days, UB will be paid for up to a further 312 days, provided you satisfy the contribution conditions at the date of your new claim (see p231). So, if you have been off work for a long time but have not yet used up the 312 days – and therefore do not need to requalify (see p10) – it may be in your interest to break your claim.

But before you decide to sign off for eight weeks, you should consider your position very carefully. First, for this purpose you cannot end your period of interruption of employment simply by not claiming. Unless you were working or genuinely unavailable for work – eg, because you were abroad or on a long touring holiday in the UK[14] – you must be able to prove to the Benefits Agency that when you failed to claim, you did not intend to avoid the need to requalify. If you cannot, you will be treated as if you had been entitled to unemployment benefit during the time that you did not claim.[15]

You should also remember that if you make yourself unavailable for work, you are likely to lose any entitlement to income support and to be credited with Class 1 contributions (see p225) for that period.

3. HOW TO CLAIM

UB is administered on behalf of the DSS by the Employment Service, an 'executive agency' of the Department of Employment. Unless you live in a rural area (see p12), you claim by attending in person at an unemployment benefit office – not necessarily in the same place as the JobCentre. This, and the subsequent claims which you will normally have to make each fortnight, is known as 'signing on'.

It is usual to sign on at the unemployment benefit office which is nearest to your home. But if a different office is more convenient for you – perhaps because it is easier to reach by public transport, you are entitled to sign on there. If you claim at an unemployment benefit office which is not near your home and you have not given a good reason, you may be suspected of fraud.

If at all possible, you should take your P45 tax form from your previous job with you when you go to sign on for the first time. Your employer is obliged to give you this immediately after paying you your last wages or salary. If s/he has not done so, or if you have mislaid it, do not delay your claim but take the P45 to the unemployment benefit office as soon as you receive or find it. In this case, the Employment Service will want to know your national insurance number (although again you should not delay your claim if you cannot remember it).

When you go to the unemployment benefit office for the first time, you will be seen by a member of staff called a 'new client receptionist'. His/her job is to provide you with a claim form and, unless this is inappropriate – eg, if you are re-claiming after a short spell of temporary work – to arrange an appointment with a 'new client adviser' (see below).

Unfortunately, there have been instances where new client receptionists (and sometimes other members of staff) have wrongly discouraged people from claiming or given incorrect advice about entitlement to UB. If this happens to you it can amount to 'good cause' for making a late claim (see p281) and/or give you grounds for suing the Employment Service for compensation for damages for negligent misrepresentation. But this is a cumbersome process and the best way to avoid being caught up in it is not to be put off at this early stage. Although an adjudication officer (see p283) may refuse you benefit (subject to your rights of appeal – see p304) no one, from the new client receptionist and the new client adviser to the Secretary of State him/herself, can stop you from making a claim for benefit and you should insist on doing so.

At your interview with the new client adviser your availability for work will be discussed (see p13) and you will be given a 'Back to Work Plan' containing details of some steps which you are advised to take to find work. For more details of the requirement that you should 'actively seek work' see p20.

Although the basic rule is that UB is a 'daily benefit' and there is a reserve power to require you to sign on on each individual day for which you wish to be paid,[1] you will usually be allowed to make fortnightly claims and, at the end of your interview with the new client adviser, will be given a regular day and time to sign on.[2] It is important that you keep these appointments – failure to attend without good cause can lose you benefit.

You must attend in person at the unemployment benefit office if you are required to do so.[3] But the Employment Service allows claimants who live more than 10 miles from the unemployment benefit office to claim by post. Those who live more than six miles but less than 10 miles away have to claim in person at the beginning but can sign on by post afterwards. You can also claim by post if the journey to the unemployment benefit office would cause you hardship, either because you are disabled or the journey is very difficult.

If you are required to sign on every day, it is probably because you are suspected of working while claiming. This decision is taken by the Secretary of State rather than an adjudication officer and therefore you cannot appeal against it (see p286). However, you can try to persuade the Employment Service that its suspicions are unfounded, and that you should be allowed to sign on less frequently.

It will occasionally be in your interest to delay making a claim (see p232) but normally you should claim UB on the very first day that you are out of work. If you do not do so, you are likely to lose money unless you have 'good cause' for a late claim (see p281).

4. AVAILABILITY FOR WORK

Capable of work

If you are unable to work because you are ill or disabled then, obviously, you cannot be available for work. For this reason, it is a condition of entitlement to UB that you should be 'capable of work'.[1] This is simply the opposite of being 'incapable of work' (see p48). For advice about signing on if you are appealing against a decision not to pay you one of the benefits described in Chapter 3 see p63.

Similarly you do not count as capable of work if you are cannot work *legally*. So, if your immigration status prohibits you from taking employment or if you could not take a job without first applying for a work permit, you are not entitled to unemployment benefit.[2]

Availability for work

As well as being capable of work, you must also be available to work as an 'employed earner' (see p175) in any job which you can reasonably be expected to do.[3] The reference to employment 'as an employed earner' means that refusal of an offer of self-employment will not be regarded as affecting your availability but also that being available for self-employment only is not sufficient.

To be available, you must be willing and able to accept any suitable job offer at once (for exceptions see 'Deemed availability' – p14).

An adjudication officer can contest your availability for work without having to show that you have actually turned down a job offer.[4]

Restricting your availability

You are treated as not being available for work if you place restrictions on the sort of job you are prepared to accept,[5] unless you can prove that you still have a reasonable chance of getting a job despite those restrictions.[6] This includes restrictions on:

- the type of work you are prepared to do; *or*
- the hours you are willing to work; *or*
- the conditions of employment you will accept; *or*
- the location of the job; *or*
- the rate of pay.

If you have a usual occupation this rule does not apply during your **permitted period**.[7] This is a short period of *up* to 13 weeks from the time you first claim unemployment benefit during which you are allowed to concentrate your search for work on vacancies in your normal line of work and to refuse to take or look for jobs that are not what you would normally do. But any restrictions you place on your availability during this period must be *consistent* with the conditions of work that are normal in your occupation. So, for example, if you are a professional footballer you will be allowed to refuse a job in a shop during your permitted period because that is not your usual occupation – but if you refuse a particular job playing football on the grounds that you prefer not to work Saturdays, you are likely to be refused benefit.

The length of your permitted period is in practice decided by the new client adviser at your interview when you first sign on. It can be, and often is, less than the maximum 13 weeks. In making the decision, s/he must take into account what your 'usual occupation' is, your skills and qualifications, the time you have spent training for and working in that occupation, how long it is since you last worked in that occupation and the availability of jobs in that area of work.[8] You have a right of appeal to a Social Security Appeal Tribunal (SSAT) if the length of your permitted period is set at less than 13 weeks and you are refused benefit as a result.

You can also place restrictions on your availability if these are reasonable in view of your physical or mental condition.[9] So, if you suffer from angina you can refuse to undertake strenuous physical work and if you are agoraphobic you do not have to take a job as a gardener. If the restrictions you impose are reasonable ones for you, then it does not matter that they mean you have no reasonable prospects of obtaining employment. But if you have no prospects at all you should consider whether you really are capable of work. If not, it may be in your interest to claim one of the benefits in Chapter 3 instead of UB. In particular, once you qualify for invalidity benefit, it is paid at a higher rate than UB, lasts indefinitely and entitles you to a disability premium when your entitlement to income support and some other income related benefits is assessed (see CPAG's *National Welfare Benefits Handbook* for further details).

Even if you impose unreasonable restrictions on the work you will do, you will still be regarded as available for work if the *only* reason they stop you from having reasonable prospects of getting a job is because of *temporary* adverse industrial conditions in your area.[10]

'Deemed' availability

The requirement that you should be available for employment immediately could, if strictly applied, prevent you from doing any work – paid or unpaid – while you are claiming unemployment benefit. There are therefore a few limited exceptions to this rule. You will be treated ('deemed') as if you were available for immediate employment if:

- you are engaged in providing a service; *and*
  - you can be available on 24 hours' notice (48 hours if you are a volunteer – see below) to start a job or attend an interview; *and*
  - it would not be reasonable to require you to be available at less than 24 hours' notice (or 48 hours if you are a volunteer).[11]

This exception applies whether or not you are being paid for the service you are providing. But it is mostly used to allow people to do voluntary work while claiming UB. You count as a volunteer if you are working for a charity or other non-profit organisation or doing voluntary work for anyone other than a member of your family *and* you do not receive any payment other than expenses.[12] For more on part-time work while claiming UB see pp25-30;

- you are
  - engaged in crewing or launching a lifeboat;[13] *or*
  - carrying out duties as a part-time firefighter;[14] *or*
  - working for the benefit of others by helping to save life, prevent injury or protect property in an emergency following a fire, flood, explosion, accident, national catastrophe or in an organised search for a missing person;[15]
- (for a maximum of 14 days – excluding Sundays – in any calendar year) you are attending a residential work camp organised by a charity or local authority providing a service of benefit to the community.[16]

There are also rules which may deem you to be available for work while a decision is being made on whether you are actually available for work (see p18).

Checking your availability

First interview

One of the forms which you will be given when you first visit the unemployment benefit office is an ES461. This form asks for a lot of information including:

- details of your last three jobs;
- your qualifications;
- the kind of job you are looking for;
- what other jobs you will accept;
- the minimum wage or salary you are seeking;

- the areas in which you are looking for, or would be prepared to accept, a job;
- when you can start;
- what hours you are prepared to work;
- whether your health imposes any limits on the work you can do; *and*
- whether you have children or dependent adults for whom you have to care during working hours.

Your answers to these questions will form the basis for your interview with the new client adviser (see p12) and subsequently for the decision on whether you are available for work. It is very important that you fill it in properly.

If possible you should not fill in the form at the unemployment benefit office but take it home and complete it in your own time. As everyone's circumstances are different there are no 'right' answers, but there are a number of general rules to bear in mind:

- Take your time, think carefully and read the notes that come with the form before answering the questions. Write out your answers in draft on a separate piece of paper if you are not sure. If English is not your first language or if you have difficulties with reading and writing, ask someone (preferably not an employee of the Employment Service) to help you.
- Be truthful. The other parts of this chapter explain what you have to do to qualify for UB. If you have doubts about whether you come within the rules, it is far better to face up to any difficulty from the beginning and see if you can rearrange things so that you can make yourself eligible. For example, if you look after children and at present are not available to start work or attend a job interview at a moment's notice, you could try to change your childcare arrangements so that you have more flexibility. Above all, it is unwise simply to write out the standard answers you may have read in advice leaflets – your new client adviser has read them too and will use the interview to explore what they actually mean in your case. As a result you will still have to answer the questions but will not have the time you would otherwise have had to consider your replies.
- Keep a copy of your answers. You will certainly be asked the same questions again if you are unemployed for more than six months and it may be sooner than that. If your answers differ, there may well be a good reason but you should be prepared to explain what it is.
- Be realistic. When you fill in the form you should describe the sort of job you would be prepared to accept and not the sort of job you would ideally like. In particular, except during your 'permitted period' (see p13), you are not entitled to insist that you will only accept a job that

pays as much as your last one – rather, it is *vital* that the minimum wage or salary you say you will accept should not be higher than the going rate for the jobs you have said you would be prepared to take. If it is, the Employment Service is likely to say that you are imposing unreasonable restrictions and have no reasonable prospects of obtaining employment (see p13). If you are not sure what figure to give, you can write 'the going rate for the job' and say that you will see what is on offer. Similarly, while it is always a good idea to emphasize that you are being flexible in your search for work, you should mention any good reasons why you cannot take certain types of job or jobs in certain areas – if you do not, it may prove very difficult to justify turning down such a job if it is offered to you later.

Certain questions on the form present particular difficulties. For example:

- The questions about dependent children or adults need careful thought. If you have children and either your partner is working or you have no partner, the new client adviser will want to know what plans you have for their care if you get a job. Because you have to be available for work at short notice, you must be able to show that you have a plan worked out or the adjudication officer is likely to refuse your claim for benefit. You may have a particular childminder lined up. If not, are you intending to find one or to make use of a relative or friend as an emergency measure if a job suddenly comes up? If so, make sure they are not claiming UB themselves before you tell the new client adviser!

- When answering the question about what hours and on which days you are prepared to work, remember that Saturday is an ordinary working day for UB purposes. If you refuse to work on it you run the risk of losing a sixth of your benefit each week. And if you are looking for jobs in areas where Saturday working is customary, a refusal to work Saturdays may lead to your being refused benefit altogether on the basis that because of this restriction on your availability, you do not have reasonable prospects of obtaining employment (see p13).

- You are normally expected to be prepared to travel for up to an hour both to and from work, unless you have a good reason. If you are too restrictive about the areas in which you say you are prepared to look for, or accept, work the adjudication officer may say that you are unavailable. The important thing is to be able to give a good reason for your answers. For example, if you do not drive and there is little public transport in your area, it may be reasonable to refuse to look for jobs beyond walking distance. On the other hand you might, in some circumstances, be expected to move if a job is offered to you.

If, at the end of the interview, the new client adviser has doubts about your availability, s/he will send your papers to an adjudication officer for a decision on this point, or perhaps you might be asked to see another adviser.

Restart interview

If you are still unemployed after about six months, you will be invited to a 'Restart' interview. This is an invitation you cannot refuse. You will be disqualified from benefit if:[17]

- you fail to attend the interview following a written request; *and*
- within 14 days of that interview, a further written notice is issued calling you to another interview; *and*
- without good cause, you fail to attend the second interview.

Benefit will be stopped from the date of your second missed interview until either you do attend an interview or the notice is revoked. If you had good reasons for not attending the interviews (eg, you did not receive the appointment, or there was a sudden emergency which you had to deal with, or you did try to attend but unexpected transport difficulties prevented you from doing so), you should put in an appeal and write directly to the person sending the notices. The latter may lead to your benefit being reinstated long before an appeal can be heard.

The form used as the basis for the Restart interview – form UB671R – is very similar to form ES461 (see p15) but goes on to ask you what you have been doing to find work and whether you need help to get back to work. You should bring with you the records you have kept of your attempts to find work (see p21).

At the interview you may be given details of a job interview. Alternatively, you may be offered one or more of a number of options, including the opportunity to join a Jobclub, a Restart course, a Training for Work scheme, the Enterprise Allowance scheme or to do voluntary work. In some inner city areas, there are also job interview guarantee schemes. Full details of these schemes are beyond the scope of this *Guide* but can be obtained from the *Unemployment and Training Rights Handbook* and other booklets published by the Unemployment Unit and Youthaid (see Appendix Five).

If you decline all offers of assistance, your case will be referred to an adjudication officer who may decide either that you are not really available for work or, if you have refused an offer of employment or training (see p37), that you should be disqualified from benefit for a specific period. You will be deemed to be available during the time that the adjudication officer takes to make up his or her mind.[18]

If you are asked to provide further evidence that you are available for work, you will also be deemed to be available for a month (or a longer period if the Employment Service agrees) to give you time to comply with the request.[19] For more on 'deemed' availability see p14.

There may be a follow up Restart interview a few weeks after the main interview when further offers may be made.

Looking for a job can be a difficult, depressing and frustrating experience and many claimants find Restart interviews – and in particular having to justify their attempts to find work to a person in authority under the threat that their benefit may be stopped – very intimidating. If you feel this way, consider whether any of the following might help:

- take a friend or relative with you to act as a witness, provide moral support and take notes. This has a number of advantages:
  - misunderstandings by the Employment Service over your answers at the Restart Interview can lead to disputes about whether you are available for and/or actively seeking employment. You are much more likely to win an appeal if someone else heard what was said and agrees with your recollection of what happened – particularly if that is backed up by contemporaneous written notes. If you have difficulties with English, it is *vital* that someone else – preferably an interpreter – should be present;
  - Employment service staff are told to treat claimants with courtesy but, as in any walk of life, a minority do not. Simply having someone else in the room is likely to inhibit discourteous or intimidating behaviour.
- If there is no one you can ask to come to the interview with you, make sure you take notes yourself.
- If you feel you have an irreconcilable personality clash with your adviser, ask for him or her to be changed.

Holidays while you are unemployed

While you are on UB, you may be allowed to take up to two weeks' holiday in a year.[20] A 'year' in this context means 'any period of 12 months', *not* a calendar year.

Example

You are unemployed and take two weeks' holiday from 8-21 August 1994. You return to work in October 1994 and requalify for benefit but lose your job again in April 1995. While you were working, you booked a holiday from 19 June-2 July 1995.

Although the two holidays are in separate calendar years, they are in the same period of 12 months. You will not get benefit if you decide not to cancel the second.

The holiday rules excuse you from actively seeking employment while you are away but you still have to be available for work and the holiday must not 'materially' reduce your chances of finding a job. This means that holidays abroad will not be accepted and that you will be disqualified if the nature of the work you are looking for means that you must be personally present when recruitment takes place (eg, casual labouring on building sites)[21] – this is because your absence will be treated as materially reducing your chances of employment.

You must tell the Employment Service before you go on holiday and you will be asked to complete a 'holiday form'. This does not guarantee payment – the important question is whether you are still available for employment. You will be asked to provide an address or addresses where you can be contacted (remember that you can pick up mail at a post office) and if you can provide a telephone number for any calls this will also be helpful. If you cannot do this, offer to phone the local office or some other number regularly to see if there are any messages. You will also be expected to give an assurance that you will be willing and able to cut short your holiday if notified of a job.

When you return from your holiday you must sign on on the very next day your unemployment benefit office is open *even if that is not your usual signing-on day*. If you do not, you may lose benefit for the whole of the period you were away unless you can show that you had 'good cause' (see p281) for failing to do so. This is because of the technical rule that you are only excused from signing on every day if you sign on when you are directed to do so.[22] The holiday form tells you to sign on as soon as possible after your return and if you fail to do so, you have also failed to claim for every day in the intervening period.

5. ACTIVELY SEEKING EMPLOYMENT

You are only entitled to UB for any particular day if that day is part of a week (see p23) in which you are (or are treated as if you were – see p22) actively seeking employment.[1]

In order to be treated as actively seeking employment, you must take reasonable 'steps' to find a job.[2] Taking one 'step' on a single occasion during a week will not be enough unless taking that step on that occasion was all that it was reasonable for you to do[3] – the implication is that taking two steps a week will generally be enough.

In order to check that you are actively seeking employment, the Employment Service will ask you from time to time to give details of the 'steps' you have taken (see below). It is therefore extremely important that you should keep records of your attempts to get a job. Apart from keeping copies of all the letters you send – and any replies you receive – the best way of doing this is to keep a diary and make a note every time you make a phone call or visit to a Jobcentre, a potential employer or an agency or do anything else which might count as a 'step' towards seeking employment. Ideally, these notes should be as detailed as possible and include the dates and times of the conversations, who you spoke to and what was said. If at all possible, it is also a good idea to keep copies of any advertisements which you reply to.

A person who cannot read or write should tell his/her claimant adviser of this. It may be possible for such a person to find a friend or relative to help compile a record (and to help to look for jobs). The Employment Service may be prepared to accept an oral report but the problem is that checks on whether or not you are actively seeking work are not carried out every single week (see p24) and without anything in writing to refresh them, memories fade over time. A written record is also much more convincing and will inevitably be more detailed.

Difficulties with English can present similar problems and a claimant adviser may be able to suggest organisations who can help maintain a record of the evidence a claimant will need to show that s/he is actively seeking work.

What counts as a 'step'?

The regulations say[4] that 'steps' include:

* making written or oral applications for employment to people who have advertised jobs or who appear to be in a position to offer employment;[5]
* seeking information from advertisements, advertisers, agencies or employers;[6]
* registering with an agency;[7] *or*
* appointing someone else to help you find employment.[8]

But this list is not exhaustive and other actions not mentioned above may count as 'steps' if they might lead to your being offered employment.

The 'steps' you take must be the ones which can reasonably be seen as the most likely to produce offers of employment in your case.[9] So, for example, if you are a hairdresser, replying to job advertisements in *The Nursing Times* probably will not count!

When the adjudication officer considers whether the steps you have taken are reasonable, s/he has to look at all the circumstances in your individual case, including:[10]

- your skills, qualifications, abilities and physical and mental limitations;
- how long you have been unemployed;
- the 'steps' you have taken in previous weeks;
- the availability and location of jobs;
- any time you have spent launching or crewing a lifeboat or acting as a firefighter, helping in an emergency, undertaking voluntary work, attending an Outward Bound course or participating in training or study;
- whether you have applied for, or accepted a place on, or participated in a course or programme supported by public (including EC) funds for the purpose of selecting, training for, obtaining or retaining employment;
- if you are homeless, the fact that you have no accommodation and the steps which you have to take to find a home.

Again the list is not exhaustive and any other factors which are relevant must be taken into account.

When are you 'deemed' to be actively seeking employment?

Even if you are not actively seeking employment you will be treated as if you were during any week (see p23):

- which is the first week for which you have claimed unemployment benefit since *either*
  - you were in employment; *or*
  - you were on an employment or training programme for which a training allowance was payable for at least six consecutive days (excluding Sunday);[11] *or*
- which includes the last day of unemployment of any spell of unemployment[12] – a 'spell' of unemployment is any one or more days of unemployment (except that two or more such periods are treated as a single 'spell' unless they are separated by more than three consecutive days on which you are not entitled to unemployment benefit);[13] *or*
- for which you have given written notice that you will be away from home.[14] This rule allows you a total of two weeks (consecutive or not) away from home in any period of 12 months;[15] *unless*
  - you are blind, in which case you are allowed a maximum of six weeks (again consecutive or not) provided you are on a training

course in the use of guide dogs for at least three days in each week;[16] *or*

– you are on an Outward Bound course, in which case you are allowed three weeks (again consecutive or not) provided you attend the course for at least three days in each such week;[17] *or*

• during which you are engaged in launching or crewing a lifeboat or acting as a firefighter or carrying out emergency duties for at least three days;[18] *or*

• (for a maximum of five consecutive weeks) during which you are on an employment or training course for which a training allowance is not payable;[19] *or*

• during which you are taking active steps to establish yourself in self-employment under the Enterprise Allowance Scheme. This only applies during a single period lasting no more than eight weeks and starting with the week during which you attend the meeting necessary before you can apply to participate in the Scheme.[20]

What counts as a 'week'?

Because the rules tell adjudication officers to look at the steps you have taken to seek employment during a particular week, the definition of 'week' is important.

Usually you are required to sign on fortnightly and the two weeks will be the two periods of seven days for which you sign on. There are special rules which apply at the beginning and end of your claim, if you do not sign on fortnightly or if your signing-on day changes.

The basic rule is that a week is a period which begins immediately after one 'relevant day' and ends with the next.[21] 'Relevant days' are:[22]

• the day immediately before the first day of a period of interruption of employment (see p251) for which unemployment benefit is claimed; *and*
• every day on which you have to sign on during your claim; *and*
• if you do not have to sign on every seven days, the day in each week which corresponds to your last relevant day; *and*
• the last day of your claim.

Since you will normally be deemed to be actively seeking employment during the first and last weeks of your claim (see p22), these rules only really affect those who are required by the Secretary of State to sign on more frequently than once every seven days – probably because they are suspected of fraud. If this applies to you, then each of the periods of seven days ending with each of the days you sign on counts as a separate 'week' – even if they overlap.[23] In practice this will mean that a 'step' taken on one day will count towards entitlement to unemployment benefit on that day and each of the following five days (excluding Sundays) but no longer.

In all other circumstances, if there would be more than one 'relevant day' in any period of seven days, all but the last are ignored.[24] The effect of this is that if your signing-on day is changed, a 'week' may last for more than seven days.

Example

You sign on fortnightly on Tuesdays. The days you sign on are 'relevant days' and so are the Tuesdays in the intervening weeks because they correspond to your previous 'relevant day'. In Week 1 you sign on on the Tuesday but are told to sign on on Friday in Week 3. Tuesday in Week 3 would normally be a 'relevant day' as it corresponds to your last such day but, as it is in the same period of seven days as Friday of Week 3, it is disregarded and the 'week' lasts ten days – from Wednesday in Week 2 to Friday in Week 3.

Checking whether you are actively seeking employment

You are not normally expected to prove that you are actively seeking employment every time you sign on (although you will have to sign a formal declaration to this effect). However, the steps you have taken will be checked at Restart interviews (see p18) and by random checks on other occasions.

The claimant adviser will want to know what jobs you have applied for and why you have not applied for others. S/he may also make other suggestions about steps which might be helpful. You should be given the opportunity to explain the steps you have taken and to say whether you agree with the suggestions which have been made and, if not, why not.

If the claimant adviser thinks you are not trying hard enough to get work, you will be given a warning letter setting out up to five steps you should take, and you will be asked to go back to an 'Actively Seeking Review'. At the Review, your efforts will be discussed further and you may be offered a vacancy or a place on a work or training scheme.

If the claimant adviser is still not happy with the efforts you are making, s/he will refer your case to an adjudication officer. If this happens, you will be told why. The adjudication officer then has to decide whether the steps you took in the relevant week or weeks were sufficient to count as actively seeking work; if you are unhappy with the decision, you can appeal.

If your claim is referred in this way, your benefit will be suspended[25] and, if you are claiming income support, it will be paid at a reduced rate.[26] Arrears will be paid if the adjudication officer decides that you have been actively seeking work. It is important that you should continue to sign on, make yourself available for work and actively seek employment in the meantime as otherwise you may lose benefit even if the adjudication officer's decision ultimately goes in your favour.

6. SPECIAL RULES IF YOU WORK PART-TIME

In a few cases you can get UB even though you have a job of some sort. This section deals with entitlement to UB in three different situations:

- you lose your job and take another for fewer days or hours each week;
- you are put on short-time working;
- your job is one where there are compulsory, unpaid holidays.

The most important thing to remember is that if you do work and claim UB during the same week, you must report the work you have done and any money you have earned to the Employment Service when you next sign on. If you do not you may have to repay any benefit which has been overpaid (see p295) and you may also be prosecuted (see p265).

Remember also that if you are claiming income support as well as unemployment benefit:

- any earnings over £5 per week (£15 in some cases) will reduce that benefit pound for pound;[1] *and*
- if you work for more than 16 hours a week, you will lose entitlement to income support altogether.[2] This in turn will mean that:
  - if your mortgage interest is being paid by the Benefits Agency this will cease;
  - any entitlement to housing benefit and council tax benefit may also be reduced; *and*
  - you will lose the automatic right to 'passport' benefits such as free prescriptions.

For further details about income support, see CPAG's *National Welfare Benefits Handbook*.

Part-time workers must also show that they are available for work on the days for which they claim. You can do this if:

- there is a reasonable prospect of obtaining part-time employment for those days of the week on which you are not already working; *or*
- the part-time work you are doing would not interfere with a potential full-time job, perhaps because it is in the evenings; *or*

- you are prepared to give up your part-time job if you are offered a full-time one.

DSS leaflet FB26 contains useful information for part-time workers.

Unemployment benefit is a 'daily benefit' – ie, entitlement to it is theoretically assessed on a daily basis. In principle, therefore, any work you do on one day should not affect your entitlement on another day. In practice, however, this would leave the system open to abuse – to take a slightly far-fetched example, it would be possible for employers and employees to agree that for a limited period they would work a full 36-hour week in three 12-hour days so that the employees could take home a normal week's wage and claim three days' unemployment benefit as well.

To prevent claimants from compressing their working hours into fewer days, and other more sophisticated schemes, a number of exceptions have been introduced to the principle of daily assessment – exceptions which can cause unfair and anomalous results.

The earnings rule

The most important exception is the earnings rule. This says that if you earn more than the lower earnings limit (currently £57 per week – see p216) in a week, you are not entitled to unemployment benefit on any day during that week. For the purposes of this rule, a week is a period of seven days (including Sunday) ending with the day of the week you sign on. [3]

The £2 rule

If you earn less than £57 in any particular week, then unless you are caught by the 'normal idle day rule' (see p27) or by the 'full extent normal' rule (see p28), you will be entitled to unemployment benefit for any day (except Sunday – see p253) on which *either*:

- you do not work (so long as you satisfy all the other conditions of entitlement – see p8); *or*
- you do work as long as you continue actively to seek employment (see p20) and all the following conditions are satisfied: [4]
  - you earn £2 a day or less; *and*
  - you are not working as an employee in your usual main occupation, unless you are working either for a charity or for a local authority or health authority providing a charitable service; *and*
  - you are available for full-time work.

Earnings over a period of work are averaged out at a daily rate. For further details of what counts as earnings and how they are calculated see p261 but note that in this context certain payments to Members of Reserve Forces are ignored.[5]

Work which you do on a Sunday (or any day substituted for Sunday in your particular case – see p253) does not count for the purposes of the £2 rule. But any money you earn will count for the purposes of the earnings rule (see p26) and Sunday work will almost certainly affect your entitlement to income support if you are claiming it.

If you work at night and your shift begins before midnight and ends afterwards, there are special rules to determine which of the two days you are treated as working on (see p253).

With these two exceptions any work you do during the 24 hours following midnight counts as work on that day.

The 'normal idle day' rule

The effect of the earnings rule and the £2 rule is that part-time workers who earn less than £57 per week in total may be able to claim UB for any day on which they earn less than £2. However, this position is complicated by two further rules, which apply if the claimant earns more than £12 per week, and which are designed to deny benefit to those who do not 'normally' work a full working week. These are the 'normal idle day' rule[6] and the 'full extent normal' rule.[7]

The 'normal idle day' rule says that in certain circumstances you cannot get unemployment benefit for a day on which in the normal course you would not work anyway. It is rarely applied in practice, but when it is, its most usual – although not its only – application is in relation to short-time working:

Example

You normally work a five-day week (Monday–Friday). You are put on two days a week short-time working (Tuesday and Wednesday). Provided you earn less than £56 on those two days, you will get unemployment benefit for three days (Monday, Thursday and Friday), but not for four as Saturday is a 'normal idle day'.

Inevitably it is not as simple as that. There is a long list of exceptions and occasions on which the rule does not apply. In particular, the rule does not apply:

• unless the claimant has a contract of employment with at least one employer which has not been terminated[8] – so if you normally work less than six days a week but lose your job altogether, you can get UB for six days a week as long as you are available for employment on those days (see p13);

- in any week during which the claimant does not earn more than £12;[9]
- if the claimant is only employed in 'casual' work;[10]
- if the claimant does not 'in the normal course' work for the employer for whom s/he is working;[11]
- if the claimant is unemployed or incapable of work (see p48) on every day of the week on which s/he would normally work except Sunday[12] (or any day substituted for Sunday – see p253);
- if the claimant's employment is suspended for at least six consecutive days (excluding Sunday or its substitute);[13]
- unless *either*
  - there is a recognised or customary working week for the work the claimant is doing; *or*
  - the claimant regularly works for the same number of days in a week for the same employer or employers.[14]

In contrast to the earnings rule, 'week' for these purposes means from Sunday to Saturday – not seven days ending with the day you sign on.[15]

The test for determining your 'normal' days of work is the same as for the 'full extent normal' rule (see below) and as a result there is a considerable overlap between the rules.

The 'full extent normal' rule

As its name suggests, this rule prevents UB from being paid during any 'week' (Sunday to Saturday) in which the claimant is employed to the 'full extent normal in his/her case'.[16] The rule differs from the normal idle day rule in that it applies even if a claimant's contract has been terminated altogether, and is not restricted by reference to a 'day'.

Example

You normally work 18 hours a week – nine hours a day on Monday and Tuesday. One week your employer asks you to work six hours a day on Wednesday, Thursday and Friday and you claim unemployment benefit for Monday and Tuesday. Under the 'normal idle day' rule you would qualify for benefit as Monday and Tuesday are not normally idle days for you. But under the 'full extent normal' rule you will not – you have worked for 18 hours and that is the full extent normal in your case.

What is 'normal'?

If you have been working full-time and become unemployed, adjudication officers will generally accept at first that part-time work is not your 'normal' employment if you have taken it while looking for a full-time job.[17] But there comes a time when that part-time work does become your 'normal' employment even if you do not want it to. There is no hard and fast rule but traditionally your past full-time employment has continued to be regarded as your 'normal' employment for at least a year.[18]

Adjudication officers sometimes argue that a job has become your 'normal' employment once you have worked the same days every week for half the year – with the effect that if you usually work the same days each week, you lose UB after only six months. However, the commissioners' decisions[19] relied on by adjudication officers for this '50 per cent test' concerned people who have had irregular work patterns in the past and ought not to be applied to you if you were usually employed for the same days each week before you claimed UB.

A period of short-time working due to temporary adverse industrial conditions is disregarded when deciding what is 'normal' in your case.[20] The current recession is not regarded as temporary but, in any event, this rule is seldom relevant because the commissioners have not tended to regard people working short-time as working to their normal extent until they have been on short-time for a year.

Compulsory holidays

You are not entitled to UB on any customary or recognised holiday while you are employed.[21]

The most common problem in this area is experienced by the employees of education authorities during school holidays when no work is done. Clearly **full-time staff** who are paid throughout the year are genuinely 'on holiday' for the whole of the school holidays. On the other hand some **ancillary staff** are only paid for two or three weeks of the holidays and it has been held that an employee in this position is entitled to unemployment benefit for the remaining weeks. Temporary teachers who are not paid during holiday periods are in a difficult position – they are usually treated as being on holiday unless they do not intend to teach again when term resumes (although it is important to investigate the precise terms of the contract with the education authority in each individual case).[22] The justification for this is that UB is meant to insure against the *risk* of unemployment, not the *certainty* of it. In other words, a person taking work as a temporary teacher is considered to have accepted long, unpaid holidays as part of the job. But, if you can show that in the past you have worked during holiday periods (and so do not accept the 'certainty' of unemployment), you may be entitled to benefit. Thus a teacher who was also a professional musician was held to have two jobs and awarded benefit during those parts of the school holidays when he was unable to obtain work playing music.[23]

If a person is employed under a series of renewable contracts, it can sometimes be difficult to tell whether a job has ended or not. This may be important as the holiday disqualification only applies if you are still employed. A good rule of thumb is that if you have not given notice but would not be in breach of your contract of employment if you did not return to work, then your job has come to an end and you are entitled to benefit. If you are unsure whether or not your job has ended, you should seek advice (see p329).

7. PAYMENTS FROM YOUR PREVIOUS JOB

This section covers a variety of different payments which you may receive when you leave a job. It is important to consider how these will affect your UB if you, or your union, are negotiating an agreement with your employers. The payments concerned are:

- compensation for unfair dismissal;
- payment in lieu of notice and other compensation for the loss of your job;
- occupational and personal pensions.

Compensation for unfair dismissal

If you take your former employers to an industrial tribunal, the money you recover may affect your entitlement to unemployment benefit in two ways:

- If the industrial tribunal orders your former employers to compensate you for loss of the money which you would have earned but for your unfair dismissal or a refusal to reinstate you, you are not entitled to UB for any day in the *future* which is covered by that award, or for a year, whichever is shorter.[1]
- If you have already been paid UB for a period in the past covered by such an award, your former employers must pay it back under the 'recoupment provisions'[2] and the amount of compensation they have to pay you will be reduced by the same amount.

These rules only apply to payments made by your former employers as a result of an order of an industrial tribunal (or, on appeal, the Employment Appeal Tribunal[3]). So if you *settle* your case without an order of the tribunal, neither you nor your former employers will have to repay anything. There is therefore a financial advantage to both sides in settling cases. Even partway through a hearing, you can always withdraw your case or ask the tribunal to record the private settlement you have reached. Neither of these counts as an *order*.

If your former employers have gone into liquidation and you would therefore have to get court consent to enforce the tribunal's award, it will not affect your unemployment benefit[4] (because the award is not 'payable'[5]). But if they are not formally in liquidation but have just stopped trading, it is up to you to force them into liquidation. You will need legal advice in order to do this and may be entitled to legal aid (see p330).

You will be refused benefit for any period covered by a tribunal award, even if the tribunal reduces your compensation – eg, because it decides you were partly to blame for your own dismissal or that you have lost earnings because you have failed to look hard enough for other work. It is the *fact* of the award rather than the *amount* which leads to the disqualification.[6] Generally speaking, you should claim income support without delay if your award is reduced for any reason.

A reduced award also has consequences for the repayment of UB which you received before the tribunal decision. If the tribunal decides that, for example, you were one-third to blame for your dismissal and your employers two-thirds, they will only have to repay two-thirds of the benefit. In that case you will have to repay the other third if the adjudication officer can prove that you have failed to disclose a material fact (see p297). To avoid this it is very important that you should tell the Employment Service at the earliest possible opportunity that you are considering going to an industrial tribunal.[7] If you tell them later, you should not have to repay any benefit after that date.

Payment in lieu of notice and other compensation for the loss of your job

If you receive any compensation from your former employer for the termination of your employment, it is assumed that part of that payment is in lieu of any notice you were entitled to but not given. Accordingly, you are not entitled to UB for any day which would have been covered by that notice and which can be treated as covered by the compensation.[8] This is known as the *'ineligible period'* (see p32).

What counts as 'compensation'?

Any payment made to you when you leave – and which would not have been made if you had not left[9] – is treated as compensation except:[10]

- any pay for the period before your employment ended[11]; *and*
- any holiday pay; *and*
- any redundancy payment to which you are entitled by statute; *and*
- any refund of contributions under an occupational pension scheme.

Although any of the above payments may affect you if you are claiming income support, your UB will only be affected if you receive other compensation as well.

How long is the 'ineligible period'?

The 'ineligible period' always begins the day after your employment ended, but when it ends depends on what your former employers say about the payment. If your former employers say either that the payment is in lieu of notice or is in compensation for the early termination of a fixed-term contract, the 'ineligible period' ends either 52 weeks after it begins or (if it is sooner) on the 'due date'.[12] The 'due date' is *either*:

- the day when any notice to which you were entitled – either by contract or Act of Parliament, whichever is longer – (or to which you would have been entitled had you not waived it) would have expired; *or*
- if you had a fixed-term contract, the date when the contract was due to expire.[13]

If you are made redundant at the same time as at least nine other employees, your employers are obliged to consult any recognised trade union at least 30 days before making the redundancies (90 days where 100 or more employees are threatened with redundancy).[14] If your employers say that the payment is in lieu of these rights the 'ineligible period' ends either when the consultation period would have ended or (if the payment also includes compensation in lieu of notice) on the 'due date' (see above) or on the 'standard date' (see below), whichever is later.[15] In any other case – including if your employers do not say anything about the payment – the 'ineligible period' ends on the 'standard date'. This is *either*:

- the 'due date' (see above); *or*
- the last day of the period (calculated in weeks by dividing the amount of the payment by £206 and rounding down to the nearest whole number.[16]

Occupational and personal pensions

If you are 55 or over, and are receiving an occupational or personal pension of more than £35 per week gross, your UB (including any increase for a dependent adult or child[17]) will be reduced by the amount of the excess.[18]

In this context, 'occupational or personal pension' means periodical payments which are made to you because your employment has ended:[19]

- from money provided wholly or partly by your former employer; *or*
- from money provided under legislation; *or*
- from most types of personal pension schemes.

This is a wide definition and will catch periodical payments made under early retirement schemes and pensions paid to those who have retired on health grounds.[20] But lump-sum payments are not included (because they are not 'periodical payments') and neither are payments made solely because you have been made redundant (unless they are made under the rules of your pension scheme).[21]

If you are receiving an increase for an adult dependant, a separate earnings rule applies if a pension is paid to her/him. For further details see p208.

8. DISQUALIFICATIONS

Even if you would otherwise be entitled to UB, you may be disqualified from receiving it if:

- you are dismissed from your job (or lose your place on an approved training scheme) for misconduct (see below); *or*
- you leave your job or give up your place on an approved training scheme voluntarily (see p37); *or*
- you do not take steps to obtain work or a place on an approved training scheme which has been recommended to you by the Employment Service or if you turn down the offer of a job or training place (see p39); *or*
- you are unemployed because of a strike or trade dispute at your place of work (see p41).

You will also be disqualified if you fail to attend a Restart interview without good cause (see p18).

Misconduct

If you are dismissed from your job[1] or lose your place on an approved training scheme[2] for misconduct you will be disqualified from UB for up to 26 weeks and any income support to which you may be entitled will also be paid at a reduced rate.

What is misconduct?

Not every breach of your contract of employment or employers' rules or instructions amounts to misconduct – everyone makes mistakes or is inefficient from time to time. Even if you were sacked or forced to resign because of inadequate work, you are only guilty of misconduct if your actions or omissions are *blameworthy*.

In one decision a former Chief Commissioner defined misconduct as being:

> conduct which is causally but not necessarily directly connected with the employment and having regard to the relationship of employer and employee and the rights and duties of both, can fairly be described as blameworthy, reprehensible and wrong.[3]

So, for example, a naturally slow worker who, despite making every effort, cannot produce the output required by his/her employers will not be guilty of misconduct. Having said that, you may be guilty of misconduct without being dishonest – serious carelessness or negligence may be enough although

> it is necessary to discriminate between that type and degree of carelessness which may have to be put up with in human affairs, and the more deliberate or serious type of carelessness which justifies withholding unemployment benefit because the employee has lost his employment through his own avoidable fault.[4]

Negligence is more likely to be treated as misconduct if it occurs while you are exercising a special skill for which you are employed – eg, as a driver. On the other hand, a bus driver, who had a clean driving record for 21 years and was dismissed for an accident which only caused slight damage, was not disqualified. It was held that an isolated error of judgement was not misconduct.[5]

Some behaviour is clearly misconduct. This includes:

- **Dishonesty** – theft, either from an employer or from fellow employees will always lead to a disqualification. Indeed a conviction for any offence of dishonesty – whether or not connected with your work – may lead to a disqualification if it causes your employers to dismiss you because they no longer trust you.[6] On the other hand, dishonesty which took place before your employment began cannot justify disqualification. For example, in one case an accountant who was dismissed when his employers found out about a previous conviction for fraud was not disqualified.[7]
- **Arson** and other forms of deliberate damage to the property of your employers or fellow employees.

- **Assaults** on your employers, fellow employees or customers.
- **Drunkenness** at work or working under the influence of illegal drugs – especially if it is repeated or endangers the safety of your fellow workers.
- **Bad timekeeping** and failing to report in time that you are sick.

The misconduct does not have to take place during working hours in order to justify disqualification. But it does have to be causally connected with the employment so as to give a reason for your employers to dismiss you. Convictions for dishonesty outside work have already been mentioned in this context. Another example would be of someone who needs to drive for his/her job and who loses his/her driving licence following a traffic offence. People in this position will usually be disqualified from unemployment benefit as well as from driving – particularly if drinking was involved – even if the offence took place outside work.

Deciding whether you are guilty of misconduct

When you claim benefit, your former employers will be sent a form asking whether you were dismissed and, if so, why. If their answer suggests there may have been misconduct, you will be sent a copy and asked to comment on it. Your remarks will in turn be passed to your former employers for further comments.

Make sure you put on record the details of your case and why you contest the allegation of misconduct. If you are going to an industrial tribunal, say so. In this case you may want to discuss your reply with whoever is advising you on your claim for unfair dismissal, as you may be asked questions at the industrial tribunal hearing about what you have said.

It is important to make your replies to the enquiries as full as possible as the adjudication officer has to decide from the information which s/he has gathered whether or not your loss of employment was due to misconduct on your part. If the adjudication officer decides against you, you should consider whether to appeal (see p304).

Very often, the facts will be disputed. If so, it is usually a good idea to appeal the disqualification – particularly if it was for the full 26 weeks (see p35) – so that the SSAT can see you in person and hear your point of view. Sometimes your former employers are asked to attend and you can ask your former workmates to give evidence. Although it is generally for the claimant to prove entitlement to benefit, the onus of proving misconduct is on the adjudication officer (who will normally have to rely upon evidence from your former employers).

Often an SSAT will recognise both sides' points of view by upholding the disqualification but reducing its length (see below).

Sometimes the same facts will have to be considered by other bodies – eg, industrial tribunals, the criminal courts, the Civil Service Board and other disciplinary and appeal bodies – as well as by the SSAT. The important thing to remember in such cases is that the questions which these other bodies have to investigate may not be the same as the ones which the SSAT must ask itself. Industrial tribunals, for example, have to consider whether a dismissal is 'fair' and, while it may be fair to dismiss a slow employee, s/he is probably not guilty of misconduct. So a finding by an industrial tribunal that a dismissal was fair does not prevent an adjudication officer or SSAT from concluding that there has been no misconduct. Similarly, although SSATs will normally accept a criminal conviction as proof that a claimant has done what is alleged, it must still go on to consider whether this was connected with your employment and whether it amounts to misconduct.

While the question of possible misconduct is being investigated, your UB will be suspended and income support will be paid at a reduced rate. You will receive arrears if it is later decided not to disqualify you.

The period of disqualification

The period of disqualification can be any length from one day to 26 weeks. The decision on how long it will be in your case is taken by the adjudication officer who decides your claim (see p285). S/he should consider your case on its individual merits.

If you feel that the period of disqualification in your case is harsh or unfair, it is worth appealing because SSATs (see p303) often reduce periods of disqualification. An appeal will give you a much better chance to put your side of the case – and to challenge your former employer's version of events – than any written comments which you may have made before the adjudication officer made his/her decision.

You will also be able to argue that 26 weeks is a maximum for really serious misconduct and that a lesser period is more fitting in your case. For example:

- a claimant was dismissed for stealing an item worth seven pence which he believed to be valueless. At the time, the maximum period of disqualification was six weeks but a commissioner imposed a period of only two weeks;[8]
- an assault on a fellow employee which had been provoked would deserve a shorter period of disqualification than one which was premeditated and without provocation.

At present, the period of disqualification 'defers' your entitlement to unemployment benefit – ie, once the period has expired, you can receive your full entitlement up to a maximum of 312 days (see p10). However, the DSS now has the power to change this so that the period of disqualification reduces your entitlement. For example, if you were disqualified for six weeks (36 days), your maximum entitlement to unemployment benefit would be 276 days (312 days – 36 days) rather than a year. This change has not yet been brought into effect.[9]

Leaving your job or training scheme voluntarily

You will also be disqualified if:

• you leave your job voluntarily without just cause;[10] *or*
• you give up your place on a training scheme voluntarily and without *good cause*.[11]

As with misconduct, the maximum period of disqualification is 26 weeks and the length of the period in any individual case should be decided according to the merits of that case. If you are also claiming income support, it will be paid at a reduced rate during the period of disqualification.[12]

Although it is normally clear whether a person has left employment or training voluntarily, that is not always the case. If you are told to resign or put in a position where you have no practical choice but to do so, you have not left voluntarily.[13]

Volunteering for redundancy does not count as leaving your job voluntarily[14] (but see p38 for the position if you volunteer for *early retirement*).

Just cause

Once it is established that you left of your own free will, it is up to you to show that you had just cause (or, if you left a place on a training scheme rather than a job, good cause). For the meaning of 'good cause' see p40 – 'just cause' is a harder test to satisfy as it involves the adjudicating authorities (see p283) balancing your interests against those of all the other contributors to the national insurance fund. You must show not only that you acted reasonably in leaving, but also that the circumstances of your case make it proper that the community should support you.[15]

So, for example:

• **If your job does not suit you,** you are expected to find, or at least seriously look for, another one before giving it up.[16]

- **If you volunteer for early retirement,** you probably will not have just cause.[17] However the circumstances in which you volunteer will be relevant to the length of the disqualification imposed, particularly if you can say that it was in the public interest for you to have taken early retirement.[18]

    This rule only applies in cases where you have genuinely volunteered to leave. 'Early retirement' is often a euphemism for being sacked or made redundant (see p37 and p32), in which case you have not left your job voluntarily. Remember also that in early retirement cases, the adjudication officer will want to be satisfied that you have not actually retired and that you are still available for and actively seeking work before awarding you UB.

- **If you leave your job for personal or domestic reasons,** you may have just cause. For example, accommodation difficulties may provide justification for giving up your job to take up an offer of proper housing in another district[19] (though a 21-year-old woman who left work to move with her parents was disqualified because it was reasonable for her to live alone[20]). Health reasons may also be sufficient, but it would be important to show that you had mentioned these to your employers when you left.[21] Married women who have left jobs to live with their husbands who have been posted elsewhere by their employers have not usually been disqualified[22] (although there can be other problems with UB if the posting is abroad even to another EC country[23]). Men who leave jobs to live with their wives should also receive the same treatment.[24]

- **If you give up work to look after a sick relative,** you probably have good cause,[25] but you may still be refused benefit because you are not available for work. Consider claiming invalid care allowance (see p158) and income support instead.

- **If you give up your job because of a change in your terms and conditions of employment,** you may have just cause (although you will be expected to use any grievance procedure first). For example, a piece-worker who left because of a substantial, unilaterally-imposed, reduction in earnings was not disqualified.[26] Neither was an apprentice who was instructed to do work clearly outside the terms of his apprenticeship.[27] If you do not feel *capable* of the new work – but your employers are satisfied that you are – you will need medical evidence to establish just cause.[28] If you give notice hastily when your terms of work are changed and then try to revoke it but are not allowed to by your employers, you should argue that the *period* of disqualification should be reduced (see p36).[29]

Trial periods

If you have not worked (or been in training or full-time education) for at least 26 weeks, an exception to the rules on giving up your job voluntarily allows you to take a job for a trial period. This means that if you give up the job voluntarily after the end of the sixth week, but before the end of the twelfth week, you will not be disqualified.[30]

The rules for calculating the six- and 12-week periods are artifical and it is important that you get the calculation right. Any week during which you did not work for at least 16 hours is ignored[31] and it is assumed that you started work on the Sunday at the beginning of the week in which your job started,[32] and the periods of six and 12 weeks end at midnight on Saturday in those weeks. So, in one case a milkman who left his job at midday on the Saturday of the sixth week was held to fall outside the trial period rules and was disqualified (although only for one day).[33] If he had left at midday the following Monday or at any time before midnight on the Saturday of the twelfth week he would not have been disqualified at all.

If you decide to accept a job on a trial basis you must also remember that if you do not claim UB for at least eight consecutive weeks, a new period of interruption of employment (see p251) will begin when you next claim. This may be to your advantage as (unless you have exhausted your 312 days' entitlement to UB and need to requalify – see p10) a fresh period of 312 days' entitlement will also begin. On the other hand you will have to serve a further three waiting days (see p9) and, more seriously, the question of whether you satisfy the contribution conditions (see p231) will be looked at again – probably by reference to later years than before. Because of this it is very important to work out whether, if you give up your job after a trial period of more than eight weeks, you will still meet the contribution conditions (see p231) when you re-claim benefit. If not, then you should make a final decision on whether you are suited to the new job after six weeks but before the eight weeks have expired.

Failing to take up a job or a place on a training scheme

If you repeatedly fail to take jobs that are offered to you, the adjudication officer may decide that you are not really available for or actively seeking work and refuse you benefit altogether. You will be disqualified from benefit if:

• You are notified of a job vacancy or a place on a training scheme and *either*:

- – you do not apply for it; *or*
  - you refuse to accept it if it is offered to you.[34]
  - A job or training place counts as having been 'notified' to you if you are told about it by or on behalf of an employer, by the Employment Service, a local education authority or by certain agencies.[35]
- You fail to take a reasonable opportunity of getting a job or a place on a training scheme.[36]
- You do not carry out reasonable written recommendations given to you by the Employment Service to help you find a job.[37]

Again, the period of disqualification is decided by the adjudication officer and should reflect the merits of the case. The minimum period is one day and the maximum 26 weeks. You can appeal against the decision to disqualify you, the length of the disqualification or both.

Good cause

These disqualifications do not apply if you have 'good cause' for acting as you did. When reaching a decision on whether there was 'good cause', the adjudication officer must take all your relevant personal circumstances into account. The regulations say that these include:

- any personal circumstances suggesting that a particular job, course of training or official recommendation might cause you serious harm or subject you to excessive physical or mental stress;[38]
- any sincerely held religious or conscientious objection;[39]
- any responsibility for the care of another member of your household;[40]
- the travelling time involved.[41] Normally you are expected to be prepared to travel for up to an hour 'by a route and means appropriate to your circumstances' (see p17) each way to and from your job or training scheme. But less might be reasonable if your health would suffer or if you are responsible for the care of another member of your household;[42]
- any expenses which would be incurred in doing the job or attending the training scheme if they would amount to an unreasonably high proportion of your income.[43]

On the other hand, the adjudication officer is not allowed to take into account your family income except in relation to your work or training expenses.[44] This means that you cannot usually refuse a job because the wage or salary is too low. But there are some limits on what you are expected to accept:

- You do not have to accept a job involving less than 24 hours' work a week.[45]
- You do not have to accept a job which is vacant because of a trade dispute – ie, you do not have to be a strike-breaker.
- During your 'permitted period' (see p13), you do not have to take a job except in your usual occupation and for at least your usual rate of pay.
- If you have trained for a job for at least two months, you do not have to accept work in any other kind of employment for four weeks after your training ends.[46]
- You do not have to take a job which you find out about by yourself[47] unless *either*:
  – you have also been notified of the job by the Employment Service;[48]
  or
  – you have worked for the employer within the past year and have a right to return (eg, after maternity leave) *and* your pay and conditions will be at least as good as before.[49]

Remember, however, that if you do not take a job you have been offered, the adjudication officer may decide that you are not available for work (see p13).

Strikes and trade disputes

You will be disqualified from UB if the reason you are not working is because:

- you have withdrawn your labour as part of a trade dispute;[50] *or*
- there is a stoppage of work due to a trade dispute at your place of employment (unless you are not 'directly interested' in the outcome of the dispute).[51]

Even if you are disqualified from unemployment benefit during a trade dispute, you may still be entitled to **income support** if you have a family – for further details see CPAG's *National Welfare Benefits Handbook*.

What counts as your 'place of employment'?

Often the answer to this question will be obvious. But if you work for a large business, you may be able to argue that a stoppage of work in another department is not taking place at *your* place of employment.

This is because there is a rule that says that if there are different kinds of work, which are commonly run as separate businesses, being carried on in the same factory but in different departments, each department is treated as a separate place of employment.[52]

'Department' refers to administrative as well as physical divisions – eg, electricians in a steel works and lorry drivers employed by a firm of ship repairers have been successful in claiming unemployment benefit when the whole organisation has been shut down by a strike, because both types of work are commonly carried out as businesses separate from the 'department' where the dispute was in progress.[53]

Who is 'directly interested' in a trade dispute?

Even if the stoppage is at your place of employment, you will not be disqualified if you can show that you are not directly interested in the dispute. This is very difficult. In effect you have to show that you have nothing to gain, either financially or in connection with your conditions of work, by the terms on which the dispute might be settled. If the outcome of the dispute will affect you because by a collective agreement or established custom, all workers have the same terms and conditions of employment irrespective of union membership, it makes no difference that you are not a member of the union or group of workers in dispute.[54]

Period of disqualification

The disqualification continues for as long as the stoppage of work, whatever your personal circumstances, unless:

- having lost your job as a result of the trade dispute, you become employed elsewhere and lose your *second* job. In this case you will qualify for benefit, providing you can prove that the second job was genuine, and not a ploy aimed at requalifying for UB;[55] *or*
- you have been made redundant during the course of the dispute. In this case you will become entitled to UB from the date of the redundancy even though the stoppage of work is still continuing;[56] *or*
- you return to work during the dispute but become unemployed again before the stoppage of work ends. In this case you will not be disqualified if your reason for leaving was unconnected with the dispute itself.[57]

9. SPECIAL RULES FOR PEOPLE OVER PENSIONABLE AGE

You cannot receive UB if you are over 65 if you are a woman or 70 if you are a man. If you are over pensionable age (60 for a woman, 65 for a man), UB will only be paid if:[1]

• you would be entitled to a Category A retirement pension (see p116) or, if you are a widow or widower, a Category B retirement pension (see pp120 and 122); *and*
• you have deferred your retirement pension by not claiming it (see p114) or by electing to de-retire (see p116).

If your pension would have been paid at a reduced rate because you do not have a full contribution record (see p235), then the rate at which UB (and any increase for a dependent adult)[2] is paid will be similarly reduced.

An increase is paid for dependent children if you receive UB and are over pensionable age. This is not reduced if your contribution record is incomplete.

The difference in the pensionable age for men and women means that men aged between 60 and 65 are treated differently from women of the same age. The difference depends on your contribution record (and on whether you have dependent children).

Example

You are a woman aged 63. You have worked and paid full contributions for the past five years but, taken over your working life as a whole, your contribution record is incomplete and would only entitle you to 50% of the full rate of a Category A retirement pension. Unemployment benefit is paid at £28.80 per week (£57.60 ÷ 2). If you were male, UB would be paid at the full under-pensionable-age rate of £45.45 per week – you would be better off if you were a man.

You are a man aged 63 and have worked and paid contributions continuously since you were 16. Although you cannot claim it until you are 65, you have already paid sufficient contributions to entitle you to a full Category A retirement pension. You live with your 15 year-old daughter. UB will be paid at £45.45 per week. If you were female, it would be paid at the full 'over-pensionable-age' rate of £57.60 and you would receive a dependant's increase for your daughter worth £9.80 per week (after the operation of the overlapping benefit rules – see p258), a total of £67.40 – you would be better off if you were a woman.

If you would be better off being treated as a member of the opposite sex, see the section on equal treatment for men and women (p267).

10. SPECIAL RULES FOR STUDENTS

Students are not entitled to UB while they are on any *full-time* course of study. It makes no difference whether you receive a grant or whether you claim during term-time or during the vacation.[1]

The regulations do not define full-time education by reference to particular courses or hours of study, so whether or not your course is full-time is judged on the particular circumstances of your case. If you disagree with the adjudication officer's decision, you can appeal (see p304). Ask your union, student welfare officer or the college authorities to help you.

Your UB will not be affected if you fill in time while unemployed by doing some limited studying – eg, evening classes, correspondence courses (such as the Open University) or a part-time course of education. However, you *must* remain **available for work**. An adjudication officer will take into account all your circumstances (including the length of the course, any fees paid and the level of commitment required) when deciding whether you are still genuinely available for work and free to take up any reasonable job offer immediately.

11. OTHER BENEFITS

The other principal benefit for people who are out of work is **income support**. This is a means-tested benefit which you can claim if your weekly income (including UB) is low enough to qualify, and your savings and other capital are below the current limit. Unlike UB, income support is paid from the first day of your claim (ie, there are no waiting days), can include a payment to cover mortgage interest payments and 'passports' claimants onto other benefits such as housing and council tax benefits and free prescriptions and legal aid. In addition, from April 1994, the basic rate of income support for a single adult aged 25 or over will be £45.70 – 25 pence higher than the standard rate of UB for people below pensionable age.

So unless you are absolutely sure that you are not entitled (perhaps because you have savings of more than £8,000 or are living with someone who is in full-time work), you should claim income support as well as UB.

The amount of income support is normally reduced if you are

disqualified from UB because you lost your job through misconduct or left it voluntarily, or because you have refused an offer of employment or training (see p33).[1] There are also special rules for those involved in trade disputes.[2]

For further details on income support see CPAG's *National Welfare Benefits Handbook*.

While you are unemployed, you are entitled to Class 1 national insurance credits (see p225).

UB is an earnings replacement benefit (see p4) and 'overlaps' with widows' benefits (except the lump-sum widow's payment). It is counted as income when calculating means-tested benefits. For the relationship between UB and retirement pensions see p43. Adult dependency increases to UB overlap with personal benefits (see p258) paid to the dependant in her/his own right (see p260).

12. TAX

UB is taxable except for increases in respect of dependent children (which are only payable if you are over pensionable age – see pp6 and 9).[1]

The tax is not deducted while benefit is being paid but reduces the refund you would otherwise receive through pay-as-you-earn (PAYE) when you return to work. As UB is low, very few people will owe more tax at the end of a period of unemployment than at the beginning.

Any tax refunds of PAYE payments will be paid to you at the end (5 April) of the tax year to which they relate. Any other tax refund will be paid only when UB ceases to be paid and the amount of refund will be affected by the amount of benefit you have received.[2]

In rare cases, you may end up owing tax. If so, your tax code will be adjusted when you return to work so that the tax deducted from your earnings will be increased until the money you owe from your period of unemployment has been collected.

13. FUTURE CHANGES

It has been announced that as part of the Government's long-term review of benefits UB and income support for people who are out of work are to be abolished in April 1996 and replaced by a benefit to be called 'Jobseeker's Allowance'.

Claimants will have to sign – and presumably keep to – a 'Jobseeker's Agreement' which will commit them to taking specific steps to find work.

For those who have paid sufficient contributions, Jobseeker's Allowance will be paid without a means test but only for six months (as opposed to a year for UB). After that, it will only be paid if you pass a means test.

Further details of the proposals will appear in CPAG publications as they become available.

CHAPTER THREE

Benefits for people incapable of work

This chapter covers:

1. Incapacity for work (p48)
2. 'Invalidity cut-off' – disputes about your capacity for work (p51)
3. Statutory sick pay (p64)
4. Sickness benefit (p73)
5. Invalidity benefit (p76)
6. Severe disablement allowance (p81)
7. Future changes (p86)

Most people who are away from work due to sickness receive statutory sick pay (SSP) from their employers for the first 28 weeks. Those who are not entitled to SSP but who are unable to work receive sickness benefit from the Benefits Agency for the first 28 weeks provided they satisfy the contribution conditions or have suffered an industrial injury. Most of those who have been entitled to SSP or sickness benefit then become entitled to invalidity benefit until they retire or are able to work again.

If you do not qualify for SSP or sickness benefit you do not get benefit for the first 28 weeks unless you are entitled to income support (IS). IS cannot normally be paid for any day before you claim, so if you are not sure you will get SSP or sickness benefit, you should claim IS at the same time (see CPAG's *National Welfare Benefits Handbook*).

Even if you are not entitled to invalidity benefit (IVB) because, for example, you have not paid enough contributions, you may be entitled to severe disablement allowance (SDA) instead after 28 weeks.

It is important to remember the difference between SSP and 'occupational sick pay'. Many employees are covered for sick pay by their contract of employment, which frequently gives a better level of payment and a longer period of entitlement than SSP. This is known as occupational sick pay. SSP is the minimum employers must pay. The amount of SSP payable is laid down by Act of Parliament.

If you are disabled you may also be entitled to one of the benefits described in Chapter 8 or to disability working allowance (DWA) (see

CPAG's *National Welfare Benefits Handbook*). If you are ill or injured because of your work you should also read Chapter 9.

I. INCAPACITY FOR WORK

A 'day of incapacity'

All the benefits covered in this chapter are theoretically 'daily benefits'. This means that you have to satisfy the Benefits Agency (or in the case of statutory sick pay (SSP), your employers) that you are unable to work on *each day* for which you want to receive benefit. In practice, the Benefits Agency will usually allow you to claim less frequently than this and most medical certificates will also cover periods of more than one day. But the fact that entitlement is decided on a daily basis still has some practical effects. You may find, for example, that Benefits Agency decisions say that periods for which you have claimed were not 'days of incapacity' when what they mean is that the adjudication officer (see p283) does not accept that you were unable to work.

If you are claiming sickness benefit, IVB or SDA, your days of incapacity must also form part of a 'period of interruption of employment' (see p251). To qualify for SSP, your days of incapacity must form part of a 'period of incapacity for work'. This is not the same as a 'period of interruption of employment' and the differences are discussed later in this chapter (see p67).

'Incapable of work'

To qualify as incapable of work you must prove:

• that you are suffering from a disease or are physically or mentally disabled; *and*
• that, as a result, you are unable to do any work which it is reasonable to expect you to do (but see below for exceptions).[1]

Even if you are able to work, the Benefits Agency will sometimes treat you as if you are not. This is known as 'deemed' incapacity. You will be treated as incapable of work if *either*:[2]

• you are under medical observation as the possible carrier of an infectious disease or have been in contact with a carrier. A Medical Officer of Environmental Health can give you a certificate 'deeming' you incapable of work; *or*
• you have a certificate from your GP stating that for convalescent or precautionary reasons, you should not work and you are under medical care *and* you do not in fact work.

If you can do some work but not your normal job

Whether or not you can get benefit if you can do some work depends on whether it is reasonable to expect you to do other jobs. At the beginning of your claim, only your normal job will be considered. Once you show you are incapable of that, your claim would be allowed. However, as time goes on you will be expected to consider other work.[3] Usually the adjudication officer does not look at this question until you have been off work for about six months. At this stage you may have some idea whether you can return to your old job and, if so, when. If you are likely to return soon, it would not be reasonable to expect you to look at other jobs. But if you are likely to be unable to do your own job for a long time, you will be expected to consider other work. When looking at what it is reasonable for you to do, your age, education, state of health and skills are taken into account.[4] The adjudication officer must also look at you as you are and not how you could be if you retrained or were more highly skilled.

If you are only able to do a limited amount of light or 'therapeutic' work this will not, on its own, affect your rights to sickness benefit, IVB or SDA (provided you meet the conditions set out below). You are not expected simply to sit at home and do nothing. However (apart from any work you may do as a local councillor[5]), the Benefits Agency may take into account any work you do, including therapeutic work, as evidence that you are not 'incapable of work'.

Work you may do while claiming

If you are claiming sickness benefit, IVB or SDA the Benefits Agency may (but does not have to) allow you to receive benefit (but not SSP) even though you are working if:[6]

- you do not earn more than £43 a week; *and either*
- you only work under medical supervision as part of your hospital treatment, either in hospital or as an outpatient; *or*
- you only do work which you have 'good cause' to do.

Such work is sometimes known as 'therapeutic' work.

Work does not necessarily count as therapeutic just because it is unpaid. The Benefits Agency may still treat you as working even if you are only doing voluntary work.

For the rules on how earnings are calculated see p261. You cannot avoid the earnings rule by not claiming earnings which are due to you.[7]

If you are a local councillor and your net allowance (after deducting expenses) is more than £43 in any week your benefit will be reduced by the amount of the excess.[8]

Members of Disability Appeal Tribunals (see p311) are deemed to be incapable of work for up to one day a week when they are hearing appeals.[9]

It is difficult to say generally when you will have 'good cause' for doing any particular work. There will certainly be good cause if, on your doctor's recommendation, you do a small amount of light work (either as exercise or to take your mind off your disability) even though that work is not actually carried out under medical supervision. It is also clear that non-medical reasons can sometimes be good cause (eg, work done in an emergency), but when non-medical good cause will exist cannot be predicted and such situations will be exceptional. In particular, commissioners have held more than once that if your reason for working is to get more money, either generally or for a particular purpose, you do not have good cause.[10] This has not always been followed by other commissioners – eg, a woman who worked to pay for contact lenses which she needed to avoid going blind and could not get on the NHS was held to have good cause.[11] But it does indicate that the commissioners are anxious to prevent the 'good cause' rule from being used to undermine the principle that the people who get incapacity benefits must be unable to work.

If your reason for working is to earn money, whether or not you succeed does not make any difference. So, claimants who have worked to develop small businesses do not have good cause even where their businesses do not make any profit.[12] This is because the claimants hoped to make money, albeit in the future, when they did the work.

Because it is much easier to show good cause if you have a doctor's recommendation, it is a good idea to speak to your GP *before* you do any work to see whether s/he agrees that it would be beneficial for you to do it. Better still, if your doctor is prepared to put that recommendation in writing, you will then be able to show it to the Benefits Agency.

Remember that the Benefits Agency does not have to allow you to do these kinds of work. It has a choice. If you are in any doubt you should contact your local office before taking a job to see if it is acceptable. If you disagree with the Benefits Agency's decision you should appeal (see p304) although you cannot appeal a refusal to approve therapeutic work in advance – you have to wait until a decision to stop your benefit has actually been made.

Training for work and incapacity for work

You cannot receive any of the benefits covered in this chapter while on a training course and receiving a training allowance.[13] However, your income will not be reduced because the training allowance is fixed at your previous benefit level, and you will also receive an extra training premium of £10 a week.

At the end of the course, your benefit is usually reinstated provided you reclaim within eight weeks of the course ending so that your periods of interruptions of employment can be linked (see p253). However, this is not automatic. If you have shown yourself to be able to work by attending the course or have acquired new skills which mean that there is now other work which you might reasonably be expected to do, an adjudication officer may decide that you are no longer incapable of work. If this happens you should claim unemployment benefit (UB) and/or income support (IS) instead and consider whether to appeal (see p61).

Proving you are unable to work

If you claim SSP or occupational sick pay, your employers will have requirements about how you prove you are too ill to work. These will be in your employment contract. But, for SSP, there are limits to what your employers can ask for (see p69).

For the DSS benefits, the general rule is that you must provide medical certificates.[14] The rules also allow you to prove that you are unable to work by using other evidence provided that it is 'sufficient in the circumstances', but this is to cover unusual cases and you should not rely on it unless it is absolutely necessary.

Normally your first certificate is the self-certification form (SC1) in which you state that you are too ill to work.[15] After seven days of self-certificated sickness, you will usually be expected to supply certificates from your GP. Doctors cannot charge for these if they are provided for social security purposes.[16] The certificate states that the doctor advises you to refrain from work. It is either a 'closed certificate', stating a date within the next two weeks on which you can return to work, or an 'open certificate', stating that you will be unfit to work for a specified period (up to six months) without stating that you will then be fit to return.

You can submit a medical certificate from other medical sources, such as an osteopath or chiropractor, or a certificate from your own GP which is not the standard national insurance one, or your evidence can be in the form of a letter rather than a certificate.

2. 'INVALIDITY CUT-OFF' – DISPUTES ABOUT YOUR CAPACITY FOR WORK

In recent years, the Government has become increasingly concerned about the growth of expenditure on incapacity benefits. One consequence of this is the proposed abolition of sickness and invalidity benefits and their replacement by 'incapacity benefit' from April 1995. More immediately, Benefits Agency procedures on keeping claims for invalidity benefit under review have been tightened up so that most people who suffer from a long-term disease or condition will at some point have to face the additional worry of having to convince the Benefits Agency that they are still so ill that they cannot be expected to work. This section explains the procedures which the Benefits Agency follows in reviewing your capacity for work and suggests steps which you or your advisers can take to ensure that your benefit is not withdrawn if you are genuinely unable to work.

There are a number of points which should always be kept in mind:

- Long-term benefits such as IVB and SDA must be awarded for an indefinite period unless there is a good reason for limiting the award to a definite length of time (eg, because a change of circumstances is reasonably expected in the foreseeable future).[1] If the adjudication officer's letter telling you that you have been awarded benefit does not say how long the award is to last, then it is indefinite.

  Unless you have come to the end of a fixed period award, the adjudication officer can only stop your benefit by carrying out a review. In practice this means that the burden of proof is on the adjudication officer to show that you no longer qualify for benefit.[2]

  The point is important and worth repeating – as long as your award of benefit has not come to an end, it is up to the adjudication officer to prove that there is work which you are capable of and which you can reasonably be expected to do: it is *not* up to you to prove that you are incapable of work.

- In every case, the question is whether you have a disease or physical or mental disablement and as a result you are unable to work at a job which you can reasonably be expected to do. Although medical evidence is obviously relevant here, this is not just a medical question. So whatever the doctors say about your state of health, it is also important for everyone concerned to think in detail about what a job will actually involve in practice when considering whether it is reasonable to expect you to do it.

There are three basic stages in an 'invalidity cut-off'. First there is the consideration of your case by the Benefits Agency Medical Service ('BAMS') which will probably involve a medical examination. Then the adjudication officer must consider the BAMS report and any other relevant medical and non-medical evidence. Finally, if the adjudication officer decides that the claimant is capable of work, there is a right of appeal to an independent tribunal.

Although you can always appeal against an adjudication officer's decision that you are capable of work, appeals are a lengthy and worrying process and, perhaps most importantly, your benefit will not be paid while the appeal is being decided. If at all possible, therefore, it is important to nip doubts about your incapacity in the bud so that you are never put in the position where you have to appeal. This section considers in detail what happens each stage of the process and suggests steps you can take to make sure the Benefits Agency or the Social Security Appeal Tribunal (SSAT) have all the information which they need to make the right decision.

The basic point is that stopping an 'invalidity cut-off' is an active process. Do not just sit back and allow things to happen. Get advice and help if necessary and make it clear at all stages how ill you are and how your illness affects you in practice.

Examination by the Benefits Agency Medical Service

When you first claim an incapacity benefit the adjudication officer will generally accept your doctor's certificate without question. But if your illness or disability proves to be long-term, the adjudication officer will look at your claim from time to time and at some stage it will be referred to a doctor employed by the Benefits Agency Medical Service (BAMS). These doctors are called Examining Medical Officers (EMOs).

There is no fixed rule about when your claim will be reconsidered, although the Adjudication Officer does have to consider (unpublished) Benefits Agency internal guidance which says the decision should be based on the nature of your illness or disability and the length of time for which you have been away from work. Normally your claim will not be referred to BAMS until you have been off work for at least six months, but there is nothing to stop it happening before then and there is no appeal against the decision to refer.

Although it is sensible to take the precautions recommended below, there is, in fact, nothing to worry about at this stage. The adjudication officer has not made a decision to stop your benefit and – unless you have given the Benefits Agency a reason for doubting your claim (eg, by working during your claim (except therapeutic work – see p49)) – s/he is probably just getting a second opinion as a matter of routine. The EMO may well agree with your own doctor that you are unable to work.

When s/he first receives your papers, the EMO will consult with your GP about your condition. In many cases, this may be sufficient to convince the EMO that you are medically incapable of work and if yours is one of those cases, you may not even know that your claim has been referred. However, if the EMO remains unsure about your condition after consulting your GP you will be asked to attend an examination.

When you get an appointment to be examined by a EMO, you should try to keep it if at all possible. You will normally be given about four weeks' notice. If you cannot keep the appointment, you should write immediately explaining why and asking for another one at a more convenient time. Alternatively, if the reason you cannot attend the examination is that you are too ill to travel, you should ask to be examined at home.

If you fail to attend an examination without a good reason you can be disqualified from receiving benefit (see p76).

The examination will probably be a short one of about 15 minutes. The EMO will ask you about your condition and your medical and employment history, examine you and assess whether, overall, you are fit to work, taking account of your degree of capacity in specific functions. The EMO has to fill in a form (Form RM9) which asks her/him to state *either*:

- that you are medically incapable of all work. In this case, the EMO will also suggest when the adjudication officer should refer your case to BAMS for a further review; *or*
- that you are incapable of work in your most recent occupation but are capable of doing other 'light' work. In this case, the EMO will suggest particular jobs which s/he believes you are capable of doing; *or*
- that you are not medically incapable of work (including your most recent occupation).

Whatever his or her opinion, the EMO is asked to give brief reasons for it.

If the EMO thinks you are capable of some work, s/he also has to consider:

- the function in your shoulders, arms, hands, eyes and ears; *and*
- your ability to carry out the various tasks such as climbing stairs and ladders, working at heights, walking, standing, kneeling, bending, lifting and carrying, prolonged sitting, driving and working outdoors in all weathers; *and*
- your ability to cope with exposure to dust, fumes and skin irritants.

The EMO will then record on Form RM9 the extent to which each of these functions is impaired on a scale from 1 to 4 where 1 is full unimpaired function and 4 is no function at all.

When you prepare for your appointment with the EMO, it is important to remember two things about doctors. The first is that they are very busy people and the second is that, however gifted they may be, they are not psychic. Doctors rely on their tests and examinations, on what their patients tell them and on medical records (which are no more than the results of previous tests and examinations and other doctors' notes – sometimes inaccurate and often illegible – about what you have said about your symptoms in the past).

The most important of these sources of information are how the patient behaves and what s/he says. There are limits to what even the most thorough and conscientious examination can discover and you should not assume, for example, that a doctor will know that you have pains in your ankle when you first get up or in cold weather if you do not tell him or her about it.

Unlike your GP who may have known and treated you for years, the EMO has probably never seen you before. S/he has to decide on the basis of a very short meeting whether you are medically capable or incapable of work. Although s/he will probably have had a letter from your GP giving an outline of your relevant medical history and the treatment which you have been receiving, this is unlikely to give as much detail as you or your GP would like (remember that GPs are also busy and rely on their notes of what you tell them). It is therefore very important that you tell the EMO in as much detail as possible exactly what is wrong with you and how it affects you in practice. If you do no more than answer questions and allow yourself to be examined, there is a real chance that something important will be missed and that the EMO will say you are capable of work simply because you have not given him or her enough information. Worse still, if you have to appeal, the tribunal may not believe you if you complain then of symptoms that you have not mentioned to the doctor.

So for example:

- Take a list of the medicines which your GP is prescribing for you, or has prescribed for you since you became unable to work. This may lead the EMO to ask questions which s/he would not otherwise have thought of.
- The doctor's surgery is often a very artificial environment and doctors' tests are inevitably limited. If, for example, the doctor asks you to bend over once or twice, it may be quite possible for you to do this without pain. But you may know from experience that if you bend over for lengthy periods, you suffer intense discomfort and could not possibly contemplate doing a job which involved repeated bending or lifting. If so, you will be the only one who knows this. Tell the doctor.
- Similarly, illness is not constant. Some diseases are recognised as involving periods of relapse and remission and all people suffering from a long-term illness can have good days and bad days. If the doctor is seeing you on a good day s/he will not necessarily know how bad things are on a bad day unless you explain.

- Many people are nervous of doctors and this is particularly under-standable when one possible outcome of an examination is that your benefit may be stopped. If you think there is a risk that you will become tongue-tied, make a note in advance of all the things you want the doctor to know. You could even leave the note with the doctor to jog his or her memory when s/he is preparing the report to the adjudi-cation officer, but if you decide to do this, make sure that you keep a copy first.
- It is also a good idea to ask a friend or adviser to come to the examina-tion with you if you feel that you may need moral support. Apart from anything else, this will be useful if there is ever a dispute about what you did or did not say during the examination. And someone who knows you may be able to help by giving the doctor more details on the practical consequences of your illness. However, it is important that anyone who comes to the examination with you should allow the EMO to do his or her job and should not try to take over or behave in a confrontational way.
- If English is not your first language, it is *vital* that someone goes with you to see the EMO. Choosing who this should be can be difficult, but ultimately a good knowledge of English is more important at this stage than personal knowledge of you and your symptoms.

If, after you have seen the EMO, you are unhappy with the way the examination went, it may be an idea to write down what the doctor said and did and what you are unhappy about before your memory fades. This may be helpful for your advisers if there has to be an appeal.

The BAMS report and the adjudication officer's decision

If the EMO agrees with you that you are incapable of work your benefit will continue to be paid and the only thing that you need to do – at least until the next time the adjudication officer looks again at your claim – is to continue to send in your medical certificates. If, on the other hand, s/he considers you are fit to do some work, s/he will inform your GP and the adjudication officer.

Note that your benefit should *not* stop automatically at this stage – the person who takes the decision on whether or not you should continue to receive benefit is the adjudication officer and not the EMO.

However you should consider carefully whether you agree that you could now try to return to work. Remember that the rules on linking periods of interruption of employment (see p253) mean that if you try to go back to work but discover that your health will not permit it, you will go straight back on to invalidity benefit without having to wait another 168 days (see p77) as long as you give up work within eight weeks. And if you are entitled to DWA (see CPAG's *National Welfare Benefits Handbook*) while you are working, this period is extended to two years.[3] In practice, these rules mean that you can go back to work for a short period on a trial basis without affecting your entitlement to incapacity benefits. And, of course, if you try to do a job and fail because of your health, that is the best possible evidence that you are incapable of doing that job when you next claim benefit.

If you feel that you are now able to work but have no job to go back to you should consider claiming UB (see Chapter 2) instead of an incapacity benefit. The Disablement Resettlement Officer at the Jobcentre may be able to give you help to find a suitable job or training.

If you do not agree with the EMO that you are capable of work there are two things which you *must* do immediately. The first is to go and see your GP and the second is to get advice (see p329).

Your GP's support is vital if you are to avoid an invalidity cut-off, so make an appointment to see him/her and discuss the implications of the EMO's report. That report is only one doctor's opinion and your GP is not bound to agree with it. On the contrary, it is most important that your GP makes up her/his own mind, rather than simply accepting the EMO's opinion. S/he has probably known you a lot longer than the EMO and has a far better idea of your true condition and your capacity for work.

The most important thing is to persuade your GP to continue to give you medical certificates. Obviously this is a matter for her/his professional judgement and you are not entitled to insist, but in practice if s/he stops giving medical certificates then – except in rare cases where your consultant supports you but your GP does not – it will mean that you cannot continue to receive an incapacity benefit. It is very difficult to persuade anyone you are too ill to work if your own doctor does not support you.

If your GP stops issuing medical certificates, you should immediately sign on as available for work and claim UB (see Chapter 2) and/or IS (see CPAG's *National Welfare Benefits Handbook*).

If your GP does not agree with the EMO and is prepared to go on issuing certificates, you should ask him/her to go further and write to the adjudication officer explaining the position in more detail. Adjudication officers are told that they should not treat the fact that a GP continues to issue certificates as evidence of disagreement with the EMO's report unless s/he specifically says so or the reason given for your incapacity changes to one which has not previously been considered by the EMO. In either of these situations, the adjudication officer will arrange for you to be seen by another EMO and if s/he thinks you are incapable of work your benefit will not be stopped.

In practice, you may find that your GP is reluctant to say in as many words that s/he thinks another doctor's opinion is wrong. S/he may however be prepared to state his or her own views in a letter to the adjudication officer. If you appeal, the adjudication officer will write to your GP and ask for his or her opinion.

As well as going to see your GP, you should also try and get advice from someone with experience of Benefits Agency procedures if you have not already done so. See p329 for suggestions about which organisations may be able to help you. Professional help is desirable because the reality of the situation is that, without it, the adjudication officer is likely to stop your benefit.

The adjudication officer has to make a decision about your capacity for work based on all the evidence, both medical and non-medical.

There is no rule that says s/he has to agree with the BAMS report if this conflicts with what your GP says. On the contrary, s/he is supposed to make a reasoned decision based on all the evidence – medical and non-medical. Despite this, it is likely in practice that the adjudication officer will prefer the EMO's evidence. For example, adjudication officers are told that 'a doctor's statement is rarely enough to undermine the report of the BAMS medical officer' and that 'unless there is substantial evidence that the GP is fully aware of the patient's medical history and work potential, his opinion should not outweigh the BAMS report merely because he has known the patient longer'.[4]

It is therefore important to give the adjudication officer as much additional evidence as possible. Consider the following:

- Ask your adviser to talk to your GP about what s/he is going to say *before* s/he writes to the adjudication officer. S/he may take more notice if a fellow professional explains why it is important that certain things are included or put in a certain way.
- You or your adviser should ask your GP to make his or her letter as detailed as possible. Why, precisely, does s/he consider you are incapable of work despite what the BAMS says? If s/he has been treating you on a regular basis for many years, then s/he should say so specifically so that there can be no doubt that s/he is 'is fully aware of (your) medical history and work potential'.
- A report from a consultant will carry more weight than your GP's views on their own. Your GP may be able to arrange for you to see one through the National Health Service. Alternatively, If your incapacity arises from an accident for which you are claiming compensation, your solicitor will probably have a consultant's report, or will be getting

one, or, if the injury is work-related, your union may be prepared to pay for a report. If you are getting IS or your income is very low you could ask for a solicitor to obtain a consultantUs report through the 'Green Form' scheme ('Pink' in Scotland) for legal assistance. If you have not seen a consultant before, then in practical terms it will probably be very difficult to see one and get a report before the adjudication officer makes his/her decision but you should still make the necessary arrangements now because a favourable consultant's report will be important if you have to appeal.

• If you have tried to work in the past but have had to give up because of ill-health, ask your former employer to write to the adjudication officer and explain what the difficulties were in practice.

If you provide the adjudication officer with further medical evidence, it is likely that s/he will ask BAMS for its comments and (if s/he is still in doubt) s/he may seek further information by asking you to come in for an interview, sending you a questionnaire to complete or referring you for another examination by a different EMO. In some areas, third referrals to BAMS are becoming increasingly common – almost as if adjudication officers are trying to set up a sufficient body of medical evidence to 'trump' the views of the claimant's own doctors if there should be an appeal.

If the adjudication officer decides that you are fit for some work, s/he will go on to suggest a specific job or jobs which s/he believes you are capable of doing.[5] This is usually done by reference to the job descriptions set out in the Standard Occupational Classification, a list of different types of jobs published by HMSO. The adjudication officer must show that the jobs s/he has suggested exist but s/he does not have to prove that there are vacancies in your area – if you are capable of doing a particular job but cannot find employment in that occupation you should be claiming UB or IS, not an incapacity benefit.

However, the adjudication officer does have to take you as you are and not how you might be in a better world. For example, if you cannot read or speak English then you cannot reasonably be expected to do a job which involves those skills – such as a clerk, or a receptionist or telephonist – even if you are otherwise physically capable of doing so. Similarly, adjudication officers are told that a job should not be regarded as suitable if you would need to undergo a prolonged course of training before you are able to do it.[6] On the other hand, it may be reasonable to expect someone to undergo a short course of training.

Job descriptions inevitably give only an outline of what is actually involved in a job. The important questions are what employers are likely to require in practice and whether that is feasible for you given your disabilities.

Example

A building labourer in his 40s suffers from asbestosis, so the job of attendant in a car park is suggested. There is no heavy work in giving out tickets and checking to see they have not expired. However, car exhaust fumes accumulate even though the car park is in the open air, and this would aggravate his breathing problems. The work is not suitable.

You should consider each job suggested by the adjudication officer and find out what difficulties there may be. Thus if you have a bad back and a job as a messenger is suggested, you can point out that a messenger often has to carry parcels, which involves bending and lifting. If possible try to get a letter from someone – preferably an employer – who knows the type of work suggested.

Another way to help your case is to ask your doctor to comment specifically on your ability to work at that particular job.

An important point to bear in mind is that the job being considered must be one that some employer would pay you to do.[7] You can argue that, as a matter of common sense, no one will pay you if you can do certain tasks only for a short time or occasionally.

Example

You have a bad back strain. You cannot sit or stand for long, must alternate between the two every 30 minutes, and cannot bend or do heavy lifting. The adjudication officer suggests a job as an assembly worker in light engineering or component manufacture. You can tell the tribunal why it is unlikely that you would be given a job. For instance, most jobs like this do not allow a worker to change position at her/his convenience. Products have to be lifted up and down and a seven- or eight-hour working day is the norm. You could also write to a local firm of this type, describing your limitations, and asking them to comment on the prospects of your being employed there. Alternatively your union representative may have wide experience and could comment.

This is not the same as saying that, as there is a lot of unemployment, you cannot get a job in your area. You are arguing that as you have got the disabilities described, *no* employer is likely to employ you.

In practice, these suggestions for influencing the adjudication officer's decision may be a counsel of perfection. You may find that an adverse decision is given as soon as the adjudication officer receives Form RM9 from the EMO without your being given any further opportunity to comment.

Some claimants have even found that – quite wrongly – the Benefits Agency is jumping the gun and sending out letters demanding the return of their order books as soon as the EMO says that they are medically capable of some work and without waiting for the adjudication officer to make a decision. If this happens to you, you or your adviser should make a formal complaint (see p301) but there is probably little that can be done in practice. Your order book is the property of the Secretary of State and if you do not return it when required to do so, you may be exposing yourself to a criminal prosecution. You should remind your local office that the Secretary of State is legally obliged to pay your benefit until the adjudication officer's decision and ask to be sent a girocheque.

If the adjudication officer does stop your benefit before you have been able to put your case fully, asking for a review of the decision (see p288) may be quicker than appealing. In most cases, however, the adjudication officer will be unwilling to change the decision and it will be necessary to appeal to an independent SSAT (see p303) if you want to challenge it.

Appealing to a Social Security Appeal Tribunal

If you are convinced that you are too ill to work, it is almost always worth appealing to an SSAT if your incapacity benefit is stopped. Indeed you may well have no other choice.

First, if you are entitled to it, IVB is more advantageous than most alternative benefits. For example, it is paid at a higher rate than UB, lasts indefinitely, is not taxable, and entitles you to disability premiums for means-tested benefits.

Secondly, it is the declared policy objective of the DSS to make a substantial saving in expenditure on IVB by reducing the number of long-term claimants. Unfortunately, that policy objective is not conducive to disinterested consideration of individual cases by the Benefits Agency and the hearing before the independent SSAT may well be the first time that your case gets considered in a proper, dispassionate way.

When deciding whether to appeal and how to prepare your case, bear in mind that the tribunal has to consider four distinct questions:

- What is the extent of your incapacity?
- What work, if any, does your incapacity allow you to do?
- Is it work that it is reasonable to expect you to do?
- What period is to be considered?

The first three of these are the same questions which should already have been considered by the adjudication officer so all the advice given previously remains relevant at this stage, particularly if you have not had a chance to get all your evidence in earlier. You may wish to consider the following points as well.

(a) What is the extent of your incapacity?

This is the major medical question and it has to be decided by the members of the SSAT, who are not doctors, assessing the reports in front of them, and your own evidence.

If you have not been able to obtain a consultant's report in any other way, you can ask the tribunal to obtain one free for you (through the adjudication officer).[8] However, this cannot be done in advance of the hearing, so if the tribunal agrees there will have to be an adjournment. Tribunals have been reminded by the commissioners of their power to obtain reports where claimants cannot afford them,[9] but they will not normally do so if the doctors agree on the diagnosis and only disagree on the effect of the claimant's condition on his or her capacity to work.

If the only evidence is the report of a single EMO and the evidence of your GP then you should argue that the latter should be preferred. The tribunal is not bound by the advice given to adjudication officers on this point (see p58) and, looked at objectively, it is only common sense that the independent opinion of your own doctor who knows you should normally be given more weight than the views of one who has seen you for 15 minutes. The fact that the EMO is employed by BAMS, the principal instrument of the DSS's policy of reducing expenditure on incapacity benefits, and is therefore not independent, must also be relevant in considering his or her opinion (although this point should be made with tact as there is a risk of alienating the SSAT).

It is often useful for a person who lives with you or knows you well to attend the hearing to describe to the tribunal the day-to-day problems you suffer.

You should take a list of any medication you are taking with you to the tribunal hearing.

If there is a dispute about whether your symptoms are genuine, a tribunal has to decide the case, partially at least, on its assessment of you. Your appearance will be important, as well as your record in claiming benefit – a lengthy history of claims may count against you.

Watch out for the term 'functional overlay' in medical reports. This means incapacity for which there is no evident physical cause. It is often taken to be a euphemism for malingering or imaginary symptoms, although it does not actually mean the same thing. Genuine symptoms should be taken into account, even if there is a psychological element partly causing them.[10]

(b) What work, if any, does your incapacity allow you to do?

As well as all the points discussed on pp59 and 60, an appeal hearing gives you the opportunity to have someone who knows about the jobs suggested as suitable for you by the adjudication officer to give oral evidence to the tribunal about what is involved. Your union may be able to help you find someone with the relevant knowledge.

(c) Is it work that it is reasonable to expect you to do?

Because this question is not addressed properly, claimants often lose appeals unnecessarily. The tribunal may accept that you are physically capable of doing some jobs without going on to ask whether it is reasonable to expect you to do them. If there are reasons why you cannot or do not want to do the jobs which the adjudication officer says you are fit for, you should tell the tribunal and back them up with evidence if possible. The reasons do not have to be related to your health (see p59).

(d) What period is to be considered?

In practice the tribunal will make a decision on whether you are capable of work for the whole of the period from the adjudication officer's decision up to the date of the tribunal hearing. It is therefore important that, if you can, you should continue to submit medical certificates showing that you are still unfit for work while you are waiting for the appeal to be heard. This is also important to ensure that, if you win your appeal, your period of interruption of employment (see p251) does not come to an end so that you have to wait a further 168 days before becoming entitled to IVB again. Sending in medical certificates is also important if you claim IS pending a decision on your appeal.

Protecting your income and national insurance credits while waiting for an appeal

Sickness benefit, IVB and SDA are not paid while your appeal is waiting to be heard. For this reason, you should claim IS (see CPAG's *National Welfare Benefits Handbook*) immediately benefit is refused. If you send in medical certificates while waiting for your appeal to be heard you will not be required to sign on as available for work in order to qualify for IS but it may still be in your interests to do so (see below). If your appeal is *successful*, you will receive arrears of benefit to make up for the difference between the rate of IS and the non-means-tested incapacity benefit which you are claiming.

   You will also need to consider whether or not to claim UB as well as or instead of IS. Normally, it will be important for you to do this even if there is no immediate financial advantage, as a successful claim for UB will mean that you receive Class 1 national insurance credits (see p225) while your appeal is waiting to be heard *whatever the outcome*. If you only claim IS, you will get credits for the period if you eventually win your appeal but not if you lose. A complete contribution record may be important to ensure you get the maximum pension when you retire and (if you are a married man) to protect your wife's entitlement to a widow's pension should you die.

The following points are also relevant:

• the contribution conditions for UB are stricter than for sickness bene-fit/IVB. You will not necessarily be entitled to the former just because you were getting the latter;
• similarly you may not be entitled to IS if you do not pass the means test (eg, if you have savings or a private income) or if, for example, you have a partner who works for 16 or more hours a week. If so, you may have no alternative but to claim UB;
• for the year from April 1994, the basic rate of IS for a single person aged 25 and over is slightly higher than the equivalent rate of UB. However, you should compare the rates of the two benefits carefully as the position may be different if, for example, you are under 25, over pensionable age or one of a couple.

There is a potential problem about entitlement to UB while waiting for an appeal against an 'invalidity cut-off'. To be eligible for UB you have to be capable of, available for and actively seeking work (see p8).[11] Logically you ought to have difficulties convincing the Employment Service that you are capable of work because you will be saying in your appeal that you are not.

Fortunately for claimants – who would otherwise be put in a very difficult position – this rarely seems to be a problem in practice and a recent com-missioner's decision says that a claim for UB should not be held against claimants when deciding the appeal. The best thing to tell the new client adviser at the Unemployment Benefit Office is that you will accept any reas-onable work within your limitations. What you should *not* say is that you are really too sick to work but have been told you have to sign on.

3. STATUTORY SICK PAY

SSP is administered and paid by your employers, *not* the Benefits Agency (although there are rights of appeal to an adjudication officer if you and your employers cannot agree). Your contract of employment may mean that your employers must also pay you occupational sick pay. But SSP is a legal mini-mum and, if you qualify for it, your employers are not allowed to pay you less.

Conditions of entitlement[1]

For every day you receive benefit:

* You must be an employee;
* You must be incapable of work (see p48);
* You must have begun a 'period of incapacity for work' (see p67) by being incapable of work for at least four consecutive days;
* The day must be a 'qualifying day' (see p69);
* Your 'period of entitlement' (see p68) must not have ended; *and*
* You must have notified your employer (see p69).

Who can get SSP?

You are entitled to SSP if you are an employee.[2] This does not mean you must have a written agreement. It is the fact that you are employed which matters rather than any documents (though documents are useful for evidence in case of a dispute). Your right to SSP cannot be taken away by any document, whether you sign it or not[3] and, if your employer sacks you to avoid paying SSP, then s/he is still liable to pay it after your contract has ended.[4] The question of whether you are an employee for SSP purposes is similar to the question of whether you are an 'employed earner' under the Industrial Injuries Scheme (see p175).

Even if you are an employee, your employers do not have to pay your SSP if they are neither resident nor present in Great Britain or if they are exempt from the social security legislation because of an international treaty.[5]

Below are some other employees who will not get SSP.[6]

(a) People over pensionable age

If you are over pensionable age (65 for a man, 60 for a woman) you will not get SSP unless your 'period of entitlement' (see p68) began before your 65th/60th birthday and has not yet ended. This unequal treatment of men and women is almost certainly contrary to EC law.[7] If you are a woman aged between 60 and 65 and are refused SSP on this ground, then provided you are not also claiming a retirement pension, you should claim sickness benefit instead (see p73). If you would be better off having SSP, apply for a decision from an adjudication officer (see p72) and be prepared to appeal if necessary (see p304). You should also read the section on Equal Treatment of Men and Women in Chapter 14.

(b) People with short-term contracts

If your contract of employment lasts for less than three months, you cannot get SSP unless your period of entitlement began when you were working under a different contract and has not ended. This will be rare (see p68).

Again it is the facts rather than what the documents say which is relevant here. If you have in fact been employed continuously for more than three months, then (unless you are ineligible for some other reason) you are entitled to SSP even if your contract of employment was originally a short-term one.

There are also rules to stop employers avoiding their liability to pay SSP by employing people on a series of short-term contracts. These say that you are entitled to SSP if you have been employed by the same employer on two or more short-term contracts separated by eight weeks or less and the total period specified in those contracts exceeds three months.

(c) People with low earnings

You cannot get SSP if you normally earn less than the lower earnings limit, currently £57 (see p216). It is your gross earnings (before tax and national insurance contributions are deducted) that are relevant here.

(d) Pregnant women

If you are entitled to statutory maternity pay (SMP)(see p88) or maternity allowance (see p95) you cannot get SSP during the 'maternity pay period' or the 'maternity allowance period'. Within the limits set out on pp90-1 (and unless your baby is born early – see p94) you have a right to choose when your maternity pay or maternity allowance period begins. So, for example, your employers cannot insist that you claim maternity allowance at the earliest possible date in order to limit the period for which they have to pay SSP.

If you are not entitled to SMP or to maternity allowance you cannot get SSP for the six weeks before the week in which your baby is due, for the expected week of confinement itself or for the 11 weeks afterwards.

(e) Prisoners[8]

You cannot get SSP for any day that you are in prison. If you become incapable of work while in prison you cannot get SSP for any of the subsequent days of the same period of incapacity for work, even if you are released in the meantime. This will apply even if you have been held on remand awaiting trial and are eventually acquitted.

(f) People involved in trade disputes

You cannot get SSP if there is a stoppage of work due to a trade dispute at your place of employment unless *either*:

• you can show that you did not have a 'direct interest' in it (see p42); *or*
• your period of entitlement began before the stoppage of work and has not yet ended.

This rule will prevent you from getting SSP during the whole period of your sickness even if the strike ends the day after you fall ill and even if you do not take part in the stoppage. You can claim sickness benefit instead if you have paid enough contributions or if you became ill as a result of an industrial injury or disease. You will not lose SSP if there is any industrial action short of a stoppage of work – eg, a ban on overtime or 'working to grade'.[9]

(g) People outside the European Community[10]

You cannot get SSP if you are not in an EC country unless you are an airman or woman, a mariner or a continental shelf worker. If you spend any time outside an EC country on the first day of your period of incapacity for work you cannot get SSP for the remainder of that period.

(h) People who have not yet started work

If you have agreed to go and work for an employer but have not yet started work and you fall ill you will not get SSP for any day during the same period of incapacity.

'Period of incapacity for work'

A period of incapacity is four or more consecutive 'days of incapacity' (see p48).[11] Every day of the week (including Sundays[12]) counts for this purpose even if they are not days on which you would normally work. Any two periods separated by not more than eight weeks are treated as a single period.[13]

For sickness benefit, odd days can be linked to form a period of interruption of employment if you are incapable of work on any two or more days in a week because you are receiving certain types of regular treatment such as dialysis (see p251). For SSP, that rule does not apply. If this prevents you getting SSP and you are receiving one of those forms of treatment, you should claim sickness benefit instead (see p73).

'Period of entitlement'

Your 'period of entitlement' begins with the commencement of a 'period of incapacity for work' (see above) and ends with whichever of the following first occurs:[14]

- the end of that 'period of incapacity for work';
- the day on which your contract of employment ends;
- the day before you are disqualified on the ground of pregnancy (see p66);
- the day on which you reach your maximum entitlement to SSP as against that particular employer;
- the third anniversary of the beginning of the 'period of entitlement';
- a day when you are not in an EC country (see p247). It is sometimes suggested that this means your period of entitlement ends when you are in international waters on your way from, say, Great Britain to France. If your SSP is stopped on that ground, you should ask for an adjudication officer's decision and be prepared to appeal (see p304). You should argue that the regulations clearly intend that you should be able to travel freely within the EC and that, otherwise, they would be contrary to EC law.[15]

If your period of entitlement ends before your period of incapacity, you will not be entitled to SSP until your current period of incapacity ends and a new one arises. In practice this means that at least eight weeks must elapse between when you recover and when you fall ill again.

If you have received sickness benefit, IVB, maternity benefits or SDA, you must also wait at least eight weeks from the end of your period of interruption of employment (see p251) before you can get SSP again.

Periods of entitlement with the same employer separated by eight weeks or less are linked and treated as a single period.[16] This is why it is possible not to have exhausted your 28 weeks' entitlement to SSP before the third anniversary of the beginning of your period of entitlement.

Periods of entitlement with different employers cannot usually be linked. However, on leaving a job you should be given a leaver's statement on form SSP1(L). Provided that you give this to your new employers within a week of your first qualifying day, the two periods can be linked.[17] This affects your maximum entitlement and allows you to transfer to IVB earlier.

'Qualifying days'

Qualifying days are usually those days of the week on which you would normally work if you were not sick. However, other days may be selected as qualifying days by agreement between you and your employer if that would provide a better reflection of your contract of employment (eg, you work a complicated shift pattern). There must be a minimum of one qualifying day in each week, which begins on a Sunday.[18] You and your employers can agree that the qualifying days are those normally worked, so there may be a different number in each week depending on your shift arrangements. Or you can average these out to give a constant pattern, eg, five days a week for two weeks, and four days a week for another two weeks. If there is no agreement as to which days are qualifying days, they are presumed to be:

- the days on which it is agreed that you are required to work; *or*
- Wednesday, if it is agreed that you are required to work no days in that week – eg, offshore oil-workers, who may work two weeks 'on' and then two weeks 'off'; *or*
- every day in the week except days where you and your employers agree that no employee works (if you can agree at least to that extent).[19]

'Required to work' means required by the terms of your contract of employment.[20] Days when you can choose whether to work or not do not count – eg, voluntary overtime shifts.

Informing your employer that you are sick

The form in which employers require you to notify them that you are sick is for them to decide, or for negotiation with you or your union. Most employers have their own rules for notification, which must be set out in the notice of terms and conditions of employment you should receive when you start work. They must take reasonable care to tell you what these are.[21] Notification should be in writing unless there is an agreement to the contrary.[22] As far as SSP is concerned the employers *cannot* insist on notification by you:

- personally;
- in the form of medical evidence (as opposed to a simple medical certificate);
- more than weekly;
- on a document provided only by the employers;
- on a printed form.[23]

You can also negotiate how quickly you have to notify the employers of your absence. For their own purposes many employers insist that they should be notified within the first hour, or in the morning, or some such other rule. For SSP purposes, however, employers cannot insist on notification before the end of the first qualifying day.[24] If there is no agreement, notification must be within seven days.[25]

Notice given in a properly addressed prepaid letter is deemed to have been given on the day the letter was sent.[26] A late claim must be accepted if there is 'good cause' for the delay, but not later than 91 days after the first day of absence. The effect of a late claim is to delay your entitlement – you will still get a total of 28 weeks' payment of SSP if you are off that long after your first valid day of absence.[27]

The DSS relies on employers to administer SSP, but if the employers are suspicious of a long period of illness they can ask BAMS to arrange an examination (see p53).

For occupational sick pay schemes most employers adopt the requirements for the sickness benefit scheme and accept self-certification for the first seven days, with medical certificates thereafter.

Amount of payment[28]

SSP is payable at two weekly rates, depending on your earnings.

Earnings £pw	SSP £pw
200 or more	52.50
57.00 to 199.99	47.80

Both rates of SSP are below the lower earnings limit (see p216), so you will not have to pay national insurance contributions. These will be credited to you (see p225) but you must claim them from the Benefits Agency by sending medical certificates to your local office as well as to your employer.

For the purpose of calculating SSP, earnings are normal gross weekly earnings averaged out over the eight weeks before the beginning of the period of entitlement.[29] Only payments actually made during the eight weeks are counted.[30] If you receive less than the relevant amount (£200 or £57) your SSP is calculated accordingly even if, in theory, you should have been paid more.

Example

You are paid £60 for 25 hours a week. You go on two weeks' annual leave (weeks 2 and 3). Your employers pay you two weeks' holiday pay in advance which you receive during week 1. You fall ill in week 10. Your SSP is based on the average wages received in weeks 2 to 9, so the total is £360, not £480. This is divided by 8 to give £45, not £60. So you get no SSP.

Previous payments of SSP count as earnings when working out your average.[31]

The daily rate [32] depends on your weekly earnings and the number of qualifying days you have in a week. Therefore if you are a shift worker and have perhaps six or seven qualifying days in a week you will qualify more quickly, but you will get less money for each day. This is irrelevant if you are off for a full week after qualifying, as the weekly rate of SSP is the same.

If you cannot work, you are entitled to SSP from any employment where you fulfil the qualifications. So you could get payments of SSP for each of two contracts with the *same* employer (you might be both a daytime teacher and an evening tutor with an education authority) or payments from two separate employers. It is possible, at the same time, to be unable to work on one contract and be entitled to SSP, but be able to work on a different contract – if, for example, you perform quite different tasks, such as manual and clerical work.

SSP is usually paid in the same way as your normal wages or salary. If you have some form of sick pay arrangement with your employers, SSP forms part of your weekly pay.

It is not paid for the first three qualifying days in a period of incapacity (see p67). These are known as 'waiting days'.[33]

Your maximum entitlement to SSP in one period of entitlement is 28 times the weekly rate in any period of incapacity for work.[34]

Other benefits

You can claim IS from the Benefits Agency (and/or housing benefit (HB) and council tax benefit (CTB) from your local authority) as well as SSP. Your net SSP payment counts as your income and so reduces the amount you would otherwise get.

A day which falls within a period of entitlement, even if you do not receive payment because it is not a qualifying day, cannot count as part of a period of interruption of employment for benefit purposes.[35] However, when SSP has run out, the next three days of incapacity are automatically treated as part of a period of interruption of employment if you are unemployed or unfit to work. So you get UB, sickness benefit or IVB immediately.[36] The time you are on SSP may count towards the 168 days you need to qualify for IVB (see p77).

Tax

SSP is treated like any other earnings and you pay tax and national insurance contributions by PAYE in the normal way.[37]

Disputes, references and appeals

In the past, employers'expenditure on SSP was largely reimbursed by the DSS. The amount of help given in this way has been progressively reduced and, from April 1994, will be withdrawn altogether except for small businesses. In practice, this is likely to lead to an increase in disputes about SSP between employers and employees. Unfortunately it is necessary for employees and their advisers to remember that people who have worked for their employer for less than two years have no rights not to be unfairly dismissed. Your employers still have to pay you SSP if they sack you when you are sick in an attempt to avoid payment. But this may be little comfort if you find that you do not have a job to go back to when you have recovered.

You have the right to request the following information from your employers within a reasonable time:[38]

- the days which they regard as qualifying days – ie, the days you are entitled to SSP;
- the reason that SSP is not payable for other days;
- the daily rate of SSP.

Your employers can require you to provide 'such information as may reasonably be required' for the determination of your claim for SSP.[39]

The intention is that your employer should administer SSP without any involvement by the DSS, but you are not left entirely at your employer's mercy because you can ask for a decision by an adjudication officer if your employer decides you are not entitled.

Employers are given detailed guidance by the DSS in leaflet NI 270, *Employer's Manual on SSP* (see Appendix Five). If your employer is not satisfied that you are really incapable of work, s/he can ask you to attend a medical examination to help her/him decide whether you can work, or can ask for DSS help in deciding whether you are capable of work. This can only be done with your consent but, since your employer could simply refuse payment, you are unlikely to gain much by not consenting.

The DSS will only help your employer in this way if you have been off work for two or three months, if your doctor has written 'NAD' (no abnormality detected) on your medical certificates or if you have been off sick for less than a week (and so have not submitted a doctor's certificate) four times within the last 12 months. If the DSS does help, a doctor from BAMS speaks to your doctor and you may be asked to attend an examination (see p53). Your employer is then simply given the medical officer's view as to whether you are capable of work but is not given any medical report or other explanation. It is still for your employer to decide whether to pay SSP.

If you are dissatisfied with your employer's decision, you should write to your local Benefits Agency office asking them to make a decision. Any question on whether you are an employee is dealt with by the Secretary of State (see pp175 and 286).[40] Most other matters are referred to an adjudication officer either by employees or by the Secretary of State, who in some cases meets most of the cost of SSP and might, in a rare case, want to object to an employer's decision to pay you.[41] Your employer has no right to refer a case because s/he can simply refuse to make any payment. The time limit for referring a matter to an adjudication officer is six months for an employee but only three months for the Secretary of State.[42] You (or your employer or the Secretary of State) can appeal against the adjudication officer's decision to an SSAT (see p304).[43]

If your employer does not pay you after an adjudication officer has decided that s/he is liable to do so, you can obtain payment from the Secretary of State instead.[44] The liability is also a debt enforceable in the county courts (Sheriffs' Courts in Scotland) and, in criminal proceedings, employers can be fined up to £400 for non-payment.[45]

4. SICKNESS BENEFIT

Sickness benefit is important for those who have no jobs or where SSP is not payable

Conditions of entitlement[1]

For every day you receive benefit:

- you must claim within the time limit (see p280); *and*
- you must be incapable of work (see p48); *and either*
- you have paid (or been credited with) enough contributions; *or*
- you became incapable of work because of an industrial injury or prescribed disease (see p164); *and*
- you are not entitled to SSP; *and*
- the day must be part of a 'period of interruption of employment' (see p251).

Amount of payment[2]

	Claimant under pensionable age £pw	Claimant of, or over, pensionable age £pw
Claimant	43.45	55.25
Adult dependant	26.90	33.10
Child dependant	–	11.00

The daily rate is one-sixth of the weekly rate.

There is an 'earnings rule' for the dependant's increase (see pp208-209). People over pensionable age may receive less than the standard amount if the contribution conditions for retirement pension are only partially satisfied (see p235). So does a local councillor whose net allowances exceed £43 a week (see p49).

You receive national insurance credits while in receipt of sickness benefit (see p225).

Tax and other benefits

Sickness benefit is not taxable but counts as income for IS purposes. Sickness benefit overlaps with other personal benefits (see p258) payable to the claimant. Any dependant's addition overlaps with other personal benefits payable to the dependant.

Payment

Payment is by girocheque, usually sent to your home address. Sickness benefit is usually paid weekly in arrears.[3] The first payment is made about 10 days after your first claim or your first becoming entitled. Payment continues for up to six months after your claim, after which you will receive IVB (see p76).

How to claim

The claim procedure differs slightly, depending on whether or not you are employed.

If you are not employed

You do not have to go to a doctor for a medical certificate for the first week of incapacity for work.[4] You fill in a self-certification form (SC1) which you can obtain from the Benefits Agency local office, your doctor's surgery or a hospital. You should send the completed certificate within the time limits to the Benefits Agency (see p280).

If you are employed

You should normally be paid SSP and any payments you are entitled to from your occupational sick pay scheme, if there is one. If your employers think that you are excluded from receiving SSP for one of the reasons listed on pp65-67 or if your entitlement to SSP has run out, they must give you form SSP1 which includes a claim form for sickness benefit. Send this to your local Benefits Agency office. If you disagree with your employers' decision you can refer the matter to the adjudication officer (see p72) but do not delay claiming sickness benefit while you do so.

People over pensionable age

You may still claim sickness benefit if you are over pensionable age but only if:

- you have deferred entitlement to a retirement pension (see p114); *and*
- you would have been entitled to a Category A (or, in the case of a widow or widower, a Category B) retirement pension if you had not done so.[5]

The standard amounts (see p73) will be reduced if the contribution conditions for the retirement pension are not satisfied in full (see p235).

The unequal treatment of men and women aged between 60 and 65 is very probably unlawful under European Community law. If you would be better off being treated as a member of the opposite sex, read the section on Equal Treatment for Men and Women in Chapter 14.

Sickness benefit and statutory sick pay

You cannot receive sickness benefit and SSP at the same time. When your SSP ends, normally after 28 weeks, you will usually go on to invalidity benefit. If SSP is not payable, you will get sickness benefit. Neither is affected by any payments from an occupational sick pay scheme.

If you are claiming sickness benefit after your SSP entitlement has run out, your employers should give you a transfer form SSP1(T). Send the form with medical certificates or similar evidence to the local office of the Benefits Agency. You may need to get your last medical certificate back from your employer if it covers a period after your SSP entitlement has ended. Do not delay your claim while you do this. It is better to claim sickness benefit immediately and tell the Benefits Agency that you are trying to get the certificate.

At the end of your claim for sickness benefit, you will be given a form by the Benefits Agency. Keep it (if you are not employed), or give it to your employers, because the 'linking rule' means that you will have to claim sickness benefit and not SSP if you are ill again within the next eight weeks.

Disqualification

You may be disqualified for up to six weeks for one of the reasons given below.[6] Normally an adjudication officer disqualifies you for the full period. You can appeal against the fact of disqualification or the period or both.

The reasons are:

- **You are incapable of work because of your own misconduct.** This is conduct which is blameworthy or wrong, and does not include playing dangerous sports and accidents. Involuntary alcoholism is not 'misconduct', but drunkenness is.[7]
- **You fail to attend a medical examination,** having had at least three days' notice in writing, unless you have good cause. In practice the Benefits Agency will not disqualify you if you tell them that you have a good reason for not attending. You may have good cause if the refusal to attend is based on a firm religious conviction.[8]
- **You do not take suitable treatment.** You are not required to subject yourself to 'invasive' treatment – eg, inoculation, vaccination or surgery (unless it is very minor). The Benefits Agency recognises that many people, perhaps irrationally, fear or mistrust such treatment and that it has risks. You can refuse any other treatment if you can show that you have a genuine, albeit irrational, fear of it, or that you are allergic to a drug or an anaesthetic.
- **Without good cause you behave in a way which will slow down your recovery.**
- **Without good cause you go away from home** (eg, to stay at a friend's or relative's house) **without leaving word** with the Benefits Agency as to where you may be found. This is so that you can be called to a medical examination if needed. Write to the Benefits Agency giving the period you will be away, and where you are going.
- **You work** (except in the circumstances described on pp49-50).

5. INVALIDITY BENEFIT — *Incapable of work.*

Invalidity benefit is the general term used to describe invalidity pension and invalidity allowance. The basic benefit is invalidity pension and, if you meet the relevant conditions, you may qualify for invalidity allowance as well. *— Counted in full for – Means-tested benefits*
Can claim – Means-tested benefit

Conditions of entitlement[1]

For each day you receive benefit:

Qualifying benefit for disability Premium
HB, CTB, IS.

Invalidity benefit [handwritten note in top-left margin]

t be incapable of work (see p48); *and*
nust be part of a 'period of interruption of employment' (see
nd *either*
t have been entitled to sickness benefit, or maternity allow-
L68 days within the period of the interruption of employment;

- you are deemed to have done so because you have received statutory sick pay (SSP) instead and satisfy the other conditions (see p78); *or*
- you qualify as a widow or widower (see p79).

If you are receiving sickness benefit you will be transferred automatically to IVB. — *Satisfy NI contributions — OR incapable of work due to industrial disease or Accident* [handwritten]

Amount of payment [2]

Invalidity pension

	£pw
Claimant	57.60
Adult dependant	34.50
Child dependant	11.00

As well as invalidity pension, you may also receive an additional sum based on your earnings under the state earnings related pension scheme (SERPS) (see p235).

A reduced rate may be payable if you are over pensionable age (see p235) or you are a local councillor and your net allowances exceed £43 a week (see p49).

A Christmas bonus is paid to those on invalidity pension (see p262). You will also be entitled to national insurance credits (see p225).

The earnings rule in respect of a spouse is more generous than for sickness benefit (see pp208-209). This means that if your spouse was earning too much to entitle you to an increase in sickness benefit, you may nevertheless be entitled to an increase in invalidity pension. You must make a separate claim for the increase. If you do not claim it within six months, you will find that only six months' arrears are paid unless you had 'good cause' for the late claim (see p281).

Invalidity allowance

This is payable on top of your invalidity pension if you are under 60 (men) or 55 (women) on the first day of incapacity for work in your period of interruption of employment (see p251). The amount is dependent on how young you were on that date. [3]

Men	*Women*	*£pw*
Under 40	Under 40	12.15
40-49 inclusive	40-49 inclusive	7.60
50-59 inclusive	50-54 inclusive	3.80

A commissioner has decided that the discrimination against women aged between 55 and 60 is unlawful under European Community law.[4] For advice on what to do if you are a woman who became incapable of work between the ages of 55 and 59 (inclusive) see pp272-274.

The amount of invalidity allowance is reduced by the amount of any pension you receive under SERPS or its equivalent if you are 'contracted-out' of SERPS.

Tax and other benefits

IVB is not taxable. It counts in full for IS purposes, though you will qualify for a disability premium or higher pensioner premium.

For five years, between 65 and 70 for a man or 60 and 65 for a woman, you can defer entitlement to retirement pension (see p114) and thus keep IVB. The advantage of this is that IVB is not taxable whereas retirement pension is. You should consider what to do carefully if you are in this position. Note that you will not gain an increased retirement pension by deferring entitlement (see p114) if you are receiving IVB.

If you were receiving invalidity allowance in the eight weeks before reaching pensionable age, it will be added to your retirement pension.[5]

If you stop claiming IVB and try to go back to work but are unsuccessful, your period of interruption of employment will not end as long as you claim IVB again within two years and you have been continuously entitled to DWA (see CPAG's *National Welfare Benefits Handbook*) in the meantime. This means that you will not have to wait another 168 days before getting IVB again.[6]

Invalidity benefit and statutory sick pay

A day for which you receive SSP cannot usually count as part of a period of interruption of employment.[7] However, for the purposes of satisfying the 168-day qualifying period for IVB, any week when you received a whole week's SSP counts as six days of entitlement to sickness benefit.[8] Odd days can also count depending on the number of days a week you usually worked. These rules only apply if you are no longer entitled to SSP and the first day of a period of interruption of employment was within 57 days of your last day of entitlement to SSP.[9]

Note also that a day when you received SSP cannot be treated as a day of entitlement to sickness benefit if it was before the first day on which you would have satisfied the contribution conditions for sickness benefit (see p231).[10]

Entitlement to invalidity allowance depends on your age on the first day of entitlement to SSP that can be treated as a day of entitlement to sickness benefit.[11]

Payment

IVB continues for any days of incapacity within the same period of interruption of employment until you reach pensionable age (65 for a man, 60 for a woman).[12] See below for circumstances in which it may be paid to people over pensionable age. You will be paid by an order book or, if your doctor is giving you medical certificates for periods of less than eight weeks, by weekly girocheques. IVB cannot be paid by credit transfer into a bank account.

People over pensionable age

If you are over pensionable age, you are entitled to IVB only if you have deferred entitlement to retirement pension (see p114) and would have been entitled to a Category A (or, in the case of a widow or widower, a Category B) retirement pension if you had not deferred entitlement.[13] The amount of your benefit will be reduced if the amount of your retirement pension would have been reduced due to an inadequate contribution record (see p235). However, if you are incapable of work due to an industrial injury or disease, the minimum payment (including any additional pension) will be £57.60 a week.[14]

A commissioner has decided that the unequal treatment of men and women aged between 60 and 65 is unlawful under European Community law.[15] The DSS is appealing against this decision and that appeal has recently been referred by the Court of Appeal to the European Court of Justice. Women claiming IVB who would be better off if they were male (including also women aged between 55 and 59 who are refused invalidity allowance – see p77) should read the section on equal treatment for men and women in Chapter 14 for further advice.

Special rules for widows and widowers

Widows and widowers may be paid invalidity pension even if they were not entitled to sickness benefit first.

A **widow** is entitled if:[16]

- her husband died or her widowed mother's allowance ran out after 5 April 1979; *and*
- her widowed mother's allowance has run out, or she was not entitled to widowed mother's allowance when her husband died; *and*
- the period of interruption of employment (see p251) began before her husband died or her widowed mother's allowance ran out; *and*
- she receives no widow's pension or she receives a reduced widow's pension because of her age at the relevant time.

The invalidity pension paid to a widow will be either (a) the standard rate, or (b) an amount sufficient to take the total of invalidity pension and widow's pension (if any) up to the rate of widow's pension which the claimant would have received had her husband died when she was over the age of 55, whichever is higher.

A **widower** is entitled if his wife died after 5 April 1979 and either he was then incapable of work or he became incapacitated within 13 weeks of her death.[17]

There is no entitlement to invalidity pension until the claimant has been incapable of work for 168 days, although all or some of that period may be before the death of the spouse. Days in receipt of SSP count towards this period (see p78).

The invalidity pension paid to a widower will be either (a) the standard rate, or (b) an amount calculated in the way a widow's pension would have been calculated but on his wife's contribution record, whichever is the higher.

In either case, an additional pension may be payable under SERPS (see p235).

A widow or widower will not receive an invalidity pension under these provisions if already over pensionable age. But if you receive an invalidity pension and reach pensionable age while you are still incapable of work, you will get a Category A retirement pension at the same rate as your invalidity pension, unless you are entitled to a higher retirement pension on your contribution record.[18]

The rule allowing a widow to claim more than 12 months' arrears if she did not know of her husband's death applies to invalidity pension and Category A retirement pension claimed under these provisions in the same way as it applies to widows' benefits (see p103). So does the forfeiture rule (see p102).

Disqualification

The rules are the same as for sickness benefit (see p76).

nd of your claim

given a form by the Benefits Agency when you recover and go
rk, or sign on for UB (if relevant), or for IS. Keep it (if you are
d), or give it to your employers, because if you fall sick again
t weeks of the end of a previous period of interruption of
t (see p251) you claim IVB and not SSP. For most people it is
better to have IVB as it has additions for dependants and is not taxable.

If you do go off work again within eight weeks your employers should
give you form SSP1(E). This, with any medical certificates, should be
sent to the local Benefits Agency.

5. SEVERE DISABLEMENT ALLOWANCE

Conditions of entitlement[1]

- You satisfy the residence conditions (see p241).
- You are incapable of work (see p48).
- You have been incapable of work for 196 consecutive days (see p82).
- Either the 196-day period began before your 20th birthday (see p84);
  or you are disabled to the extent of 80 per cent (see p84) and have been
  so disabled for 196 consecutive days; or you have previously been
  entitled to non-contributory invalidity pension (see p85).
- You are not under 16 (nor under 19 if you are in ordinary full-time
  education at a university, college, school or comparable institution –
  see p83).
- You are not over pensionable age (but see p83 for exceptions).

Amount of payment[2]

	£pw
Claimant	34.80
Adult dependant	20.70
Child dependant	11.00

An age-related addition is also payable if you are young enough. The
amount depends on your age on the first day of the 196-day qualifying
period.

Age	£pw
under 40	12.15
40-49 inclusive	7.60
50-59 inclusive	3.80

You will also be entitled to a Christmas bonus (see p262). If you are a local councillor, the amount of your benefit is reduced by the amount by which your net councillor's allowances exceed £43 in any week (see p49).

A common problem is that older married women are not getting the correct age addition. A woman may have been incapable of work for many years but unable to claim a non-contributory invalidity pension (the benefit which was replaced by SDA) because of the discriminatory 'normal household duties' test (see p85). The Benefits Agency often treats the 196-day period as beginning immediately before a woman's claim for SDA. This is wrong. If you can prove that you have been continuously incapable of work before your 40th or 50th birthday, whether or not you claimed benefit then, you may be entitled to a higher age addition than the one you are getting. You should apply for leave to appeal late (see p318) and, if you are unsuccessful, seek a review (see p288). If you claimed a non-contributory invalidity pension, but were turned down because of the 'normal household duties' test, the Benefits Agency may have documents on file which will prove when you became incapable of work. If not, you may need to rely on the evidence of your doctor and of family or friends.

Tax and other benefits

SDA is not taxable. It counts in full as income for IS purposes but will qualify you for a disability premium or higher pensioner premium. There are special rules for 16- and 17-year-olds[3] who receive SDA and who also claim IS, which mean your IS will be paid at the higher 18- to 24-year-old rate. Together with the disability premium this means that your IS may exceed your SDA and you will be paid the difference as income support. The Benefits Agency often overlooks this point. If you are refused IS, appeal and seek advice.

If you stop claiming SDA and try to go back to work but are unsuccessful, your period of interruption of employment will not end as long as you claim it again within two years and you have been continuously entitled to DWA (see CPAG's *National Welfare Benefits Handbook*) in the meantime.[4] This means that you will not have to wait another 196 days before getting SDA again.

You are not entitled to SDA for any day which falls within a period of entitlement to SSP (see p68).[5]

Calculating the 196 days

The 196 days must be consecutive, and for this purpose Sundays count, so that 196 days is 28 weeks. Days spent in prison or other detention in legal custody cannot count towards these 196 days.[6]

People over pensionable age

Under British legislation you are excluded from SDA if you are over pensionable age, unless you were entitled to it or to non-contributory invalidity pension immediately before reaching that age (or you would have been but for the rules about 'overlapping'[7] (see p258)). However, the European Court has held that this is contrary to European Community law because it involves treating men and women unequally.[8]

The consequence is that both men and women can claim SDA up to the age of 65 simply by satisfying the usual conditions. If you are over 65, the position is more complicated, but see p161 for a suggestion as to how the law works, as the rules for invalid care allowance are exactly the same.

When you reach pensionable age, you might become entitled to sickness benefit and then IVB instead of SDA. That is because your contribution record may not have been good enough for you to qualify for sickness benefit when you were under pensionable age but it may be good enough when you are over that age because the contribution conditions are different (see p74).

Full-time education[9]

The exclusion of those in full-time education applies only to those aged *under* 19. Full-time education means 21 or more hours a week. In calculating the 21 hours, any special education or tuition designed for those with a physical or mental disability is ignored.[10] Temporary interruptions of education are disregarded. Periods of private study are also not included in the 21-hour limit.

Routes to qualifying

SDA is paid only if you are both incapable of work (having been incapable for 196 days) and you satisfy one of three further qualifying conditions:

- you were under 20 when your 196 days of incapacity started;
- you have a disablement which is assessed at 80 per cent or above;
- you were previously entitled to non-contributory invalidity pension.

You were under 20 when incapacity started

If your 196 days of incapacity started before your 20th birthday and you are still incapable of work, you can qualify without satisfying further conditions about your disablement. You can still qualify by this route if you broke your period of incapacity (eg, by trying a job) in your late teens or early twenties. You will be allowed the benefit of this provision if:[11]

• you were incapable of work for one complete period of 196 days which started before your 20th birthday; *and*
• you have now been incapable of work for 196 days again; *and*
• the gap between these two periods is less than 182 days in aggregate; *and*
• the gap started when you were older than 15 years and 24 weeks.

Disablement assessed at 80 per cent

Appendix Two sets out the rates of disablement that have been adopted in the industrial injuries scheme. They apply to SDA as well.[12] For instance, 80 per cent disablement is the equivalent of the amputation of a leg close to the hip or an arm close to the shoulder. The difficulty is that many claimants are likely to have less defined disabilities. The guidance given on pp117-174 about the assessment of disablement for disablement benefit purposes applies equally to SDA. You should apply if you think that your illness or disability is severe. The 'disablement questions' (ie, the extent of your disablement and the period to be covered by your assessment) are decided by the adjudicating medical authorities (see p287). You can appeal to a medical appeal tribunal (see p308).

In a wide variety of circumstances you are 'deemed' to satisfy the 80 per cent rule. You are automatically regarded as 80 per cent disabled for the purposes of the allowance if:

• you receive the higher or middle rate of disability living allowance (DLA) care component (see p134), the higher rate of DLA mobility component (see p127), attendance allowance or war pensioner's mobility supplement;
• you have previously been assessed for industrial injuries purposes or a war disablement pension as 80 per cent disabled;
• you are receiving a vaccine damage payment;
• you are registered blind or partially sighted, or have an invalid tricycle or car allowance from the DSS.[13]

Previous entitlement to non-contributory invalidity pension

Non-contributory invalidity pension was a benefit replaced by SDA in November 1984. Entitlement to it did not depend on your being 80 per cent disabled provided you were incapable of work.[14] Nor did entitlement depend upon a claim having been made.[15] However, at the time, married women and women living with men as husband and wife were obliged by British legislation to show that they were not only incapable of work but were also incapable of performing normal household duties. That discrimination has been held to have been unlawful under the law of the European Community.[16]

You are entitled to SDA now if you were entitled to non-contributory invalidity pension immediately before both 10 September 1984 and 29 November 1984, and your present claim falls within the same period of interruption of employment.[17] It is not necessary for you to show that you were receiving benefit at the time but you will not obtain more than a year's arrears of benefit if you make a claim now.

Married or cohabiting women who were refused, or did not claim,[18] non-contributory invalidity pension or SDA because of the old (discriminatory) rules may establish entitlement to SDA now if:

* you were incapable of work for 196 days before both 10 September 1984 and 29 November 1984; *and*
* you have been incapable of work ever since then except for gaps of less than eight weeks.

If these apply to you but you did not claim non-contributory invalidity pension, you should still get benefit for the future and at least 12 months' arrears. It is possible that you will also be entitled to arrears going back to November 1984 but these will not be paid until after a case now going to the European Court of Justice has been decided.[19] Details of developments on this case will be published in the *Welfare Rights Bulletin* as soon as they are available. Ask your adviser to contact CPAG's Citizens' Rights Office for further details.

If you did make a claim before then you can either seek leave to appeal out of time (see p318) against the old refusal of benefit or, alternatively, apply for a review (see p288) of that decision. On a review only 12 months' arrears of SDA will be paid pending the European Court's decision, whereas on a late appeal arrears will be paid back to the date of claim and possibly 12 months before that if you had good cause for a late claim (see p281). However, a chair of a tribunal does not have to give you leave to appeal out of time.

Claims

A claim for the allowance should be made in writing to the local office as soon as you think the conditions are fulfilled. On your first claim, backdating of up to one month can be allowed,[20] or up to a year if you had good cause for the delay (see p281). DSS leaflet NI252 incorporates a claim form. Mentally handicapped people aged 16 and over are a large category of claimants of this benefit. The benefit can be claimed on their behalf by another adult where they are not able to make the claim themselves (see p278). When a claim is submitted late, the question is whether the claimant, ie, the mentally handicapped person, had good cause for being late and not whether the person acting for her/him had good cause for being late unless someone had been *formally* appointed to act for her/him (see p282). The 80 per cent disablement test is referred to the adjudicating medical authorities (see p287).

If you have at one stage been receiving SDA, you can make a further claim during the same period of interruption of employment. Provided you have become incapable of work again, you do not have to satisfy the principal conditions of a further 196 days of incapacity or 80 per cent disablement.[21]

Disqualification

The rules are the same as for sickness benefit (see p76).[22]

7. FUTURE CHANGES

With effect from April 1995 sickness benefit and IVB are to be abolished and replaced by a new benefit called 'incapacity benefit'. The lower rate of SSP is also to be abolished.

It is proposed that the new benefit will have two components – a short-term benefit payable for the first 52 weeks of incapacity and a long-term benefit payable indefinitely thereafter until the claimant either becomes capable of work or reaches pensionable age. It will be paid at the sickness benefit rate for the first 28 weeks, SSP rate for the next 24 and IVB rate after that. There will be an increase in the long-term rate of benefit if the claimant is under 45 when s/he first becomes incapable.

Perhaps most controversially, there is to be a new test for incapacity for work. For the first 28 weeks, the test will be whether the claimant is medically capable of carrying out his or her own occupation (if s/he has one). Otherwise the test will only consider 'objective' medical factors (ie, it will be consider whether the claimant is physically capable of doing any type of work).

The details of this test and of any transitional arrangements for existing sickness benefit and IVB claimants remain to be announced but will be published in the *Welfare Rights Bulletin* when they are known. The 18th edition of this *Guide* (to be published in April 1995) will contain a full account of the new arrangements together with practical advice for claimants and their advisers.

CHAPTER FOUR

Maternity pay and benefits

This chapter covers:

1. Statutory maternity pay (see below)
2. Maternity allowance (p95)
3. Future changs (p96)

Statutory maternity pay (SMP) and maternity allowance are paid to women who are pregnant or who have recently given birth. **SMP** is paid by employers on the same lines as statutory sick pay (SSP), and **maternity allowance** is paid by the Benefits Agency to women (including the self-employed) who have paid sufficient contributions but who do not qualify for SMP. Maternity grants have been abolished, but those receiving income support (IS) or family credit (FC) may be entitled to a £100 payment per child from the social fund (see CPAG's *National Welfare Benefits Handbook*).

If you do not qualify for SMP and maternity allowance, perhaps because you have a difficult pregnancy and are away from work for more than 18 weeks, you may be entitled to one of the benefits described in Chapter 3.

I. STATUTORY MATERNITY PAY

Conditions of entitlement[1]

To receive statutory maternity pay (SMP) for any day, you must:

* be an employee, who is not excluded from the scheme (see p91);
* be employed for at least one day in the 'qualifying week' (see p89) and have been continuously employed by the same employers for at least 26 weeks ending with that week;[2]
* have given your employers the appropriate notice and information (see p92);
* satisfy the earnings condition (see p93);
* not do any work for the employers paying you SMP;
* not work for other employers after the birth (but see p91 for an exception);

• be expecting a child within 11 weeks, or have recently given birth.

SMP is the minimum amount of wages that the law requires employers to pay during maternity leave. Many groups of employees have negotiated better rates of pay and/or periods of entitlement. Your trade union representative should be able to tell you your rights, or your employers' personnel department should give you the basic information. Your written particulars of employment might contain details of your entitlement. *You do not have to return to work with the same employers in order to qualify for SMP.*

A 'week' is defined as the period of seven days beginning at midnight between Saturday and Sunday.[3]

The 'qualifying week' is the fifteenth week before the week in which your child is expected (or the 'expected week of confinement' as it is sometimes called).

Amount of payment

SMP is paid by your employer, not the Benefits Agency. There are two rates of SMP depending on how long you have been in paid employment.[4]

The higher rate is nine-tenths of your average weekly earnings and is paid for the first six weeks of SMP for which you qualify.[5] After this, you will receive the lower rate.[6] These earnings are calculated over the eight weeks immediately before the qualifying week (see above).[7] The problem is that if your earnings are low for any reason, such as short-time working, sickness or lay-off, you may fail to qualify. You are entitled to this higher rate if you have been working for your employers *either*:

• full-time (16 or more hours a week for at least two years) ending with the qualifying week (see above); *or*
• part-time (at least eight but under 16 hours for at least five years) ending with the qualifying week (see above).[8]

If you are not entitled to the higher rate you will receive the lower rate, currently £48.80 a week for the full period.[9]

As with SSP, if you satisfy the conditions with more than one employer, you can get SMP from each of them. You do not have to give up both jobs at the same time if you feel fit enough to carry on with one of them, because, for instance, it is less physically demanding than the other.

Tax and other benefits

SMP is treated as earnings and you pay tax and national insurance contributions as appropriate.[10] The lower rate is below the lower earnings limit so, unless your employers add to it, you do not pay national insurance contributions on it and, if you claim them, you will receive national insurance credits throughout the maternity pay period (see below). If you have insufficient income after SMP is paid to you, you may claim IS. Alternatively, if you have a partner working over 16 hours a week and have at least one child already, claim FC. SMP is counted in full as income for calculating IS but not for FC or disability working allowance (DWA).[11]

You cannot get SMP for the same day as either SSP, unemployment benefit (UB), sickness benefit or maternity allowance. SSP is not payable for any day in a maternity pay period. This period is not part of a period of interruption of employment (see p251),[12] but the maternity pay period can count towards the qualifying period for invalidity benefit (IVB) if:

• you are suffering from a disease of disablement which would have made you incapable of work (see p48) even if you had not also been pregnant; *and*
• immediately before your maternity pay period began you were entitled to SSP or sickness benefit (or would have been entitled to sickness benefit if you had claimed it).

If you become entitled to IVB during the maternity pay period as a result of these rules, your IVB will be reduced by the amount of your SMP.[13]

Payment and periods of entitlement

SMP is usually paid in the same way as your normal wage or salary.[14] It cannot be paid in kind or by way of services or the provision of lodgings. You should not have to collect it in person and it is not paid in a lump sum but according to your normal wage payment periods – weekly, monthly, etc. The maximum period of payment of SMP is 18 weeks, known as the 'maternity pay period'.[15]

Rules specifying when the maternity pay period starts and ends are complex. There is a core period of 13 weeks which starts with the sixth week before the week in which the baby is due. The other five weeks can be taken before or after the core period, or partly before and partly after, depending on when you finish work. So, the earliest at which you can take maternity leave to obtain your full SMP is 11 weeks before the expected week of confinement, and the latest is six weeks.[16]

Therefore if you intend to claim the maximum entitlement to SMP, your last working week should be at least six weeks before the week in which you expect your baby to be born. If you work for a week or part of a week after this you will lose SMP for that time. It is entirely up to you when you give up work and start to draw SMP.

The maternity pay period starts with the week after you stop work or the sixth week before the expected week of confinement, whichever is earlier. Therefore the earliest time you can give up work and then claim SMP is the last day of the twelfth week before the baby is due. Your SMP will start the next week, ie, the eleventh.[17]

If you prolong your work to the last possible date before the SMP period starts, you will be entitled to SMP until 11 weeks after the expected week of confinement (ie, six weeks before *plus* the week of confinement *plus* 11 weeks after = 18 weeks).[18]

When working out your maternity pay period, remember that, as is usually the case with social security benefits, a week begins on Sunday and ends at midnight on Saturday. It does not mean any period of seven days.[19]

If you work for another employer before your confinement, your entitlement to SMP is unaffected. However, if you work for another employer after your confinement you will usually lose your entitlement to SMP for the rest of your maternity pay period, even if you stop working again.[20] The only exception to this rule arises if the other employer is one for whom you were working immediately before the 'qualifying week' (see p89) but who is not liable to pay you SMP. Working for such an employer does not affect your entitlement to SMP at all.[21]

Employers, employees and excluded employees

An employee is a person who either pays, or should pay, primary Class 1 national insurance contributions[22] (see p220). Employers are the persons or firm paying national insurance contributions for you.[23]

Employers cannot restrict your right to SMP by their own rules or 'contract' with you – it is a right established by statute. Nor can employers require you to contribute towards the cost of SMP.[24] They cannot avoid liability by dismissing you once you have qualified for SMP. They are also liable if they dismiss you before you qualify and dismissal was 'solely or mainly' to avoid paying SMP. Provided you were employed for eight weeks or more by that employer, you are deemed to be entitled to SMP.[25]

The only employees excluded from entitlement are those who:

- have normal gross earnings below the lower earnings limit (currently £57 a week);
- go abroad, outside the EC;
- are in legal custody, eg, prison.[26]

If your employers think that you are in an excluded group they will give you a completed form SMP1 and return your maternity certificate. This allows you to claim the benefit known as maternity allowance (see p95). You can challenge the employers' decision (see p93).

If you are not entitled to either SMP or maternity allowance, you will be regarded as incapable of work and may be entitled to sickness benefit for at least the period beginning six weeks before the baby is expected until two weeks after the date of birth.[27]

Notification and information

You must give your employers details of the expected date of birth and notice of when you intend to stop work.[28] The details of the expected date of birth are on form MAT B1 which you will be given by your GP, clinic or midwife. Your employers need to see this certificate, or a copy, to work out your SMP, and you have to provide this within three weeks of the start of the maternity pay period. To ensure that you are eligible to return to work you should also tell your employers, in writing, that you do intend to return. You have a statutory right to return to work if you work until the start of the eleventh week before the expected date of confinement and have, at that time, been continuously employed by your employer for at least two years. Remember also that your contract with your employers may contain more favourable terms than the statutory rules.

If you do not have form MAT B1 the employers can require, or accept, other medical evidence. The time limit for presenting this is extended to the end of the thirteenth week if you have good cause for the delay.[29]

You must give your employers notice of leaving at least 21 days before you mean to stop work, or as soon as practicable after that.[30] It is up to your employers to say what form such notice should take – most require it in writing. If you are late handing it in the employers must decide whether your reason for delay is acceptable. If they do not accept your reason you can challenge that decision (see p93).

You have to keep your employers informed of any change of circumstance (eg, going abroad) which may affect your entitlement and you *must* tell your employers if you start working for someone else.[31]

If you are requested to supply information by the local office of the Benefits Agency, in the name of the Secretary of State, you *must* do so within ten days or risk prosecution.[32]

Notification to employers or the Benefits Agency counts once it is put in the post.[33]

Disputes and appeals

If you consider that you are owed SMP by an employer or you are paid an amount you consider to be wrong, you can ask them for a written statement showing:

- if SMP has been refused, the reason why;
- if SMP is being paid, how many weeks they consider it should be paid for, and the amount they will pay.[34]

If you disagree with either part of the statement you should ask the adjudication officer at the local Benefits Agency office to give you a ruling on the question. Employers cannot seek a ruling, although they can ask an adjudication officer for advice. The adjudication officer will ask both sides to put their case in writing. Take care to deal with the main points logically and clearly. When the adjudication officer gives a decision both sides have a right to appeal to a social security appeal tribunal (see p303). If the tribunal finds in your favour and the employers do not pay, or become insolvent, the Secretary of State may make the payments in default.[35]

Before applying to the adjudication officer you should consult your trade union representative and try to resolve the problem using the grievance procedure if there is one, but you must not leave it for more than six months from the first day which is in dispute or you will lose your right to have the adjudication officer make the decision.

The earnings condition[36]

To qualify for SMP your average weekly earnings for the period of eight weeks (up to the last pay day before the end of the qualifying week – see p89) must be at least the lower earnings limit for national insurance contributions (currently £57). In calculating your average weekly gross earnings, your employers must take into account bonuses, overtime, SSP and any other earnings.[37] Gratuities (tips) and money paid from a holiday fund, a trust scheme, or through a profit-sharing scheme are excluded.[38]

Continuous employment rule[39]

You must have worked for your employers for a continuous period of 26 weeks including at least one day in the qualifying week (see p89). Periods when you were previously on maternity leave, sickness benefit or SSP, away from work, or on short-time working all count.[40] A strike does not break your continuity of employment, but neither does it count towards the 26 weeks.[41] If your employment is transferred from one employer to another as a result of a commercial deal, or you are transferred from one local authority or health service employer to another (and in certain other circumstances), your employment is unbroken.[42] The rules are broadly the same as those for calculating continuous employment when looking at redundancy pay and unfair dismissal.

What happens if your baby is born early?[43]

If your baby is born before your expected date of confinement your SMP rights may change.

• If you have your baby after you have started your maternity pay period, SMP is not affected even if the birth is earlier than you expected.
• If your baby is born more than 11 weeks before the week in which it was expected, your maternity pay period will begin the following week. You must give your employers notification of the date of confinement within 21 days or as soon as practicable. The eight weeks for satisfying the earnings condition are the last eight weeks before the week of the birth. You satisfy the continuous employment rule if you would have done so had the baby been born on the expected date.
• If your baby is born less than 11 weeks before the week in which it was expected, but before your maternity pay period was due to start (because you had not given notice to your employers, or had told them that you would not be giving up work till later), the normal rules apply. However, you must give your employer notice of your confinement within 21 days.

If the birth takes place earlier than expected, it does not entitle you to more than the 18 weeks' maximum period of SMP – the maternity pay period simply starts, and ends, sooner (see p90). You can go on to SSP or sickness benefit if you are still off for medical reasons at the end of the period.

Multiple or stillbirths

No additional SMP is payable if you are expecting or giving birth to more than one baby.

If a stillbirth occurs after 24 weeks of pregnancy, SMP is payable in the same way as for a live birth.[44] If earlier, SMP is not payable but SSP or sickness benefit may be while you are incapable of work.

2. MATERNITY ALLOWANCE

You cannot get SMP if you have recently given up or changed your job, or have been self-employed, but you may get maternity allowance.

Conditions of entitlement[1]

• You satisfy the contribution condition (see p232).
• You are either expecting a child within the next 11 weeks, or have recently given birth (see p96).
• You are not working.[2]
• You have been employed or self-employed for at least 26 weeks in the year (52 weeks) ending at the end of the 'qualifying week' (see below).

The 'qualifying week' is the same as for SMP. But, unlike SMP, the period of 26 weeks need not be continuous and you do not have to have worked for the same employer for the whole of that period.

Amount of payment[3]

	£pw
Claimant	44.55
Adult dependant	26.90

Tax and other benefits

Maternity allowance is non-taxable but is taken into account when calculating IS. Once you are within the maternity allowance period in your pregnancy (see p96), you can receive IS without having to be available for work.[4]

You are not entitled to SSP during the maternity allowance period. If you are already claiming SSP when you reach this period, your employers should give you form SSP1(T) explaining that you are no longer entitled. If you continue to work into the maternity allowance period and fall sick, your employers should give you form SSP1(E) explaining that you are excluded from entitlement to SSP (see p66).

You cannot receive maternity allowance for any week when you are entitled to SMP.[5]

Any day within the maternity allowance period (see p96) counts as a day of incapacity for work for the purposes of making a period of interruption of employment[6] (see p251). This may help you later when claiming sickness or unemployment benefit.

Period of payment

The allowance is payable for 18 weeks. The earliest it can start is from the beginning of the eleventh week before the week of the expected birth. The period of 18 weeks is known as the 'maternity allowance period'.

The rules for the calculation of the period, and late or early confinement, are the same as those for SMP[7] (see pp90 and 94).

How to claim

If you are working you may be entitled to SMP. You should claim from your employers. If your employers do not consider that you are entitled, they must give you form SMP1 with which you can claim maternity allowance.

You must normally provide a certificate from your doctor or midwife giving the expected date of birth of your child.[8]

If you have already stopped working by the beginning of the maternity allowance period, you should claim the allowance in the three weeks preceding the eleventh week before the expected date of birth. If you continue working after the beginning of the eleventh week before, you should claim as soon as you stop working.[9]

3. FUTURE CHANGES

From the end of July 1994, the rules for SMP and maternity allowance will be significantly improved. These changes, which have been introduced to implement the *EC Directive on the Protection of Pregnant Women at Work*, are as follows:

- All women who qualify for SMP because they have worked continuously for the same employer for 26 weeks will be entitled to be paid 90 per cent of their earnings (see p89) for the first six weeks of the maternity pay period (see p90);
- For the remaining 12 weeks of the maternity pay period, the lower rate of SMP will be increased from £48.80 to £52.50 a week;
- Maternity allowance will be increased from £44.55 to £52.50 and the period of 52 weeks for payment of the 26 Class 1 or 2 contributions (see p232) will be extended to 66 weeks;
- If you are on sick leave because of your pregnancy, the maternity pay and maternity allowance periods will start automatically at the beginning of the sixth week before the expected week of confinement (see p89) unless you have chosen to start them earlier.

These changes will only apply to women whose expected week of confinement (see p89) commences after 15 October 1994.

CHAPTER FIVE

Widows' benefits

This chapter covers:

1. Introduction (see below)
2. Widow's payment (p104)
3. Widowed mother's allowance (p105)
4. Widow's pension (p106)
5. Industrial death benefit for widows (p108)
6. Special rules for polygamous and invalid marriages (p109)

1. INTRODUCTION

The three main widows' benefits are:

- **Widow's payment** – a lump-sum payment of £1,108.
- **Widowed mother's allowance** – a weekly benefit paid to widows who have children or who are pregnant.
- **Widow's pension** – a weekly benefit paid to widows who are aged at least 45 (formerly 40) when their husband dies or their widowed mother's allowance ceases.

Entitlement to these benefits depends on whether your late husband satisfied the contribution conditions.

If your husband died as the result of an industrial accident or disease, you are treated as though he had satisfied the contribution conditions for the above benefits. This provision has replaced **industrial death benefit** (see p108) for widows whose husbands died after 10 April 1988, but industrial death benefit is still paid to the widows of those who died before 11 April 1988.

Non-contributory benefits are paid only to the widows of men who were already aged 65 on 5 July 1948 – ie, you can only get them if your husband would be 110 years old if he were still alive. For the year from April 1994, non-contributory widows' benefits will be paid at a standard rate of £34.50 per week. Readers are referred to the 16th edition of this *Guide* for more details on the conditions of entitlement and the circumstances in which this weekly rate may sometimes be reduced.

Widowhood

A widow is a woman who was legally married to a man at the date of his death.

In **Scotland** (but not the rest of Great Britain) this includes a woman who was married to a man 'by cohabitation with habit and repute' without having gone through a formal wedding ceremony.[1] Note however that this is more than simply living together – there must be something about the relationship from which consent to marriage can be inferred and nothing which would have prevented a valid marriage having been contracted (eg, either party already being married to someone else).[2]

Polygamous marriages do not always give rise to a right to claim widows' benefits even if they are recognised as valid in Great Britain for other purposes. Section 6 of this Chapter (p109) covers what to do if the Benefits Agency says that you are not entitled to benefit because your marriage was polygamous or because it was in some way invalid (perhaps because it was bigamous).

Divorce

If you were divorced when your ex-husband died, you are not a widow. But a divorce becomes effective only when the *decree absolute* is pronounced. So, if you were in the process of obtaining a divorce, you are still entitled to widows' benefits as long as your husband died before the decree was made absolute.

If you were living apart from your husband when he died – but without being divorced from him – you are still his widow. This applies even if you were judicially separated as long as you were not actually divorced. But see p99 for more details of what happens if you are cohabiting with another man.

Losing contact with your husband

If your husband disappears and has not been seen or heard of for at least seven years by those who would be expected to have seen or heard of him, then it is assumed that he has died.[3] In these circumstances, a woman can get an order from a court declaring her husband to be dead and – if she has not already divorced him on the ground of five years' separation – ending the marriage so that she is free to marry again.

But this should not be necessary for social security purposes. Even without a decision from a court, an adjudication officer may presume your husband to be dead – and award you widows' benefits – after seven years' absence (although s/he will want to make his or her own enquiries first). And if you have persuaded a court to declare that your husband is dead, the adjudication officer should certainly accept that you are a widow.

Remarriage

If you remarry, you lose all entitlement to widows' benefits based on your first husband's contribution record. This is less favourable than the rule for cohabitation (see below) when widows' benefits are only suspended, not stopped altogether. If you have been widowed more than once, your entitlement to widows' benefits depends on the contribution record of your most recent husband.

If you were a widow immediately before your 60th birthday and then remarried after 4 April 1971, you can still claim a Category B retirement pension based on your first husband's contributions, even though you cannot claim widows' benefits on them (see p121).

Cohabitation

You are not entitled to widows' benefits while you and a man to whom you are not married are living together as husband and wife. The benefits stop only during the period of cohabitation and are payable again if the cohabitation stops.[4]

Defining 'cohabitation' or 'living together as husband and wife' is complicated. The extreme positions are clear. The widow who lives with Mr Jones and calls herself Mrs Jones is likely to be cohabiting. So also are the man and woman who share their money, eat together, sleep together and spend most of their leisure time together. On the other hand, a widow who has a 'boyfriend' who stays with her two or three nights a week, but who has a separate address and does not eat with her regularly or contribute to the household fund, is unlikely to be cohabiting. A widow with a male lodger should not lose her benefit unless there is substantially more to the relationship than the provision of board and lodging for payment. Each case depends on its own circumstances.

'Living together as husband and wife'

Your benefit can be stopped only if you and the man with whom you are alleged to be cohabiting are 'living together as husband and wife'. The burden of proof lies on the adjudication officer.[5]

If the man has a different address which he regards as 'home', that is very strong evidence that you are not 'living together'. But living under the same roof does not necessarily involve 'living together' because 'living together' implies a common household.[6] So, if you keep separate stocks of food, do your cooking and washing separately, have separate televisions and so on, you are unlikely to be regarded as 'living together'. Sharing some facilities does not necessarily mean that you are 'living together'. It is a matter of degree.

Even if you are 'living together', it does not necessarily mean that you are 'living together as *husband and wife*'. It is still necessary for the adjudication officer to consider any sexual relationship, any financial relationship and your general relationship.[7]

The relevance of any sexual relationship

A sexual relationship is an important part of any marriage. So, if there has never been any sexual relationship between two people then that is strong evidence that they are not living together 'as husband and wife'.[8] If you are in this situation, it is important that you should tell the adjudication officer that you have never slept together because s/he will probably not ask you unless you bring the subject up first. Even though this may cause you some embarrassment, you may lose benefit which you ought to get if you do not let the adjudication officer know the true situation. If there is, or has been, a sexual relationship, that is evidence of the affection and trust between the parties. However, an occasional sexual relationship does not imply cohabitation if the rest of the relationship is casual and unlike a marriage.

The relevance of any financial relationship

It is not necessary for the adjudication officer to show that one party is supporting the other. For cohabitation the relationship should usually be such that one party would support the other *if necessary*. For that reason, you should borrow from someone other than your alleged cohabitee if you need money after your benefit is stopped, or at least make it quite clear that the money is a loan. Money lent out of friendship should not lead to a finding of cohabitation, but it can be misinterpreted.

The financial relationship between lodger and landlady often comes in for scrutiny. Adjudication officers sometimes say the payments are too high or too low and so indicate that the relationship is not purely financial. There are a number of things which can be said in reply. First, an adjudication officer seldom, if ever, produces any evidence of other charges made in private arrangements, so that an adjudication officer's idea of too high or too low is just one opinion. Second, many widows have no idea of what other landladies charge and merely charge enough to cover their expenses and provide something towards the mortgage repayments. They often do not increase charges to keep up with inflation. It is important to explain how the charge came to be as it is. However silly the charge may look in retrospect, it is the reasoning which led to it at the time which is important. Third, a widow may have many motives for having a lodger apart from purely commercial ones or cohabitation. She may well want another adult in the house to do occasional babysitting or simply to talk to. Friendship between lodger and landlady does not mean they are cohabiting.

Your general relationship

It is always most important to explain your general relationship because it provides the context for any sexual or financial relationship. You have to explain how you see each other. The extent to which you lead separate lives should be emphasised, with particular reference to other men friends and women friends. The way you organise the household is also relevant, and the reasons for doing it that way are even more important. If you have moved home together in the past, that will also have to be explained. In one case, a disabled widow and a disabled widower who had been friends for years moved in together at the suggestion of a social worker who pointed out that they would have one rent to pay. They had never had a sexual relationship and did not share a bedroom but shared other accommodation. Household chores were managed jointly and meals and leisure were usually taken together. The widower paid the bills. These circumstances taken together were not sufficient to establish that the couple were living together as husband and wife.[9]

Died 'as a result of' an industrial accident or disease

For the meaning of industrial accident or disease, see pp164-170.

The industrial accident or disease must have been a cause of death, but it need have been only one of several causes and need not have been a direct cause.[10]

If your husband died when entitled to constant attendance allowance (see p177), he is deemed to have died as a result of the relevant injury or disease. This also applies if constant attendance allowance had been stopped solely because he was in hospital.[11]

Death is also deemed to have been due to the relevant disease if your husband was, at the time of his death, assessed as at least 50 per cent disabled due to pneumoconiosis or byssinosis and he died from a lung disease.[12]

The forfeiture rule

The forfeiture rule is a general rule of law which prevents people gaining anything from their own crimes. It prevents you from obtaining widow's benefit (or any other benefit based on your late husband's contributions) if you unlawfully killed your husband unless it is decided that it should not apply in your particular case.

Any question concerning the forfeiture rule is decided by a social security commissioner rather than an adjudication officer or tribunal (see p315).[13]

If you have been convicted of **murder**, the forfeiture rule must be applied and no widow's benefit is payable.[14] If you have been convicted of **manslaughter** or of some other offence or you have not been convicted at all, the commissioner may decide that the forfeiture rule may be modified so that you should lose only some benefit. S/he could decide that you should receive only part of your benefit or that benefit should be reduced or withheld for a limited period of time.[15]

The rule can be applied even if you have not been convicted of any offence but, if you have been charged with manslaughter and acquitted, you are unlikely to lose any benefit unless the acquittal was on a technicality or the jury did not hear all the evidence.[16]

A commissioner may direct that her/his decision should affect any future claim by you.[17] However, a decision on the forfeiture rule may be reviewed by a commissioner on the ground that there has been a change of circumstances.[18] A decision may also be reviewed on the ground that it was made in ignorance of, or was based on a mistake as to, a relevant fact.

To apply for a review, write to one of the commissioners' offices (see p316).

Earnings

There is no limit to the amount you may earn while remaining entitled to widows' benefits.

Tax and other benefits

The lump-sum widow's payment is not taxable. Other widows' benefits are taxable apart from any increase in respect of children.[19]

There are special rules to help widows claim invalidity benefit (see p79) and retirement pensions (see p119). Widows are also entitled to credited contributions for some other purposes (see p228).

If you are entitled to a widow's benefit and invalidity benefit you may receive both basic benefits subject to a maximum of £57.60 a week. You are also entitled to both additional pensions under SERPS, subject to a maximum (equal to the amount one person could theoretically receive as an addition to one benefit). Usually, the widow's benefit is paid in full, with any additional benefit being paid as invalidity benefit (IVB).[20] However, as IVB is not taxable, it may be advantageous to apply for the full IVB, with widow's benefit merely topping it up. Payment of IVB also has the advantages that you will be entitled to a disability premium for the purposes of means-tested benefits – eg, income support, housing benefit and council tax benefit; and that you will be credited with Class 1 contributions (see p226).

Widows' benefits are counted in full as income for income support (IS) purposes.[21] If you are over 50 *and* have not worked for the last ten years *and* would not have been required to be available for work during that period (eg, because you were bringing up children), you are not required to be available for work as a condition of entitlement to IS, unless you have a real prospect of future employment.[22] As a single parent, a widowed mother receives an extra £5.10 a week IS, but one parent benefit is not payable if you receive widowed mother's allowance.[23]

If you receive IS, family credit, housing benefit or council tax benefit, you may be entitled to a grant for funeral expenses from the social fund. Your widow's payment is not treated as capital for this purpose.[24] Any such grant will be recovered from your husband's estate if there is enough money in it.

For general practical advice about preparing funerals and registering deaths, obtain DSS leaflet D49, *What to Do After a Death*.

Claims and payments

You will usually have to provide the adjudication officer with your husband's death certificate and your marriage certificate. You get an extra copy of the death certificate for social security purposes when you register the death and, if you complete the form on the back, you will be sent the claim form for widows' benefits. Arrears will be paid up to a maximum of 12 months. Do not delay just because you do not have a certificate. Make sure you get your claim in within the 12-month period.

The 12-month limit on arrears will be waived only if:[25]

- you did not make a claim for widow's benefit before 13 July 1990; *and either*
- your husband's body has not been discovered or identified, *and*
  - an adjudication officer (or tribunal, etc) has determined that he has died or is presumed to have died, *and*

- you claimed widow's benefit within 12 months of that determination; *or*
- you did not know that your husband's body had been discovered or identified, but you found out within 12 months of it having been identified *and*
  - you claimed widow's benefit within 12 months of your finding out about the identification.

Widow's benefit is then payable from the date of death or presumed death. This is useful where a marriage has broken down and a woman has lost touch with her husband, provided that either she finds out about his death within a year of his body being identified or the DSS has also lost track of him and it has to be presumed that he has died.

The benefits are normally paid weekly in advance, but widowed mother's allowance and widow's pension may be paid into your bank account four-weekly or quarterly in arrears if you prefer (see DSS leaflet NI105).

2. WIDOW'S PAYMENT

Conditions of entitlement[1]

- Your husband satisfied the contribution condition (see p233); *or*
- your husband died as the result of an industrial injury or disease (see p101); *and either*
- you were under 60 when your husband died; *or*
- if you were 60 or over, he was not entitled to a Category A retirement pension when he died (eg, because he was under 65, or had deferred entitlement, or he had an inadequate contribution record); *and*
- you claimed within 12 months of his death.

Amount of payment

A lump sum of £1,000.[2] Widow's payment is not the same as a funeral grant from the social fund and if you are not receiving a means-tested benefit, you may be entitled to both. See CPAG's *National Welfare Benefits Handbook* for more about the social fund.

Disqualification

No payment is made if at the time of your husband's death you were living with another man as his wife (see p95).[3]

3. WIDOWED MOTHER'S ALLOWANCE

Conditions of entitlement[1]

- Either your husband satisfied the contribution conditions (see p233); or
- your husband died as the result of an industrial injury or disease (see p101); *and either*
- you are expecting a child by your husband; *or*
- you are pregnant as a result of artificial insemination or *in vitro* fertilisation *and* you were residing with (see p206) your husband immediately before his death; *or*
- you are entitled to child benefit in respect of a qualifying child (see below); *or*
- you have residing with you a person under the age of 19 who would be a qualifying child for whom you would have been in receipt of child benefit if s/he had not been abroad at the relevant time. It may be sufficient that the person lives with you at weekends only, and a temporary absence does not matter even if it lasts several months.

Amount of payment[2]

	£pw
Claimant	57.60
Child dependant	11.00

An additional pension may be paid if your husband died after 5 April 1979 (see p235).

Increases in respect of child dependants are payable only if the children are qualifying children (see below) and the usual conditions are also met (see p205).

You may receive less if your husband's contribution record was incomplete (see p235).

You are also entitled to a Christmas bonus (see p262).

The allowance is paid as long as your children qualify you for it. It ceases if you remarry, and is suspended during any period in which you are cohabiting (see p99).[3] You may become entitled to widow's pension after widowed mother's allowance ceases (see below).

'Qualifying children'

The following count as qualifying children:[4]

- a child of yourself and your late husband;

- a child for whom your husband was entitled to child benefit immediately before his death;
- if you were residing with your husband immediately before his death, a child for whom you were then entitled to child benefit.

If you have been twice widowed, your second husband is treated as having been entitled to child benefit in respect of a child if:[5]

- your first husband was entitled to child benefit for the child immediately before his death. (If you were living with him or being maintained by him and you were receiving child benefit, he is treated as having been entitled to it.); *and*
- you were entitled to child benefit for the child immediately before the death of your second husband.

4. WIDOW'S PENSION

Conditions of entitlement[1]

- Either your husband satisfied the contribution conditions (see p233); *or*
- your husband died as the result of an industrial injury or disease (see p101); *and*
- you are not entitled to widowed mother's allowance; *and either*
  - your husband died before 11 April 1988 and you were over 40 but under 65 either at the date of his death or when you ceased to be entitled to widowed mother's allowance (eg, because your children had grown up); *or*
  - your husband died on or after 11 April 1988 and you were over 45 but under 65 either at the date of his death or when you ceased to be entitled to widowed mother's allowance; *and*
- you are still under 65.

Amount of payment

The basic rate is £57.60 a week.[2]

You may receive an additional pension based on your husband's earnings if you were widowed after 5 April 1979 (see p235).

The basic amount may be reduced if your husband had an incomplete contribution record (see p235).

If you were widowed after 10 April 1988, your pension is reduced if you were under the age of 55 when you first qualified for your pension. The amount of widow's pension you would otherwise receive is reduced by 7 per cent for every year that you were under the age of 55 on the relevant date.[3] That proportion remains the same for as long as you continue to receive widow's pension.

Example

You would be entitled to £60 a week by way of basic and additional pension, and you were 49 when you ceased to be entitled to widowed mother's allowance. Your pension is reduced by

6 years (55–49) × 7% of £60 pw = 42% of £60 pw = £25.20 pw

You receive £34.80 pw.

If you were widowed before 11 April 1988, the pension is reduced by 7 per cent for every year that you were under 50 (instead of 55) at the relevant date.[4]

You will be entitled to a Christmas bonus (see p262).

The pension is paid for as long as the conditions are satisfied, but ceases if you remarry. It is suspended while you are living with a man as his wife (see p99).[5]

When you reach 60, you become entitled to a Category B retirement pension payable at the same rate as your widow's pension (see p120). This means that between the ages of 60 and 64 you will be entitled to either widow's pension or Category B retirement pension depending on which you claim. Many of the rules for retirement pensions are more favourable to claimants but the Benefits Agency will continue to pay widow's pension until you are 65 unless you claim a retirement pension.

It may be particularly important to claim your retirement pension instead if:

• you are cohabiting (see p99); *or*
• you are considering marrying again (see pp118 and 121); *or*
• you have paid some national insurance contributions in your own right and wish to take advantage of the rules which allow you to combine your late husband's contribution record with your own to get a Category A retirement pension (see p119). Unlike a widow's pension or Category B pension, a Category A pension will not be reduced if you were younger than 55 (or 50) when your husband died or when you ceased to be entitled to widowed mother's allowance (see above).

On the other hand, it may be important *not* to claim a retirement pension until you are 65 if you are receiving invalidity benefit as well as a widow's pension (see pp79 and 116).

If you are in any of these situations, you should take advice. Your adviser will need to obtain full details of your own contributions record and those of your late husband and, if applicable, the man you are planning to marry.

5. INDUSTRIAL DEATH BENEFIT FOR WIDOWS

If your husband died after 10 April 1988, you will not be eligible for industrial death benefit. However, if his death was due to an industrial accident or disease, he will be deemed to have satisfied the contribution conditions for widow's payment, widowed mother's allowance and widow's pension.

Conditions of entitlement[1]

- Your husband died before 11 April 1988; *and*
- your husband died as a result of an industrial accident or disease (see p101); *and either*
- you were 'residing with' (see p206) your husband when he died; *or*
- you were receiving periodical payments for your maintenance at the rate of at least 25 pence a week (or would have been but for the accident or onset of the disease); *or*
- although you were not actually receiving such payments, you were entitled to receive them because of a court order, trust or agreement which you had taken reasonable steps to enforce.[2]

Amount of payment

Benefit is paid at two different rates. The **higher permanent rate**[3] is £57.60 a week and is payable if:

- you are entitled to industrial death benefit in respect of a child (see p199); *or*
- you are residing with a person under 19; *and either*
- your husband was, at the time of his death, entitled to child benefit for that person; *or*
- he would have been entitled to child benefit if that person had been under 16 or not been abroad; *or*
- you were over 50 when your husband died; *or*
- you were over 40 when you ceased to be entitled to industrial death benefit for a child, or you ceased to reside with a person under 19 as above; *or*

- you were permanently incapable of self-support when your husband died.

The **lower permanent rate**[4] is £17.28 a week and is payable if you do not qualify for the higher permanent rate.

You will be entitled to a Christmas bonus (see p262).

Disqualification

You cease to be entitled if you remarry and the benefit is suspended if you are living with a man as husband and wife (see p99).[5]

If you have children residing with you, cohabitation does not affect your right to receive industrial death benefit in respect of them (see p199). Remarriage, however, does.

6. SPECIAL RULES FOR POLYGAMOUS AND INVALID MARRIAGES

Polygamous marriages

As a general rule, the law in England, Wales and Scotland does not treat a man and a woman as being legally married unless their marriage is a monogamous one.[1] However, there are occasions when a polygamous marriage can give rise to an entitlement to widows' benefits (and most other benefits which depend on marital status – eg, increases for adult dependants).

A marriage is polygamous if the law of the country where it is celebrated permits either party to have another wife or husband.[2] Usually it is the husband who is allowed to have more than one wife but the rules apply in the same way if it is the wife who is permitted two or more husbands.[3]

For entitlement to social security benefits, the crucial question is whether or not either the husband or wife actually has another spouse[4] – the marriage is treated as being monogamous on any day when it is *potentially polygamous* (ie, if neither the husband nor the wife has ever had more than one spouse) or when it is *formerly polygamous* (ie, if the husband or wife have had other spouses in the past but all such spouses have now died or been divorced) but not on any day when it is *actually polygamous* (ie, the husband has more than one wife or the wife more than one husband).

This means that you are treated as a widow if, on the day he died, your husband had no other wife and you had no other husband.

If you are refused widow's benefit because your marriage was polygamous, you should take advice. The law on the recognition of polygamous marriages is complex and it is quite possible that even if you think your marriage is polygamous, the law will not agree with you.

This will depend on whether you were your husband's first wife and on where you and your husband were *domiciled* at the time of your marriage and any subsequent marriage. Domicile is a difficult legal concept but – in very general terms – means the country which you have chosen to make your permanent home.[5] Domicile is not the same as *presence* (see p244), *residence* (see p244), *ordinary residence* (see p245) or *nationality*.

In particular, no one who is domiciled in England and Wales is allowed to contract a polygamous marriage anywhere in the world even if the local law would allow it.[6]

Example

At the time of your wedding, you and your husband were domiciled in Pakistan and you were married under Islamic law. After the wedding you came to live in England and made your permanent home here. Later your husband returned temporarily to Pakistan and married a second wife. As your husband was domiciled in England and Wales rather than Pakistan at the time of the second marriage, English law does not recognise that marriage and therefore regards you as your late husband's only wife. Provided you meet the other conditions of entitlement, you are entitled to widows' benefits.

The Benefits Agency has a special section called the Validity of Marriage Unit to which adjudication officers refer any questions about whether a marriage is to be treated as monogamous.

Invalid marriages

Sometimes the law will treat even a monogamous marriage as invalid even though you have been through a formal wedding ceremony. An invalid marriage can be either *void* or *voidable*. The difference is that while a *voidable* marriage (eg, one that has not been consummated) has to be annulled by a court order to allow the parties to remarry, a *void* marriage (eg, a bigamous one) does not exist at all and, from a legal point of view, has no consequences and can simply be ignored (although for most practical purposes, it will be necessary to confirm the position by getting a court order).

For social security purposes, this means that if your marriage is void it cannot give rise to any entitlement to widows' benefits (or any other benefit – eg, an increase for an adult dependant (see pp202-203) – which is based on marital status) even if it has not been annulled.[7] For the same reason, if you have been widowed more than once and your most recent marriage is held to be void, you may be entitled to widows' benefits based on the contributions of your previous husband.

On the other hand, a marriage which is *voidable* is treated as a marriage until a *decree absolute* of annulment is pronounced.[8] So, if your husband dies before your marriage is finally annulled, you may claim as his widow. If you are widowed and then enter a voidable marriage, then that marriage will end your entitlement to widows' benefits based on the contributions of your first husband even after it is annulled.

As with polygamous marriages, questions about the validity of marriage can be deceptively difficult. For example the Benefits Agency may claim that your marriage was bigamous (and therefore void) because it claims that English or Scottish law does not recognise the validity of a divorce given by a foreign court.

The Validity of Marriage Unit (see p110) also decides questions in this area. If they claim that your marriage was invalid, you should take advice (see p329).

CHAPTER SIX

Retirement pensions

This chapter covers:

1. Introduction (see below)
2. Category A retirement pension (p116)
3. Category B retirement pension for a married woman (p119)
4. Category B retirement pension for a widow (p120)
5. Category B retirement pension for a widower (p122)
6. Category D retirement pension (p123)
7. Graduated retirement benefit (p124)
8. Future changes (p124)

1. INTRODUCTION

There are three main categories of retirement pension:

- **Category A** retirement pension is payable on *your* contribution record.
- **Category B** retirement pension is payable on your *spouse's* contribution record. There are different conditions depending on whether you are a married woman, a widow or a widower.
- **Category D** retirement pension is a non-contributory pension payable to those over 80.

The vast majority of male pensioners receive Category A retirement pensions. Women usually receive either Category A or Category B retirement pensions or both.

Category C retirement pensions are non-contributory pensions which are paid to:[1]

- men who are at least 110 years old; *and*
- women who are at least 105 years old *or* who are married to (or in some cases divorced from) a man who is at least 110 years old *or* who are widows *and* whose husbands would now be at least 110 years old if they had lived.

Given these rules (and the fact that there is also a residence test), not many people now qualify. If you think you might be one of them, please see the

15th edition of this *Guide*. The current rates for the Category C pension are set out in the table at the beginning of this book.

Pensionable age and retirement

To get a retirement pension:

- you must have reached 'pensionable age'. Pensionable age is 65 for a man and 60 for a woman.[2] This rule discriminates on grounds of sex but is not contrary to EC law (see p270);
- you must claim. You do not automatically become entitled to your retirement pension just by reaching pensionable age. If you do not claim you will be treated as having deferred' your retirement (see p114). If you are getting invalidity benefit or severe disablement allowance you should take advice before claiming (see p116) but do not wait for more than a year after reaching pensionable age before making a decision or you may lose out (see below);
- you do *not* have to retire. You can choose whether or not to give up work. If you decide to go on working your earnings will not reduce the pension you receive (although if your spouse is still working you may not be able to get an increase in your pension for her/him (see p208)).

Claiming your retirement pension

A claim should be made within 12 months of your becoming entitled to the pension. If you claim later, only 12 months' arrears will be paid.[3]

Claims for retirement pensions may be made up to, but no more than, four months in advance.[4] You should take full advantage of this provision as it takes a long time to sort out your contribution position. Normally the Benefits Agency will send you an application form about four months before you reach pensionable age. If you have not received a form three months before you want to receive the pension, ask for one.

If the DSS tells you that you have not paid enough contributions, you may still be able to get your pension if you make up the missing contributions now. The DSS does not always tell you this, so it is worth asking specifically whether or not this rule applies to you.

Proving your age

It is up to you to prove that you have reached pensionable age. For most claimants it will be enough to produce your birth certificate but problems can occur if you were born in a country which did not have a formal system of registering births. If you are in this position, you should consult

CPAG's *Ethnic Minorities Benefits Handbook* for detailed advice on what other evidence of your age the DSS will accept.

Payments

Payments are usually made by giving you a book of orders which you may cash weekly in advance. However, you can choose to be paid by direct credit transfer into a bank account either four-weekly or quarterly in arrears if you prefer, in which case you should obtain a copy of Benefits Agency leaflet NI105 and complete the form attached to it.

Deferring your retirement pension

During the first five years after you reach pensionable age, you are allowed to defer entitlement to a Category A or Category B retirement pension. In return for doing so, you later become entitled to a higher rate of pension.

For each week you defer entitlement, the pension you eventually receive is increased by one-seventh of 1 per cent.[5] The same applies to graduated retirement benefit (see p124).[6] This means that if you defer entitlement for the whole five-year period, you will then receive slightly over 37 per cent extra retirement pension each week.

The benefits which are increased in this way include any additional pension under the state earnings related pension scheme (SERPS), an invalidity increase and any increase resulting from your late spouse's deferment, but not increases for dependants or age addition.[7]

If you are a **widow** and your husband had deferred his entitlement to pension, you become entitled to the increase he would have gained through his deferment provided you do not remarry before you reach the age of 60. A **widower** can similarly become entitled to an increase resulting from his wife's deferment, but only if he was over pensionable age when she died.[8]

The rules for people who reached pensionable age before 6 April 1979 are different – in particular, you need eight weeks of deferment to gain a 1 per cent increase.[9]

It is important to realise that any day on which you receive any of the other benefits described in Chapters 2 to 6 of this guide will not be counted when your increased pension is calculated[10] – nor will any day for which you would have been disqualified from receiving a Category A or B retirement pension because you were in prison.[11]

From 5 August 1992, this rule also applies to graduated retirement benefit (see p124).[12] As payments of **graduated retirement benefit** are usually very small, this can mean that an increment to a Category A or B retirement pension worth many pounds can be lost because of payments of graduated retirement benefit of as little as a few pence per week. This is a problem which particularly affects married women (see below), but everyone should think carefully, and if necessary take advice, before claiming graduated retirement benefit unless they are claiming their retirement pension at the same time (particularly since the graduated retirement benefit will itself be increased if you defer claiming it).

Before 5 August 1992, receipt of graduated retirement benefit did not affect increments.[13] People who have been refused increments because they claimed graduated retirement benefit before that date are referred to the 16th edition of this *Guide* and to the sections on the 'anti-test-case rules' and 'late appeals' in this edition (see pp284 and 318).

Many married women have no choice about whether to defer their Category B retirement pensions. This is because they cannot claim them until their husband reaches pensionable age and claims his own Category A retirement pension (see p116). Anyone who does have a choice should think very carefully before deferring their pension now that the earnings rules for retirement pensions have been abolished. Even if you can afford to live without the money from your pension at present, you may be better off claiming it now and investing it. Apart from anything else, if you die within five years of reaching pensionable age, any money you have claimed and invested will go to your family, but if you die before you claim, only your spouse, and not other members of your family, can benefit from the deferment of your pension, and even then only in certain circumstances (see p114). Your entitlement to means-tested benefits such as income support, housing benefit and council tax benefit will not be affected as long as you do not allow your total capital to rise above £3,000.

One situation where you might want to consider deferring your pension (or de-retiring – see p116) is if you are a married man who is terminally ill and whose wife is over 60. This is because if you are not receiving a Category A retirement pension when you die, your widow may be able to receive the £1,000 lump sum widow's payment (see p104). And if you do not claim any other contributory benefit either, her widow's pension may also be increased to take account of the deferment of your Category A pension (see p114). But if you are in this position you should take advice before deciding to defer to ensure that you do not lose more in pension payments than your wife is likely to gain. One possibility – if you are under 70 – might be to prepare and sign an election to de-retire and authorise someone to send it to the Benefits Agency by recorded delivery post shortly before your death. The election takes effect as soon as it is posted.[14]

De-retirement

You can usually defer your retirement pension simply by not claiming it but, once you have become entitled, you may only defer by notifying the Benefits Agency of your intention on the proper form.[15] You may 'de-retire' in this way at any time during the first five years after you reach pensionable age.[16] You can also cancel your deferment at any time, but you cannot then de-retire a second time.[17]

You cannot de-retire if you are a man who is entitled to a Category A retirement pension and you have a wife who is entitled to a Category B retirement pension by virtue of your contributions, unless your wife consents or withholds her consent unreasonably.[18]

Tax and other benefits

Retirement pensions are taxable except for increases for children.[19]

You can continue to receive invalidity pension or severe disablement allowance when over pensionable age. If you are entitled to these benefits, there may be tax advantages in not retiring. This is because they are – at least for the moment – non-taxable, whereas retirement pensions are taxable; and because people receiving invalidity pension receive a higher rate of income support and some other means-tested benefits than most people with retirement pensions.

Retirement pensions are taken fully into account for income support purposes, but pensioners receive a higher rate of income support.[20]

2. CATEGORY A RETIREMENT PENSION

Conditions of entitlement[1]

- You must claim within the time limit (see p113), but see p117 for exceptions.
- You satisfy the contribution conditions (see p233) on the basis of your own contribution record (unless you are a widow, a widower or divorced).
- You are over pensionable age.

Amount of payment[2]

	£pw
Claimant	57.60
Adult dependant	34.50
Child dependant	11.00

In addition, you may receive:

- **an age addition** of 25 pence a week if you are over 80;
- **graduated retirement benefit** based on earnings between 1961 and 1975 (see p124);
- **an additional pension** based on SERPS if you reached pensionable age after 5 April 1979 (see p235);
- **a higher pension** if you deferred entitlement to pension (see p114);
- **invalidity allowance** if you were receiving this within eight weeks of reaching pensionable age (see p77). If you were over pensionable age on 5 April 1979, the allowance is payable under the old rules and you receive the higher rate only if you were under 35 on the first day of incapacity for work (see p252) in the relevant period of interruption of employment (see p251), and the middle rate only if you were under 45.[3] If you have an additional SERPS pension, any invalidity allowance to which you are entitled is set off against it;[4]
- **a Christmas bonus** (see p262).

You may receive less than the standard amount of pension if you only partially satisfy the contribution conditions (see p235).

Exceptions to the rule on claiming [5]

Provided you meet the other conditions of entitlement you need not claim your Category A retirement pension if *either*:

- you are a woman aged over 65 and receiving widowed mother's allowance; *or*
- you are a woman aged under 65 and receiving a widow's pension.

If you fall into either of these categories you should be paid your pension automatically when you either cease to receive widowed mother's allowance or reach the age of 65.

Special rules for divorced people

There are special rules which may help you qualify for a Category A retirement pension, if you cannot qualify on the basis of your own contributions.[6] These rules apply if:

- you have been divorced; *or*
- your marriage was voidable (not void) and has been annulled by a court; *and either*
- your *decree absolute* of divorce or nullity is dated after you reach pensionable age; *or*

- your *decree absolute* of divorce or nullity is dated before you reach pensionable age and you do not remarry before you reach that age.

Those rules mean that you will be treated as satisfying the first contribution condition (see p233) for a Category A retirement pension if your former spouse did so in any year of his/her working life (see p233) up to and including the year in which your marriage ended.[7]

In addition, you can use your former spouse's contribution record instead of your own in order to increase the number of years in which you satisfy the second contribution condition (see p233).[8]

To do this, you divide the number of years in which your former spouse met the second contribution condition by the number of years in his/her working life (in both cases up to but *excluding* the year in which your marriage ended). You can then *either*:

- multiply the number of years in your own working life (up to and including the year in which your marriage ended) by this figure and then round up to the next whole number and add the number of years after that year in which you satisfy the second contribution condition; *or*
- multiply the number of years for which you were married (including both the year in which you were married and the year in which your *decree absolute* was given) by this figure and then round up to the next whole number and add the number of years – both before and after your marriage – in which you personally satisfied the second contribution condition.

You are then taken as having satisfied the second contribution condition for whichever number of years is higher.[9]

In practice this means that if your former spouse had a full contribution record, you can use it to replace your own either for all the years in your working life up to and including the one in which you were divorced or for all the years during which you were married. If your former spouse's contribution record was incomplete you will not be treated as satisfying the second contribution condition for all of those years – only some of them. But this may still be more than you would qualify for on the basis of your own contributions.

These rules may mean that if your spouse is continuing to work and pay contributions, it is to your advantage not to get divorced when your marriage breaks up, unless and until one of you wants to remarry.

If you are considering remarrying, have an incomplete contribution record, and are approaching pensionable age, you should think carefully about the timing of your wedding as it may be to your financial advantage to postpone it until after you have reached pensionable age.

Conversely, in some cases there may be a financial advantage in bringing the wedding forward. This will depend both on whether you are male or female and on the contribution records of your former and your prospective spouses. You should take advice.

If you have been married more than once, only your most recent marriage counts for these purposes.[10]

These rules do not apply to you if:[11]

• you had already reached pensionable age by 5 April 1979 (ie, if you are now a woman aged 75 or over or a man aged at least 80); *and*
• your decree absolute is also dated on or before 5 April 1979.

Special rules for widows and widowers

The rules for divorced people (see p117) also apply to all women who are widows on the day they reach pensionable age.[12] They apply to widowers in the following circumstances:

• your late wife died before you reached pensionable age and you did not remarry before you reached that age;[13]
• you are a man and were widowed after you reached pensionable age but before your late wife's sixtieth birthday[14] (a woman in the equivalent position would not need to use these rules because of her entitlement to Category B retirement pension at the widow's rate and the rules discussed below).

Widowers cannot benefit from the rules if they had already reached pensionable age by 5 April 1979 unless their late wife did not die until after that date.[15]

In addition, if you are entitled to both a Category A pension at a reduced rate on your own contributions and a Category B pension on the contributions of your late spouse there are special rules which allow you to add the two together up to a maximum of £57.60 per week (see p259).[16] This rule applies only to widows and widowers – not if you are divorced.

3. CATEGORY B RETIREMENT PENSION FOR A MARRIED WOMAN

Conditions of entitlement[1]

• You must claim within the time limit (see p113).
• Your husband has satisfied the contribution conditions (see p233).
• You and your husband are both over pensionable age.

- Your husband has become entitled to a Category A retirement pension.

If your husband was receiving an increase of Category A retirement pension in respect of you before you receive this pension, that increase will be replaced by this pension, which will normally be paid at the same rate.

Amount of pension [2]

	£pw
Claimant	34.50
Child dependant	11.00

In addition, you may receive:

- **an age addition** of 25 pence a week if you are over 80;
- **a higher pension** from deferring entitlement to pension (see p114);
- **a Christmas bonus** (see p262).

You may receive less than the standard rate because your husband only partially satisfies the contribution conditions (see p235, but see also p119).

4. CATEGORY B RETIREMENT PENSION FOR A WIDOW

Conditions of entitlement [1]

You must claim within the time limit (see p113), but see p122 for exceptions; *and either*

- your husband satisfied the contribution conditions (see p233); *or*
- your husband died as a result of an industrial injury or disease (see p101); *and either*
- you were 60 or over when he died; *or*
- you were a widow immediately before you reached the age of 60 and you are entitled to a widow's pension (or would be but for one or more of the reasons given below).

If you were under 60 when your husband died, but are not receiving a widow's pension, you are still entitled if the reason you are not receiving the widow's pension is one or more of the following: [2]

- you have failed to claim it; *or*

- you are receiving widowed mother's allowance instead; *or*
- you are cohabiting; *or*
- you have remarried since your 60th birthday (but only if after 4 April 1971); *or*
- you are disqualified under the 'overlapping benefits' rules (see p258) or for any other reason (other than being abroad); *or*
- you are over 65.

Effectively, only widows who fail to qualify because they were too young when their husband died, or when their children grew up, are not entitled.

A widow who is approaching 60 and considering remarriage should assess her position and, if necessary, take advice. There may be considerable financial benefits in postponing any wedding so that she is still a widow immediately before attaining pensionable age.[3]

Widows whose widow's benefit was suspended before they were 60 because they were cohabiting are entitled to have any Category B pension to which they may be entitled paid from their 60th birthday. But to get this you *must* claim the pension. If you do not, the Benefits Agency will continue to treat you as entitled to widow's benefit (and will therefore continue to suspend payment during cohabitation) until your 65th birthday (see 'Exceptions to the rule on claiming' pp122 and 117).

Amount of payment[4]

	£pw
Claimant	57.60
Child dependant	11.00

In addition, you may receive:

- **an age addition** of 25 pence a week if you are over 80;
- **graduated retirement benefit** based on your husband's graduated contributions between 1961 and 1975 (see p124);
- **a higher pension** if your husband deferred entitlement to pension (see p114);
- **an additional pension** based on your husband's earnings after 5 April 1979 under SERPS (see p235);
- **a Christmas bonus** (see p262).

You may receive less than the standard amount of pension because your husband only partially satisfied the contribution conditions (see p235, but see also p119).

If you formerly received widow's pension which was reduced because you were under the age of 55 when your husband died, or when you ceased to be entitled to widowed mother's allowance, your Category B retirement pension will be reduced in the same way.[5] An identical reduction is made if you would have been receiving a widow's pension but you were disqualified (eg, while you were living with a man as his wife).[6]

Period of payment

The pension is paid indefinitely and does not cease if you remarry (as long as your remarriage was after 4 April 1971) or if you live with a man as his wife.[7]

Exceptions to the rule on claiming

These are the same as for Category A retirement pension (see p117).

5. CATEGORY B RETIREMENT PENSION FOR A WIDOWER

Conditions of entitlement[1]

* You must claim within the time limit (see p113).
* Your wife has satisfied the contribution conditions (see p233).
* You reached the age of 65 after 5 April 1979.
* Your wife died when you and she were both over pensionable age.

Amount of payment[2]

	£pw
Claimant	57.60
Child dependant	11.00

In addition, you may receive:

* **an age addition** of 25 pence a week if you are over 80;
* **graduated retirement benefit** on your wife's graduated contributions between 1961 and 1975 (see p124);
* **an additional pension** based on your wife's earnings after 5 April 1979 (see p235);
* **a higher rate pension** if your wife deferred entitlement to pension (see p114);
* **a Christmas bonus** (see p262).

You may receive less than the standard amount because your wife only partially satisfied the contribution conditions (see p235, but see also p119).

The different conditions of entitlement for widows and widowers discriminate against men on the grounds of sex (because a man can never receive a Category B pension if his wife died before she reached pensionable age) but this is probably *not* contrary to EC law (see p270). Note, however, that if your wife died before she was 60 you may be able to use her contributions to help you get a Category A pension (see p119).

Period of payment

The pension is paid indefinitely and does not cease if you remarry or live with a woman as her husband.[3]

6. CATEGORY D RETIREMENT PENSION

Conditions of entitlement [1]

- You must claim within the time limits (see p113, but see below for an exception).
- You satisfy the residence conditions (see p242).
- You are aged 80 or over.
- You are entitled either to no other retirement pension or to an amount of retirement pension less than the current rate of a Category D retirement pension.

Amount of payment [2]

	£pw
Claimant	34.50

In addition, you will receive:

- **an age addition** of 25 pence a week because you are over 80;
- **a Christmas bonus** (see p262).

Exception to the rule on claiming [3]

Provided you meet the other conditions of entitlement you need not claim Category D retirement pension if you were 'ordinarily resident' in Great Britain (see p2) on your 80th birthday and you are already receiving another retirement pension.

7. GRADUATED RETIREMENT BENEFIT

Between 1961 and 6 April 1975, those paying flat-rate Class 1 contributions also paid graduated contributions. For every £7.50 contributed by a man, or £9 contributed by a woman during that period, that person is now entitled to £7.48 pence a week.[1]

From 7 June 1993 you are entitled to an age addition of 25 pence a week if you are receiving graduated retirement benefit but are not (for some reason) receiving any other retirement pension.[2] This rule seems only to affect people who are not eligible for a Category D pension either because they fail to meet the residence conditions or who failed to make a claim for it. It is not necessary to make a separate claim for the age addition.[3]

If you are a **widow**, you may add half your husband's entitlement to your own. Similarly, a **widower** entitled to a Category B retirement pension (or who would be if he did not have a Category A retirement pension) may also add half his wife's entitlement to his own.[4]

Graduated retirement benefit may be paid even if you are not entitled to any retirement pension. But if you are entitled to only a very small amount, you will receive a lump-sum payment instead of weekly payments. It is increased if you defer entitlement in the same way as for retirement pension (see p114).[5]

The contribution conditions for graduated retirement benefit discriminate against women on the grounds of their sex and would appear to be against EC law (see p267).

8. FUTURE CHANGES

The Government has announced[1] that pensionable age for women will be increased from 60 to 65 between 2010 and 2020. These changes will affect all those who were born after 5 April 1950. Women born after 5 April 1955 will reach pensionable age at 65 and those born between 6 April 1950 and 5 April 1955 at an age between 60 and 65.

It is also proposed to equalise the rules for Category B retirement pension and for increases for adult dependants to Category A retirement pension on the same (more favourable) basis as they currently apply to women.

The five-year maximum time limit for the deferment of retirement pension is to be abolished and each year of deferment will produce an increment of 10 per cent as opposed to 7.5 per cent at present.

These changes mean that there will also be changes in the contribution conditions for retirement pensions and in the rules for home responsibilities protection (see p229) and additional pensions under SERPS (see p235). These are discussed in Chapter 12 (see p239).

Further details on these changes – and in particular a table showing when women who are presently aged between 39 and 44 will reach pensionable age – are contained in DSS Leaflet EQP1 – *Equality in State Pension Age* – which can be obtained free of charge by telephoning 0345 825522. Your telephone call will be charged at local rates.

~~Benefits Severely disable~~ ; ~~Disability Benefit~~

DLA = Mobility – Higher eg Virtually or unable to walk
Lower – Supervision.

Care – Higher – DAY plus NIGHT Supervision Attention
Middle – Day OR Night.
Lower – Cooking test / Limited Attention Condition.

Note Cooking test 0–16. Can not satisfy cooking tests.
– Above conditions Plus "Substantially access") test
P135.

CHAPTER SEVEN

Benefits for severely disabled people

[handwritten: Mobility = Walk - DLA in Supervision in/out of doors]

[handwritten: ✻ See notes at back]

This chapter covers:

[handwritten: CARE Comp checkers.]

1. Introduction (see below)
2. Disability living allowance mobility component (see p127)
3. Disability living allowance care component (see p134)
4. Attendance allowance (see p142)
5. Matters common to both disability living allowance and attendance allowance (see p144)

[handwritten: Not over-lapping benefits.]

I. INTRODUCTION

The benefits available to severely disabled people were reorganised from 6 April 1992. The old mobility allowance, and attendance allowance for those under 65, were incorporated into a new benefit, **disability living allowance** (DLA), which has both mobility and care 'components'. These also have new, lower rates with less stringent qualifying conditions. Attendance allowance remains for those aged 65 or more when their care needs start. There were also changes to the rules about qualifying periods and a new adjudication structure was introduced.

So far there have been no significant decisions by commissioners on the new rules introduced. The old case law on the provisions that have been carried over from the former attendance and mobility allowance remains valid.

People entitled to these benefits may also qualify for other benefits mentioned elsewhere in this *Guide*.

See Appendix One for benefits and services not usually regarded as social security benefits but which are available to people with disabilities (p331).

(handwritten: Living Allowance)

(handwritten: 2 Rates Higher/lower)

BILITY LIVING ALLOWANCE MOBILITY
PONENT *(handwritten: — For care or mobility needs — Replaced ... Allowance + mobility allowance for people)*
ns of entitlement *(handwritten: under 66.)*

- You satisfy the residence conditions (see p242).
- You are five or over but under 66 when you <u>first claim</u>.
- You are likely to be able to benefit from time to time from 'facilities for enhanced locomotion'.
- You satisfy the 'disability' conditions: *(handwritten: — 1 condition.)*
  - **For the higher** rate of the mobility component (the former mobility allowance) *either*:
    you must be suffering from a physical disability such that you are unable to walk; *or*
    you must be suffering from a physical disability such that you are virtually unable to walk; *or* *(handwritten: — See next page.)*
    you are both deaf and blind; *or*
    you were born without feet or are a double amputee; *or*
    you are severely mentally impaired; *and* have severe behavioural problems; *and* qualify for the highest rate of the care component.
  - **For the lower** rate of the mobility component you need to show that although you are able to walk you are so severely disabled, physically or mentally, that, ignoring any familiar routes, you are unable to take advantage of your walking abilities outdoors without guidance or supervision from another person most of the time.[2]
  - **For both rates** you must have satisfied one of these conditions for at least the past three months and you must be likely to satisfy it for the next six months (unless you are terminally ill).

(handwritten in left margin: Higher Rate jctor Physical — 0 Connection of work un-means tested)

Amount of payment *(handwritten: * NOTE * If receiving Middle or higher rate Care Comp. — Qualify for SDP for IS, HB, CTB)*

- The higher rate of mobility component is £31.95 per week.
- The lower rate of mobility component is £12.15 per week.

Rules about age

The mobility component cannot be paid to anyone under the age of five. However, the three months before the fifth birthday can be the qualifying period resulting in payment from the fifth birthday.

For the lower rate mobility component, those aged between five and 16 also have to show *either*:

- that they require substantially more guidance or supervision than persons of their age in normal physical and mental health would; *or*
- that persons of their age in normal physical and mental health would not require such guidance or supervision.[4]

The upper age limit for claiming either rate of the DLA mobility component is normally 65. Those who are aged 65 but who have not yet reached 66 are able to claim if they can show that they have met the residence and presence test (see p242) and that their disability had begun on the day before their 65th birthday. The three-month retrospective qualifying period runs from the date the disability began, provided that it was before the date of their 65th birthday. You cannot claim the mobility component for the first time once you have reached the age of 66.[5] But once you become entitled, it can then be paid for life.

Unable or virtually unable to walk –

This is the commonest route to the higher rate mobility component. The regulations say that a person shall be treated as suffering from a physical disablement that makes her/him unable or virtually unable to walk only if:

his physical condition as a whole is such that without having regard to circumstances peculiar to that person as to the place of residence or as to place of, or nature of, employment:

- he is unable to walk; *or*
- his ability to walk out of doors is so limited, as regards the distance over which or the speed at which or the length of time for which or the manner in which he can make progress on foot without severe discomfort, that he is virtually unable to walk; *or*
- the exertion required to walk would constitute a danger to his life or would be likely to lead to a serious deterioration in his health.[6]

'Physical disablement'

To qualify for the higher rate of the mobility component, the cause of your incapacity to walk must be physical and not psychological, so people with agoraphobia (who are frightened of going out) do not qualify for the higher rate mobility component (although they may qualify for the lower rate, see p132). To qualify as virtually unable to walk, you may need to show that 'behavioural problems' which limit your mobility have a physical cause. Often, what are referred to as behavioural problems are the result of a mental disability which has an organic, physical basis.

'Unable or virtually unable to walk'

Ability to walk is considered after taking into account any artificial aid you habitually wear or use, or which would be suitable for you.[7] You will not qualify if you are able to walk with a stick or crutches. However, the term 'walk' is important here. A man with one leg and no artificial limb may be able to get about with crutches but getting about in this way cannot mean the same thing as being able to 'walk'. He qualifies because he is simply unable to walk without it being necessary to consider whether he is virtually unable to walk.[8] Since April 1991 people with no feet have qualified automatically.

'Out of doors'

The test is whether you can walk out of doors, not indoors. If you have problems with your balance on uneven pavements and roads, or you have a lung or other condition which is made worse by wind or rain, these will be relevant factors in deciding your claim.[9]

'Distance'

The regulations do not say that if you are able to walk a certain distance you are automatically ineligible for the mobility component. In one case, an appeal tribunal's decision that a person who had walked less than 50 yards was not virtually unable to walk was upheld.[10] But other appeal tribunals have accepted that a person was 'virtually unable to walk' even when able to cover 300 yards or more. One relevant consideration may be how long it takes you to recover after walking a certain distance – eg, 50 yards. If you can walk another 50 yards after only a minute's rest, your walking ability is obviously greater than that of a person who has to lie down for an hour after walking such a distance.

'Without severe discomfort'

If, when you walk, you feel severe discomfort – eg, pain and breathlessness brought on by walking[11] – you should make this clear. The point of this part of the regulation is to ignore any walking that can be achieved only with severe discomfort when considering whether you are virtually unable to walk.[12] However, pain is difficult to measure, and may be as much a subjective phenomenon as an objective one.

'The exertion required to walk'

This provision has been commented on in one case:

> It is 'exertion required to walk' which must lead to the danger to life or a serious deterioration in health. The expression includes . . . a condition

which might be induced or precipitated by walking. It then has to be shown as a matter of probability that the exertion would constitute a danger to life or lead to a serious deterioration in health.[13]

But this leaves unclear what distance has to be considered when applying this test. It may be that it is the limited distance of, say, 50 yards that would be considered in a conventional 'virtual inability to walk' case. Or it may be that the distance to be considered is that which a person in reasonable health could walk.

It is not necessary for the possible serious deterioration in your health to be permanent or long-lasting.[14]

In practice, few claimants seem to qualify under this route. Even those with heart problems, who might be thought most likely to do so, are rarely advised not to walk on medical grounds (indeed, exercise is often advised by their doctor). However, it may well be that their walking tolerance is so limited by pain or breathlessness that they are virtually unable to walk.

'Without having regard to circumstances peculiar' to the claimant

Your personal circumstances are not taken into account. It is not, for instance, relevant that you do not have sufficient mobility to get to your nearest bus stop to go shopping,[15] or that you are no longer able to use public transport.

People without feet

People without feet are automatically treated as being unable to walk. A person needs to fit within this precise definition:

he has both legs amputated at levels which are either through or above the ankle, or, he has one leg so amputated and is without the other leg, or is without both legs to the same extent as if it, or they, had been so amputated.[16]

Blind and deaf claimants

You are treated as being unable to walk if:

- the degree of disablement resulting from your loss of vision is 100 per cent; *and*
- the degree of disablement resulting from your loss of hearing is 80 per cent on a scale where 100 per cent represents absolute deafness;[17] *and*
- the combined effects of the blindness and deafness mean that you are

unable to walk to any intended or required destination while out of doors, without the help of another person.[18]

The legislation does not explain how your loss of vision and loss of hearing should be assessed. So, you should argue that 100 per cent loss of vision is to be assessed by reference to the scale used for severe disablement allowance and disablement benefit on which 100 per cent is the assessment for 'loss of sight to such an extent as to render the claimant unable to perform work for which eyesight is essential' (see p338).[19] That is something less than total blindness.

Since absolute deafness is assessed as 100 per cent on the same scale, the statutory test for industrial deafness cases can be used to decide whether your disablement from loss of hearing is 80 per cent. On that basis, you qualify if adding together the hearing loss in each ear due to all causes at 1, 2 and 3 kHz and dividing the result by two gives an average loss of at least 87 dB.[20] In practice, adjudication officers accept a person as having 80 per cent loss of hearing if s/he is unable to understand a question asked from a distance of one metre.

Claimants with severe behavioural difficulties

There is a route to the higher rate mobility component of DLA for those with severe behavioural difficulties.

A claimant qualifies if:

- s/he is severely mentally impaired; *and*
- s/he displays severe behavioural problems – ie:
  - s/he exhibits disruptive behaviour which is extreme; *and*
  - s/he regularly requires someone else to intervene and physically restrain them in order to prevent them causing injury to themselves or others, or damage to property; *and* ~ Pg 13 1
  - s/he is so unpredictable that another person has to be present and watching over them whenever they are awake; *and*
- s/he qualifies for the higher rate of the care component.[21]

Many people likely to pass this test may live in hospitals or other accommodation where the care component is not payable. They may, therefore, need to put in a claim for the care component and satisfy the Benefits Agency that they would qualify for it at the higher rate (even though it will not be payable to them). They would then be able to receive the mobility component under these rules.

People with severe behavioural difficulties who are already in receipt of mobility allowance may have been awarded it for a limited period only, at the end of which they will need to make a renewal claim in the standard way. They may not meet all of the elements of the test for the higher rate mobility component – eg, they may not be sufficiently unsettled at night to get the higher rate care component. However, if they qualified previously on the basis that they were virtually unable to walk, there is nothing to stop them continuing to qualify for the higher rate component via that route. The same applies to new claimants who might also be unable to fit themselves within the newer test. This will involve arguing that the claimant's disability prevents her/him from walking effectively, causing so many refusals to walk that the person can be said to be suffering from 'temporary paralysis' and thus be virtually unable to walk.[22]

The lower rate mobility component

Claimants who lacked 'directional mobility' – ie, people with disabilities such as blindness or learning difficulties – had problems with the previous mobility allowance. They had legs and could walk but for various reasons found it difficult to get about.

Some of these claimants will now meet the test of severe mental impairment and thus qualify for the higher rate mobility component. However, that test is restrictive and intended to benefit only those with severe behavioural problems. Not all people with learning difficulties qualify for the higher rate.

Many people with learning difficulties have problems finding their way on unfamiliar routes or lack road sense. Others may have behavioural difficulties but not receive the higher rate care component. They, and many blind and partially sighted people who cannot walk effectively out of doors with an aid (eg, a stick or guide dog), qualify for the lower rate mobility component. They can show that (ignoring any familiar routes) they are unable to walk outdoors 'without guidance or supervision from another person most of the time'.

People with dementia and similar conditions, who are not so severely disabled as to qualify for the higher rate mobility component, should also qualify under this test. People with agoraphobia, whose fear of going outside means that they need another person to be with them, and those who need to be accompanied because of the effect of unpredictable fits or blackouts, may also qualify.

'Guidance' would be most likely to cover people with visual disabilities, while 'supervision' would be more likely to cover those with mental disabilities.

'To benefit from enhanced facilities for locomotion'

This test applies to both rates of the component. Very few people fail it.

You should receive DLA if you are in hospital or in an institution such as a children's or old people's home, provided that you can still benefit from a trip out, even if, for instance, you have to be carried into a taxi for a ride. It is not essential that you be interested in or enjoy going out provided that it would be beneficial for you to do so. [23]

Even if, in practice, it would be very hard for the claimant to go out at all, because of behavioural problems or a very disabling physical condition, it should be argued that if there were a theoretical chance that they could do so were sufficient resources available to them, then they should not be excluded under this provision. The only people who should be excluded are those who are in comas or who cannot be moved because, for medical reasons, it would be dangerous for them.

Terminal illness

A terminally ill claimant is defined in the same way for the mobility component as for the care component (see p138). However, unlike the care component, a terminally ill person is not automatically deemed to satisfy the qualifying conditions for the mobility component. The only special treatment given is that where a claim is made specifically on the basis that the claimant is terminally ill, s/he does not have to satisfy either the three-month retrospective or the six-month prospective qualifying conditions. [24] It is hoped that such claims will usually be processed within 10 days.

The mobility component and invalid vehicles

The Benefits Agency used to provide invalid vehicles and help with car running costs for people with disabilities. If you still have a vehicle or assistance, the mobility component will not be paid. [25]

The only exception is if the Secretary of State certifies that: [26]

- you have purchased or obtained on hire, hire purchase or lease, a car of your own, or intend to do so; *and*
- you intend to keep the car for at least six months (or such other period as the Secretary of State determines) and to learn to drive within that time; *and*
- you are using the mobility component during that period to help obtain the car.

You may surrender a vehicle or end the assistance and receive the higher rate of the mobility component instead. You can transfer on to the mobility component when you are over the age of 65. You will continue to receive the component provided that you continue to satisfy the residence and presence conditions, and provided that your physical condition does not improve to the extent that you would no longer have qualified for the vehicle.[27]

Motability

Motability is a charity incorporated by Royal Charter. It runs a scheme to help you lease or buy a car if you receive the higher rate mobility component.

You pay your DLA mobility component direct to Motability. You may also have to make a down payment and if you drive more than 12,000 miles a year you may also have to make further annual payments. For further information write to Motability, Gate House, Westgate, Harlow, Essex CM20 1HR. Motability produces leaflets on its schemes for car leasing and hire purchase of new cars, used cars and electric wheelchairs.

3. DISABILITY LIVING ALLOWANCE CARE COMPONENT — Rates — Satisfy for 3 month s next six months

Conditions of entitlement[1]

- You must satisfy the residence conditions (see p242).
- You must not be resident in certain types of accommodation (see p144).
- You must also satisfy the 'disability' conditions (see p136):
- *either* you satisfy one or more of the attention or supervision conditions (see pp139 and 141); *or*
- you are over 16 and can pass the 'cooking test' (see p138); *and, in either case*:
  - you have done so for a continuous period of three months immediately before your claim;
  - you are likely to continue to satisfy those conditions for the next six months; *or*
- you are terminally ill (see p138).

Amount of payment[2]

The care component is paid at three weekly rates:

- the lower rate of £12.15 – for satisfying *either* the cooking test *or* the limited attention condition;
- the middle rate of £30.55 – for satisfying any one other disability condition;
- the higher rate of £45.70 – for satisfying *both* a day *and* a night disability condition *or* for being terminally ill.

Rules about age

There is no lower age limit for claiming the care component. However, as with other claimants, a baby has to meet the qualifying conditions for three months before the allowance becomes payable, unless they are terminally ill.

Children (ie, those under the age of 16) cannot qualify for the lower rate care component via the cooking test. A child can otherwise qualify provided s/he meets one of the following additional conditions:

- s/he has attention or supervision requirements 'substantially in excess of the normal requirements of a person of his age'; *or*
- s/he has substantial attention or supervision requirements 'which younger persons in normal physical and mental health may also have but which persons of his age and in normal physical and mental health would not have'.[3]

The upper age limit for claiming the care component is normally 65, although those who are aged 65 are able to claim if they can show that their disability had begun and they had met the residence and presence test on the day before their 65th birthday. You cannot claim it once you have reached the age of 66. If you are above this age limit you have to claim attendance allowance.

There is no upper age limit for receipt of the care component once you qualify.

The rules about qualifying periods for those in receipt of disability living allowance care component above the age of 65 are the same as those for attendance allowance. Thus, those who are above the age of 65 and whose condition worsens have to show that they have met the qualifying conditions for the higher rate care component for six months before it can be awarded, not three months. Those aged over 65 who receive the middle rate component, and whose condition improves, lose the allowance altogether. They cannot move down on to the lower rate component.[4]

The disability conditions

'So severely disabled physically or mentally'

The law provides that a person has to be 'so severely disabled physically or mentally' that they require attention or supervision from another person. This should rarely be a difficult area. However, in one case someone who engaged in violent and irresponsible behaviour was held not to be suffering from any severe physical or mental disability, even though he had a personality disorder.[5]

'Requires'

The law refers to the attention or supervision that you 'require' from another person. This does not mean only 'medically required' – it simply means 'reasonably required'.[6] In the past this area has been a source of disputes. For example, those adjudicating on the claim would suggest that claimants did not have an attention need as it was not medically necessary for someone to have their bedding frequently changed if they were incontinent, if they had adequate padding and their skin was not too vulnerable. However, this was unlawful. What mattered was that it was *reasonable* to change the bedding frequently.

This also arises in relation to a person's requirement for supervision. It has been suggested that a claimant should be 'sensible' and avoid doing anything which might cause a risk. They will then need no supervision. A problem group have been those who are at risk of falls as a result of their condition. A person can avoid most risks by staying in a chair all day but that may be totally unreasonable.[7] It may not be reasonable to expect the disabled person to avoid all situations in which they might fall.[8] However, it will still be necessary to show that the risk of falling is a risk of a substantial danger.

In considering the need for continual supervision, the adjudication officer should regard the fact that such supervision is in fact provided as strong evidence that it is 'required'. As one chief commissioner said: 'Mothers would be unlikely to exhaust themselves by providing it unnecessarily for years.'[9]

Night and day

An adult who needs help going to the toilet at 3am, a time when most people are asleep, clearly needs that help at night. Problems do sometimes arise when children need supervision or attention in the evening or where an adult requires assistance in the late evening or early morning.

'Night' has been rather unhelpfully defined as 'that period of inactivity, or that principal period of inactivity, through which each household goes in the dark hours' beginning when 'the household, as it were, closes down for the night'.[10] This may be somewhere between 11pm and 7am, but the pattern of activities of the particular household needs to be taken into account. The definition of 'night' for a child is the same as for an adult, so that attention given to a child in the evening before the adults have gone to bed will count only towards satisfaction of the day condition.[11]

Attention or supervision

The difference between, on the one hand, attention, and on the other, supervision or watching over, is often straightforward. 'Attention' involves some services of an 'active nature'[12] whereas supervision is passive and 'may be precautionary or anticipatory, yet never result in intervention'.[13]

However, where supervision does lead to intervention, the supervisor is providing 'attention', so you should not regard the two categories as completely separate. For example, if you need to be supervised because you are likely to fall and injure yourself, you receive attention every time your carer gives you a steadying hand or warns you of an obstacle you were about to trip over.[14] If that attention is 'frequent' you will qualify even if the supervision is not 'continual' throughout the day. And, sometimes, an act can be both supervision and attention.

It is therefore probably wise for advisers and claimants to emphasise the extent of the disabled person's disabilities and needs without trying to fit them neatly into either attention or supervision categories.

Renal dialysis

Special regulations apply if you are undergoing renal dialysis on a kidney machine.[15] To qualify, you need to have such treatment regularly for two or more sessions a week. You also need to show that either the dialysis is of a type which requires the attendance or supervision of another person or that you in fact require attention or supervision from another person while you are dialysing. You will receive the middle rate care component. These rules also apply to those who dialyse in hospital and have no help from any member of the staff. Others who dialyse in hospital will not qualify by this special route. There is nothing to prevent those who undergo renal dialysis in a manner that does not qualify them under this route from qualifying for the care component of DLA under the ordinary conditions.

Terminal illness

A terminally ill claimant is treated as satisfying the conditions for the higher rate care component and as having done so for the preceding three months.[16] So, all terminally ill claimants are entitled to DLA except those abroad or in hospital or similar accommodation (see p144). The Benefits Agency is usually able to deal with claims within 10 days. They are referred to as claims under the 'special rules'.

A person is regarded as 'terminally ill' if s/he is suffering from a progressive disease and can reasonably be expected to die within six months as a result of that disease.[17] Note that this does not mean that it must be more likely than not that the person will die within this period. It simply means that death within six months would not be unexpected.

The special rules apply only if the claim is made on that basis, or if an application for review or an appeal on an existing claim is made on that basis. Any notification to the Benefits Agency that a person is terminally ill should be treated as an application for a review or a claim, provided that the notification refers to DLA or attendance allowance. Someone else is allowed to make a claim or seek a review on behalf of a terminally ill person without her/his knowledge or authority.[18]

The 'cooking test'

This test provides access to the *lower* level of the allowance for those who can show that they are so severely disabled physically or mentally that they cannot prepare a cooked main meal for themselves if they have the ingredients. This test does not apply to those under the age of 16.[19]

Satisfying the 'cooking test'

In parliamentary debate, a government spokesman said that this was 'an abstract test' – ie, you do not need physically to demonstrate that you are unable to cook.[20] It seems that the meal for the test is a traditional one, cooked in a conventional oven. You need to show that your disability makes you unable to perform the tasks that are needed to cook such a main meal. The claim form asks about your ability to peel and chop vegetables, use taps, cooking utensils, a cooker, cope with hot pans, and plan a meal.

Thus, you need to be able to manage both the physical tasks (eg, lifting, carrying, bending, and making fine movements), and the mental tasks (eg, concentrating and planning) examined in the test.

It may be argued that those with epilepsy and other similar conditions satisfy this test. Although they might physically and mentally be able to cook, in practice they would not because it would be potentially too dangerous an activity for them. Those with visual impairments, perhaps unable to read labels and instructions, or use a cooker safely, may also in practice avoid cooking. Some forms of mental illness, such as severe depression, may also lead people not to cook. Only those who could reasonably be expected to prepare a cooked main meal should be regarded as being able to do so.

In addition, the degree of stamina required to cook a main meal must be taken into account. It may be that there are disabled people able to undertake any one of the tasks involved in the test but overall they would be unable to prepare the meal because of fatigue.

Rules about attention

You need to show that you are so severely disabled physically or mentally that you require, in connection with your bodily functions, from another person:[21]

— Most satisfy one of them.

- attention for a significant portion of the day, whether during a single period or a number of periods; this is the new lower rate 'limited attention' condition; *or* *—12.15.*
- frequent attention throughout the day; this is the day attention condition; *or*
- prolonged or repeated attention during the night in connection with your bodily functions; this is the night attention condition.

Attention in connection with bodily functions

The attention you require must be in connection with bodily functions. These include:

breathing, hearing, seeing, eating, drinking, walking, sitting, sleeping, getting in or out of bed, dressing, undressing, eliminating waste products and the like, all of which an ordinary person who is not suffering from any disability does for himself. But they do not include cooking, shopping, or any of the other things which . . . generally . . . one of the household does for the rest of the family.[22]

This list has now been extended by more recent decisions of the social security commissioners.

Although cooking is not directly a form of 'attention in connection with your bodily functions', the special selection and very precise weighing and measuring of a very specialised diet may qualify as such because it is part of your overall treatment.[23] This approach has been extended to include those whose disabilities mean that they have extra laundry needs.[24]

If you are profoundly deaf and cannot speak properly you may qualify if you can show that you need attention from another person to enable you to communicate.[25]

The 'limited attention' condition

This test provides a route to the lower rate of the care component. You need to show that you need attention for a 'significant portion of the day'. This can be either during a single period or a number of periods.

People qualify for this lower rate care component who do not meet the attention conditions for the middle or higher rates of the component – eg, those who need help with 'getting up' activities such as dressing and washing at the beginning of the day, and with 'going to bed' activities such as undressing and washing at the end of the day, but are otherwise able to care for themselves without help.

It remains unclear how long a 'significant portion of the day' is. A government spokesman said this was 'an hour or thereabouts' in the debate on this provision.[26]

Frequent attention throughout the day

To satisfy the day attention condition you need to show that attention is required frequently throughout the day. There is likely to be a thin line between some of those who meet the 'limited attention condition' and some of those who satisfy the 'frequency condition'. A 'frequent' need might include help with toiletting (whether that be to reach the toilet, use a commode, or deal with zips and buttons), or needing help to walk within your own home. For this test, it is the pattern of the needs across the day which is crucial. These are both examples of activities which most people would reasonably engage in with some frequency during the course of a normal day. However, most people who satisfy this test will have a range of care needs. These should be added together and looked at to see whether the person needs frequent help throughout the day.

Prolonged or repeated attention during the night

This night attention condition is more clearly defined than the day attention condition. This is because the help that needs to be given in the night has to be either 'prolonged' or 'repeated' – both of which are more easily measured than the 'frequency' condition which must be met during the day (see above). The Benefits Agency usually regards 20 minutes of attention as 'prolonged'. 'Repeated' simply means twice or more. It is not necessary for the attention to be required every night or even on most nights, provided that it is a fairly regular feature. In fact, fewer people satisfy the night condition simply because most people sleep through the night and so do not require attention.

It should be noted that sleeping is a 'bodily function' (see p139). This means that soothing a child back to sleep counts as giving attention in connection with a bodily function.[27]

Rules about supervision and 'watching over'

You need to show that you are so severely disabled physically or mentally that you require:

- by day, continual supervision from another person in order to avoid substantial danger to yourself or others; *or*
- by night, another person to be awake for a prolonged period or at frequent intervals to watch over you in order to avoid substantial danger to yourself or others.

Continual supervision in order to avoid substantial danger

This provision applies to the amount of supervision required in the daytime. It has been held to consist of four parts.[28]

- There must be a **substantial danger to yourself or someone else as a result of your medical condition**. What constitutes a 'substantial danger' must be decided on the facts of each case.
- **The substantial danger must be one against which it is reasonable to guard**. This involves weighing the remoteness of the risk and the seriousness of the consequences should it arise. While the risk of a house catching fire may be remote (but not fanciful), the consequences of leaving a disabled person who is unable to move alone in a house which did catch fire would be catastrophic. Thus, it can be argued that such a person reasonably requires continual supervision.[29] In another case it was said:

  > If a small child, escaping the supervision of its mother, runs out of the house on to a public highway, that may well be an isolated incident. But it only requires one such incident for the child to be killed by passing traffic. In my view, the fact that the incidents in question were isolated is nothing to the point.[30]

  In assessing the likelihood of danger, the adjudication officer must look not only at what has happened in the past but at what may happen in the future.[31]

- **There must be a need for the supervision**. As with the attention conditions, there have in the past been many arguments as to whether supervision need be 'medically required' or only 'reasonably required' (see p136). People may still qualify who, although they do not receive much by way of supervision (perhaps because they live alone), clearly require it.

- **The supervision must be continual.** This is something less than 'continuous', but supervision which is required only occasionally or spasmodically is insufficient. The 'characteristic nature of supervision is overseeing or watching over considered with reference to its frequency or regularity of occurrence'.[32] Supervision can be precautionary and anticipatory. It does not necessarily involve direct intervention. Some claimants liable to epileptic fits without warning may need continual supervision, although attention for the period between the fits is not required.[33] Even if you have warning of the fits so that you can prevent yourself from falling, you may require continual supervision if you suffer from prolonged periods of confusion afterwards.[34] A parent with a young child may need supervision so that there is someone to look after the child when the parent has a fit.

People with mental health problems have long had particular difficulties in qualifying for the allowance because of their supervision needs. It is not acceptable for those adjudicating on the claim to assume, without fully investigating the case, that someone really at risk of harming themselves would be a hospital in-patient, particularly in the light of policies which encourage disabled people to live in the community.[35] Further, in the case of someone at risk of committing suicide, it is not only wrong to assume that if this really were the case they would be an in-patient, it would also be wrong to suggest that no amount of supervision would prevent a determined suicide attempt and supervision is therefore not required. The correct approach would be to decide whether supervision would result in 'a real reduction in the risk of harm to the claimant'.[36]

Watching over in order to avoid substantial danger

This provision applies to the amount of watching over that is required at night time. The person watching over you has to be awake for a prolonged period or at frequent intervals. A 'prolonged period' may well mean 20 minutes or more, similar to the night attention condition. 'Frequent intervals' probably means more than twice.

2 Rates + Amounts same as DLA Care -

4. ATTENDANCE ALLOWANCE - 65.

2 Rates Higher = Some DLA.

Attendance allowance is for people over the age of 65. The rules follow those for the higher and middle rates of the DLA care component. The

2-Rate - Higher- Rate Same as DLA   Same qualifying
lower - Rate middle as DLA conditions

over 65

:edure and the structure of adjudication are described in
low.

ns of entitlement [1]

fy the residence conditions (see p242).
- You are not resident in certain types of accommodation (see p144).
- You satisfy the disability conditions:
  - you meet one or more of the day or night conditions (see pp139
    and 141); *and*
  - you have done so for a continuous period of six months
    immediately before your award begins; *or*
  - you are terminally ill (see below).

Amount of payment [2]

Attendance allowance is paid at two weekly rates:

- the lower rate of £30.55 – for satisfying either a day or night
  condition;
- the higher rate of £45.70 – for satisfying both a day condition, and a
  night condition, or for being terminally ill.

The attention and supervision conditions

These are the same as for the middle or higher rates of the DLA care component. The guidance given above (see pp136-142) applies, but there is
no equivalent of the lowest rate care component.

The qualifying period

If you claim attendance allowance you have to show that you have met
the conditions about needing attention and/or supervision for six
months before the benefit can be awarded to you.

Renal dialysis

The same rules apply as for the DLA (see p137). [3]

Terminal illness

A terminally ill claimant is deemed to satisfy the conditions for the higher
rate of attendance allowance and to have done so for the preceding six
months. [4]

5. MATTERS COMMON TO DISABILITY LIVING ALLOWANCE AND ATTENDANCE ALLOWANCE

Tax and other benefits ~DLA / AA

- Attendance allowance is not taxable nor is any part of DLA.[1]
- These benefits may be paid in addition to any other benefits described in this *Guide* *except that*:
  - attendance allowance and the care component of DLA overlap with constant attendance allowance under the industrial injuries or war pensions schemes (see pp177 and 332); *and*
  - the mobility component of DLA overlaps with the war pensioners' mobility supplement payable under the war pensions scheme.
- If you are receiving the higher or middle rates of the care component, or attendance allowance, and someone regularly looks after you, that person may be entitled to invalid care allowance (see p158).
- Receipt of attendance allowance or any rate of DLA will entitle you to a Christmas bonus (see p262).
- Neither attendance allowance nor any part of DLA is taken into account as income for the purposes of income support (IS), family credit (FC), housing benefit (HB) or council tax benefit (CTB) (unless you receive the care component or attendance allowance and are in residential care or a nursing home).
- If you or a partner or a child in your family is entitled to attendance allowance or DLA, IS, HB and CTB will be paid at a higher rate than usual, via the premiums for disabled adults, disabled children and disabled pensioners. There is a special premium, the severe disability premium, for people who receive attendance allowance or the higher or middle rates of the care component who are treated as living alone, or who live with someone else who is also receiving attendance allowance or that level of that component. For further information see CPAG's *National Welfare Benefits Handbook*, the companion work to this *Guide*, which deals comprehensively with means-tested benefits.

Special rules for certain types of accommodation[2]

It has always been the policy intention that DLA care component and attendance allowance should not be paid to people when they are living somewhere where their care needs are being met out of central government or local government funds. This is to avoid double provision. There are thus a series of restrictions on rights to receive these benefits in hospitals, local authority run homes, and since April 1993, in residential care and nursing homes.

The mobility component of DLA is unaffected by stays in either hospital or in other forms of accommodation paid for out of public funds.

Hospitals

Attendance allowance or the care component can no longer be paid once someone has been maintained free of charge and is receiving in-patient treatment in hospital for more than 28 days for adults and 84 days for children. Two or more distinct periods, separated by 28 days or less, will be added together towards the 28- or 84-day limit as appropriate.[3] Only a complete period of 24 hours, midnight to midnight, counts as a day in hospital. Thus someone who is out of hospital during the day (eg, working or attending college) may be able to claim benefit for that day.[4] Similarly, where someone lives in a house in hospital grounds (typically as part of a process of moving back into the community after a long stay in hospital) they may also be able to get benefit. The powers under which their accommodation is provided will need to be looked at closely.[5]

Someone cannot be paid attendance allowance or the care component of DLA if they first claim when they are living in hospital. However, it may be worth claiming nevertheless, because the person will receive the initial 28-day concession payment if they spend even one day outside. Those who are moving into the community from hospital often start by spending limited periods outside in accommodation where the allowance is payable.

Hospices

The definition of a hospice since April 1993 has been a hospital (but not a health service hospital) or other institution 'whose primary function is to provide palliative care for persons resident there who are suffering from a progressive disease in its final stages'.[6] Where someone is terminally ill and residing in such accommodation, attendance allowance and the care component of DLA can be paid.

Other accommodation provided out of public or local funds

Where a restriction is imposed on a person's right to receive the care component of DLA or attendance allowance in these sorts of accommodation, benefit will not be payable once 28 days has been spent there. Unlike hospitals, the period is the same for both adults and children. Two or more distinct periods, separated by 28 days or less, will be added together towards the 28-day limit.[7] Only a complete period of 24 hours, midnight to midnight, counts as a day in such accommodation.

From 1 April 1993 some of the rules in this area were changed following the introduction of community care policies. They mainly affected those living in residential care and nursing homes. Many people in these homes also need to claim IS. For a detailed description of the rules in relation to that benefit see CPAG's *National Welfare Benefits Handbook*.

Whether a person can continue to receive DLA care or attendance allowance in residential care, or even in some forms of private dwelling, often depends on whether they were resident on 31 March 1993, or whether the local authority is or could be funding their accommodation.

The allowances cannot be paid where the accommodation is provided under Part III of the National Assistance Act 1948 (often referred to as 'Part III accommodation') or, in Scotland, Part IV of the Social Work (Scotland) Act 1968 or section 7 of the Mental Health (Scotland) Act 1984.

Also excluded is any accommodation where the cost is or may be borne wholly or partly out of public or local funds under the above Acts or under any other enactments relating to 'persons under disability or to young persons or to education or training'.[8]

These broad provisions are intended to prevent payment of the allowances not only to those in local authority run accommodation, but also to those who have been accommodated by local authorities under their community care responsibilities.

However, there are a range of situations in which people will usually be entitled to receive attendance allowance or DLA care component without restriction:

- those who live in private dwellings. Sometimes there are practical problems for those who live in group homes with intensive social work support. It can be argued, though, that the local authority is not funding the accommodation. The authority is merely providing domiciliary services to a private dwelling.[9]
- those who were living in, or were only temporarily absent from, a care home with less than four residents where board and personal care was being provided on 31 March 1993 and which had to apply to be registered by 1 April 1993 as a residential care home, and who were entitled to these benefits on that date.[10]
- those who were living in, or were only temporarily absent from, a registered care or nursing home as at 31 March 1993. For IS purposes these people are referred to as having a 'preserved right' to IS.[11] Their entitlement is not affected if they claim these benefits after that date. However, if they do receive IS to help pay their fees then these benefits will be taken into account as income.
- those who are living in residential care or nursing homes and are wholly funding the cost of the accommodation themselves, ie, not

receiving IS, HB, or any form of funding from their local authority (but see below).[12]

Usually, in any of the above cases, if the local authority is *actually* funding, in whole or in part, the cost of the accommodation, then people will not be able to receive these benefits. But there are some exceptions which relate mainly to young people. Even where the local authority *is* funding the accommodation DLA care component can still be received without restriction by:

- students receiving grants or loans or attending colleges which receive funds from funding councils;[13]
- children under the age of 16 who are being looked after by a local authority and have been placed by that local authority into a private dwelling (ie, fostered);[14]
- young people in private dwellings, who are under 18 and to whom section 17(10)(b) or 17(10)(c) of the Children Act 1989 applies (ie, they need services because of impairment to their health and development or because they are disabled);[15]
- anyone under 18 being educated abroad who is having the costs met by their local authority (eg, at the Peto Institute in Hungary).[16]

There are also situations in which people will not usually be entitled to receive attendance allowance or DLA care component. These include:

- those who live in local authority owned residential accommodation (often referred to as 'Part III' accommodation). The restriction applies even if they are paying the full cost of their accommodation;[17]
- those who were in residential care or nursing homes prior to 31 March 1993 who have been, or are now being, helped with the costs of the accommodation by their local authority;
- those who moved into residential care or nursing homes after 31 March 1993 for whom their local authority has taken responsibility for paying the costs of the accommodation.[18] However, if the person subsequently refunds the costs to the local authority, eg, from the sale of their former home, *and* has not had help from IS with their fees, then it is arguable that their attendance allowance or DLA care component should not just be restored to them forthwith but should also be refunded to them for the whole of the period for which it was withdrawn. If you are in this situation you should seek advice;
- people who live in accommodation where the cost is being borne or may be borne under any enactment relating to 'persons under disability or to young persons or to education or training'.[19]

Where the person is living in accommodation where the cost *is not* but *could be* borne out of public or local funds, these restrictions will also usually apply. However, they do not apply if the claimant is:

- living in accommodation as a privately fostered child; *or*
- living in accommodation provided for homeless people by local authorities under section 65 of the Housing Act 1985.[20]

The 'may be borne' provision also cannot usually be applied to anyone who lives in a private dwelling. However, it is supposed to apply where the private dwelling that the disabled person lives in is a residential care home. It should also bite where the person was moved from somewhere where the costs were borne wholly or partly out of local funds, 'at the instigation of the body which bore the cost', into a residential care home.[21]

The reason why there is a confusion in this area is that the local authority only has a power to provide this sort of accommodation under s21 of the National Assistance Act. This is a power of last resort and the local authority cannot therefore necessarily be held responsible for accommodating people under that power. This is most relevant to those who go into residential or nursing care without any assessment of their needs by the local authority, or who have been assessed but not been found to require such accommodation. The allowances will therefore remain payable as the cost may *not* be borne by the local authority.[22] However, as most homes charge more than the potential combined benefit income from IS and attendance allowance or DLA care component, there is likely to be a shortfall which will require the financial intervention of the local authority. Nevertheless, this 'self-funding' option may be financially attractive to those who have their former home for sale and who are able to have any shortfall met, perhaps by relatives. If they were financially assisted by the local authority, then that assistance would be recouped by a charge on their property, while help in the form of IS and attendance allowance or DLA care will not be recovered once the property is sold.

Respite care

Note that two periods separated by less than 28 days are linked and count as one period. This may particularly affect you if you need 'respite care'. If you go into hospital or residential care more than once every four weeks the odd short periods when you are in such accommodation will be added together and, after 28 such days, your attendance allowance or DLA care component is no longer paid while you are in such accommodation. This can be avoided if it is possible for you to remain at home for over four weeks at a time every now and then, because the link is then broken. If you are unable to break the link, it may be useful to have your allowance paid by direct credit transfer rather than by order book because the necessary adjustments can be made with less inconvenience both to the Benefits Agency and yourself.

You are paid the allowance at a daily rate of one-seventh of the weekly rate for odd days of entitlement between periods in hospital or other accommodation disqualifying you from the allowance.

Claims and decisions

All initial decisions on claims are made by an adjudication officer.[23] There is a DLA Advisory Board which gives guidance to adjudication officers and the Secretary of State but this body does not actually decide any cases.

A claim for attendance allowance or DLA should be made on the relevant DSS claim form, either a DS2 or a DLA1. These forms have undergone a number of revisions and may well change again in the future. They are not generally available to the public. However, you can get one by ringing or visiting your local DSS office. Alternatively, you can ring the DSS Freephone benefit enquiry line for people with disabilities on 0800 882200 or send in the tear-off slip requesting a claim form from the leaflet DS702 for attendance allowance or DS704 for DLA. You will then be sent a claim form. (It may be wise to keep a record of the date you asked for it.) The claim form will be date-stamped, and provided that you return it within six weeks, your claim will be treated as being made on the date you requested the form.[24]

The forms are also available through citizens' advice bureaux and other advice agencies. These will not be date-stamped. The date of claim will be the date the claim form is received by the DSS, in the normal way.

Completing the claim form

The DLA claim pack is large and runs to 40 pages. The attendance allowance claim pack has over 20 pages. Both packs come in two parts. The first asks for various factual details about the person claiming the allowance, the second about the sort of help they need with personal care and/or getting around. If you find it difficult to complete the form, you can get help with this. The Benefits Agency can arrange to ring you to help you complete the form or in some circumstances send a visiting officer to do so. Most advice agencies will also willingly help you complete the form. It is the first part of the pack which is technically the benefit claim. If you are going to take a while to complete the second part, do not delay sending the first part back.

The process is similar for both benefits. In the second part of the form you are asked to assess your abilities across a range of tasks and activities and to describe the nature of your condition. You are also asked to give the names of two people who can confirm what you have said. One of these is a person who knows you well in a professional capacity, the other someone who knows you personally. These might be, therefore, your doctor and your carer. Your doctor will not charge you for completing that page of the form. If you are unable to get other people to complete the form you should send it in anyway, as the Benefits Agency will arrange for this to be done.

The DLA claim form covers both mobility and care needs, but you do not need to complete both sections. It is quite possible, for example, to complete the questions that relate only to mobility needs because you only want to claim for the mobility component. When you complete the second part of the form you should look carefully at the descriptions of the qualifying conditions for the various rates of the allowances given earlier in this chapter.

If you are claiming for the higher rate mobility component of DLA, be cautious when completing the part of the form which asks you to say how far you can walk without experiencing 'severe discomfort'. It is often difficult to judge distances accurately. Get a relative or friend to check that any estimate you make is right. Make sure that if walking becomes painful after you have gone a short distance, or you have to stop after a short distance, it is that short distance that you put down, not the total distance that you can achieve. Remember that this is supposed to be a test of your ability to walk out of doors. If you have a walking problem which is worse when you are out of doors you should make this clear.

The attendance allowance and DLA claim forms ask many detailed questions about your need for personal care, including dressing, undressing, getting in and out of bed, eating, drinking, toiletting, etc. However, no form can be comprehensive. There is plenty of opportunity given for you to add your own comments, over and above replying to the set questions. Do give details of any needs you have which are not asked about on the form.

It is hard for someone who may qualify under the 'supervision' criteria to complete the form accurately, especially if they have a mental health problem. There are questions about being kept safe and about fits, blackouts and falls but the emphasis is on the frequency with which help is required. Remember that someone can qualify under the supervision criteria if they need continual supervision to prevent even occasional dangers if they are serious enough.

It is particularly difficult to complete the DLA care component part of the form for a child. Remember that the test of their care needs involves a comparison with the amount of help that a non-disabled child of the same age would need. Again, the best approach may be to try to give as much detail as possible of the child's needs, over and above completing all of the questions on the form.

For both care and mobility elements the form asks regularly about how many times a week you need help or have a walking problem. It is your *overall pattern of needs* or problems that will be looked at. Something is most likely to be taken into account if it happens more often than not, that is, on four days a week or more, or on most of the occasions when you try to walk outside.

Claiming for terminally ill people

If a claim is being made on the basis that a person is terminally ill, it may be made without the ill person's knowledge or authority. This applies equally to claims for attendance allowance, the care component of DLA, or the mobility component of DLA (although in this latter case, as explained above, terminal illness will only exempt the claimant from the rules about 'qualifying periods').[25]

These claims are known as claims under the 'special rules'. People claiming under these rules need to provide a form DS1500, completed by their GP or consultant, detailing their medical condition. They do not need to fill in the parts of the claim form relating to their need for personal care. If they wish to claim for the mobility component, then they do need to fill in that part of the form.

It is possible for someone acting on behalf of a terminally ill person to request a review of an unfavourable decision and even to appeal to a disability appeal tribunal, without the ill person's knowledge or authority. Such claims will normally be dealt with within 10 days.

Renewal claims

If you have been awarded DLA or attendance allowance for a limited period you will be invited to make a renewal claim before the current award runs out. Even if you fail to do so promptly you may still not lose out as benefit can be backdated to the end of the previous award, provided that you submit a renewal claim within six months and throughout have met all of the qualifying conditions.

The position is different where your award has ended for a reason other than a failure to make a renewal claim, perhaps because your condition has improved. If you reclaim within two years you can be paid from the date of claim, without again having to serve the standard three- or six-month qualifying period, provided that you meet all of the other qualifying conditions.[26]

Transitional rules about claims

People who prior to April 1992 had mobility allowance or attendance allowance under the old system were transferred over into their equivalents in the new benefits structure. The details of these provisions were given in the 15th edition of this *Guide*.

It was possible, between April 1992 and April 1993, for people to make 'top-up' claims where they had either attendance or mobility allowance prior to April 1992, but not both, and wanted to try for the other element which they did not have. Such people were thus safeguarded against the unexpected loss of their existing component, as that would not normally have been considered afresh. Some claims of this type may still be outstanding. Note that they can be backdated to 6 April 1992 if they were received before 5 April 1993.[27]

The administration of claims

Claims are initially dealt with by regional disability benefit centres. A claim is first checked to see that it does not fail on grounds other than the claimant's disability, eg, that the claimant is abroad or the wrong age. If your claim fails on these grounds you have the right to challenge the decision by means of a review, although if you wish to take the matter any further you will need to appeal to a social security appeal tribunal.

Your claim is then checked by the adjudication officer to see what information is needed to come to a decision on your case and if anybody needs to be contacted about it. S/he may choose to contact someone you have named on the form for more information, perhaps your doctor. S/he may also arrange for you to be given a medical examination by a doctor acting on behalf of the DSS.[28]

The Secretary of State has the power to refer claimants to doctors for examinations either in order to monitor the operation of DLA, or to provide the adjudication officer with further information in connection with the claim.[29] He may also direct that certain classes of case are always referred to doctors. The doctors themselves may refer such special cases to the DLA Advisory Board for advice.

If you refuse to attend a medical examination at the request of the adjudication officer or the Secretary of State 'without good cause to do so' then the adjudication officer will have to decide your claim against you.[30]

Period of payment

Either allowance can be awarded for limited periods or for life.[31] In practice, a limited period award is likely where the claimant is a child or has a medical condition which is receiving active treatment, but limited period awards are in any event common on first claims. If you think benefit should be awarded for longer, perhaps because your condition is such that your care or mobility needs will not decrease, or because you needed a longer period award of the mobility component to take advantage of the Motability scheme, you should consider asking for a review (see p154). If the award is for a limited period you will be invited to make a renewal claim shortly before the award runs out.

Between April 1992 and April 1993 people who qualified for both the care and mobility components of DLA, either by claiming them for the first time after April 1992, or because they had their previous equivalents, still technically had separate awards of the two components.[32] These could therefore be for different periods. From 27 December 1993 such people had their two separate awards terminated. They were given a new combined award of both components. If one award was for life and the other for a limited period, then the new combined award runs until the award which is for a fixed period expires. Thereafter the beneficiary will have only a life award of the other component (although the component which has stopped may well become payable for a further fixed period, or for life, when a renewal claim is made). If both awards were for a fixed period, then the end date of the new combined award will always be the earlier of the end dates of the two previous awards.[33] Those who have claimed and been awarded both components since 27 December 1993 can have a life award of one component and a limited period award of the other. If they are given both components for limited periods, then both of those awards must end on the same day.

Payment to children

The care and mobility components of DLA for a child (ie, someone under the age of 16) are usually paid to an adult with whom the child is living, whom the Secretary of State appoints to act on their behalf. This will normally be the child's mother or father. If the child is not living with either parent, then whomever the child is living with may be appointed to act for them.

The allowance can continue to be paid even when the child and appointee are not living together, including during a temporary separation of up to 12 weeks, or when the child is absent at a boarding school, or when the child is in hospital. The allowance will cease to be paid immediately when the child is being looked after by a local authority or any similar arrangement, unless the arrangement is not intended to last for more than 12 weeks.[34]

Reviews

If you are dissatisfied with the decision on your claim, you can ask for a review. If you ask for the review within three months of the decision this can be 'on any ground', so it is enough that you simply think the decision is wrong.[35] Your should write to the DLA unit or attendance allowance unit within three months of the decision being sent to you. This three-month limit can be extended if your request for a review was delayed in the post by industrial action.[36]

A review is carried out by a different adjudication officer from the one who took the original decision. The second adjudication officer is based at the relevant central unit, not the regional disability benefit centre where your claim was initially decided. The adjudication officer conducting the review decides what further evidence is needed in order to come to a decision, and how to collect this. Medical evidence from a GP or consultant may well be helpful at this stage. However, evidence from a carer or a diary of your walking and/or care needs over a period may be equally useful.

If you are refused at this review stage and you wish to take your case further, this will normally be by way of an appeal to a disability appeal tribunal (although see below as a further review can occasionally be more appropriate).

It is also possible for an adjudication officer's decision to be reviewed outside these time limits if the adjudication officer conducting the review accepts that:

- the earlier decision was made in ignorance of, or was based on a mistake about, some material fact; *or*
- there has been any relevant change of circumstances since that decision was made; *or*
- it is anticipated that there will be a relevant change of circumstances; *or*
- there was an error of law in the decision; *or*
- the decision was to make an award wholly or partly after the claim was made but on the basis that some condition would be fulfilled in the future and that condition has not been fulfilled; *or*
- the decision was that someone was terminally ill and there has been a change of medical opinion in relation to that.[37]

There are a number of situations where this form of review (an 'at any time' review) may be used.

First, adjudication officers may use it. Some of the grounds listed above are clearly most appropriate to them.

Secondly, this is the form of review sought by those claimants whose condition has worsened, who are asking to be awarded a higher rate than they had before. If a claimant is dissatisfied with a decision on such a review application, typically because the adjudication officer takes the view that their condition has not worsened sufficiently to qualify them for the rate they were requesting, then they may seek a further review (a review 'on any ground') of that decision. If still dissatisfied, the claimant can then appeal against the decision on review to the disability appeal tribunal in the standard manner.

Thirdly, it may sometimes be the best route to follow for someone who has been refused on an initial claim.

Example

You suffer from a number of disabling conditions. You have claimed the care component. Because you were embarrassed about it you did not specifically refer to your problems with incontinence and the help you need with managing this. When you asked for the initial review you were so annoyed at being turned down that you did not send in any detailed explanation of your care needs. You have now been sent a further refusal, and seen all the papers considered by the adjudication officer. You realise that your incontinence problems and the help you need have been overlooked. Although you could appeal to the tribunal at this stage, it may be quicker and easier to seek a further review on the basis that the adjudication officer made his decision 'in ignorance of a material fact' (ie, that you also need help in connection with your incontinence). A letter from your GP or consultant explaining your problem would be very helpful. You may be able to receive the allowance by this route without the stress of having to attend a tribunal

---

If you do go down this route there are some further complications.

The first is that if the adjudication officer reviews the decision but does not alter it in your favour, you cannot then appeal immediately to a tribunal. You will be given the opportunity to seek a further review 'on any ground' (within three months). You can only appeal to the disability appeal tribunal against a negative decision on an 'on any ground' review.[38]

The second complication is where the adjudication officer does not review the original 'on any ground' review decision. This might be because s/he does not agree that the decision was made in ignorance or mistake of material facts. S/he thinks these were all taken into account and you were properly refused. How do you take your case further? You should request a further 'on any ground' review of the decision not to review your case (within three months). If that is unfavourable, you can then appeal to the tribunal against that decision. However, this will mean that your case goes before the tribunal much later than it would have done if you had simply appealed to the tribunal at the first opportunity.

In any event, you should always think carefully before requesting a review. A review is a fresh hearing of your case. That means that your case is looked at completely anew. So there is a risk that, if you have been awarded a component of DLA or attendance allowance at a particular rate, and you seek a review because you think you should have got more than you were awarded, you may lose what you had. This happens only rarely.

There is a further, small risk in seeking a review, which arises from the combination of attendance and mobility allowance into DLA in April 1992. Some people seeking a review may be doing so because they have not been awarded one component of DLA when they are already in receipt of the other. Or they may be seeking a review of the rate they have been awarded of one component when they are quite satisfied with the rate they receive of the other. In these circumstances the adjudication officer need not consider the component which is not the subject of the review, although s/he may.[39]

Further, if a person has been awarded a component of DLA for life, then the adjudication officer should not consider the rate of that component, or the length of time for which it has been awarded, unless the review has been asked for on that basis, or 'information is available to the adjudication officer which gives him reasonable grounds for believing that entitlement to the component, or entitlement to it at the rate awarded or for that period, ought not to continue'.[40]

It may be possible to secure backdated benefit from a review. You will need to show that you have 'good cause' for your late request for review.[41] The test of what constitutes good cause should be the same as that described in 'good cause for a late claim' (see p281). Note that if a person has an appointee acting for them, which is often the case with these benefits, then it is the appointee, not the disabled person, who has to show good cause. Arrears can only be paid for more than 52 weeks in this sort of case in a limited range of circumstances.[42]

Example

An elderly woman is in receipt of attendance allowance at the lower rate. She then has a devastating stroke and is in hospital for some months. When she leaves she lives with her daughter who cares for her. Some time later the daughter seeks advice about her mother's benefits. She is advised that her mother should have asked for a review requesting the higher rate of the allowance (a review 'on any ground'). The mother has no appointee acting for her and has been far too ill to seek a review herself during this period. Good cause may be shown for the late request for review and arrears of the higher rate backdated. Because of the rules about qualifying periods, arrears could only be payable from six months after the date on which the mother's condition deteriorated.

Appeals

You may appeal against the decision of the adjudication officer on your review. This is to a disability appeal tribunal, if your dispute relates to a 'disability question', otherwise it will be to a social security appeal tribunal (see p303). If you are still dissatisfied, you may then appeal to a social security commissioner against any decision of a disability appeal tribunal, but only on a point of law (see p313).

Reviews and appeals concerning DLA and attendance allowance

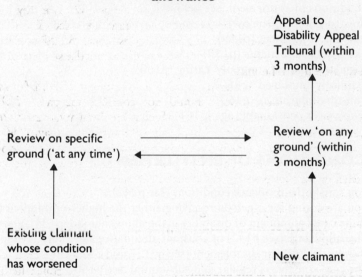

Appeal to
Disability Appeal
Tribunal (within
3 months)

Review on specific
ground ('at any time')

Review 'on any
ground' (within
3 months)

Existing claimant
whose condition
has worsened

New claimant

CHAPTER EIGHT

Invalid care allowance

This chapter covers:

1. Conditions of entitlement (see below)
2. How to claim (see below)
3. Amount of payment (p159)
4. Tax and other benefits (p159)
5. 'Regularly and substantially' caring (p160)
6. 'Gainfully employed' (p160)
7. 'Full-time education' (p160)
8. People over pensionable age (p161)

[handwritten: Premium get it entitled but not get because of overlapping / only get dep addition or ICA.]

1. CONDITIONS OF ENTITLEMENT [1]

- You satisfy the residence conditions (see p242).
- You are caring for a person receiving either the higher or middle rates of the care component of disability living allowance (see p134), attendance allowance (see p142) or constant attendance allowance in respect of industrial or war disablement (see pp177 and 332).
- The care you give is regular and substantial (see p160). *[handwritten: 35hr per wk.]*
- You are not gainfully employed or in full-time education (see p160).
- You are not under 16 or over 65 (but see p161 for exceptions).
- You claim within the time limit (see below).

2. HOW TO CLAIM

You should claim the allowance from your local Benefits Agency office within 12 months of becoming entitled. If you claim later, only 12 months' arrears will be paid.[2]

A claim for income support or unemployment benefit *may* be treated as a claim for invalid care allowance (ICA).[3] This is a decision for the Secretary of State, so there is no right of appeal (see p286) and he does not have to treat the claim as one for ICA.[4] You will win if it is felt that a reasonably alert official, asking the proper questions, would have recognised

e entitled to ICA. If you fail, contact your MP and/or con-
ining to the Ombudsman (see p301).

NT OF PAYMENT [5]

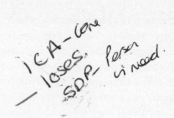

	£pw
Claimant	34.50
Adult dependant	20.65
Child dependant	11.00

While receiving ICA, you are credited with Class 1 contributions (see p227). You are entitled to a Christmas bonus (see p262).

4. TAX AND OTHER BENEFITS

ICA is taxable except for any increase in respect of dependent children.[6]
There can be both advantages and disadvantages to claiming ICA because of its effect on other benefits. There are a number of factors that you need to take into account.
If you are a married woman, your husband cannot claim an increase of his benefit in respect of you.[7] This may be important if he receives invalidity pension because an increase in invalidity pension in respect of a wife is not taxable. On the other hand, ICA now has a more generous earnings rule.
If you receive ICA you are not required to be available for work as a condition of entitlement to income support (IS).[8] If you are not receiving ICA, but you are regularly and substantially caring for a person who receives or has claimed attendance allowance or the higher or middle rates of the care component of disability living allowance (DLA), you are likewise not required to be available for work.[9]
If you receive ICA (or are entitled to it but do not receive it because of the effect of the overlapping benefit rules), you will get a carer's premium of £12.40 per week included in the calculation of your IS, housing benefit or council tax benefit.[10] Your IS will be reduced by the amount of any ICA you receive as it is taken into account in full as income as it is for other means-tested benefits (so you will be the value of the carer's premium, £12.40, better off each week).[11] However, if you actually receive ICA the person you care for will not be able to get the severe disability premium for the purposes of those benefits.[12]
ICA attracts a credited Class 1 contribution (but your contribution record may be protected anyway through home responsibilities protection (see p229)).

5. 'REGULARLY AND SUBSTANTIALLY' CARING

To qualify for the benefit you must be engaged in caring for the disabled person 'regularly and substantially'. You satisfy this requirement during any week in which you are (or are likely to be) engaged and regularly engaged in caring for her/him for 35 hours or more.[13] You can be treated as meeting this rule if some of the time you spend on caring in the week is time spent preparing for the disabled person to come to stay with you, or clearing up after their visit.[14] However, it is not possible to meet the rules if caring for 35 hours per week 'on average' by showing that you care for more than 35 hours in some weeks and less in others. The rules require that the carer cares for 35 hours a week in the week in question.[15] You will also not qualify if you are caring for two or more disabled people for a total of 35 hours a week. You will have to show that you are caring for one of the disabled people for at least 35 hours a week.[16]

Once you have been caring for the disabled person for a while, temporary breaks in your care do not lead to the loss of your benefit. You can have a break, provided that you were caring for them for 14 of the previous 26 weeks and that you would have been caring for 22 of those weeks but you or they were in hospital. That means you can have four weeks' holiday in any period of six months.[17]

ICA stops if the disabled person's attendance allowance or DLA stops because they are in hospital. If they are an adult this will be after they have been an in-patient for more than four weeks. If they are under the age of 16 they do not lose their DLA until they have been in hospital for 12 weeks.

6. 'GAINFULLY EMPLOYED'

You cannot qualify if you are gainfully employed or in full-time education. You are considered to be gainfully employed if your earnings are £50 a week or more (for the way earnings are calculated, see p261). Your earnings will be ignored if you are working during a period when you are not actually caring for the disabled person because s/he is in hospital or you are on your four weeks' holiday (see above). They will also be ignored during any week when you are on leave from work, even if that is a week of paid absence from work.[18]

7. 'FULL-TIME EDUCATION'

If you are attending a university, college or school for more than 21 hours a week you will be treated as being in full-time education and will not be able to receive the allowance. In calculating the 21 hours you include only the hours spent in supervised study. You ignore any time spent on meal breaks or unsupervised study. The effect of this rule is that some people who might conventionally be regarded as 'full-time students', such as many undergraduates and postgraduates, are not disqualified from receiving the allowance. You will be treated as still being a student during vacations and any temporary interruptions of the course, but not if you have abandoned the course or been dismissed from it. [19]

8. PEOPLE OVER PENSIONABLE AGE

Under UK legislation, you are not entitled to ICA once you are over pensionable age (65 for men, 60 for women) unless you were entitled to it immediately before you reached that age (or you would have been but for the overlapping benefit rules, see p258). [20] However, in the light of advice from the European Court of Justice, the House of Lords has decided that the difference in the ages when this rule applies amounts to sex discrimination – which is unlawful under European Community law. [21] The effect of this is that women as well as men are now able to claim ICA up to the age of 65 simply by satisfying the usual conditions.

If you are over 65, you are entitled to ICA only if you were receiving it immediately before you reached *either* the age of 60 *or* the age of 65. These alternatives arise because the UK legislation prescribes the two different pensionable ages for men and women. Men can claim to be discriminated against by the choice of 65 and women can claim to be discriminated against by the choice of 60. Both sexes can choose either age depending on which suits their claims.

If you are a woman entitled to ICA immediately before you reach the age of 65, you can continue to receive the benefit even if you have ceased to look after a disabled person and even if you start working full-time. Under UK legislation this only applies to a man if you are entitled to ICA immediately before you reach the age of 70. [22] However, it is arguable that European law again has the effect that the sexes should be treated equally so that men too may continue to receive ICA once over the age of 65, even if they have ceased caring for an invalid and have perhaps also started full-time work.

The overall effect of this is that, whether you are a man or a woman:

- if you are aged under 65, you are entitled now provided you satisfy the usual conditions;
- if you are aged over 65 and you were receiving ICA immediately before

you reached 60 but not immediately before you reached 65, you are entitled now provided you satisfy the usual conditions;

- if you are aged over 65 and you were receiving ICA immediately before you reached 65, you are entitled now even if you have ceased caring for an invalid or have started full-time employment.

Although the Benefits Agency is now willing to pay ICA to women aged between 60 and 65 claiming for the first time, you may have to appeal in order to get benefit under some of the more obscure permutations discussed here. Ask a local advice agency to contact CPAG's solicitors if you need further help.

injured Result of industrial Accider /or proscribed industrial disease. / employee. only. Qualify for.

NINE

Injuries benefits (handwritten)

trial injuries benefits

This chapter covers:

1. Introduction (see below)
2. Industrial accidents and diseases (p164)
3. Disablement benefit (p175)
4. Reduced earnings allowance (p179)
5. Retirement allowance (p186)
6. Industrial death benefit (p186)

Not overlap (handwritten)

I. INTRODUCTION

Benefits under the industrial injuries scheme are paid to people who are disabled as a result of an accident at work or a disease caused by their job. The main benefit is disablement benefit (see p175). There are also a number of benefits which are paid as increases to disablement benefit. The most important are constant attendance allowance (see p177) and exceptionally severe disablement allowance (see p178). There are three other benefits – reduced earnings allowance, retirement allowance and industrial death benefit – but these are being phased out and will only be relevant if your accident or disease occurred before October 1990 (for reduced earnings allowance and retirement allowance) or if your spouse died before April 1988 (for industrial death benefit).

Even though you do not meet the usual contribution conditions, you will also be able to receive full sickness or invalidity benefit if you are incapable of work as a result of an industrial accident or disease (see p73).

For all these benefits (except industrial death benefit and non-contributory sickness/invalidity benefit) you must show:

- *either* you have suffered a 'personal injury' in an 'industrial accident' (see p164); *or*
- you are suffering from a 'prescribed industrial disease'; (see p168) *and*
- as a result of that accident or disease you have suffered a 'loss of faculty'; *and*

- as a result of that loss of faculty you are **'disabled'**; *and*
- you were an **'employed earner'**.

You are not covered by the scheme if your disability was caused by an industrial accident which happened before, or by a disease the onset of which was before, 5 July 1948. However, you may still be able to claim allowances under either the Workman's Compensation (Supplementation) Scheme 1982 or the Pneumoconiosis, Byssinosis and Miscellaneous Diseases Scheme 1983. See leaflets WS1 and PN1, available from the Benefits Agency.

If you have been injured by your work you may also have the right to sue your employer. Legal aid and help under the Green Form scheme (Pink Form in Scotland) may be available and you may be able to get a free consultation with a solicitor under the Accident and Legal Advice Service (ALAS) scheme. Your right to compensation from your employer is separate from your rights to benefit under the industrial injuries scheme (although your compensation may be reduced if you have received benefits from the Benefits Agency, see p263).

2. INDUSTRIAL ACCIDENTS AND DISEASES

A 'personal injury'

Defining a personal injury is not normally difficult. You will usually know whether you have been injured or not and if you are in doubt you should claim anyway. Personal injury includes the obvious, such as broken legs or arms,[1] but also covers the less obvious such as strains and psychological injury.[2] So an assault at work causing slight physical injury might give a far greater injury to the mind by causing agoraphobia or a breakdown. In difficult cases, the question is whether or not you have suffered a physiological or psychological change for the worse. It is not enough just to suffer pain if the pain is merely a symptom of an existing condition and does not make that condition substantially worse.[3] The damage must be to your body or mind but some permanent prostheses will be treated as part of your body even though they are not living tissue – eg, dislocation of an artificial hip joint counts as a personal injury,[4] but damage to a pair of spectacles[5] or an artificial leg,[6] does not.

An 'industrial accident'

An industrial accident is defined as 'an accident arising out of and in the course of your employment'.[7] It is important to realise that despite the name, it is not only industrial workers who can suffer from industrial accidents – any accident while you are doing your job can qualify. For example, if you are an office worker and a badly loaded filing cabinet tilts and falls on you, that would count as an industrial accident.

'Accident'

The 'accident' must be an 'unlooked-for occurrence' or 'mishap'.[8] If you do a heavy or dangerous job where accidents are common, a resulting injury is just as much an accident as if your job is sedentary and comparatively safe. If your heavy lifting causes a heart attack, it is the heart attack which is the accident, not the heavy lifting.[9] Deliberate acts by third parties can be accidents – eg, assaults on security workers or on staff in shops and hospitals.[10] However, if you start a fight at work and injure your hand punching somebody, that is not an industrial accident!

One of the most difficult questions in this area is the distinction between an 'accident', for which benefit is payable, and a 'process', for which it is not, unless it causes a 'prescribed disease' (see p168). Clearly, to fall from a ladder and break your leg is an accident – equally clearly, to work for many years as a heavy manual worker and have a sore back is a cumulative process.[11] However, sometimes a series of events, over a period of time, can be viewed as an accident for the purposes of the benefit.[12]

Example

Your job is trimming excess rubber from hot water bottles with a pair of scissors. A particularly hard batch of rubber comes through and each cut requires greater strength. Over two or three days you suffer a strain injury in your hand. The series of cuts constitutes a series of accidents that meets the definition.

It will be easier to establish the series of events as an accident if the period of time is fairly short,[13] or is noticed at an identifiable moment.[14] An accident is proved if you can establish that an identifiable occurrence must have happened, even if it is impossible to prove when.[15]

'In the course of... employment'

The accident must arise 'in the course of' employment. It has been said that 'an accident befalls a man in the course of his employment if it occurs while he is doing what a man so employed may reasonably do within a time during which he is employed, and at a place where he may reasonably be during that time to do that thing'.[16] Difficulties arise when work rules are broken, or when you do something not directly connected with work. The guidelines given below are literally only guidelines –there are exceptions to nearly every rule.

Generally speaking, when you arrive at your employers' factory or shop, and are on their private property, you are in the course of your employment. You do not have to have clocked in or have reported to your actual workplace. If you arrive early to get ready for work, or to have a meal in the works canteen,[17] you are covered, though if you arrive early to fit in a game of billiards you are not.[18] You are probably covered during breaks from working if you remain on the employers' property,[19] but probably not if you go elsewhere. So if, during a tea-break, you go to a local shop to buy a snack, you are outside the course of your employment.[20] If you are allowed to have a snack either at home or at work while still on duty (such as may happen with a police officer) you are covered.[21] While at work most activities are considered to be 'in the course of' work.[22] Smoking,[23] chatting,[24] or passing sweets[25] are all 'reasonably incidental' to the employment, provided they are not done in breach of instructions.[26] Even if you were doing something in breach of instructions you are still covered if what you were doing was done for the purposes of, or in connection with, your employment.[27]

Example I

You work as a labourer in a paper factory where there is an absolute ban on riding on the load of a fork-lift truck. You are seen riding on the load, fall off and are injured. Usually you would not be covered, but you saw the load was slipping and rode on the truck in order to hold it on. This was done for the purposes of your employment and so, this time, you are covered.

Example 2

A supervisor works in an office where central heating has been removed, but not replaced or the holes patched. It is cold and her staff are threatening not to work in the draught. The employers do not respond to her pleas for help. She goes onto the roof to patch the holes with papers and falls through it. She is in the course of employment even though the employers would have stopped her activities.

As more people are injured on journeys to and from work than are injured at work itself, accidents while travelling have been a source of much dispute. You are not in the course of your employment during ordinary journeys to and from work unless you are travelling on transport operated by or on behalf of your employer or by arrangement with your employer and not in the ordinary course of public transport service.[28]

Many employees have no set place of work, eg, lorry drivers, local authority home-helps, gas and electricity board employees. Obviously a lorry driver is at work when driving her/his lorry, but gas board workers, travelling directly from home to their first job of the day are not always in the course of employment even if driving a gas board van. It depends on the circumstances, including the rules for the use of the van.[29] A home-help has been found to be in the course of her employment travelling between jobs, but not going to the first job or from the last. This is because she became engaged in her employment once she started at the first job and remained engaged until the end of the day.[30] However, a home-help who had to go out of her way to the first job to get special sugar for a diabetic client was in the course of her employment when injured travelling from the shop.

Some employees with no fixed hours of work may be regarded as covered from the moment of leaving home.[31] Recent cases have eased the rules on travelling, eg, to conferences or meetings. You must look at all the factors in a common-sense way when deciding whether or not you were in the course of your employment. So a police officer who had to travel about 40 miles from home to a training course was in the course of his employment while travelling.[32] Provided you go reasonably directly, with no marked deviation from a proper route, and do not embark on activities unrelated to the journey, you may be covered.

One important factor in deciding whether you are in the course of your employment will be whether you receive wages for travelling.[33] If you receive a flat-rate travelling allowance, as compensation for having to work at a workplace other than your normal base, this may not be enough to make your journey to your alternative workplace part of your work.[34]

In putting forward your claim or arguing your case at an appeal, you should consider all aspects of the employment, including the wording of your contract and the degree of flexibility in the arrangements between you and your employers.[35]

'Out of . . . employment'

As well as arising in the course of your employment, the accident must arise 'out of' your employment, so that it can be said that in some way the employment contributed to it. The fact that you suffered a displaced retina at work is not sufficient to show it arose 'out of' the employment, but medical evidence which shows that it was caused by sudden head movements while inspecting a production line will enable a finding of 'industrial accident' to be made. An unexplained fracture while walking at work is not an industrial accident;[36] but it is if you slip and the fracture occurs while you are falling onto the ground. You are covered even if you are more susceptible to injury because, for example, your bones are brittle[37] or your eyes are weak.

Example

A farm worker, doing his normal job of digging, suffers sudden pain in the groin. It is found that a previous hernia, which had been surgically repaired, has given way again. The adjudication officer says that this could have happened at any time and so did not arise 'out of' the employment. The claimant's doctor says it could have happened any time but probably did so at *that* time because of the heavy digging.

A tribunal awards him benefit.

An accident also arises out of your employment if it arises in the course of your employment, *and*

- it is caused by another's misconduct, skylarking or negligence, *or*
- by the behaviour or presence of an animal (including bird, fish or insect), *or*
- it is caused by your being struck by any object or by lightning; *and*
- you did not directly or indirectly induce or contribute to the happening of the accident by your conduct outside the employment or by any act not incidental to the employment.

An accident is deemed to be 'out of and in the course of your employment' if you are helping people in an emergency, or trying to save property at or near where you are employed.[39] A milkman was covered when he went to help at a bungalow which had caught fire and to which he was delivering milk.[40]

A 'prescribed industrial disease'

Not every disease you suffer because of your work will qualify you for benefit. It is necessary for the disease to be 'prescribed'. This means it is on a list, produced by the DSS, of diseases which are known to have an occupational link.[41] This list is reproduced in full in Appendix Three (see p340).

Whether or not you suffer from a prescribed disease is known as the 'diagnosis question' and is decided by a special procedure (see p285).

If the Benefits Agency accepts that you are suffering from a prescribed disease, other diseases which result from it (eg, amnesia resulting from methyl bromide poisoning (C12)) will be included when assessing your loss of faculty and disablement.[42]

'Prescribed occupations'

Different diseases are 'prescribed' for different types of jobs because different jobs have different health risks. To qualify for benefit on this ground it is not enough to be suffering from a disease which happens to be on the list. You must also prove:

- that you have worked in one or more of the jobs for which that disease is prescribed; *and*
- that your job caused the disease.

It can sometimes be difficult to say whether a particular job is included on the list or not. Commissioners have had to decide whether workers suffering from occupational deafness (prescribed disease A10) who had respectively been employed in a steel rolling mill[43] and on the surface of a coal mine[44] had worked with a 'forging press plant engaged in the shaping of metal' and 'in mining coal'. The answers (no and yes respectively) are of less general importance than the fact that the decisions illustrate how complicated the questions can be. As can be seen from Appendix Three, the definitions are complex. If the Benefits Agency refuses to accept that you have worked in a prescribed occupation you should take advice, preferably from your union if you have one, or from another advice agency. An expert's report may help to prove your case.

For most prescribed diseases you do not have to have worked in a prescribed occupation for any minimum length of time. You can also claim at any time, even if it is many years after you worked in that occupation. However, there are exceptions to these general rules. If you are suffering from occupational deafness (A10) you have to have worked in a prescribed occupation for 10 years and to claim within 5 years of having done so.[45] If you have occupational asthma (D7) you have to claim within 10 years of working in a prescribed occupation.[46] If you have chronic bronchitis or emphysema (D12) you have to have been working in a prescribed occupation for 20 years.

Causation

You must prove that the disease is due to your occupation, but it is normally assumed that if you suffer the disease in the prescribed occupation within a month of last working in that occupation, the occupation caused the disease.[47] With carpal tunnel syndrome (A12), inflammation of the mucous membrane (D4) and dermatitis (D5) there is no such presumption. The presumption operates with slightly different time conditions for occupational deafness (A10), tuberculosis (B5), pneumoconiosis (D1), byssinosis (D2) and chronic bronchitis and emphysema (D12). The connection for carpal tunnel syndrome, dermatitis and inflammation of the mucous membrane will therefore have to be proved. Dermatitis is quite a common industrial disease. The Benefits Agency will investigate this, and you may need to ask your GP or consultant to help with a report linking the disease to your occupation. DSS guidance on the diagnosis of diseases is available (see Appendix Five, p352). However, it is *not* necessary to prove the link beyond any reasonable doubt and to rule out all other possibilities. It is necessary only to establish the link 'on a balance of probabilities'; in other words, it is more likely than not that there is a connection.

Example

A hospital cleaner uses a new cleaning material. A rash develops on his hands and he has to give up the job. The medical evidence shows that the cleaning material could have caused the problem but so could several things with which the cleaner had been in contact outside work. There is a strong argument that the cleaning material was what caused the rash because the rash developed so soon after using it.

'Onset' and 'recrudescence'

The 'onset' (date of starting) of a prescribed disease is taken as the date of the first day you suffer the relevant loss of faculty (see p171). In deafness cases it is the later of either the date you first suffered the loss of faculty or the date you successfully claimed benefit.[48]

With diseases other than deafness, asthma and respiratory conditions, you can improve and then worsen again. It is important to know whether it is a 'recrudescence' (fresh outbreak) or a completely new attack. The first enables an immediate review;[49] with the second, a claim will have to wait for 15 weeks before disablement benefit can be claimed. If a further attack commences during a current period of assessment, it is assumed to be a recrudescence unless the contrary is proved. There is a special procedure (see p285) for deciding this recrudescence question.

Pneumoconiosis, byssinosis and diffuse mesothelioma

If you are suffering from pneumoconiosis, byssinosis or diffuse mesothelioma (or you are the widow or were another dependant of someone who died while suffering from one of those diseases) and you cannot get compensation from the employer, you may be able to get a lump-sum payment in addition to any industrial injuries benefit. For further details see Appendix One.

The disablement questions

In addition to showing the link between your injury or disease and your occupation, you also need to establish that you have suffered a loss of faculty and are disabled. There are three disablement questions:[50]

- Has the relevant accident or disease resulted in a loss of faculty?
- What is the extent of disablement resulting from a loss of faculty?
- What period is to be taken into account by the assessment?

These questions are decided not by adjudication officers but by adjudicating medical authorities (see p287) and on appeal by medical appeal tribunals (see p308). It is here that most disputes about disablement benefit arise. The DSS guidance for adjudicating medical authorities is available to the public (see Appendix Five).

Loss of faculty

A loss of faculty is simply an 'impairment of the proper functioning of part of the body or mind'.[51] A decision of an adjudication officer that there has been a personal injury resulting from an industrial accident does not itself prevent the medical authorities from finding that there is no loss of faculty, but this will be rare.[52]

If you are turned down on the ground that there is no loss of faculty, ie, the accident has had either no effect on you, or only a very marginal effect (less than 1 per cent), you should be realistic as to whether this is true. If it is not, and you feel there has been a loss of faculty, you should appeal. You may not get to the 14 per cent 'barrier' for payment of disablement benefit, but, if your accident or disease occurred before 1990, you will need a finding of at least 1 per cent to claim for reduced earnings allowance (see p179) if there is any income loss. In addition, if you are unlucky enough to suffer another industrial accident, the percentages of disablement can be added together and may entitle you to benefit, even if neither accident would do so on its own.

Loss of faculty is *not* the same as disablement (see below).

Disablement

The extent of your disablement is assessed on a percentage basis. If the total disablement from all industrial accidents and diseases is more than 20 per cent, it is rounded to the nearest multiple of 10 per cent with multiples of 5 per cent being rounded upwards.[53] Any assessment between 14 per cent and 19 per cent is treated as 20 per cent (except for those entitled to disablement gratuities – see p176).[54]

Some degrees of disablement are laid down by regulations.[55] These include various amputations – eg, loss of a hand, or a leg – and degrees of hearing loss (see Appendix Two). However, even in these cases the adjudicating medical authorities must take into account the real disablement resulting from an injury[56] – eg, the loss of a right hand will be more disabling for a right-handed person than for a left-handed person. Apart from age, sex and physical and mental condition, the personal circumstances of a claimant must be ignored, so that particular problems you may have, like the location of your office, or the distance to the nearest bus stop, are ignored. Disablement is assessed by reference to a person of the same age and sex whose physical and mental condition is normal.[57]

When no degree of disability is laid down (and these form the vast majority of cases), the authorities must assess you on the basis of their experience and use the prescribed degrees as a guide.[58] In particular, you should note that 100 per cent is given to people who are far from totally disabled (eg, those with no disabilities other than total deafness) and other assessments should reflect this. The DSS *Industrial Injuries Handbook for Adjudicating Medical Authorities* gives further guidance based on medical appeal tribunal decisions (see Appendix Five).

It is important that you are very straightforward with the examining doctors. The authorities have checks to establish that your symptoms are consistent with the injury, and that your movements are consistent with the disablement you claim. Therefore how you walk into the room, and how you undress, will be examined as carefully as how you respond to the examination.

If a disability has two causes, the rules for assessment are complex. If the other disability is congenital or arose before the industrial one, it is deducted from the total disability.[59]

Example
You lose a hand, which would normally be 60 per cent, but you had previously lost its index finger. So 14 per cent is deducted, leaving 46 per cent (rounded up to 50 per cent).

The reduction is often known as the 'offset'. Mistakes are sometimes made because the authority incorrectly bases your assessment on the loss of faculty instead of on the disablement resulting from the loss of faculty.

Example
You have a back injury as a result of an industrial accident. An authority has reduced your assessment by, say, 5 per cent on the ground of a pre-existing disability of which you knew nothing. Many people have spines that are slightly curved due to lifting things. The authority may have looked at an X-ray, correctly considered that your curved spine is not due to the relevant accident and then incorrectly reduced your assessment.

What the authority should have done was to consider whether the pre-existing loss of faculty (the curved spine) really has led to disablement which would have occurred even if the industrial accident had not happened. The authority should therefore have considered, among other things, whether the loss of faculty led to disablement before the industrial accident occurred. There was no physical disablement if you did not suffer any pain or restriction of movement and it was therefore wrong to reduce your assessment unless there was some good reason for deciding that disablement would have arisen during the period of assessment even if the industrial accident had not occurred. You should appeal if this happens to you.

The authority also should bear in mind that even if you did have a pre-existing problem which caused a disability, the accident may worsen the effects of it, as well as causing a new problem. The assessment should reflect the increase in the original problem as well as the new disability.

No reduction is made if 100 per cent is a reasonable assessment for the industrial accident.[60]

If the other disability arose *after* the industrial accident then the authority has first to assess the purely industrial injury – if it is less than 11 per cent any disability from the other cause is ignored; if it is more than 11 per cent any extra disablement caused by the effect of the industrial injury on the other disability is added.[61]

Example 3
You lose a little finger in an industrial accident and are assessed as 7 per cent disabled as a result. You then lose the other fingers of that hand in a non-industrial accident. You continue to be assessed as 7 per cent disabled due to the industrial accident.

Example 4
You lose the middle, ring and little fingers of one hand in an industrial accident and are assessed as 30 per cent disabled as a result. You then lose the index finger of that hand in a non-industrial accident. Your total disablement (assessed according to the Schedule) is now 50 per cent. But loss of the index finger only would have been 14 per cent. The disablement resulting from your industrial accident is therefore reassessed at 36 per cent (50 per cent – 14 per cent) which is rounded up to 40 per cent.

If you have two or more industrial accidents you may also end up in a situation where the second or later accident is made worse by the interaction with the effect of the previous accident or accidents. The assessment process can allow for this.[62] Your most recent assessment should include an increase for any such interaction.[63] The same would apply where an industrial disease interacts with the effects of an industrial accident.

Example 5
You have a fall at work and seriously injure your left leg. You receive a life assessment of 10 per cent. Years later, you have a further fall and seriously injure the other leg. You are assessed as 10 per cent disabled for that accident, with a further 5 per cent for the extra disability you suffer as a result of the interaction between the two injuries. The total of 25 per cent is rounded up, resulting in payment of a 30 per cent pension.

In pneumoconiosis cases there are special rules. Any effect of tuberculosis is assessed with the effects of the pneumoconiosis.[64] If you are assessed at 50 per cent due to the pneumoconiosis, any added disability due to chronic bronchitis or emphysema will be added.[65] If you have made a claim for pneumoconiosis you cannot make an effective separate claim for chronic bronchitis or emphysema.[66]

Period of assessment

The authority or medical appeal tribunal makes an assessment for a period 'during which the claimant has suffered and may be expected to continue to suffer from the relevant loss of faculty'. It must begin on a specified date and normally ends on a specified date. Assessments are for a set percentage and are usually made for six months, one year or two years, or will be given for life.[67]

An assessment will be either **final** or **provisional**.[68] It will be provisional when there is doubt as to what will happen in the future, and you will be automatically called for assessment at the end of the period.[69] Life assessments are of course final. If you are given a final assessment for a fixed period but you think that the effects of the accident or disease will last for longer than that, you should consider an immediate appeal against that assessment (see p308). If your condition deteriorates during a period of assessment, or if you still have a disability at the end of a period for which you have been given a final assessment, you should apply for a review (see p292). If your assessment was awarded by a medical appeal tribunal, you must ask a tribunal to give leave for such a review to take place.

An assessment of disablement benefit for occupational deafness is always provisional for a period of five years.[70] If the later assessment shows that your hearing loss is lower than the 50 decibels minimum loss for benefit to be paid, no benefit is then paid.[71] This does not mean that your hearing has got better (the condition generally worsens, in fact) but different means of testing give different results. If a re-assessment does take you down to just under the 50 decibel mark it is worth asking your GP or trade union to arrange for you to have a further examination to try to get grounds for appeal.

Employed earner's employment

You can claim industrial injuries benefits only if you were an employed earner whose accident or disease was caused by your employed earner's employment.[72] This rule excludes the self-employed.[73] It also excludes most trainees on employment training and youth training schemes although they are likely to be covered by a similar scheme run by the Department of Employment.

If you pay, or ought to pay, Class 1 contributions as an employed earner (see p217) you are covered by the scheme. This includes those paying Class 1 (and, in the case of volunteer development workers, Class 2 – see p222) contributions while abroad.[74] You are also covered if your earnings are too low to pay contributions – mostly this is because of part-time work. Finally, you are treated as being in employed earner's employment if you are an apprentice, mine inspector or rescue worker, special constable, taxi-driver, office cleaner, agency worker, minister of religion, lecturer, member of an aircrew, mariner, or – in some situations – an offshore oil or gas worker.[75]

You are treated as *not* being an employed earner if:[76]

- you are employed by your spouse *and either* your employment is not for the purpose of her/his employment *or* your earnings are normally below the lower earnings limit (see p216). So a man employed by his wife to help run her shop, and earning £60 a week, is covered; *or*
- you are employed by a near relative (parent, step-parent, grandparent, son, daughter, step-child, grandchild, brother, sister, half-brother or half-sister) in a private house where you both live, and your employment is not for your relative's trade or business carried out there; *or*
- you are a member of visiting Armed Forces, or a civilian employed by them, unless you are normally resident in the UK.

3. DISABLEMENT BENEFIT

Conditions of entitlement

- You suffer from loss of physical or mental faculty, as a result of one or more industrial accidents or prescribed diseases or injury.
- Your resulting disablement is assessed as being at least 14 per cent (1

per cent in the case of pneumoconiosis, byssinosis and diffuse mesothelioma).
• Ninety days (excluding Sundays) have elapsed since the date of the
  accident or onset of the prescribed disease or injury.

Amount of payment

The amount of benefit depends on the extent of your disablement (see
p171).[1]

Extent of disablement	Benefit £pw Claimant aged under 18 and not entitled to an increase in respect of a dependant	Benefit £pw Any other claimant
100%	57.10	93.20
90%	51.39	83.88
80%	45.68	74.56
70%	39.97	65.24
60%	34.26	55.92
50%	28.55	46.50
40%	22.84	37.28
30%	17.13	27.96
11-20%	11.42	18.64
1-10%	5.71	9.32

There are also increases of benefit (see p177).

Since 1 October 1986, disablement benefit has been paid only if the
assessment of disablement is at least 14 per cent,[2] except in the cases of
pneumoconiosis, byssinosis and diffuse mesothelioma, when benefit is
paid if the assessment is at least 1 per cent.[3]

Until 1 October 1986, disablement benefit was paid in respect of any
assessment of disablement of at least 1 per cent. The old rules are still in
force for assessments following claims made before that date.[4] That is
most important where there have been a series of provisional assessments, because any new assessment is then regarded as following from
the original claim which may have been made some years ago.

Under these old rules, an assessment of less than 20 per cent results in
entitlement to a lump-sum disablement gratuity.[5] The amount of the
gratuity depends on the maximum disablement gratuity in force at the
beginning of the period of assessment (rather than at the date of the
award). The maximum is now £6,190 and is awarded if the assessment is
19 per cent disablement for life. The gratuity is reduced by 5 per cent for
every 1 per cent by which the assessment is lower than 19 per cent.

A life assessment is treated as equivalent to an assessment for seven years and, if the assessment is for a shorter period, the gratuity is reduced proportionately.

Example
A pre-1986 accident giving rise to an assessment of 10 per cent disablement for two years from 1 May 1993 results in a disablement gratuity of:
$$£6,190 - 55\% - 2/7 = £972.71$$

Before 1 October 1986, those entitled to special hardship allowance (now replaced by reduced earnings allowance) could choose to have a small weekly pension instead of a gratuity. This was called a 'pension in lieu' of a gratuity. That option has now been abolished, but those already entitled to such pensions continue to receive them with their reduced earnings allowance. [6]

Tax and other benefits

Disablement benefit is not taxable. [7]

It is taken into account in full for income support purposes.

Increases of disablement benefit

Constant attendance allowance

You are entitled to constant attendance allowance if: [8]

- you are entitled to a basic disablement pension based on a degree of disablement assessed at 100 per cent; *and*
- you require constant attendance as a result of the relevant loss of faculty (see p171).

Disablement as a result of pre-1948 industrial accidents and diseases, war injuries and injuries suffered while on police or fire duty, may be taken into account in considering the degree of your disablement. [9]

Invalid care allowance may be paid to someone looking after you while you are receiving constant attendance allowance (see p158).

The **higher weekly rate**, £74.80, is paid if a person is 'so exceptionally severely disabled as to be entirely, or almost entirely dependent on (constant) attendance for the necessities of life, and is likely to remain so dependent for a prolonged period and the attendance so required is whole-time'. [10]

The **lower weekly rate**, £37.40, is paid if a person is 'to a substantial extent dependent on (constant) attendance for the necessities of life and is likely to remain so dependent for a prolonged period'. This may be increased up to £56.10 a week if 'the extent of such attendance is greater by reason of the beneficiary's exceptionally severe disablement'. If attendance is part-time only, the amount payable is 'such sum as may be reasonable in the circumstances' (usually £18.70 a week).[11] Some claimants may be better off claiming the care component of disability living allowance or the ordinary attendance allowance instead (see pp134 and 142).

Exceptionally severe disablement allowance

This is paid at the weekly rate of £37.40 if you are entitled to a constant attendance allowance (or would be if you were not in hospital) at a rate in excess of £37.40 a week, and are likely to remain so permanently.[12]

Unemployability supplement[13]
Hospital treatment allowance[14]

These were abolished in April 1987, except for claimants who were then in receipt of them. For more information, refer to earlier editions of this *Guide*.

Claims

Disablement benefit, including constant attendance allowance and exceptionally severe disablement allowance, should be claimed within three months of your becoming entitled. If you claim late, only three months' arrears can be paid, unless you have 'continuous good cause' for claiming late (see p281).[15] The usual absolute bar on any payment in respect of a period more than 12 months before the date of your claim does *not* apply to disablement benefit.

You can apply for a declaration that you have had an industrial accident. You do this on form BI 95 from your local Benefits Agency office. This may be a wise precaution where you have had an accident but are not sure whether you wish to proceed with a claim to benefit.

There are special time limits for people suffering from occupational deafness (A10) or occupational asthma (D7). Although at one time it was held that the time limit in respect of occupational deafness had been imposed unlawfully, this has now been made valid retrospectively.[16]

Chronic bronchitis and emphysema for miners (D12) were prescribed from 13 September 1993. There was a two-stage process for accepting claims.[17] Those who were at least 70 years old on that date, or who were in receipt of the higher rate of attendance allowance or the care component of disability living allowance (DLA), could claim from then until 28 February 1994. All others can only claim from 1 March 1994. Any claim received before 31 August 1994 will be backdated to 13 September 1993.

Reviews

Any decision of an adjudicating medical authority or a medical appeal tribunal may be reviewed by a medical board (see p292) if satisfied by fresh evidence that the decision was given in ignorance of a material fact or was based on a mistake as to a material fact.[18] Furthermore, any assessment of the extent of disablement may also be reviewed by a medical board on the ground of 'unforeseen aggravation of the results of the relevant injury'.[19] This gives very wide powers to reopen cases – even long after the expiry of a final assessment of disablement.[20] But if the original decision was made by a medical appeal tribunal, an application for a review may be made only with the permission ('leave') of a medical appeal tribunal.[21] In practice, tribunals often seem to require medical evidence before they will give such leave, even though there is no specific requirement for this. Permission is not required for a review following recrudescence of an attack of a prescribed disease or injury (see p170).[22] The period taken into account for a review on the ground of unforeseen aggravation may include any period not exceeding three months before the date of application for the review (or the date of claim leading to a 'recrudescence question' on which the review was based).[23] In order to succeed, you will need to show not only that your condition has worsened, but also that such deterioration was not allowed for in the original assessment. You may appeal against a decision by a medical board on review to a medical appeal tribunal (see p308).[24]

Disqualification

You may be disqualified for misconduct on the same grounds as for sickness and invalidity benefit (see p76), except that you are not liable to be disqualified for behaving in a manner likely to retard your recovery.[25]

4. REDUCED EARNINGS ALLOWANCE

This is now available only to those who had accidents or started to suffer from diseases before 1 October 1990. A successful first claim can still be made now by someone who has had such an accident or disease.

Conditions of entitlement [1]

- You suffer from loss of physical or mental faculty due to an industrial injury before 1 October 1990 or an industrial disease, the onset of which was before that date (see p170); *and*
- your resulting disability is assessed as being at least 1 per cent (see p171); *and*
- as a result of the relevant loss of faculty *either*:
  - you are incapable and likely to remain permanently incapable of following your regular occupation and are incapable of following employment of an equivalent standard which is suitable in your case ('the permanent condition'); *or*
  - you are, and have been at all times since the end of the 90-day qualifying period for disablement benefit, incapable of following your regular occupation or employment of an equivalent standard which is suitable in your case ('the continuing condition'); *and either*
- you are under pensionable age; *or*
- you have not given up regular employment (see p182); *and*
- you have not been in receipt of reduced earnings allowance since 1 October 1990 and subsequently ceased to be entitled to it for at least one day (see p185).

In addition to those rules of entitlement, if you were entitled to reduced earnings allowance on either 10 April 1988 or 9 April 1989 and on that date you were over pensionable age and were retired, or were treated as retired, you remain entitled to the allowance for life. For the meaning of 'retired or treated as retired', see p69 of the twelfth edition of this *Guide*.

Reduced earnings

The fact that you are losing money as a result of an industrial injury is not, in itself, enough. You must meet either the permanent or continuing conditions outlined below. Some people fall through the gap caused by the regulations – you can have gone back to work after the accident for long enough to miss out on the continuing condition, and are now losing money, but cannot show that you are likely to be *permanently* incapable of your regular occupation.

The permanent condition

Only incapacity at the time of claim and in the future are relevant. The phrase 'likely to remain permanently incapable' relates only to the 'regular occupation' and not to 'employment of an equivalent standard'.

So you do not need to prove at a tribunal that you are likely to remain incapable of employment of an equivalent standard; just that you are not likely to be able to perform your normal job.

A person suffering from pneumoconiosis, who is advised not to work by a medical board, is deemed not to be able to work unless the adjudication officer proves otherwise.[2]

If your condition could be improved by an operation, and you refuse to have it, the adjudication officer may disqualify you, but only if the operation is a very minor one.[3] You have the right to refuse a more serious operation even if the result of not having it is permanent incapacity.

The continuing condition

Only incapacity at the time of claim and in the *past* are relevant, so there is less scope for argument than when assessing the future. However, if you returned to work but were 'sheltered' by your workmates, you can still argue that you were 'incapable' of following your regular occupation. Specific provision is made so that, if you have worked since the end of the 90-day period, but this work was approved by the Secretary of State or done on the advice of a doctor for rehabilitation, testing or training, it can be disregarded. So, also, is employment before obtaining surgical treatment, and six months of employment thereafter.[4] If you have given up work due to pneumoconiosis on the advice of a medical board you are deemed to have been continuously incapable of following that regular occupation.[5]

Regular occupation

This involves looking at your work history (part-time[6] as well as full-time) and the content of the job, as opposed to its title. For example, a docker, still employed to work as a docker but unable to earn as much because he is unable to do the full range of his duties, was found incapable of his regular occupation.[7]

If an accident happens when you have just started a new job your intentions and prospects will be relevant,[8] unless it was just a stop-gap occupation, say during ill-health.[9] If you are a full-time student, any part-time work will count as your regular occupation;[10] otherwise subsidiary employment will not count. If you would have been fairly sure to have been promoted by the time of your claim, but for the accident, then the promoted position may count as the regular occupation.

If you suffer from a prescribed disease and, because of this, gave up a job before you applied for benefit, it may count as the regular occupation.[11]

Employment of an equivalent standard which is suitable

Employment is of an equivalent standard if the normal earnings are the same as the normal earnings in your regular occupation.[12] If these earnings include a great deal of overtime, so that you have to do a lot more hours to earn the same, that is disregarded. It is the total earnings 'package' that matters, not how it is made up. Suitability is judged by looking at your education, experience, training, work history and general health.[13] Only employed earner's employment can be treated as suitable, so self-employed work will not be considered.[14]

If your regular occupation was part-time, full-time work is not of an equivalent standard even if you are medically fit to do it. Like must be compared with like. However, if there are no jobs of the same number of hours, different work for a similar number of hours may be regarded as equivalent.[15]

Retaining reduced earnings allowance

Giving up 'regular employment'

If you are over pensionable age, you lose entitlement to reduced earnings allowance if you give up 'regular employment' (unless you were entitled to the allowance on 10 April 1988 or 9 April 1989 and were then already over pensionable age and retired).

'Regular employment' is now defined in this connection as employment for at least 10 hours a week in a week within a period of five or more weeks of such employment. Hours are averaged over any period of five weeks but you are regarded as not having given up regular employment in any week in which you have one or more days of interruption of employment (ie, days of unemployment or incapacity for work – see pp252 and 253).[16] There was no such statutory definition of 'regular employment' before 1 April 1990. There is no specific rule that you must not be in receipt of retirement pension, or that you have to be under 'retirement age' (70 for a man, 65 for a woman).

During any period when you are not entitled to reduced earnings allowance because you have given up regular employment, you will receive retirement allowance instead (see p186). This will be paid to you at a much lower rate.

This means that it may be important for you to defer entitlement to a retirement pension (see p114) when you reach pensionable age and claim unemployment benefit, sickness benefit or invalidity benefit instead. Note that although these benefits may no longer be paid to you when you reach retirement age it may still be important for you to preserve your right to reduced earnings allowance by continuing to claim them, by showing that you are available for work or sending in sick notes. It is possible to do one of these at the same time as claiming your retirement pension.

Indeed, if you can show that you are now sick or unemployed, you may be able to show a continued entitlement to reduced earnings allowance, even if you now receive retirement pension or are over retirement age. You may need to make a late appeal against the decision to move you on to retirement allowance, or seek a review of that decision. If you are in this position you should seek advice. You will not be able to do this if you were entitled to the allowance on 10 April 1988 or 9 April 1989 and were then already over pensionable age and retired.

The effects of European law

In the light of the above it should be clear that, in practice, most people who lose reduced earnings allowance will do so because they reach retirement age. This is 65 for a woman, 70 for a man. It can now be clearly argued that there is no necessary connection between the overall rules about pensions and retirement age, and the discriminatory effect they have in this and other situations of withdrawing benefits from women at an earlier age than men.[17] This rule is therefore in breach of the EC directive 79/7, which provides that men and women should be treated equally in the social security systems of EC countries (see p267). In this situation a woman would be very likely to be in receipt of invalidity benefit on a non-contributory basis (see p73). That may also be reduced for a woman at age 65 when she goes on to retirement pension, which could be little or nothing. Again, this would not happen to her until the age of 70 if she were a man.

Example

You are a woman who has just reached the age of 65. You are told that this is your 'retirement age' and that your reduced earnings allowance of £37.26 a week has to be turned into retirement allowance of £9.32 a week. You are also told that your non-contributory invalidity benefit of £61.40 a week will cease. As you do not meet the contribution conditions for a retirement pension and your husband is not yet himself retired, you will receive nothing in place of your invalidity benefit. If you were a man this would not happen to you until you were 70.

You should appeal against both decisions to reduce your benefit and seek further advice.

Amount of payment

The amount of the allowance is the amount by which your current earnings, or earnings in a job which it is considered you could do, are less than the current earnings in your previous regular occupation.[18] Earnings include overtime. For most claimants this is a fairly routine calculation. However, if you are unemployed, the DSS's doctors are asked for your limitations; the Department of Employment's disablement resettlement officers are asked to say what job they think you could do; and the JobCentre is asked to quote a wage which such a job would command in your area. This leads to a number of possible areas of argument – they will be contrasting an income from the regular occupation, which may be an estimate, with the notional income of a notional job which the adjudication officer, advised from a number of sources, considers that you can do! You should look carefully at all the elements of the calculation, and assess whether the jobs quoted are realistic for you to do, whether the wages seem correct, and if a proper allowance has been given for you as an individual.

Example

You were employed as a 'silver service waitress' but injured your knee, and cannot manage walking very easily. You are unemployed, and there are few jobs of any description in the area for someone of your age (mid-50s) and physical restriction. You would have been earning £95 a week including tips. The disablement resettlement officer suggests that you could become a receptionist and quotes £70 – £90 as a range. The adjudication officer usually takes an average and so allows you £95 – £80 = £15 a week. You argue that, given your disabilities and lack of experience, an employer would pay at the very bottom of the range. You find adverts for jobs offering less than £70. At worst you should be able to argue for £95 – £70 = £25 a week for at least a year or two.

Once the first assessment has been made the amount is usually increased in line with earnings in that industry or workplace, unless that 'regular occupation' has ceased to exist.[19] In that case, it is calculated as rising in line with the nearest 'occupational group' as defined by the Department of Employment. You can ask for a fresh assessment to take into account your normal prospects of advancement, though here you have to show that promotion would have happened, say at the end of a period of employment or training, not just that it may have happened if you had been particularly diligent.[20]

The maximum amount you may receive for any one award is £37.26 a week (£22.84 a week if you are under 18 and not entitled to an increase for a dependant).[21] The total you can receive by way of disablement benefit and reduced earnings allowance (whether for one or more awards) is 140 per cent of the standard rate of disablement benefit, £130.48 a week.[22] If you were over pensionable age and retired before 6 April 1987 your allowance would be reduced if it would otherwise mean that you would be receiving more than 100 per cent disablement pension.[23]

A person who qualified for reduced earnings allowance and was retired, or treated as retired, on either 10 April 1988 or 9 April 1989 will continue to receive the allowance at the same rate. Its value will therefore erode over time.[24]

Tax and other benefits

Reduced earnings allowance is not taxable. It is taken into account in full as income for income support purposes.

The withdrawal of reduced earnings allowance

It is still possible for someone to make a first claim for reduced earnings allowance now, provided that they meet the standard qualifying conditions, and that the accident or disease occurred before 1 October 1990.

It is also possible to make a claim by showing good cause for not having claimed from an earlier date. The standard 12-month bar on the payment of arrears does not apply to reduced earnings allowance. Many claimants have been successful at tribunals because publicity for reduced earnings allowance (and special hardship allowance which it replaced) was so poor. The disablement benefit claim form, later redesigned, simply had a note saying that a leaflet was available, with no indication that a separate claim was needed. You should argue that this expected too much of claimants.[25] Further, it implied that help was available only to those who had at the time of making the claim lost earnings as a result of their accident. This would not have assisted those who were able temporarily to return to their regular occupation but might in future have become unable to do so because of the effect of their accident.

Because of the withdrawal of the allowance from those who were entitled prior to 1 October 1990 but who then failed to meet the qualifying conditions for one day or more, there are difficulties in advising those who have missed out on the allowance. Some one who might, for example, arguably be able to show good cause back to an accident in 1988, but who worked in 1991 for a few weeks in well-paid work, might be better off not raising the issue of good cause but merely claiming from now.

5. RETIREMENT ALLOWANCE

This is really a reduced rate of reduced earnings allowance for people over pensionable age. As reduced earnings allowance is phased out, so too will be retirement allowance.

Conditions of entitlement [1]

• You are over pensionable age (although see p183 above about the possible effects of European legislation if you are a woman).
• You have given up regular employment (see p182).
• You were entitled to reduced earnings allowance at a rate of at least £2 a week (in total, if you had more than one award) immediately before you gave up regular employment.
• You are not entitled to reduced earnings allowance.

Amount of payment [2]

The amount of payment is £9.32 a week or 25 per cent of the amount of reduced earnings allowance you were receiving, whichever is the lower.

Tax and other benefits

Retirement allowance is not taxable. It is taken into account in full for income support purposes.

6. INDUSTRIAL DEATH BENEFIT

Introduction

Industrial death benefit is payable only in respect of deaths due to industrial accidents or diseases which occurred before 11 April 1988. The conditions of entitlement for **widows** are covered on p108 and for **children** on p199. The conditions for **widowers** are covered below.

If a man dies as a result of an industrial accident or disease after 10 April 1988, he is deemed to have satisfied the contribution conditions for widows' benefits and Category B retirement pension, so his widow is likely to be entitled to one or more of those benefits. Otherwise, there are now no special rules or benefits for people who die following industrial accidents and diseases.

Industrial death benefit for widowers

Conditions of entitlement [1]

- Your wife died before 11 April 1988 as a result of an industrial accident or disease (see p101).
- At the time of her death, you were being wholly or mainly maintained by her (or would have been but for the relevant accident or disease).
- At the time of her death, you were permanently incapable of self-support.

Amount of payment

Benefit is paid at the rate of £57.60 a week for life.[2] It does *not* stop if you remarry or live with a woman as man and wife.

CHAPTER TEN

Benefits for children

This chapter covers five benefits paid specifically in respect of children:

1. Child benefit (see below)
2. One parent benefit (p195)
3. Guardian's allowance (p196)
4. Child's special allowance (p198)
5. Industrial death benefit for children (p199)

Disability living allowance is also available for children (see Chapter 7).

1. CHILD BENEFIT

Conditions of entitlement [1]

- You and the child satisfy the residence conditions (see p242); *and either*
- the child lives with you; *or*
- you contribute to the maintenance of the child (see p192)at the rate of at least the amount of child benefit for that child; *and*
- you have priority over other potential claimants (see p192)

Amount of payment

Child benefit is payable at the weekly rate of £10.20 for the eldest child for whom benefit is payable and £8.25 in respect of each other child. [2]

'A child'

A child is: [3]

- a person under 16; *or*
- a person under 19 receiving full-time secondary education either in a recognised educational establishment (or elsewhere if the Secretary of State is satisfied with the education); [4] *or*
- a person under 18 who has ceased full-time education but is still within the 'extension period'.

Full-time education

A person is receiving full-time education if s/he is attending a course of education for more than 12 hours a week including instruction, tuition, supervised study, exams, practical work and experiments or projects provided for in the curriculum, but excluding meal breaks and unsupervised study.[5]

'Supervised' study requires the close proximity of a teacher or tutor to enforce discipline and provide encouragement and help.[6]

If your child's education is interrupted, the absence from school can be ignored for up to six months if it is 'reasonable in the circumstances', or for longer if it is because of illness or disability.[7] If your child leaves full-time education but returns after a period of work or unemployment, child benefit becomes payable again until your child is 19.

Child benefit is not payable if your child is doing an advanced course, ie, above A-level, OND, Scottish Higher Certificate or the equivalent level[8] or if s/he is on a youth training scheme and receiving a training allowance or if s/he receives income support in her/his own right.[9]

A child ceases to qualify for child benefit *either*:

- the week after becoming 19; *or*
- on the Sunday after the first of the following dates after leaving school or college
  - first Monday in January
  - first Monday after Easter Monday
  - first Monday in September
  whichever is *earlier*.

A child who has been entered for an external examination before ceasing full-time education at a school or college is treated as still being at the school or college until after the examination or until her/his name is withdrawn from entry.[10]

The 'extension period'

After a child becomes 16 or ceases full-time education, child benefit continues to be paid during an 'extension period' if s/he:[11]

- is under 18; *and*
- is registered as available for work or youth training; *and*
- is not in remunerative work for 24 hours a week or more; *and*
- is not receiving income support; *and*
- is not on a youth training scheme.

The extension period begins on the day s/he reaches 16 or is treated as leaving full-time education (whichever is later). If that day is on or after the first Monday in September but before the first Monday in January, the extension period ends on the day before the first Monday in January. If it is on or after the first Monday in January but before the first Monday after Easter Monday, the extension period ends on the day before the 14th Monday of the year. If the extension period begins at any other time of the year, it ends on the 14th Monday after Easter of that year.[12]

Example

Your 16-year-old daughter leaves school in June 1994. She is treated as being in full-time education until 11 September 1994. The extension period then starts on the next day and continues until 1 January 1995.

Child benefit is payable during the extension period *only* if it was payable immediately before the period started *and* you apply in writing.[13]

Children in care

If a child is away from home and is *either*:

- in the care of a local authority;[14] *or*
- (in Scotland) subject to supervision and residing in residential accommodation under the Social Work (Scotland) Act 1968;[15] *or*
- being provided (or treated as being provided) with accommodation by a local authority under the Children Act 1989[16]

child benefit is not payable after the first eight weeks of absence.[17]

However, if the child actually stays with you in any of the above situations child benefit is payable if:[18]

- the child 'actually' lives with you throughout the week; *or*
- the child 'actually' lives with you for part of a day in that week and then for the whole of the next six days; *or*
- the child 'actually' lives with you for a *whole* day in that week and for the whole of the six previous days; *or*
- the child ordinarily lives with you for at least *one whole day each week* even if the child is not actually at home in that particular week.

A 'week' means seven days beginning with a Monday.[19] A 'day' means from midnight to midnight.[20] This effectively means that the child has to stay with you for two nights to be regarded as living with you for one day.

Example

Your child is in care and comes home for half-term from Friday night in one week until Tuesday morning 10 days later. You are entitled to three weeks' child benefit because your child stayed with you for a whole week, with a day in both the week before and the week after.

The requirement that a child 'actually' be living with you is regarded very strictly, and even one night's absence by a child in hospital can result in benefit being lost. On the other hand, absence by you for two nights or so may be regarded less severely.[21] This is not a problem if the child 'ordinarily' lives with you at least one day a week because then it does not matter if the child is away during any particular week.

If you qualify for child benefit under these rules, you will still not receive it if you are receiving a boarding-out allowance from the local authority, unless the child has been placed with you for adoption and you were entitled to child benefit before 6 April 1987.[22]

Entitlement to child benefit is not affected by private fostering arrangements.

DSS Leaflet CH4A – *Social Security and Children Being Looked After by a Local Authority* – contains useful information.

Other children for whom child benefit is not payable

Child benefit is not payable in respect of a child who is:

* married[23] (unless the child is not living with her/his spouse or her/his spouse is in full-time education. A spouse can never be the claimant even in these circumstances[24]); *or*
* in remunerative work for at least 24 hours a week; [25] *or*
* receiving severe disablement allowance (see p81) or income support in her/his own right;[26] *or*
* receiving an allowance under the youth training scheme;[27] *or*
* in prison or other custody (see p258).[28]

A child 'living with' you

To be living with you, the child 'must live in the same house or other residence as [you] and also be carrying on there with [you] a settled course of daily living'.[29] This does not mean the same as 'residing together' or 'presence under the same roof'.[30] A child may be 'living with' you even while temporarily away. An absence for any reason of up to 56 days in 16 weeks is ignored.[31]

A child is still treated as living with you while receiving full-time education at a boarding school.[32]

You remain entitled to child benefit for a total of 12 weeks when a child goes into hospital, or into certain other forms of residential accommodation for medical purposes.[33] After this period, the child is treated as living with you only if you are regularly incurring expenditure in respect of her/him.[34] As long as you are making visits, this condition is likely to be satisfied.

Contributing to the maintenance of a child

To satisfy this condition you must contribute at the rate of at least the current rate of child benefit.[35]

Contributions must be regular although the odd hiccup may be ignored.[36] Payments may be in kind rather than cash.[37] If a husband and wife are residing together, any contribution by one may be treated as a contribution by the other.[38] Similarly, if you and another person each contribute less than the relevant rate to the maintenance of a child but your total contributions are greater than that amount, one of you will be treated as contributing the whole of it. If you do not agree on which one of you it is to be, the Secretary of State will decide.[39]

See p207 for the way the amount of contribution is calculated in difficult cases.

Priority between claimants

It is usually possible for more than one person to claim child benefit for the same child. For example, the child may be living with one parent and maintained by the other. There is an order of priority which governs who receives child benefit when two or more people would otherwise be entitled.

No one is entitled without making a claim for child benefit and this must be done before the priority rules apply.[40] Even if the new claim carries priority over an existing claim, child benefit continues for the next three weeks on the first claim.[41]

After that, claimants take priority in the following order:[42]

- person having the child living with her/him;
- wife, where husband and wife are 'residing together' (see p193);
- a parent (this includes a step-parent, adoptive parent and both parents of an illegitimate child);[43]
- mother, where the parents are unmarried and are residing together (see p193);
- in any other case, a person agreed by those entitled;
- a person selected by the Secretary of State.

If someone else has priority over you, the result is not just that child benefit cannot be *paid* to you. You are not *entitled* to benefit even if you fulfil all the other conditions of entitlement. So, for example, if your claim is refused because the child is living with someone else and s/he then comes to live with you, you must make a new claim even if you have been contributing to her/his maintenance at the appropriate rate all the time s/he was not living with you.

A person who has claimed child benefit and has priority can agree that someone else with lower priority should receive it by writing to the local Benefits Agency office.[44] It may be important to concede priority to a person looking after a child so that s/he can claim home responsibility protection (see p229). A couple may also think that it is fair for the person looking after the child to receive the child benefit.

The rules for deciding whether a couple are 'residing together' (or 'residing with' each other)[45] are not the same for child benefit (and one parent benefit – see p195) as for other benefits (see p206).

Married couples are treated as residing together unless *either*:

* they have been formally divorced or separated by a court order or deed of separation[46] (a *decree nisi* of divorce or judicial separation counts for this purpose; you do not have to wait until the *decree absolute*);[47] *or*
* they have been absent from each other for at least 91 consecutive days[48] (13 weeks); *and*
  - the reason for the absence is not that one or both of them is not an in-patient at a hospital;[49] *and*
  - the separation is likely to be permanent.[50]

The 13-week waiting period for a parent who is not formally separated or divorced applies even if the couple have never lived together.[51]

It is possible to be *absent* from your spouse even if you are living under the same roof as long as you are living as separate households.[52]

If a child's parents are **unmarried**, they are treated as residing together only if any absence from each other is temporary.[53]

Claims

You make a claim for child benefit on forms CB2 and CB3 obtainable from your local Benefits Agency office or by filling in the coupon in Benefits Agency Leaflet FB8 – *Babies and Benefits* – and sending it to the Benefits Agency by post.

Child benefit is administered from the Child Benefit Centre, PO Box 1, Newcastle upon Tyne, NE88 1AA. The public telephone number is 091-417 9999 but it is often engaged so it is best to send queries in writing, except in emergencies.

If you claim late you may receive up to six months' arrears of benefit,[54] unless someone else was receiving child benefit in respect of the same child.[55] That person's entitlement will usually continue for three weeks after your claim and then the benefit will be paid to you if you have priority over that person (see p192).

You cannot claim before a child is born because you will not know the precise date of birth. In other situations you can claim up to three months before you expect to be entitled to benefit, eg, when a child is returning from care, or when you have made an agreement over future receipts of child benefit.[56] On a first claim you will be asked to send the child's birth or adoption certificate.[57]

Payment

Child benefit is generally paid four-weekly in arrears either by order book or by credit transfer into your bank account (see p294).[58]

Weekly payments can be made only if:

- you were receiving child benefit before 16 March 1982, and you applied in writing before, or within 26 weeks after, your first four-weekly payment[59] (or from your return from abroad as a member or the partner of a member of the Forces[60]); or
- you are entitled to one parent benefit;[61] or
- you or your spouse or the person with whom you are living as husband and wife are entitled to income support or family credit;[62] or
- the Secretary of State is satisfied that four-weekly payment 'is causing hardship'.[63]

Weekly payment of benefit can be particularly important if you are receiving income support or family credit or are otherwise on a low income. Even if you are in one of these categories, you need to inform the Benefits Agency in writing that you want to receive the benefit weekly. In an urgent case you should contact your local Benefits Agency office; otherwise write to the Child Benefit Centre.

Special rules for parents from abroad

You are not entitled to child benefit for any week during which you (or your spouse if you are residing with him/her – see p193) have earnings on which you do not have to pay UK income tax because of double taxation treaties or rules giving exemption from liability to tax to foreign officials.[64]

One of the residence conditions for child benefit is a presence test for the claimant which means that she or he must physically present in Great Britain[65] (although temporary absences of up to eight weeks are discounted). If a child has more than one parent, one of whom spends a lot of time out of the country, it may be advisable for the other parent to claim child benefit even if he or she would not normally have priority (see p192). For more on the residence conditions and what happens if you or your child goes abroad see p243 and CPAG's *Ethnic Minorities' Benefits Handbook*.

Tax and other benefits

Child benefit is not taxable.[66]

If you are a single parent, you may be entitled to one parent benefit on top of child benefit (see p188).

If you are entitled to other social security benefits, you may be entitled to an increase in respect of a child for whom you receive child benefit (see p205). However, the 'overlapping benefits' rules (see p258) mean that the amount of the increase will be reduced by £1.20 to £9.80 per week for the eldest child (see p261).

Child benefit is taken into account as income for the purposes of income support.[67] If you have a child and are in full-time work but have a low income, you should ask your Benefits Agency office about family credit. Despite its misleading name, this is a weekly benefit and *not* a loan. Your child benefit order book tells you how much you can have for a family of your size so you can decide whether it is worth applying.

If your child is living with you, s/he will continue to be treated as your dependant for the purpose of means-tested benefits during the child benefit extension period (see CPAG's *National Welfare Benefits Handbook*).

2. ONE PARENT BENEFIT

Conditions of entitlement[1]

- You must be entitled to child benefit for a child who is living with you (see p191). For this benefit, it is not enough that you are contributing to his/her maintenance.
- You must not be residing together with your spouse if you are married (see below) or living with anyone else as husband or wife (see p193).
- You must not be residing together with (see p193) a parent of the child (unless you are entitled in respect of another child and are not residing with the parent of that child).

There are certain limitations if you are in receipt of other benefits (see p196).

The rules for deciding whether couples are *residing together* – and in particular the 91-day waiting period for couples who separate informally – are the same as for child benefit (see p193). In practical terms this means that a woman who is deserted by her husband (or a man who is deserted by his wife) and left to look after the children cannot get one parent benefit for 13 weeks.

Amount of payment

One parent benefit is £6.15 a week.[2]

It is payable as an addition to child benefit in respect of the eldest child who qualifies.

Tax and other benefits

One parent benefit is not taxable[3] but is taken into account as income for income support purposes.[4]

One parent benefit is not payable if you are being *paid* certain other benefits, in particular, child's special allowance or an increase of retirement pension, a widow's benefit or invalid care allowance in respect of the same child.[5] If you are *entitled* to one of these benefits but it is not being paid (perhaps because of the 'overlapping benefits' rules (see p258)), you can still be entitled to one parent benefit.

If you receive an increase of any other benefit in respect of the child, the increase will be reduced by the amount of your one parent benefit.[6]

Claims and payments

You claim on a form which is contained in DSS leaflet CH11. Alternatively, if you fill in the coupon in Benefits Agency Leaflet FB8 – *Babies and Benefits* – a claim form will be sent to you. The benefit is paid as part of your child benefit.

3. GUARDIAN'S ALLOWANCE

Guardian's allowance is a benefit paid to those looking after children who are effectively orphans.

Conditions of entitlement[1]

- The residence conditions must be satisfied; *and*
- you must be entitled to child benefit for the child; *and*
- the child must be a qualifying child (see p197); *and either*
  - the child must be living with you (see p191); *or*
  - you must contribute to the maintenance of the child at the rate of at

- least £11 a week in addition to any payment you are making to qualify you for child benefit (see p188).

Amount of payment

Guardian's allowance is £11 a week in respect of each child.[2]

Tax and other benefits

Guardian's allowance is not taxable.[3] It is taken into account as income for income support purposes[4] but not for other income-related benefits.[5] Guardian's allowance is not payable if you are receiving an increase of a social security benefit in respect of the child,[6] but since 12 April 1993 it can be paid in addition to one parent benefit (see p195).[7]

Claims

You claim on form BG1 – see DSS leaflet NI14 for details. You should claim within six months of being entitled to guardian's allowance. If you claim later, only six months' arrears will be paid.[8] If you are looking after a child of whom you are not a parent and you do not qualify for guardian's allowance you might consider approaching the local authority social services department for a fostering fee.

Children who qualify

A child will qualify if:[9]

- both the child's parents have died; *or*
- one of the child's parents has died and the whereabouts of the other parent are unknown and were unknown at the time of the death of the first parent (you must show that you have taken reasonable steps to find the missing parent, including asking known relatives and friends and checking on old addresses[10]); *or*
- one of the child's parents is dead and the other is sentenced to a term of imprisonment greater than five years (see p198).

A **step-parent** does not count as a parent and so may be entitled to guardian's allowance in respect of a step-child.[11]

If a child is adopted, her/his adoptive parents are the ones who count as parents.[12] Guardian's allowance will be payable if both the adoptive parents have died or if one has died and the other has disappeared or is in prison. If a child is adopted by one person only, a claim can be made for guardian's allowance if that one person dies. If a child's adoptive parents have died, the child's natural parents may claim guardian's allowance.[13] However, adoptive parents may continue to receive guardian's allowance if they were entitled to it immediately before the adoption.[14]

If a child is illegitimate, guardian's allowance is payable after the death of the mother, provided that paternity has not been clearly established or admitted by the father.[15]

If a child's natural or adoptive parents were divorced, and one parent has died and the other did not have custody of the child (and was neither maintaining the child nor liable under a court order to do so), guardian's allowance is payable to a claimant other than the surviving parent.[16]

Prison sentences

The rules for calculating the length of a parent's prison sentence are complicated.[17] They apply to other custodial sentences (such as detention in a young offenders' institution).

No period before the death of the other parent is taken into account.

Any period on remand (after the death of the other parent) is added to the sentence. This is despite the fact that the sentence will be treated as reduced by the period on remand for the purpose of calculating the date for the prisoner's release. The result is that a parent sentenced to four and a half years' imprisonment after being in custody on remand for nine months counts, whereas a person who receives the same sentence after being on bail does not. This is even more surprising because no benefit is payable for a period before sentence is passed and the person who has been in custody on remand can expect to be released sooner than the person who was on bail.

Consecutive sentences are added together but, if they are not imposed on the same date, any part of a short sentence served before the imposition of a later sentence (which takes the total to over five years) is ignored.

The allowance ceases to be payable when the parent is released from prison unless the release is only temporary. If the parent is transferred to hospital or escapes, guardian's allowance continues to be payable until the date when the sentence would have been served (without remission). If s/he is then returned to prison after the allowance has ceased to be payable, s/he is treated as serving a sentence equal to the remainder of the original sentence (plus any further consecutive sentence).

4. CHILD'S SPECIAL ALLOWANCE

Child's special allowance, designed to provide some assistance to a woman who did not receive widowed mother's allowance because she was divorced from her ex-husband before he died, was abolished on 6 April 1987.[1] However, if you were receiving it on that date you will continue to be paid until:[2]

- you cease to be entitled (or to be treated as entitled – see p206) to child benefit for a child; *or*
- you remarry; *or*
- you and a man live together as husband and wife (see p99).

The rate of payment is £11 a week for each child.[3]

5. INDUSTRIAL DEATH BENEFIT FOR CHILDREN

This is not payable if the death was after 10 April 1988. However, usually either an increase of widowed mother's allowance or guardian's allowance is payable instead.

Conditions of entitlement [1]

- The deceased person died before 11 April 1988.
- The deceased person died as a result of an industrial accident or disease (see p101).
- At the time of her/his death, the deceased was entitled to (or, treated as entitled to) child benefit in respect of the child.
- The widow of the deceased is entitled to industrial death benefit.
- The claimant is entitled (or may be treated as entitled – see p206) to child benefit in respect of the child.
- *Either* the claimant is the widow; *or* the widow was, immediately before the claim, entitled to death benefit at the higher permanent rate (see p108) *and* she has not ceased to reside with the child.

The effect of this last condition is that industrial death benefit for a child continues to be paid if a widow lives with a man as husband and wife. The reason for this is that the widow remains *entitled* to industrial death benefit in respect of herself even though it is not *payable* while she is cohabiting.[2] The benefit may be claimed by the man with whom she is living.

Children who qualify

Benefit is paid for a child in respect of whom the deceased was entitled to child benefit. The deceased is also treated as if s/he had been entitled to child benefit if the child:[3]

- was a child of the deceased and either the deceased or his wife was either living with (see p191) the child or contributing to the child's maintenance (see p192) at the appropriate rate (or would have been but for the relevant accident or onset of the disease); *or*
- was a posthumous child of the deceased; *or*
- was wholly or mainly maintained by the deceased at the time of her/his death (or would have been but for the relevant accident or onset of disease); *or*
- was a child living with or maintained by the deceased's wife if she had been widowed before and her previous husband had been living with or maintaining the child when he died.

Amount of payment

Death benefit is paid at the rate of £11 a week in respect of each child.[4]

CHAPTER ELEVEN

Increases for dependants

This chapter covers:

1. Introduction (see below)
2. Extra money for your wife (p202)
3. Extra money for your husband (p203)
4. Extra money if you are not married (p203)
5. Extra money for your children (p205)
6. Residence and maintenance (p206)
7. The earnings rules (p208)
8. Trade disputes (p210)
9. Tax (p211)
10. Miscellaneous rules (p211)

I. INTRODUCTION

If you are getting:

- invalid care allowance;
- invalidity benefit;
- severe disablement allowance;
- Category A or C retirement pension;

or if you are over pensionable age and are getting:

- unemployment benefit; *or*
- sickness benefit;

you may get extra money for your dependants (ie, your wife, husband, child or someone who looks after your child for you) on top of the basic benefit.

If you are getting:

- Category B retirement pension; *or*
- widowed mother's allowance;

you may be able to get extra money for any children who you look after (but not for any adult dependant).

If you are getting:

- maternity allowance;

or if you are under pensionable age and are getting:

- unemployment benefit; *or*
- sickness benefit;

you may be able to get extra money for an adult dependant (but not for any child).

2. EXTRA MONEY FOR YOUR WIFE

Conditions of entitlement [1]

- you must be entitled to the basic benefit; *and*
- you must also make a separate claim for the increase within the time limits (see p280);[2] *and either*
- you are 'residing with' your wife (see p206); *or*
- you are 'contributing to the maintenance' of your wife (see p207) at a weekly rate equal to or greater than the standard amount of the increase (see below).

If you are getting **invalid care allowance** you must 'reside with' your wife to get the increase. You cannot qualify just by contributing to her maintenance.

Even if you meet these conditions there is an **earnings rule** (see p208) which may disqualify you from being paid an increase if your wife is working or has an occupational pension of her own.

The **overlapping benefits** rules (see p258) apply if your wife is claiming a benefit in her own right. This is a frequent source of overpayments (see p295) and it is very important that when you complete the claim form your statement of the benefits which your wife is receiving is accurate.

Amount of benefit

Increases are paid as follows:[3]

	£pw
Unemployment benefit (claimant not over pensionable age)	28.05
Unemployment benefit (claimant over pensionable age)	34.50

Sickness benefit	
(claimant not over pensionable age)	26.90
Sickness benefit	
(claimant over pensionable age)	33.10
Invalidity benefit	34.50
Severe disablement allowance	20.70
Maternity allowance	26.90
Invalid care allowance	20.65
Category A retirement pension	34.50

3. EXTRA MONEY FOR YOUR HUSBAND

If you are a woman, you can get an increase for your husband in the same circumstances and at the same rates as a man can get one for his wife. But there are two exceptions:

- a woman cannot ever get an increase in her Category C retirement pension to cover her husband; *and*
- a woman can only get an increase in her Category A retirement pension to cover her husband if:
  - immediately before she became entitled to the basic pension she was entitled to unemployment benefit, sickness benefit or invalidity benefit including an increase for him; *and*
  - she has not stopped residing with her husband or contributing to his maintenance at the appropriate weekly rate for a single day since she became entitled to the basic Category A pension. [1]

These rules discriminate directly against women, but a commissioner has held that the rule on Category A retirement pension is not unlawful discrimination because it falls within an exception to the EC Equal Treatment Directive (see p270) which allows discrimination where it is the consequence of setting different retirement ages for men and women. [2] In the light of more recent cases (see pp271-274) this decision may well be incorrect. [3] If you are a woman and are refused an increase which you would get if you were a man, you should appeal and ask your local advice agency to contact CPAG's solicitor for advice.

4. EXTRA MONEY IF YOU ARE NOT MARRIED

Even if you are not married (or are married to someone else) you may get an increase if your dependant is looking after a child for whom you are responsible.

Most people who benefit under these rules are living together as husband and wife with one partner looking after the child rather than working.

But other people can benefit as well. In particular, it is not necessary for you and your dependant to be of different sexes, so gay or lesbian couples may be entitled as may, for example, two widows with children who live together for mutual support.

Conditions of entitlement [1]

* you must be entitled to the basic benefit; *and*
* you must also make a separate claim for the increase within the time limits (see p280);[2] *and*
* your dependant has care of a child; *and either*
* you are entitled to child benefit for that child; *or*
* you are treated as entitled to child benefit for that child (see p206); *and*
* you reside with your dependant (see p206); *or*
* you contribute to the maintenance (see p207) of your dependant at a rate equal to at least the standard rate of the increase; *or*
* you employ your dependant at a cost to you of at least the standard rate of the increase and the employment started before you became unemployed, incapable of work or retired (whichever applies to you) unless the need for you to employ your dependant arose afterwards; *and*
* you do not also get an increase for your husband or wife.

If you are getting **invalid care allowance** you must 'reside with' your dependant to get the increase. You cannot qualify just by contributing to her/his maintenance or employing her/him.

There is the same **earnings rule** as for dependent wives and husbands (see p208) except that any money which you pay your dependant for caring for the child is ignored.

If your dependant is claiming benefit in her/his own right the **overlapping benefits** rules apply (see p258). This is a frequent source of overpayments (see p295) and it is very important that when you complete the claim form your statement of the benefits which your wife is receiving is accurate.

If you are getting **Category A** or **Category C retirement pensions**, your dependant must be a woman.[3] You may be able to argue that this rule is indirect discrimination and unlawful under EC law (see p267). If you are a woman with a male dependant and would be entitled to an increase if he were female; you should appeal and ask your local advice agency to contact CPAG's solicitor for further advice. You should do this as soon as possible because you will have to prove as a fact that more men have female dependants to whom they are not married and who look after their children than vice versa. This will have to be done at your appeal to the SSAT (see p303) because social security commissioners only have jurisdiction to decide questions of law (see p313).

Amount of benefit

The increase is paid for the same benefits and at the same rates as for spouses (see p202).[4]

5. EXTRA MONEY FOR YOUR CHILDREN

Conditions of entitlement [1]

- *Either* you are entitled to invalidity benefit, severe disablement allowance, invalid care allowance, a Category A, B or C retirement pension, widowed mother's allowance (or the corresponding, non-contributory benefit); *or*
- you are over pensionable age (see p113) and entitled to unemployment benefit or sickness benefit; *and*
- you make a separate claim for the increase within the time limits (see p280);[2] *and either*
- you are entitled to child benefit for a child; *or*
- you are treated as entitled to child benefit for the child (see p200); *and either*
- the child lives with you; *or*
- you contribute to the maintenance (see p207) of the child at a rate of at least £11 a week in addition to the amount you must contribute in order to entitle you to child benefit (see p188).

There is an **earnings rule** (see p208) which may stop you getting the increase if you are living with your husband or wife or cohabiting and your partner has a job or occupational pension.

If you are getting an increase in widow's benefit, retirement pension or invalid care allowance for a child, you cannot also get one parent benefit. In addition, the overlapping benefits rules (see p261) mean that if you are getting one parent benefit for a child, an increase in any other benefit for that child will be reduced by the amount of the one parent benefit. They also mean that guardian's allowance cannot be paid if there is an increase for the child. Only one increase may be paid for any individual child even if more than one person meets the conditions of entitlement.

Amount of benefit

The increase is payable for invalidity pension, severe disablement allowance, invalid care allowance and Category A, B and C retirement pensions. It is also payable for unemployment and sickness benefit but only if you are over pensionable age (see pp6 and 201-202). Widowed mother's allowance and the corresponding non-contributory widow's benefit are increased only for qualifying children' (see p105).

The basic rate of the increase is £11 for each child[3] but this will be reduced by £1.20 for the eldest child because of the overlapping benefits rules (see p261).

When can you be treated as entitled to child benefit?

If you do not yourself receive child benefit for a child, you will still be treated as doing so if:[4]

• you are residing with (see below) a parent of a child who is receiving child benefit; *and either*
• you are also a parent of the child; *or*
• you are 'wholly or mainly maintaining' the child (see p208).

This means that if a child lives with both parents and the mother receives child benefit, the father may still claim an increase for the child. But a stepfather can only claim the increase if he is 'wholly or mainly maintaining' the child (see p208).

If you do not benefit from these rules, you may still qualify for an increase if you arrange for child benefit to be transferred to you (see p193).

6. RESIDENCE AND MAINTENANCE

'Residing with'

'Residing with' means that you and your husband, wife or other dependant have a common household. This rarely causes difficulties in practice.

Temporary absences do not stop two people from being treated as residing with each other[1] and you are also treated as residing with your husband or wife when either or both of you are in hospital, even if the stay in hospital is likely to be permanent.[2]

It does not mean the same as 'living with' (see p191) and the rules on whether a couple are residing with each other for the purposes of dependency increases are not the same as for child benefit and one parent benefit (see pp193).

'Contributing to the maintenance'

'Contributing to the maintenance' means that you are making **regular** payments to or on behalf of a person. Generally, a payment covers you only for the week after it is made, but payments will be spread over a longer period if that is what you originally intended.[3] For example, you can make regular monthly payments and they will be treated as covering the month beginning with the week after they were made. Payments may be in kind.[4]

If you make a regular payment **for more than one person**, the total payment will be allocated between your dependants in the way that is most advantageous to you (even if you pay under a court order which specifies the amounts in respect of each person).[5] If the payment includes an element of arrears it is ignored.[6]

Example

You receive invalidity benefit and pay under a court order £60 a week representing £10 to your wife, £20 for each of your two children and £10 off outstanding arrears. You will be treated as paying £50 a week which will be allocated as £34.50 to your wife and £11 to your first child so as to enable you to claim increases for them. You, therefore, receive £45.50 a week by way of increases rather than just £22 a week for two children.

If you have stopped maintaining a person, you cannot later cover yourself by making a payment in arrears.[7] A broad view is taken of an interruption in otherwise regular payments.[8] If you are not paying enough, but think you are, a payment of arrears may be taken into account.[9] A woman entitled to an increase of unemployment or sickness benefit who becomes entitled to a higher increase is deemed to have been contributing at the higher rate if she was contributing sufficient to be entitled to the lower increase.[10]

If more than one member of a household contributes to the household income, the extent to which any member of the household supports any other is calculated using the **family fund test**.[11] To apply this, you calculate the unit cost of each member of the family by dividing the household income by the number of members of the family (treating each child as half an adult). Each person who contributes more than her/his unit cost is then treated as contributing to the maintenance of all the others. The amount of the contribution to any individual is calculated by dividing that individual's deficit proportionately between those providing a surplus.

This calculation is made before you became unemployed, incapable of work or retired.[12] Subsequent changes are ignored but you must contribute the amount of the increase to remain entitled to it.[13]

If you are contributing to the family fund out of income support which you are claiming, you are still treated as making the contribution from your own funds.[14] Remember, the conditions of entitlement for the increases mean that it is *never* necessary to prove that you are 'contributing to the maintenance' of an adult dependant if you are residing with' her/him.

'Living with'

'Living with' means the same as for entitlement to child benefit (see p191).

'Wholly or mainly maintaining'

'Wholly or mainly maintaining' means that:[15]

- while you are on benefit you are contributing towards the maintenance of your dependant at a weekly rate equal to or greater than the amount of the increase; *and*
- before you claimed benefit you contributed more than half the actual cost of maintaining your dependant (unless your dependant did not become dependent until after you claimed benefit).

If two or more people are 'wholly or mainly maintaining' someone between them, they may agree by a majority that one of them will get the increase. The agreement must be in the form of a signed letter to the Secretary of State.[16]

If there is no agreement the increase will be paid to the person .who contributes most (even if, on her/his own s/he contributes less than half the cost of maintaining the dependant) or, if everyone contributes equally, to the eldest.[17] It may be necessary to use the 'family fund test' (see p207) to decide who is contributing what to whom.

7. THE EARNINGS RULES

Adult dependants

If you are residing with your dependant *and* are claiming an increase in invalidity benefit, severe disablement allowance or Category A or C retirement pension, your increase will not be paid if, in the previous week, your dependant earned more than £45.45.[1]

This limit does not apply if you have been continuously entitled to an increase *in the same benefit* [2] since 14 September 1985, although in that case if your dependant's earnings exceed £45 the increase will be reduced by five pence for each complete 10 pence above that figure up to £49, and five pence for each complete five pence your dependant earns after that. [3] Unless your dependant's income is between £45.10 and £45.44 – in which case the normal rule will be applied to you – this is more favourable than the normal rule where you could lose all your increase (up to £34.50 per week) if your dependant's earnings went a penny over £45.45.

In any other case (ie, if you are not residing with your dependant or if you are claiming an increase in any other benefit), your increase will not be paid if your dependant's earnings in the previous week were more than the standard rate of the increase which you have claimed (see pp202-203). [4]

Because the earnings rule is more generous for invalidity than for sickness benefit, you may not have been entitled to an increase while you were receiving sickness benefit but may qualify after you transfer to invalidity pension. It is then necessary to make a separate claim for the increase.

For how earnings are calculated, see p261.

If your dependant's earnings fluctuate, you will not automatically lose your entitlement to the increase every time your dependant earns too much in a particular week (although you will have no right to be paid benefit during the following week if that happens). [5] This is important. It means that you do not have to make a fresh claim every time your dependant's earnings exceed the limit. It also means that if you were claiming on 14 September 1985 you can continue to benefit from the more generous earnings rules which were in force before that date (see above).

A decision of the Court of Appeal [6] means that many claimants whose adult dependants had an occupational pension but no job and whose increases were refused or reduced because of the earnings rule may be entitled to substantial arrears. You are affected if:

- You are a man and at any time between 11 March 1988 and 5 December 1992 you were entitled to a Category A or C retirement pension; *and*
  - your wife was under 60; *and*
  - you were 'residing with' her (see p206); *and*
  - she had an occupational pension; *but*
  - she had no job.
- You are a man and at any time between 11 March 1988 and 5 December 1992 you were entitled to invalidity benefit or severe disablement allowance; *and*

- you were 'residing with' your wife; *and*
- she had an occupational pension; *but*
- she had no job.
- You are a woman and at any time between 11 March 1988 and 5 December 1992 you were entitled to a Category A retirement pension and an increase of that pension for your dependent husband; *and*
  - your husband had an occupational pension; *but*
  - he had no job.

People who receive an unemployability supplement to their disability pension (see p178) may also benefit.

Anyone who is affected should take advice immediately as the DSS are relying on the 'anti-test-case' rules (see p284) to refuse to pay arrears. You should apply to the chair of your local SSAT for permission ('leave') to make a late appeal (see p318). If this is refused ask the adjudication officer at your local Benefits Agency office for a review (see p288). This will probably be decided against you and you should then appeal. Ask the clerk to the tribunal not to list your appeal until the *Bate* case (see p285) has been decided by the Court of Appeal.

The Court of Appeal decision has also raised the possibility that there has been no legal basis for an earnings rule for any dependants' increases for the claimants of any benefit (except invalid care allowance) between 16 September 1985 and 4 December 1992 – even in those cases when the dependant was working. If so, many more claimants would be entitled to arrears. A further test case will be brought to clarify the position and developments will be reported in CPAG's *Welfare Rights Bulletin*.

Child dependants[7]

If you are living with your husband or wife or cohabiting, you will not get an increase for your first child for any week if in the previous week your partner earned more than £120; for each complete £16 per week s/he earns, in addition to £120, you lose entitlement for another child. So if you have three children and your partner earns £136 a week, you will get an increase for only one child.

8. TRADE DISPUTES[1]

If your dependant is disqualified from unemployment benefit because of a trade dispute (see p41) (or would have been disqualified if s/he had claimed unemployment benefit) you are not entitled to an increase. If you have been claiming an increase since before 14 September 1985, the benefit of the 'tapered' earnings rule (see p209) will be lost forever as a result of even a one-day strike.[2]

9. TAX [1]

Increases of unemployment benefit and retirement pensions for adult dependants are taxable. Other increases (including all increases for children) are not.

10. MISCELLANEOUS RULES

Increases may be affected if you or your dependant go into hospital (see p256) or to prison (see p257). It is important to note that your increase may not be affected in the same way as your basic benefit. Increases are also treated separately under the overlapping benefits rules (see p260).

PART THREE

General provisions

CHAPTER TWELVE

Contributions and earnings-related pensions

This chapter covers:

1. Introduction (see below)
2. Payment of contributions (p217)
3. Credits and home responsibilities protection (p225)
4. Contribution conditions for benefits (p231)
5. The State Earnings Related Pension Scheme (SERPS) (p235)
6. Future changes (p239)

1. INTRODUCTION

As was mentioned in Chapter 1, many of the benefits described in this guide are financed from the national insurance fund which is made up of the social security contributions paid by employees, their employers, the self-employed and other people who choose to make them.

In turn, entitlement to those benefits – and, for long-term benefits, the amount paid – depends upon the contribution record of the claimant or, in the case of widows' benefits, of her husband. For the contribution conditions for benefits, see p231.

Fixed percentages of social security contributions go towards the cost of the National Health Service. The rest is paid into the national insurance fund.[1]

Most contributions are collected for the DSS by the Inland Revenue but the ultimate responsibility for ensuring that contributions are paid correctly lies with part of the DSS called the **Contributions Agency**. The Contributions Agency also keeps the records of your contributions throughout your working life.

Classes of contribution

There are five different classes of contribution.[2] The class you pay depends upon whether you are an **employee, self-employed** or a **voluntary contributor**. Not all classes of contributions count for all benefits.[3]

Class of contribution	Payable by	Giving entitlement to
Class 1	employed earners and their employers	all benefits with contribution conditions
Class 1A	employers of employed earners	no benefits
Class 2	self-employed earners	all benefits with contribution conditions except unemployment benefit (but see p222)
Class 3	voluntary contributors	widows' benefits and retirement pensions
Class 4	self-employed earners	no benefits

The amount of Class 1 or Class 4 contributions you pay depends upon your earnings. However, you do not necessarily gain more benefit by paying higher contributions.

Employed earners and self-employed earners

The distinction between being employed and self-employed is usually clear but there are sometimes grey areas.

An **employed earner** is defined as 'a person who is 'gainfully employed in Great Britain either under a contract of service, or in an office (including elective office) with emoluments chargeable to income tax under Schedule E'.[4]

A **self-employed earner** is anyone 'gainfully employed in Great Britain otherwise than in employed earner's employment'.[5] If you have two jobs it is possible to be both employed and self-employed.

There is not usually much dispute over whether you hold an office or not. Office-holders are such people as company directors, registrars of births, deaths and marriages and so on.

The usual area of dispute is whether you are employed under a contract *of* service or a contract *for* services. This can be a complicated question and the Secretary of State must take into account a number of factors such as how closely your work is supervised, whether you can employ a substitute to do your job for you, the method of payment, whether the contract is for a fixed period, whether you have to provide your own equipment, where you work and the amount of freedom you have to decide when you work and how much work you must do. No one criterion is conclusive and different aspects may have different weight attached to them in different cases.[6]

Certain people are deemed to be employed earners.[7] These are office cleaners, many agency workers, people employed by their spouses for the purposes of their spouses' employment, lecturers, teachers and instructors (but not if the instruction is for no more than three days in any three months or is given as public lectures) and most ministers of religion. Conversely examiners, moderators and invigilators are deemed to be self-employed.[8]

You do not have to pay contributions if your job is:[9]

- employment in your home by a close relative if you *both* live in the home *and* the employment is not for the purposes of any trade or business carried on there. Close relatives are parent, grandparent, step-parent, son, daughter, step-son, step-daughter, brother, sister, half-brother or half-sister;
- employment by your spouse if it is not for the purposes of your spouse's employment;
- employment as a self-employed earner if you are not ordinarily self-employed; employment as a returning officer (etc) at an election;
- employment by certain international organisations or foreign armed forces (but only in certain circumstances).

Upper and lower earnings limits

Contributions are now paid by reference to the tax year (ie, 6 April to 5 April).[10] For each tax year there is an **upper earnings limit** and a **lower earnings limit**.[11] Employees are liable to pay Class 1 contributions on weekly earnings between those limits. Since the present system was adopted in 1975, the earnings limits have been as follows:

Year	Lower earnings limit	Upper earnings limit
1975-76	£11.00	£69.00
1976-77	£13.00	£95.00
1977-78	£15.00	£105.00
1978-79	£17.50	£120.00
1979-80	£19.50	£135.00
1980-81	£23.00	£165.00
1981-82	£27.00	£200.00
1982-83	£29.50	£220.00
1983-84	£32.50	£235.00
1984-85	£34.00	£250.00
1985-86	£35.50	£265.00
1986-87	£38.00	£285.00
1987-88	£39.00	£295.00
1988-89	£41.00	£305.00
1989-90	£43.00	£325.00
1990-91	£46.00	£350.00
1991-92	£52.00	£390.00
1992-93	£54.00	£405.00
1993-94	£56.00	£420.00
1994-95	£57.00	£430.00

Earnings factors

The amount of earnings upon which your Class 1 contributions have been paid is said to be the 'earnings factor' derived from those contributions. Each Class 2 and Class 3 contribution gives rise to an earnings factor equal to that year's lower earnings limit. [12]

Earnings factors are used to calculate entitlement to basic benefits and the additional pension payable under SERPS (see p235).

Decisions relating to contributions

These are made by the Secretary of State [13] and not by an adjudication officer, which means that you cannot appeal to a tribunal, although there are other ways of contesting a decision (see p286). One issue the Secretary of State must decide is whether you are employed or self-employed. Disputes can also arise over a person's contribution record. The Secretary of State relies heavily on a Contributions Agency computer at Newcastle-upon-Tyne but will often accept that the computer is not perfect if you can explain why you think the computer record is wrong.

2. PAYMENT OF CONTRIBUTIONS

Age limits

Contributions are intended to be paid during a normal working life. They are not therefore payable by those under the minimum school-leaving age of 16,[1] nor by those over pensionable age (65 for men, 60 for women).[2] The DSS should send you a certificate of age exemption when you reach pensionable age. Ask at your local office if it does not. Employers of employees over pensionable age still have to pay contributions at the full (contracted-in) rate.

These rules discriminate against men (and in some circumstances also against women) on the grounds of sex but the European Court has held that they are not contrary to EC law (see p273).[3]

Residence and presence in Great Britain

Class 1 contributions must usually be paid by employees who are employed in Great Britain[4] and either resident or present (except for temporary absence) or ordinarily resident in Great Britain at the time of the employment.[5] However, if you are employed by an overseas employer and are not ordinarily resident or employed in the UK, you are not liable for Class 1 contributions until you have been resident in Great Britain for a year.[6] This also applies to certain foreign students and apprentices.[7]

If you are working abroad, you must still pay Class 1 contributions for the first year if your employers have a place of business in Great Britain, you were resident in Great Britain before your employment started and you are still ordinarily resident in Great Britain.[8] After that year you are entitled, but not obliged, to pay **Class 3 contributions**.[9]

Class 2 contributions are compulsory if you are self-employed in Great Britain and are either ordinarily resident in Great Britain, or have been resident here for at least 26 weeks during the last year.[10] If you are present in Great Britain, they may be paid voluntarily if you are not required to pay them.[11] If you are self-employed outside Great Britain, you may pay Class 2 contributions if you wish, provided you were employed or self-employed immediately before you left Great Britain and, *either*:

- you have been resident in Great Britain for a continuous period of at least three years at some time in the past; *or*
- you have paid contributions producing an earnings factor of at least 52 times the lower earnings limit in each of three years in the past. Each set of 52 flat-rate contributions paid before April 1975 counts as satisfying that condition in respect of one year.[12]

You may also pay Class 2 contributions if you are a **volunteer development worker** resident in Great Britain but employed outside Great Britain and not liable to pay Class 1 contributions. These are paid at a special rate and give entitlement to unemployment benefit, but are payable only if the Secretary of State certifies that it would be consistent with the proper administration of the legislation to allow you to do so.[13]

Class 3 contributions are always voluntary. They may be paid if you are resident in Great Britain during the course of the year in respect of which you wish to pay the contributions. They are payable while you are abroad if you satisfy either of the conditions which would allow you to pay Class 2 contributions but it is not necessary for you to have been employed or self-employed before you left Great Britain. You may also pay them if you have been paying Class 1 contributions while abroad.[14]

Class 4 contributions are payable only if you are resident in the UK for income tax purposes.[15]

For those who pay Class 2 or 3 contributions, the old system of buying stamps at the post office each week was abolished in April 1993. Instead, the Contributions Agency will send you a bill each quarter or you may ask to pay by direct debit. For more details, see DSS leaflet CA05 – *Self-Employed and Voluntary Contributors* – 'Payment by Quarterly Bill'.

If you wish to pay contributions while abroad, obtain DSS leaflet NI38 which contains an application form.

When you return to Great Britain, it is a good idea to notify the Contributions Agency so that you can be told of any deficiency in your contribution record that you might remedy, and so that your future contribution record is accurately tied in with your past record.

The meaning of the terms 'resident' and 'present' are explained on p244. Members of the Armed Forces are deemed always to be present in Great Britain and there are special rules for aircrew, mariners, share fishermen and offshore workers on the continental shelf.

For the factors which are taken into account in deciding where you are ordinarily resident see p245.

It should also be noted that Northern Ireland and Isle of Man contributions count towards British benefits and so can contributions paid in other countries in some circumstances. Also you may be entitled to benefits from other countries while you are in this country (see Chapter 13).

Reduced liability for married women and widows

Newly married or widowed women now pay the same level of contributions as anyone else. Until 5 April 1977 they could choose to pay a reduced Class 1, or no Class 2, contribution. Women who had done so were able to choose to continue payment at this reduced level of contribution.[16] The disadvantage is that there is no later entitlement to any benefit except industrial injury and no right (except for widows) to receive credits when these would otherwise be made, eg, during sickness.[17]

A married woman whose husband dies while she is taking advantage of this provision loses her right to continue to do so unless she is receiving a widow's benefit. The right is lost at the end of the tax year in which her husband dies or the end of the next year if he dies after 30 September.[18]

The right to opt for reduced liability is also automatically lost:[19]

- on divorce or annulment of marriage;
- at the end of the tax year in which she stops receiving a widow's benefit;
- after two tax years with no earnings;
- at the end of a tax year in which a Class 1 contracted-out contribution (see p221) is paid by mistake but the woman wishes to pay such contributions;
- when a Class 1 contracted-in contribution (see below) is paid by mistake but the woman wishes to continue paying it, has asked for no refund, has not since paid any reduced or contracted-out rate contributions and confirms to the Secretary of State that she wishes to

pay the full rate before the end of the calendar year after the tax year in which she starts to pay the full contributions, eg, 31 December 1994 for the tax year 1992-93.

It is worth thinking carefully about your position if you are currently taking advantage of the reduced liability. Once lost, the right cannot be reclaimed. On the one hand, if you continue with the reduced liability, you are not accumulating entitlement to contributory benefits. On the other hand, you can still receive widows' benefits and Category B retirement pension on your husband's record, non-contributory benefits (such as attendance allowance or disability living allowance), and means-tested benefits (such as income support). Bear in mind the extent to which your pension entitlement will be improved by paying contributions now, but remember that home responsibilities protection (see p229) is only available if the election to pay the reduced amount is revoked. Also you could gain an additional pension under SERPS if you start paying full Class 1 contributions now, but you could consider putting the money into a private scheme instead.

It is very difficult to give general advice. Quite a lot depends on individual circumstances, such as the amount you earn, the security of your employment, your state of health, your age and whether you are sufficiently well-off to be disqualified from income support. Ask your union or local citizens' advice bureau for advice.

To revoke your election, fill in the form in DSS leaflet NI1 for married women or NI51 for widows.

Class 1 contributions

Class 1 contributions are paid both by **employed** earners (see p175 – known as primary contributors) and their **employers** (secondary contributors).[20] Both your liability and your employers' liability depend upon the amount of your earnings in relation to the lower and upper earnings limits (see p216). These earnings limits are currently £57 and £430 a week. If your earnings are monthly, the earnings limits are multiplied by $4^{1}/_{3}$ to give monthly equivalents.[21]

If you are **not contracted out of SERPS** (see p235), the rate of your contribution is 2 per cent of earnings below the lower earnings limit plus 10 per cent of your earnings between the lower and upper earnings limits.[22]

Example

If your weekly earnings are £177 your Class 1 contribution is:

2% of £57 + 10% of £120 = £1.14 + £12 = £13.14

The most an employee can have to pay is £38.44 a week (ie, 2 per cent of £57 plus 10 per cent of £373).

If you are **contracted out of SERPS** (see p235), the rate of your contribution is 2 per cent of earnings below the lower earnings limit plus 8.2 per cent of your earnings between the lower and upper earnings limits.[23] So, the most you can have to pay is £31.73 a week.

Although your contributions to the national insurance fund are lower if you are contracted out, you probably pay more than 2 per cent of your earnings into your occupational pension scheme instead.

If you are a member of an **appropriate personal pension scheme** (see p236), you pay Class 1 contributions at the contracted-in rate but the Secretary of State then pays to the scheme a sum equal to the difference between the contracted-in and contracted-out rates.[24]

If you are a **married woman or widow with reduced liability** for contributions (see p219), you pay 3.85 per cent of your earnings up to the upper earnings limit but your employers pay at the usual rate.[25]

There are also **special rates** for members of the armed forces and the employers of certain mariners employed on foreign-going ships.[26]

If you have **more than one job**, obtain DSS leaflet NP28 which gives details of the arrangements which apply. Basically, contributions are payable on all earnings up to a maximum figure which is equal to the maximum that would be payable if you had only one employment.[27]

Your employers' liability is calculated differently from yours. Again, there is no liability if your earnings are below the lower earnings limit. If they are above that, your employer pays a contribution calculated as a percentage of your earnings. There are reduced rates if you earn below £200 a week but, unlike you, your employers must pay the same rate on your earnings below the lower earnings limit and on any earnings above the upper earnings limit (unless you are contracted out of SERPS).[28]

Weekly earnings £pw	Rate of contribution (%)
57-99.99	3.6
100-144.99	56
145-199.99	7.6
200 and above	10.2

If you are contracted out of SERPS, your employers pay three per cent less on that part of your earnings between the lower and upper limits.[29]

Example
If you are contracted out of SERPS and your weekly earnings are £140, your employers' contribution is:

5.6% of £57 + 2.6% of £83 = £3.19 + £2.16 = £5.35

If you are contracted out of SERPS and your weekly earnings are 475, your employers' contribution is:

10.2% of £57 + 7.2% of £373 + 10.2% of £45
= £5.81 + £26.86 + £4.59 = £37.26

Your employers should deduct your Class 1 contributions from your earnings and pay them with their own contributions to the Inland Revenue.[30] See p224 for what happens if they do not.

Class 1A contributions [31]

Class 1A contributions are paid by **employers**. They are only payable if an employee has the use of a company car and is charged at 10.2 per cent of the 'cash equivalent' of the benefit to the employee of the car and any fuel. This is calculated in the same way as for income tax.

Class 2 contributions

Class 2 contributions must be paid by **self-employed earners** (see p215) unless you have a certificate of exemption on the grounds of income p223 a certain level (£3,200 in 1994-95; £3,140 in 1993-94; £3,030 in 1992-93).[32]

You must apply for a certificate as soon as possible because it can only be backdated up to 13 weeks before the date of application, [33] although repayment of contributions is now possible – see below. The application form is included in DSS leaflet NI27A. It is sometimes possible to have the calculation of your earnings deferred until the end of the year (see DSS leaflet NP18) and thus wait and see if you do or do not have sufficiently low earnings. Usually your earnings are estimated; your earnings will be estimated as below the minimum level if they were below that level in the previous year and there has been 'no material change of circumstances'. Expenses are excluded from earnings.[34]

You *must* pay contributions unless you have a certificate; you *may* pay them even if you do have a certificate.[35] Married women and widows with reduced liability for contributions (see p219) are not liable for Class 2 contributions.

Class 2 contributions are payable at a flat rate.[36] The current and recent rates are:

1992-93	£5.35 a week
1993-94	£5.55 a week
1994-95	£5.65 a week

Volunteer development workers overseas (see p218) and **share fishermen**

pay contributions at special rates (£3.19 and £7.75 a week respectively) which count towards unemployment benefit, unlike other Class 2 contributions.[37]

The methods of payment are set out in DSS leaflet NI41. If you are self-employed part of the time and also have a job as an employed earner you pay both Class 1 and Class 2 contributions, subject to a maximum (see DSS leaflet NP18).[38]

If you have paid Class 2 contributions, you can apply to have them repaid to you if your earnings in that year were in fact low enough to entitle you to exception. The application must be made in writing after the end of the relevant contribution year (5 April) and no later than 31 December of the same calendar year.[39]

Class 3 contributions

Class 3 contributions are purely **voluntary**.[40] They give entitlement only to widows' benefits and retirement pensions and are not payable if your earnings factor is otherwise sufficient in that tax year to meet the second contribution condition for those benefits (see p233).[41] Any accidental overpayment of contributions should be refunded if you make a written application.[42]

Class 3 contributions are paid at a flat rate. The current and recent rates are:[43]

1992-93	£5.25 a week
1993-94	£5.45 a week
1994-95	£5.55 a week

The introduction of home responsibilities protection (see p229) has lessened the need for payment of Class 3 contributions. However, if your contribution record for long-term benefits would otherwise be imperfect (eg, because you have been abroad or in prison) you may still consider it a good idea to pay them. Ask at your local Benefits Agency office if you are in doubt.

Class 4 contributions

Class 4 contributions are paid by **self-employed earners** (see p215). They are levied at a percentage of profits or gains between certain sums.[44] The current and recent rates are:

Year	Payable on earnings between	Percentage
1992-93	£6,120 and £21,060	6.3
1993-94	£6,340 and £21,840	6.3
1994-95	£6,490 and £22,360	7.3

The profits and gains are those chargeable to income tax under Schedule D, and Class 4 contributions are usually collected with your income tax by the Inland Revenue. You may apply for permission to defer payment for a specified period if the amount to be paid has not yet been established.[45]

If you are liable to pay both Class 1 and Class 4 contributions, the total is limited to the maximum which could be paid under one class only.[46]

Pre-1975 contributions

The present contribution system was introduced on 6 April 1975. Between 5 July 1948 and 5 April 1975 there were no Class 4 contributions, and Class 1 contributions were paid by way of a 'flat-rate stamp' in the same way as Class 2 and Class 3 contributions. Graduated contributions giving entitlement to graduated retirement benefit (see p124) were introduced in 1961 but were collected separately.

Before 6 April 1975, contribution years were not the same as tax years – as they are now. Instead each person was allocated a contribution year which might have begun in December, March, June or September depending on the last letter of your national insurance number. There were complicated transitional arrangements in both 1948 and 1975 so that you may well have had a contribution year which was not 12 months long. That may explain what would otherwise be anomalies in your contribution record.

Before 5 July 1948, there was a contributory scheme under the Widows', Orphans' and Old Age Contributory Pension Acts 1936-41, which may still give entitlement to an enhanced rate of pension (see p234).

Non-payment or late payment of contributions

It is an offence not to pay contributions on time (unless, of course, they are voluntary).[47] As far as Class 1 contributions are concerned, it is your employers' responsibility to make sure that contributions are deducted from your earnings and then paid to the Inland Revenue. But if you connive with your employers in order to avoid paying contributions, you too could be prosecuted. In practice, the Contributions Agency is usually more interested in collecting the appropriate contributions than in prosecuting people.

If your employers have deducted Class 1 contributions from your earnings but have failed to pay them to the Inland Revenue, you are treated as though they had been paid unless you have been negligent, or consented to or connived in that arrangement.[48]

Class 2 contributions should technically be paid in the week in respect of which they are due.[49] In practice, payment is by quarterly bill or direct debit. (See Contributions Agency leaflet CA-OS.) At the end of the tax year you will know whether or not it is necessary to pay Class 3 contributions if you want to fill any gap in your record.

In any event, contributions may still count for benefit purposes if paid late provided that they are paid within two years (Class 1) or six years (Class 2 or Class 3) after the end of the tax year in which they were due.[50] Students, apprentices and prisoners may pay Class 3 contributions to cover their period of education, apprenticeship or imprisonment at any time before the end of the sixth complete tax year after that period finished.[51] However, contributions give no entitlement to benefits, until they have actually been paid (and, in the case of unemployment or sickness benefit, until six weeks *after* they have been paid).[52]

Voluntary contributions may be paid on behalf of a contributor after her/his death provided they are paid no later than s/he would have been allowed to pay them.[53]

3. CREDITS AND HOME RESPONSIBILITIES PROTECTION

If you do not pay social security contributions, there will be gaps in your contribution record. However, in a large number of circumstances you will be 'credited' with a contribution. A credited contribution is usually known simply as a 'credit'.

Credits help you satisfy the *second* contribution condition for those benefits with two contribution conditions. You are credited with an amount of earnings equal to the lower earnings limit (except starting credits, which give you a Class 3 credit).

You receive only sufficient credits in any tax year to meet the contribution condition which allows credits to count.[1] For example, if you earn £4,000 as an employee between April and October 1994 you receive no credits during the rest of 1994-95 because you have already paid contributions with an earnings factor of more than £2,964 (the minimum required to count for long-term benefits; 52 times the lower earnings limit of £57).

Married women currently opting for reduced liability for contributions (see p219) are not entitled to credits other than starting credits.[2]

Home responsibilities protection (see p229) helps you satisfy the second contribution condition for long-term benefits by reducing the years for which you would otherwise have to satisfy the contribution condition.

Credits for weeks of unemployment or incapacity for work

You can get a credit for a week in which you are signing on as unemployed or covered by a medical certificate. More precisely, you get one Class 1 credit[3] for *either*:

- each week of six days of unemployment or incapacity for work; *or*
- each week of five days of unemployment, provided that on the other day you do not earn more than the current lower earnings limit (see p216); *or*
- each week of six days where you are working, provided that this is for less than eight hours a week and you are still available for work. The work must be other than your usual main occupation unless done for, or organised through, a charity or public body for a similar purpose.

The week runs from Monday. Days count if you claim late or if you are receiving income support because you are either incapable of work or unemployed.

Credit entitlement is one reason why you might continue to sign on at the unemployment benefit office, even though you are getting no immediate benefit from doing so. Therefore, if you do not have a good enough contribution record to claim unemployment benefit or your entitlement to unemployment benefit has run out and you are unable to claim unemployment benefit or income support in your own right, you should consider whether it is still worth signing on to protect your right to benefits.

You are also entitled to a credit if you are receiving **statutory sick pay**, and not otherwise paying contributions, for that week. But, unlike other credits, these are not awarded automatically. It is important to send a copy of your medical certificate to your local office to claim them otherwise you may lose rights to benefit in future.

These credits will only help you towards qualification for **unemployment benefit** and **sickness benefit** if, during the relevant contribution year, *either*:

- you have *actually paid* contributions giving an earnings factor of at least 25 times the lower earnings limit in one of the two years before the beginning of the relevant benefit year (see p231). For unemployment benefit this earnings factor must have been derived from Class 1 contributions; *or*
- you were entitled to invalidity benefit, invalid care allowance or unemployability supplement for at least one day; *or*
- you claimed and satisfied the contribution conditions for unemployment benefit, sickness benefit or maternity allowance; *or*

- you were credited with a contribution for approved training (see below); *or*
- you received the credits on the ground of unemployment or incapacity for work after you had exhausted your right to unemployment benefit or sickness benefit or while in receipt of statutory sick pay.[4]

Credits for caring for an invalid

You receive a Class 1 credit for each week you receive **invalid care allowance** (see p158).[5] You also receive credits if the only reason that you do not receive invalid care allowance is that it overlaps with a **widow's benefit**.

If you are looking after an invalid but are not entitled to credits under these provisions, you may receive home responsibilities protection instead (see p229).

Starting credits

You receive Class 3 credits for the contribution year in which you were 16 and for the next two years if you would otherwise have an insufficient contribution record for long-term benefits.[6]

This is intended to help those who have stayed on at school after the minimum school-leaving age. No credits are made under this provision in respect of years before 6 April 1977.

Education and training credits

You receive Class 1 credits for the purposes only of **unemployment benefit** and **sickness benefit** for any week of a course of full-time education or full-time (or, for a person who is registered as disabled, part-time – at least 15 hours a week) training to acquire occupational or vocational skills or apprenticeship provided that:

- in one of the two contribution years in which you must satisfy the second contribution condition for the benefit, you have an earnings factor of 50 times the lower earnings limit without recourse to this provision; *and*
- you are 18 or will become 18 during the current tax year, *and*
- you were under 21 when the course started.[7]

You also receive Class 1 credits for the purposes of all benefits for each week you are undertaking an approved training course[8] provided that:

- the training is full-time unless either you are disabled or it is an introductory course; *and*

- the training is not part of your job; *and*
- the training is intended to run for less than one year (except in certain circumstances if it is a course for disabled people); *and*
- you were 18 or over at the beginning of the contribution year in which the credit is claimed.

All courses run by the Training Enterprise and Education Directorate count. Other courses are considered on their merits. You should apply through your local DSS office on form CF55C.

Credits for maternity pay period

You are entitled to a Class 1 credit for each week of the maternity pay period (see p90) for which you receive statutory maternity pay.[9] This will be important only if you are receiving maternity pay at a rate less than the lower earnings limit (currently £57 a week). You must claim these credits in writing before the end of the 'benefit year' (see p231) following the tax year in which the week falls, but the time may be extended if it is reasonable to do so.

Credits for jury service

You are entitled to a Class 1 credit for each week after 6 April 1988 when you spend part of the week on jury service.[10] Again, you must claim these credits in writing before the end of the benefit year (see p231) following the tax year in which the week falls (or such further period as is reasonable).

Credits for widows

If you are a widow, you may receive credits to enable you to satisfy the second contribution condition for unemployment benefit or sickness benefit. This is, of course, important only if you are not receiving widowed mother's allowance or widow's pension at the full rate.

You receive Class 1 credits for each year in which widow's allowance (a benefit abolished in April 1988) or widowed mother's allowance was paid, if payments have ceased for a reason other than remarriage or cohabitation.[11] Since a widow in this position is deemed to satisfy the first contribution condition for unemployment benefit or sickness benefit,[12] the effect of this provision is effectively to waive the contribution conditions for widows altogether.

Credits for men aged 60 or over

Women are not entitled or required to pay contributions once they are 60 or over. Men aged over 60 must continue to pay contributions if they are liable even if their contribution records are already sufficient to qualify them for a full Category A retirement pension. This rule discriminates against men (and also in some limited circumstances against women) on grounds of their sex but is *not* contrary to EC law because it is a 'necessary consequence' of having a differential retirement age.[13]

Men receive Class 1 credits for the contribution year in which they become 60 and for the next four years if credits are needed to allow the year to count for the purposes of the second contribution condition for any benefit.[14] This means that if you take early retirement at 60 you will still have the last five years of your 'working life' counted in full towards satisfaction of the second contribution condition for your retirement pension when you reach 65. These are sometimes known as 'autocredits'.

Credits for disability working allowance claimants

Disability working allowance is a means-tested benefit paid to people who are in work but who have a disability which puts them at a disadvantage in the labour market. For more details see CPAG's *National Welfare Benefits Handbook*.

You are entitled to a Class 1 credit if you are getting disability working allowance during any week *and either*:[15]

- you are employed and earn less than the lower earnings limit (currently £57); *or*
- you are self-employed but have been granted exemption from paying Class 2 contributions because your earnings are below the small earnings limit (see p222).

Home responsibilities protection

A year of home responsibilities is one:[16]

- throughout which you receive child benefit for a child aged under 16; *or*
- throughout which you are allowed to receive income support without being required to be available for work because you are looking after an invalid; *or*
- in 48 weeks of which you spend 35 hours looking after someone receiving either the higher or middle rates of disability living allowance care component, attendance allowance (see p142) or constant

attendance allowance (under the industrial injuries or war pensions schemes, see pp177 and 331).

A year should be automatically recorded as a year of home responsibilities if you qualify because you receive child benefit or you receive income support while caring for an invalid. If you qualify only on the third of the above grounds, or you qualify for part of the year on one ground and the rest on another, you should apply at your local DSS office. This should be done at the end of any contribution year when your earnings do not exceed 50 times that year's lower earnings limit. Ask your local office for Form CF411.

Note that for the first of the above grounds, you have to be entitled to child benefit. If you are a man *and*:

- you are looking after children *and either*:
  - you do not work; *or*
  - you do not earn sufficient to pay national insurance contributions; *and*
- their mother lives with you; *and*
  - is in work; *and*
  - earns enough to pay national insurance contributions; *and*
  - is receiving child benefit

you should ask her to stop claiming the child benefit so that you can claim it instead. When you claim the child benefit, you should include a letter from her saying that she no longer wishes to claim. It is not enough for you to say that your name is or should be on the child benefit order book *together* with hers.

A year in which a woman has elected reduced liability for contributions cannot be a year of home responsibilities.[17] It may be worth revoking such an election (see p220).

No year before 6 April 1978 can be a year of home responsibility.

Home responsibility protection helps towards satisfaction of the second contribution condition for the long-term benefits (see p233). Years of home responsibilities in which you do not satisfy the contribution conditions are deducted from the number of years for which you would otherwise have to satisfy the contribution conditions.[18]

Example
You left school at age 16 in 1976. You will be 60 in 2020. Your working life for retirement pension purposes will be 44 years and the number of years in which you would normally have to satisfy the contribution conditions is 39 (see p234). The effect of home responsibilities protection for 10 complete years of looking after children, and three of looking after a disabled relative receiving attendance allowance, is to reduce the requisite number of years in

which you must satisfy the contribution conditions for a retirement pension on the basis of your own contributions to 26 (ie, 39 – 13).

Home responsibilities protection can reduce the requisite number of years (see p234) to 20 or half what it would otherwise be, whichever is lower.[19] Because women reach pensionable age at 60 rather than 65, their maximum 'requisite number of years' (see p234) is 39 years rather than 44. This means that the maximum number of years of home responsibilities protection is 19 for a woman and 24 for a man.

4. CONTRIBUTION CONDITIONS FOR BENEFIT

Contributory benefits have two contribution conditions *except* in the case of maternity allowance and widow's payment. To help you satisfy the second condition, you may be credited with contributions to fill gaps in your record (see p225). However, the first contribution condition must always be satisfied by contributions which have actually been paid.

Unemployment benefit and sickness benefit

The first condition

You must have actually paid, in one contribution year, the appropriate class of contributions producing an earnings factor (see p217) at least 25 times that year's lower earnings limit (eg, £1,400 in 1993-94, 25 times £56).[1] For sickness benefit, they may have been paid in any tax year; but for unemployment benefit they must have been paid in one of the last two complete tax years before the 'relevant benefit year' (see below).

The contributions may be either Class 1 or 2 for sickness benefit; they must be Class 1 for unemployment benefit (except for share fishermen and volunteer development workers, see p222).[2] They must be paid before a claim for unemployment benefit or sickness benefit is made.

Benefit years are almost the same as calendar years and run from the first Sunday in January.[3] The 'relevant benefit year' is the benefit year in which begins the period of interruption of employment that contains the claim begins (see p251).[4]

A **widow** who loses her entitlement to widow's allowance or widowed mother's allowance for some reason other than remarriage or cohabitation (eg, she loses her widowed mother's allowance because her children grow up) will be deemed to have satisfied this contribution condition (and may well be credited with contributions to satisfy the second condition – see p232).[5]

For sickness benefit, this condition is satisfied by 25 flat-rate contributions of the kind payable before 6 April 1975.[6]

The second condition

You must have either paid or been credited with contributions producing an earnings factor (see p217) equal to 50 times the lower earnings limit in each of the last two complete contribution years ending before the relevant benefit year (see p231).[7]

In rare cases, this may mean that you should delay a claim so that you can draw on a different year's contribution record. This is because the relevant contribution year(s) for unemployment benefit or sickness benefit depend(s) on the benefit year in which the *first* day of your period of interruption of employment (see p251) falls. Thus, if you claim on or after Monday 2 January 1995, the relevant contribution years for unemployment benefit purposes will be 1992-93 and 1993-94, whereas if you claim on or before Saturday 31 December 1994 they would be 1991-92 and 1992-93.

Any day for which you do not claim does not count as a day of unemployment or incapacity for work,[8] so it is easy to postpone your period of interruption of employment. However, if you claim and are refused benefit because the contribution conditions are not satisfied, your period of interruption of employment will have started.[9] You would then have to stop claiming for more than eight weeks and make a fresh claim after that period. The eight-week gap would break the period of interruption of employment.

Example

During 1991-92, you spent time at home looking after your children and have only done paid work and made contributions since April 1992. In 1994 you are made redundant and (after payments in lieu of notice were taken into account), your period of interruption of employment is due to start on 12 December 1994. Your husband is in full-time employment so you are not entitled to income support. It is plainly in your interest to wait until Monday 2 January 1995 before you claim unemployment benefit.

Credited contributions will not always help you fulfil the second contribution condition for unemployment benefit or sickness benefit (see p226).

Maternity allowance

The only contribution condition for maternity allowance is that you must actually have paid Class 1 or Class 2 contributions for at least 26 weeks in the 52 weeks ending at the end of the 15th week before the expected week of confinement. The earnings factor is immaterial, but contributions paid by a married woman or widow at the reduced rate do not count.[10]

Widow's payment

The only contribution condition for widow's payment is that your husband must actually have paid, in any one tax year before his death, contributions of Classes 1, 2 or 3 producing an earnings factor (see p217) of at least 25 times the lower earnings limit (eg, £1,425 in 1994-95, 25 times £57).[11]

Any paid contributions may be counted if he became liable to pay contributions only in the tax year in which he died or the previous tax year, or if he had ever successfully claimed unemployment or sickness benefit.[12] The payment of 25 flat-rate contributions in a contribution year prior to 6 April 1975 satisfies this condition.[13]

Widowed mother's allowance, widow's pension and Category A and B retirement pensions

The first condition

The contributor (ie, you for Category A retirement pensions, your late husband for widows pension and either you, your husband or your late spouse for Category B retirement pensions) must actually have paid in any one tax year before death or pensionable age, contributions with an earnings factor of 52 times that year's lower earnings limit (eg, £2,964 in 1994-95, 52 times £57).[14]

This condition is deemed to be satisfied if the contributor was receiving invalidity benefit in the year of death or of reaching pensionable age, or in the preceding year.[15] Fifty flat-rate payments in a contribution year before 6 April 1975 also satisfy this condition.[16]

The second condition

The contributor must have paid or been credited with contributions with an earnings factor of at least 52 times that year's lower earnings limit for each of the requisite number of years.[17]

The number of years you need to satisfy this condition depends on the length of your 'working life'. This is the period inclusive of the tax year in which you reach the age of 16 up to but exclusive of the year in which you reach pensionable age or in which you die.[18]

If you were over 16 on 5 July 1948, your working life is taken as having started either on 6 April 1948 or on 6 April of the year between 1936 and 1948 that you first started paying contributions, if you paid contributions before 5 July 1948.[19]

A year of home responsibility looking after a child or invalid does not count as a year of your working life unless your earnings factor in that year was at least 52 times the lower earnings limit (see p216 for exactly how this works).

The requisite number of years is then calculated as follows:[20]

Length of 'working life'	*Requisite number of years*
1-10 years	Length of working life minus 1
11-20 years	Length of working life minus 2
21-30 years	Length of working life minus 3
31-40 years	Length of working life minus 4
41-50 years	Length of working life minus 5

Since contributions paid before 6 April 1975 do not produce an earnings factor (see p17), the number of years before that date in which the contribution condition is satisfied is calculated by adding together all the contributions paid or credited before 6 April 1975, and dividing the answer by 50. If that does not produce a whole number the result is rounded up, as long as that would not produce a number greater than the number of years of the working life before 6 April 1975. A credit is given for each of the 13 weeks between 6 April and 4 July 1948 if those form part of your working life but you did not contribute then.[21]

Example

You are a man who reached pensionable age in July 1994. You did not contribute to any pre-1948 scheme and paid or had credited 1,300 contributions between 1948 and 1975. For every year from 6 April 1975 to 5 April 1994 you paid contributions with earnings factors above the minimum level of 52 times the lower earnings limit. Your working life began on 6 April 1948 and ended on 5 April 1994 – a total of 45 years. The requisite number of years is therefore 41. You have satisfied 16 years since 1979. Between 1948 and 1975 you paid or had credited 1, 300 contributions, which equals 26 years (1,300 divided by 50). You therefore satisfy the condition for 45 years, four more than the requisite number that you need.

Note that widows, widowers and divorcees may be able to combine their own contribution records with those of their late or former spouses in order to claim a Category A retirement pension (see pp117-119).

Insufficient contributions

Benefits are paid at a reduced rate if the second contribution condition is not satisfied for the requisite number of years, provided it is satisfied in at least 25 per cent of the requisite number. The benefit is paid at a percentage of the amount which would otherwise be paid; the percentage is calculated by expressing the number of years in which the condition is satisfied as a percentage of the requisite number of years and rounding it up to the nearest whole number.[22] Thus, if you are a widow and your husband's working life was 12 years, so that the requisite number of years is ten years, and if he only satisfied the condition in eight years, you receive 80 per cent of the standard rate of widowed mother's allowance.

Increases for an adult dependants are reduced in the same proportion, but increases for children are always paid in full.[23]

It may be possible for you to pay voluntary contributions (see p223) to bring the number of years in which the second contribution condition is satisfied up to the 25 per cent figure needed for a minimum pension or to enhance the rate at which the pension will be paid. This can be very worthwhile. For example, if you are only one year short of the minimum number of years, payment of £288.60 (52 Class 3 contributions £5.55 each) may secure you a pension of £14.40 per week (£57.60 × 25%) for the rest of your life. You will get your money back in a little over 20 weeks.

5. THE STATE EARNINGS RELATED PENSION SCHEME (SERPS)

The State Earnings Related Pension Scheme (SERPS) provides for earnings-related pensions to be paid to those who have paid Class 1 contributions in excess of the minimum required for entitlement to basic retirement pensions. It provides similar pensions for widows and widowers and for invalidity pensioners.

Everyone who has paid Class 1 contributions before April 1991 is in SERPS for invalidity benefit purposes.

For the purposes of widows' benefits and retirement pensions you are not in SERPS if you either are either contracted out by your employers (see below) or are a member of an appropriate personal pension scheme (see p236).

Contracting out

You may be contracted out of SERPS by your employers if your service counts for the purpose of either a salary-related occupational pension or if your employers make certain minimum payments to a 'contracted-out money purchase' scheme. To enable you to be contracted out, either sort of scheme must be covered by a certificate from the Occupational Pension Board.[1]

The effect of being contracted out is that you and your employers pay national insurance contributions at a lower rate than other employees and their employers (see pp221-222).[2] This means that you do not build up any entitlement to pensions under SERPS (although, until April 1991, you did as an addition to invalidity pension).[3] However, you will have to contribute to your employers' scheme and will receive a benefit from that.

An employer cannot compel you to be a member of any particular scheme, so you can opt out and join an appropriate pension scheme of your choice (see below).[4]

Appropriate personal pension scheme

If a personal pension scheme satisfies certain conditions, the trustees or managers of the scheme may obtain an 'appropriate scheme certificate' from the Occupational Pension Board.[5]

If you then choose to become a member of an appropriate personal pension scheme, the Secretary of State will pay to the scheme the difference between your contracted in national insurance contributions and those you would have paid had you been contracted out [6] and, if you are over 30 at the beginning of the tax year in question, an additional sum representing 1 per cent of your income between the upper and lower earnings limits.[7] The effect of this is to place you in much the same position as a person in a contracted-out money purchase scheme[8] or, if you are over 30, to give you an incentive to opt out of SERPS. The main difference is that it is your decision to join the scheme and not your employers'.

You are then treated as not contributing to SERPS and must look to your personal pension scheme instead.

Calculating the additional pension

The method of calculating additional pensions will change in 1999.[9] Only the present system is explained here and, of course, only for those in SERPS. For the calculation from 1999, see DSS leaflet NP46.

Until 5 April 1991, everyone was regarded as being in SERPS in order to calculate additional pensions for invalid pensioners. However, no year after 1990-91 will count as a relevant year (see below) for invalidity pension purposes.[10]

For invalidity pension or Category A retirement pension, the additional pension depends on your 'earnings factor' (see p217) in each 'relevant year' in which you have paid contributions. For widows' benefits or Category B retirement pensions, the additional pension depends upon your spouse's 'earnings factor' in each 'relevant year' in which s/he has paid contributions.[11]

'Relevant years' are:

- in the case of invalidity pension, contribution years from 1978-79 up to, but excluding, the year in which you became entitled to invalidity pension or to 1990-91, whichever is earlier;
- in the case of Category A retirement pension, contribution years from 1978-79 up to, but excluding, the year in which you reached pensionable age;
- in the case of widowed mother's allowance, widow's pension or Category B retirement pensions, contribution years from 1978-79 up to, but excluding, the year your spouse reached pensionable age or died under that age.

For each relevant year, you take the 'earnings factor' and increase it by the appropriate percentage to take account of inflation. The appropriate percentages are those coming into force during the final relevant year. If the last relevant year was 1993-94, the percentages are:[12]

1978-79	310.4%	1985-86	76.6%
1978-79	262.0%	1986-87	62.2%
1979-80	202.5%	1987-88	51.1%
1980-81	188.2%	1988-89	38.9%
1981-82	141.6%	1989-90	25.8%
1982-83	119.3%	1990-91	17.3%
1983-84	103.3%	1991-92	6.5%
1984-85	88.2%	1992-93	5.0%

You deduct, from each of those figures, 52 times the lower earnings limit in force in the *last* relevant year. You then add together the resulting figures and multiply the total by 1 per cent to give the total additional pension you will receive for a year.[13] You divide that figure by 52 to obtain a weekly figure.

Once that calculation has been done for the first time, it is not repeated each year. Instead, the additional pension is simply increased in line with inflation.[14] Thus, any additional pension paid up to April 1994 was then increased by 1.8 per cent.

Example

You retire in May 1994 and claim Category A retirement pension. You were self-employed until July 1984 and then became employed. In 1984-85 your earnings factor was £6,032, and in 1985-86 it was £7,134. You were made redundant in March 1986 and remained unemployed until May 1990. Your earnings factor in 1990-91 was £8,835, in 1991-92 it was £9,916, in 1992-93 it was £10,527 and in 1993-94, your last relevant year, it was £11,209.

For each of the years when you were wholly self-employed or wholly unemployed, your earnings factor will not be higher than the lower earnings limits for those years so they do not count towards an additional pension.

For the remaining years, the calculation is as follows:

	1984-85 £	1985-86 £	1990-91 £	1991-92 £	1992-93 £	1993-94 £
earnings factor	6,032	7,134	8,835	9,916	10,27	11,209
increased for inflation	× 1.976 11,919	× 1.854 13,226	× 1.231 10,875	× 1.118 11,086	× 1.050 11,053	× 1.000 11,209
less 52 × 56	2,912 9,007	2,912 10,314	2,912 7,963	2,912 8,174	2,912 8,141	2,912 8,297

Adding those together gives £51,896

1¼% of £51,896 = £653.33

£653.33 ÷ 52 = £12.48

So your additional pension is £12.48

If you do not have all the necessary figures available to you, or if you wish to check the Contributions Agency records, you should fill in the form on leaflet NP38 and the Contributions Agency will tell you how much additional pension they think you are entitled to at current values and their estimate of the additional pension which you will receive if you continue working.

In certain circumstances, a **widow** or **widower** may be entitled to an additional pension based both on her/his own contributions and on those of her/his spouse (see p119).

Invalidity allowance is reduced by the amount of any additional pension (see pp77 and 117).

6. FUTURE CHANGES

The way in which entitlement to an additional pension under SERPS is calculated will change in 1999.[1]

As a result of the Government's proposals to equalise pensionable age for men and women at 65 (see p124), it is also proposed to change some of the rules on national insurance contributions, home responsibility protection and credits:[2]

- Women aged between 60 and 65 will become entitled to 'autocredits' (see p229) in the same way as men;
- From 1999 onwards, family credit and disability working allowance will be treated as if they were earnings for pensions purposes;
- The maximum number of years by which the 'requisite number of years' in a person's 'working life' can be reduced by home responsibilities protection (currently 19 for women and 24 for men) will be equalised at 22 for both sexes;
- There will be further changes to the SERPS scheme (see p235). At present most of these have still to be announced but the government has said that the rules on home responsibilities protection will be extended to SERPS.

CHAPTER THIRTEEN

Residence conditions and going abroad

This chapter covers:

1. Introduction (see below)
2. Residence and presence conditions (p241)
3. Absence from Great Britain (p245)
4. Northern Ireland, the Isle of Man and the Channel Islands (p247)
5. The European Community and the European Economic Area (p248)
6. Reciprocal agreements (p250)

1. INTRODUCTION

If you spend time outside Great Britain (ie, England, Wales and Scotland) your benefits may be affected in three different ways, none of them advantageous:

- all *contributory* benefits depend on your contributions record and the rules for paying contributions depend in turn on your being resident or present in Great Britain. These rules are set out in Chapter 12 and if, as a result of going abroad, you do not meet them, it may mean either that you are not *entitled* to the contributory benefit you are claiming (because you do not satisfy the contribution conditions) or, in the case of long-term benefits, that your benefit may be *paid* at a reduced rate;
- all *non-contributory* benefits have residence or presence conditions attached to them. This means that before you can become *entitled* to them you must have been resident or present in Great Britain in the past. These conditions are covered in section 2 of this chapter;
- even once you have become *entitled* to a benefit, there is a general rule which means that it will *not be paid* to you for any period during which you are absent from Great Britain. This applies to all benefits, contributory and non-contributory.

However, there are a large number of exceptions to these general rules. In particular:

- for some, but not all, benefits, temporary absence abroad may not disqualify you. The rules for this are discussed on p245;
- there are special rules for other parts of the UK (see p247);
- European Community (EC) law may mean that periods of residence and/or presence in another EEA country count as residence and/or presence in Great Britain. EC law also has rules which may allow you to 'export' your claim for benefit so that it can be paid in another EEA country (see p247);
- there are special agreements with some, but not all, other countries which allow you to claim benefits while you are there (see p250).

Matters affecting the payment of benefit while you are abroad, or when you have recently come from abroad, are dealt with by the Benefits Agency Overseas Branch, Newcastle-upon-Tyne, NE98 1YX. Adjudication officers there make decisions, but appeals are held wherever in Great Britain is convenient for you.

The Overseas Branch will answer any questions that you may have and it also advises local Benefits Agency offices when necessary. Write to them if you want information.

For more advice on the rules for entitlement to benefits (both means-tested and non-means-tested) if you have come from abroad and on how those rules link up with UK immigration law see CPAG's *Ethnic Minorities' Benefits Handbook*.

2. RESIDENCE AND PRESENCE CONDITIONS

Severe disablement allowance

You are entitled if *either*:[1]

- you are *ordinarily resident* in Great Britain (see p245); *and*
- you are present in Great Britain (see p244) and have been present for at least 26 weeks in the past year; *or*
- you were entitled to severe disablement allowance on any day between 30 March and 5 April 1992 (inclusive); *and*
- you are present (see p244) in Great Britain and have been present for at least 24 weeks in the last 28 weeks; *and*
- you have been resident (see p244) in Great Britain for 10 out of the last 20 years. If you are under the age of 20, you must have been resident in Great Britain for at least 10 years since your birth.

Once you satisfy these residence conditions you are not subject to continuing residence conditions on subsequent days of incapacity during the same period of interruption of employment (see p251)[2] although payment may be affected if you leave the country after the start of your claim (see section 3 below).

The rules are relaxed for members of the armed forces.

Invalid care allowance, disability living allowance and attendance allowance

You are entitled if:[3]

- you are *ordinarily resident* in Great Britain (see p245); *and*
- you are *present* in Great Britain (see p244); *and*
- you have been *present* in Great Britain for a total of 26 weeks, in the last 12 months.

People who make a claim for attendance allowance or disability living allowance (DLA), or apply for a review on the basis that they are terminally ill, are exempted from the rule that they have to have been present in Great Britain for the last 26 weeks.[4] If claims are made for DLA for babies who are less than six months' old, they only have to have been present for 13 of the last 26 weeks.[5]

For **disability living allowance** and **attendance allowance**, you are treated as being present during any temporary absence of less than 26 weeks, and during any further absence for the purpose of treatment. (You must obtain a certificate from the Secretary of State to the effect that the further absence is reasonable.[6])

For *invalid care allowance* you are treated as being present during any temporary absence of up to four weeks. You are also treated as present during any temporary absence for the purpose of caring for your patient provided, of course, that your patient's DLA care component, attendance allowance or constant attendance allowance is still payable.[7]

Category D retirement pension

You are entitled if:[8]

- you have been *resident* (see p244) in Great Britain for at least 10 of the last 20 years; *and*
- you were *ordinarily resident* (see p245) in Great Britain either on the day you reached the age of 80, or on the date of your claim.

Child benefit and guardian's allowance

For **child benefit**, there are separate conditions for the *child*, the *claimant* and, if different, the *child's parents*.

- The child must generally be in Great Britain.[9] However, the child may be abroad where:[10]
  - someone was entitled to receive child benefit immediately before the absence; *and*
  - the absence, when it began, was intended to be temporary and continues as such; *and*
  - *either* the child has not been abroad for more than eight weeks; or the child has not been abroad for more than 156 weeks receiving full-time education at a recognised education establishment; *or* the child is abroad during a period agreed by the Secretary of State which is for the specific purpose of medical treatment for a condition which existed before s/he left.

There are special rules if a child was born abroad during a temporary absence of the mother.[11]

- The claimant must be in Great Britain.[12] However, someone already receiving child benefit may continue to do so for eight weeks while abroad on an absence which was intended when it began, and continues, to be temporary.[13]
- The claimant *and either* the child or one of the parents must have been in Great Britain for more than 182 days in the last year.[14] There are complicated exceptions to this.[15] In particular, if the claimant is now in Great Britain and is likely to remain here for a total of at least 183 consecutive days (disregarding up to 28 days' temporary absence), s/he is treated as satisfying this condition if *either·*
  - s/he has worked and been liable for Class 1 or 2 national insurance contributions during that period of 183 days but before the start of the week for which the claim for benefit is made;[16] *or*
  - s/he has been entitled to child benefit within the past three years;[17] *or*
  - her/his spouse was entitled to child benefit within the past three years; *and either* the spouse is residing with (see p193) the claimant at present; or the spouse was residing with the claimant at the time when the spouse was entitled to benefit.[18]

Entitlement to **guardian's allowance** depends upon entitlement to child benefit, so the above conditions must be satisfied. However, if the only bar to your entitlement to child benefit and, therefore, guardian's allowance is that neither the child nor either of her/his parents had been in Great Britain during the last year, that condition is waived.[19]

A further condition of entitlement to guardian's allowance is that at least one of the child's parents was born in the UK or had, at some time after reaching the age of 16, spent a total of 52 weeks in any two-year period in the UK.[20]

'Present' and 'absent'

To be 'present', subject to the special rules below, you must be *physically* present. To satisfy a presence condition, you must prove that you were present throughout any day in question.[21] 'Absent' is the opposite of present. If the adjudication officer seeks to disqualify you because you are absent from Great Britain, the burden is upon her/him to prove that you were absent throughout any day in question.[22]

For the purpose of satisfying presence conditions, you are treated by special rules[23] as being in Great Britain if you are:

- a member of the armed forces serving abroad;
- a spouse, son, daughter, parent or parent-in-law of a member of the armed forces serving abroad and living with her/him;
- a master, member of crew or other person employed on board a ship under a contract entered into in the UK;
- a pilot or member of crew or other person employed on board an aircraft under a contract entered into in the UK;
- a person employed on an oil or gas rig on the continental shelf.

The rules do not always apply in the case of guardian's allowance: members of the family of a serving member of the armed forces are not covered. In the case of child benefit, the circumstances in which the rules apply are also limited.

A worker on an oil or gas rig on the continental shelf is not disqualified from benefit if s/he is in the area of an oil or gas field or is travelling to it from another such area or from Norway or a member state of the EC (see p247).[24]

Under EC law presence in another EC member state (or EEA states) may count as presence in Great Britain (see p247).

'Resident' and 'ordinarily resident'

You are usually 'resident' in the country where you have your home for the time being.[25] It is possible to be resident in more than one place at a time but it is unusual.[26] You can remain resident in a place during a temporary absence but this depends on the circumstances.[27] So if you go abroad to work on one particular project of limited duration, intending to return on its completion, you remain resident in Great Britain. But if you go abroad for a considerable period, you may not remain resident in Great Britain even if you do expect to return eventually. Important factors in deciding the issue are where the rest of your family live, the sort of accommodation you have – a hotel does not suggest residence – and where your furniture and other personal effects are kept. If you move, intending to settle at your new address, you are regarded as resident there from the very first day.

You are '**ordinarily resident**' if there is a degree of continuity about your residence so that it can be described as settled.[28] So if you live mostly in Great Britain but also live elsewhere from time to time, you remain ordinarily resident in Great Britain throughout the shorter periods of residence elsewhere.

The burden of proof lies on you to show that you are or were resident in Great Britain at the relevant time.[29]

Under EC law residence in another EC member state (or EEA states) may count as residence in Great Britain (see p247). Some reciprocal agreements with other countries contain similar rules.

3. ABSENCE FROM GREAT BRITAIN

The general rule is that you are disqualified from receiving benefit while you are absent from Great Britain.[1] Various exceptions are set out below. Note, however, that there are special arrangements with other countries (see pp247 and 250). There are also limited exceptions for aircrew, mariners, members of the armed forces and offshore oil and gas workers.[2]

Sickness benefit, invalidity benefit, severe disablement allowance and maternity allowance

These are payable during the first 26 weeks of any temporary absence if the Secretary of State has certified that payment would be 'consistent with the proper administration of the Act' *and*:[3]

- your absence from Great Britain is for the specific purpose of being treated for an illness which began before you left this country; *or*
- in the case of sickness or invalidity benefit arising from an industrial injury or disease, your absence is for the specific purpose of receiving treatment which is appropriate for that injury or disease; *or*
- when you left this country you had been continuously incapable of work for six months and you have been continuously incapable of work since your departure.

Whether an absence is temporary is a question which depends on the circumstances of each individual case. An absence does not cease to be temporary just because no date is fixed for your return: but the absence must be for a limited period only.[4]

Benefit is payable for the whole of any temporary absence (not just the first 26 weeks) if:

* You have been continuously absent from Great Britain since 7 March 1994, *and* one of the conditions on p245 applies to you then and continues to apply to you now[5]
* You are living with a member of the armed forces and you are his or her spouse, son, daughter, parent or parent-in-law *and either*:
  - one of the conditions on p245 applies to you; *or*[6]
  - you are receiving a severe disablement allowance.[7]

It is not necessary for the Secretary of State to certify that payment is 'consistent with the proper administration of the Act' in either of these cases.

Widows' benefits, retirement pensions and guardian's allowance

These are payable while you are abroad, but you are not normally entitled to upratings of benefit after you have ceased to be 'ordinarily resident' (see p245) in Great Britain.[8] You cannot de-retire (see p116) while abroad.[9]

In the case of **widow's payment**, two further conditions are that:[10]

* you or your husband were in Great Britain when he died; *or*
* the contribution conditions for widowed mother's allowance or widow's pension are satisfied.

Attendance allowance, disability living allowance and invalid care allowance

Once you have become entitled to attendance allowance, DLA or invalid care allowance (ICA), an absence abroad does not disqualify you as long as you continue to satisfy the residence and presence conditions on p242.[11]

Child benefit

This is payable while the child, the claimant and (if one of them is not the claimant) the child's parents are abroad as long as the conditions described on pp242 to 243 remain satisfied.[12]

Disablement benefit and reduced earnings allowance

Disablement benefit (except constant attendance allowance and exceptionally severe disablement allowance) is unaffected while you are abroad.[13]

Constant attendance allowance and **exceptionally severe disablement allowance** are payable during a temporary absence for up to six months, or such further period as the Secretary of State may allow.[14]

Reduced earnings allowance is payable during a temporary absence if:[15]

- you have been away less than three months, or such further period as the Secretary of State may allow; *and*
- your absence is not for work purposes; *and*
- you claim before you go; *and*
- you are entitled before you go.

If your accident occurs abroad or your disease is contracted abroad, your entitlement to disablement benefit or reduced earnings allowance arises only from the date of your return to Great Britain.[16]

Increases for dependants

If your **spouse** is abroad, you remain entitled to an increase during any period your spouse is 'residing with you' (see p206).[17] No increase is paid while another adult dependant is abroad.

If your **child dependant** is abroad, you remain entitled to an increase while you are entitled to child benefit (see pp246 and 242). If you are not entitled to child benefit, but you would be if you were not abroad, you are still entitled to the increase if there is no one else who is entitled to child benefit in respect of the child.[18]

4. NORTHERN IRELAND, THE ISLE OF MAN AND THE CHANNEL ISLANDS

The rules described in this *Guide* apply only to Great Britain (ie, England, Wales and Scotland). However, although Northern Ireland and the Isle of Man have their own social security legislation, any contributions paid there count as though they were paid in Great Britain and vice versa; and for most practical purposes the systems may be treated as identical. You will not lose any benefit by moving between Northern Ireland or the Isle of Man and Great Britain.[1]

Jersey and Guernsey (including Alderney, Herm and Jethou), have their own social security systems but there is a reciprocal agreement under which you can receive British benefits while on those islands (see DSS leaflet SA4, from the Overseas Branch, see pp241).[2] You will also remain entitled to benefits under British legislation while in any other part of the Channel Islands.[3]

5. THE EUROPEAN COMMUNITY AND THE EUROPEAN ECONOMIC AREA

The European Community (EC) consists of Belgium, Denmark, Germany, France, Greece, the Irish Republic, Italy, Luxembourg, the Netherlands, Portugal, Spain and the UK (including Gibraltar). On 1 January 1994, the EC joined with Austria, Finland, Iceland, Norway and Sweden – all of which are members of the European Free Trade Association (EFTA) – to form the European Economic Area (EEA) and the rules described below which used to apply only to the EC were extended to nationals of those countries. It is anticipated that Liechtenstein – also an EFTA country – will join the EEA at some point in the future.

You may qualify for benefit while abroad within the EEA because the basic rules about going abroad apply. However, you may also qualify for benefit either under EC/EEA law (which overrides British law if there is a conflict) or under a reciprocal agreement. If EC/EEA law does apply to you, you cannot rely on a reciprocal agreement even if that would be more favourable to you.[1]

The main EC/EEA legislation applies only to employed people, self-employed people, those who were formerly employed or self-employed and the families of such people. You are counted as employed or self-employed if you are insured under a national social security scheme (ie, you either pay contributions or ought to do so as an employed or self-employed person).[2] If the EC/EEA legislation does not apply to you, you may benefit from one of the reciprocal agreements.

All the benefits covered in this *Guide* used to be within the scope of this legislation. But the law changed on 1 June 1992 and, from that date on, **attendance allowance** (see p142), **invalid care allowance** (see p158) and **disability living allowance** (see pp127 and 134) are excluded.[3]

EC/EEA social security law provides only for the 'co-ordination' of different national schemes and not for their 'harmonisation'.[4] In very general terms, this means that while the benefits available may differ from country to country, periods of residence or contributions paid in one EEA country count towards entitlement to benefits in others and that benefits from one country can be paid in any of the others.

The general rule is that you can receive benefit only from the last country where you were insured, but it is a matter of controversy whether that prevents you from gaining entitlement to benefit from another country under national law alone. In one case, the European Court of Justice has made a decision which would have the effect that you could not qualify for, say, disability living allowance under British law if you happened to have been last insured in France and were accordingly entitled to French invalidity benefit.[5] However, that decision was made by a court of only three judges and it is arguable that it is not consistent with an earlier decision where, in a different context, it was decided that the removal of rights acquired under national law alone was inconsistent with the EC Treaty.[6] If you need further advice about this, ask a local advice agency to contact CPAG's solicitors.

Wherever you claim, the claim is referred to the relevant social security institution in the country where you were last insured. Only that institution calculates the amount of benefit due.[7] The calculation of benefit involves treating periods of insurance or residence in other countries as though they were periods in the country where you were last insured. The detailed rules are much too complicated to be covered here. Benefit is usually paid through the relevant social security institution in the country where you are living and that institution carries out medical examinations, etc.

So, if you last worked in Italy but are now ill and living in Great Britain, you can claim through your local Benefits Agency office and you will receive benefits calculated by the Italian authorities but paid through the Benefits Agency. Similarly, if you last worked in Great Britain but are now abroad, you can claim British benefits in the country where you are now. For the purpose of satisfying time limits for claims, your claim is treated as having been made when you send it to the relevant institution in the country where you are living.[8]

Once you have acquired (whether under national law or EC/EEA law) the right to IVB, SDA, widow's benefit, a retirement pension, an industrial injuries benefit or guardian's allowance, you are entitled to travel anywhere within the EEA without losing it – provided, of course, that you continue to satisfy any conditions other than residence conditions.[9] Residence conditions are perfectly legitimate for the purpose of deciding whether or not you acquire entitlement to the benefit in the first place.

An unemployed person retains the right to unemployment benefit while looking for work in another country only in quite limited circumstances. You must register as available for work under the local procedures in each country where you go and the maximum period for which you retain the right to unemployment benefit is three months.[10] If you fail to register, you are disqualified even if the failure was due to the Department of Employment not having advised you properly before you went.[11] In some countries, it was necessary to satisfy additional conditions. Thus, in Spain, it was necessary, until 31 December 1992, to have obtained permission to seek work there from the authorities before you went. The Overseas Branch (see p241) will deal with specific queries and will send you the relevant guide from a series published by the Commission of the European Communities. These guides cover:

No. 1   *People going to work for an employer in another member country.*

No. 2   *People going for temporary stays in another member country.*

No. 3   *People sent by an employer in the United Kingdom to work in another member country.*

No. 4   *Pensioners living in one member country and entitled to benefit from another.*

No. 5   *People living in one member country and dependent on a person working in another.*

You must say which country is relevant, so that the appropriate edition is sent to you.

European Community law on social security benefit for people moving between countries within the EEA is covered in greater detail in CPAG's *Ethnic Minorities' Benefits Handbook* (see Appendix Five).

6. RECIPROCAL AGREEMENTS

There are several countries with which Great Britain has reciprocal agreements. These mean that you receive some British benefits while in the other country and vice versa.

There are agreements between Great Britain and Australia, Barbados, Bermuda, Canada, Cyprus, Israel, Jamaica, Malta, Mauritius, New Zealand, the Philippines, Switzerland, Turkey, and the United States of America. There are also agreements with all the EC countries (and the five non-EC countries which are members of the EEA – see p248) but these cannot help you if you are covered by the EC/EEA legislation (see p248).

The agreement with the former Yugoslavia is being honoured by the remaining regions of what was the Federal Republic of Yugoslavia and by the newly independent states of Croatia, Slovenia and Bosnia-Herzegovina. The arrangements are described in leaflets available from the Overseas Branch (see p241). Child benefit arrangements are explained in DSS leaflets CH5 and CH6.

CHAPTER FOURTEEN

Other general provisions

This chapter covers:
1. Periods of interruption of employment (see below)
2. Hospital in-patients (p254)
3. People in legal custody (p257)
4. Overlapping benefits (p258)
5. Calculating earnings (p261)
6. Christmas bonus (p262)
7. Recovery of benefit from compensation payments (p263)
8. Deductions from benefit (p265)
9. Criminal offences (p265)
10. Equal treatment for men and women (p267)

1. PERIODS OF INTERRUPTION OF EMPLOYMENT

The rules on periods of interruption of employment apply to unemployment benefit (UB), sickness benefit, invalidity benefit (IVB) and severe disablement allowance (SDA). UB (see Chapter 2) is paid for days on which you are unemployed, and sickness benefit IVB and SDA (see pp73, 76 and 81) are paid for days on which you are too ill to work. But even if you satisfy all the other conditions of entitlement, you may not get benefit if you are sick or out of work only for a short period. Single days have to be joined together to form a 'period of interruption of employment' before benefit can be paid.

The minimum length of time which can count as a period of interruption of employment is *either*:

- two 'days of unemployment' (see p252). These need not be consecutive as long as they are within a period of six consecutive days of each other;[1] *or*
- four consecutive 'days of incapacity for work' (see p252);[2] *or*
- if you are having regular weekly kidney dialysis, plasmaphoresis, chemotherapy or radiotherapy, two days of incapacity for work.

Again, these days do not have to be consecutive as long as they are within the same period of six consecutive days.[3]

Example

You are unemployed on Friday for two consecutive weeks and Thursday in the third week. The first two Fridays do not form a period of interruption of employment as the period in which they both fall – Friday and Saturday of the first week and Monday-Friday in the second – is seven days long, not six. But the second Friday and the Thursday do make up a period of interruption of employment because, when you ignore Sunday, they are within the same period of six consecutive days. (Note, however, that the rules on waiting days may mean that you will not actually be paid UB for these two days unless you have been out of work or sick in the recent past and the 'linking rule' applies – see p253.)

The length of a period of interruption of employment can, of course, be much longer than two or four days. So, for example, if you are out of work for four of the six days in the week or ill for three weeks – or even three years or more – all the days will count as part of a period of interruption of employment.

Days of unemployment

A 'day of unemployment' is a day upon which you satisfy the conditions of entitlement for UB (see p8) and are not disqualified from receiving that benefit for any of the reasons set out in Chapter 2.[4] Some days are 'deemed' to be days of unemployment when your period of interruption of employment is worked out even though you will not be paid UB for them. These are:

- days upon which you attend certain training courses;[5]
- days upon which you are entitled to income support (IS) without being required to be available for work because you are 60 or over;[6]
- days between the first day (6 April) of the tax year during which you reach 60 and the day before your 70th birthday (or your 65th birthday if you are a woman) when you cannot receive UB because:
  - you have exhausted your entitlement (see p10); *or*
  - you do not satisfy the contribution conditions (see p231); *or*
  - your occupational pension is too high.[7]

Days of incapacity for work

As its name suggests, a 'day of incapacity for work' is a day on which you are incapable of work (see p48) *and* on which you are not disqualified from receiving benefit for any of the reasons on p76.[8] Days on which you are entitled to maternity allowance (see p95) also count as days of incapacity[9] so that, for example, if you are still unable to go back to work after the maternity allowance period (see p96) ends, you may be able to claim either sickness benefit, IVB or SDA immediately as long as you meet the other conditions of entitlement.

If you work at night

There are special rules to help people who work night shifts. If you work a shift that starts before midnight on one day and ends the following day, then:

- if the time spent working before midnight is longer than the time spent after it, you are treated as having worked only on the first day;[10]
- if the time spent working after midnight is the same as or longer than the time spent working before it, you are treated as having worked only on the second day.[11]

In either case, the day on which you are treated as not working can be a day of unemployment or incapacity for work if you are sick or do no other work apart from your night shift during it.[12]

Sundays

Sundays cannot normally count as days of unemployment or incapacity for work and are ignored when working out any period of consecutive days.[13]

For UB only there are two exceptions to this rule:

- if you normally work on Sunday and have another day (or days) off instead;[14] *or*
- if you do not normally work on Sunday but object to working some other day on religious grounds and do not mind working on Sunday;[15]

then as long as you claim UB for Sunday and satisfy the conditions of entitlement on that day, the other day is disregarded instead of Sunday.

The linking rules

Two or more periods of interruption of employment are joined together to form a single period unless they are separated by at least eight consecutive weeks.[16]

This is known as the 'linking rule'. It has a number of important consequences:

- If you become unemployed within eight weeks of a previous spell of unemployment or illness, you do not have to serve a further period of three 'waiting days' before UB is paid (see example on p9).
- The question of whether or not you satisfy the contribution conditions for UB or sickness benefit is decided once and for all at the beginning of the period of interruption of employment. For this reason, it may sometimes be in your interest to delay a claim for UB (see p232).
- The 168 days of incapacity needed to qualify for IVB must be in the same period of interruption of employment, but because of the linking rule, they do not need to be consecutive.
- Your entitlement to invalidity allowance (see p77) is based on your age on the first day of incapacity for work in the period of interruption of employment, not the day (168 days of incapacity later) when you become entitled to IVB. If you have been ill sporadically, this may have been some years previously and this may entitle you to invalidity allowance at a higher rate.

Provided that they are not more than eight weeks apart, you can link two periods of interruption of employment even if one is made up of days of unemployment and the other days of incapacity. An example of how this works is given on p9.

There is also an extended linking rule for people receiving IVB or SDA which is intended to encourage them to try to go back to work. If you do try, but find that ill-health forces you to give up, your period of interruption of employment can be linked back for up to two years provided that you have been continuously entitled to disability working allowance (DWA) (see CPAG's *National Welfare Benefits Handbook*) while you were working. This means that you can go straight back on to IVB or SDA without having to wait a further period of 168 or 196 days.[17]

2. HOSPITAL IN-PATIENTS

The amount of benefit which you receive may be affected by the fact that you are spending a period in hospital receiving continuous, free in-patient treatment. The amount may also be affected if an adult dependant or child for whom you are claiming is in hospital. Two periods separated by less than 28 days are counted as one period; periods of less than a full day (midnight to midnight) do not count.[1] Benefit should be paid in full during short periods at home during treatment, but you will need to tell the Benefits Agency that you are out of hospital.

Sickness and invalidity benefit, severe disablement allowance, widows' benefits and retirement pensions

All these benefits are unaffected by your first six weeks in hospital. The effect of a longer stay in hospital depends on whether you have dependants. Your dependants for these purposes are:[2]

- people for whom you are entitled to an increase of benefit or would be but for the overlapping benefits rules (see p258);
- your spouse, if temporarily abroad for the treatment of an illness which began before departure from Great Britain.

After six weeks in hospital:[3]

- if you have no dependants, your benefit is reduced by £23 a week;
- if you have dependants, your benefit is reduced by £11.50 a week.

The reduction will be less if you would otherwise be left with less than £11.50 a week (not including increases for dependants).

After 52 weeks in hospital:[4]

- if you have no dependants, your benefit is reduced to £11.50 a week;
- if you have dependants, your benefit is reduced by £23 a week. £11.50 a week of that is paid to you. The balance, with any increases for dependants, is paid to your dependants or someone else on their behalf. You have to agree to the money being paid to your dependants or another person but, if you do not, the money is kept by the Benefits Agency and you still do not receive more than £11.50 a week.

However, **after a year** in hospital all payment of benefit to you may cease if:

- you are unable to act for yourself; *and*
- the benefit is payable on your behalf to the hospital board or other authority in control of the hospital where you are staying; *and*
- the doctor treating you certifies that no sum of money, or only a part of what you would otherwise receive, can be used for your personal comfort or enjoyment.[5]

Disability living allowance

The mobility component of disability living allowance (DLA) is unaffected by any period spent in hospital, whether by an adult or a child. It will remain payable unless you become unable to benefit from 'enhanced facilities for locomotion' (see p133).

The care component of DLA stops after four weeks in hospital for an adult or 12 weeks in hospital for a child (anyone under the age of 16).[6]

Attendance allowance

This ceases after four weeks.[7]

Disablement benefit

Disablement benefit (including exceptionally severe disablement allowance but not other increases) is unaffected. Constant attendance allowance ceases after four weeks.[8] Unemployability supplement is treated like IVB (see p255). If you were already entitled before 6 April 1997, you continue to receive **hospital treatment allowance**, which was equal to the difference between the amount of disablement benefit (excluding increases) paid and what would have been paid if the extent of disablement were 100 per cent.[9]

Other benefits for adults

There are no specific rules governing other benefits. So, maternity allowance, reduced earnings allowance and retirement allowance are unaffected. Entitlement to invalid care allowance (ICA) depends on whether you are still treated as 'regularly and substantially caring' for your patient (see p160). UB inevitably ceases to be payable as you are no longer available for work. Sickness benefit or IVB is payable instead.

Increases for adult dependants

While you are in hospital, these continue to be paid at the usual rate even if your basic benefit is reduced, but you need to make a special application after 52 weeks.

If your wife or husband goes into hospital there is no reduction in the increase paid in respect of her/him during the first six weeks.

After this period, the following rules apply.[10] After six weeks, the increase is reduced by £11.50 a week, but it does not drop below £11.50 a week.

After 52 weeks, the increase is reduced to £11.50 a week. That is payable *only* if you are regularly incurring expenditure for the dependant (eg, by visiting, buying presents).

An increase for any other adult dependant ceases as soon as s/he goes into hospital, as s/he will not be caring for a child, and so does not meet the requirements for the increase (see p204).

Benefits for children

Child benefit, one parent benefit, guardian's allowance and increases of other benefits paid in respect of children are all affected in the same way. If your child is living with you (see p191), there is no reduction during the first 12 weeks the child is in hospital. **After 12 weeks** the benefits stop altogether, unless you are regularly incurring expenditure for the child (eg, by visiting, buying presents, etc) *and* are satisfying the other requirements for the benefit.[11] In practice, the benefits continue, since a child is treated as continuing to live with you as long as you are regularly incurring expenditure by visiting. That is enough to entitle you to both child benefit and increases of other benefits.

3. PEOPLE IN LEGAL CUSTODY

Legal custody means imprisonment, or detention in a young offenders' institution, and includes being remanded in custody before trial.

The general rule is that you are disqualified from benefit while in legal custody,[1] but there are exceptions.

Adults

Most benefits are payable if you are in custody **on remand** (awaiting trial), unless you receive a custodial sentence at the end of your case. These benefits are sickness benefit, IVB, attendance allowance, DLA, child's special allowance, SDA, maternity allowance, widows' benefits, retirement pensions, disablement benefit, reduced earnings allowance (REA) and retirement allowance.[2]

They are suspended while you are on remand and you are then paid arrears if you do not receive a sentence of imprisonment (including a suspended sentence[3]), or detention in a young offenders' institution. If you do not receive a custodial sentence, you should also check that the Contributions Agency has credited you with contributions for the time you were on remand.

Disablement benefit (other than increases) is paid for up to a year in addition to any period on remand when the increases are payable.[4]

If you are transferred to a mental hospital while serving a sentence and are detained in the hospital, the disqualification ends on the date on which you would otherwise have been released[5] Others detained in mental hospitals are always treated as being hospital in-patients (see p254) rather than being 'in legal custody'.

If your husband or wife is in legal custody, you cannot receive an increase in respect of her/him. If your spouse is *remanded* in custody, your increase is merely suspended, and is paid if no custodial sentence is awarded.[6]

You are treated as residing with your husband or wife even though one of you is in prison, unless your marriage has broken down and your separation is likely to be permanent.[7]

You will not receive an increase for any other adult dependant while that adult is in custody.[8]

Children

You can still claim child benefit[9] and guardian's allowance while you are in legal custody.[10]

If your child goes into legal custody, child benefit ceases after eight weeks, so guardian's allowance and any increase of benefit for the child also stops.[11] However, as with adults, arrears will be paid at the end of any period of remand if your child does not receive a custodial sentence.[12]

If you are looking after the child of someone in legal custody and the child's other parent is dead, you may be entitled to guardian's allowance (see p196).

4. OVERLAPPING BENEFITS

You cannot receive two or more **earnings replacement benefits** (see p4) at the same time. There are also overlapping provisions covering some other benefits.

Personal benefits

You cannot usually receive more than one of the following benefits for the same period. You receive the one which is worth most[1] (but see pp259 and 103 if you are entitled to IVB and widows' benefits).

Unemployment benefit	Invalid care allowance
Sickness benefit	Widowed mother's allowance
Invalidity pension	Widow's pension
Severe disablement allowance	Non-contributory widow's benefit
Maternity allowance	Retirement pension

A **training allowance** paid by a government department or training agency causes any of these benefits to be reduced by the amount of the training allowance.[2]

y **supplement** (under the industrial injuries scheme or
me, see pp178 and 331) causes any of these benefits
allowance to be reduced by the amount of the
upplement.

aid to an adult (under the industrial injuries scheme or
eme – see pp108, 199 and 331) does not affect UB,
sickness benefit or maternity allowance but causes any of the other
personal benefits to be reduced by the amount of the death benefit
(except in the case of an invalidity pension or Category A retirement
pension which is not reduced below the amount of the basic component
based on your own contributions – ie, not including any additional
pension under SERPS or any part of the pension based on your former
spouse's contributions or the fact that you are a widow or widower).[3]

You cannot receive more than one **retirement pension** at a time.[4] But
there are special rules if you would otherwise be entitled to both a
Category A (see p116) and a Category B retirement pension (see
pp119-123) and your Category A pension would be paid at a reduced
rate because you have not paid enough contributions (see p235). In this
case your Category A pension will be increased *either*:

• by the amount of a basic Category B pension; *or*
• to the full amount of a basic Category A pension;

whichever is less.[5]

If you are a widow or widower, you will then also be entitled to both
an additional pension on your own contribution record and one on your
spouse's record, subject to a maximum equal to the maximum additional
pension a person could theoretically receive on one contribution record.[6]

A **widow** entitled to both invalidity pension and either widowed
mother's allowance or widow's pension may receive both benefits subject
to a maximum of £57.60 a week.[7] She will also be entitled to both additional pensions subject to a maximum equal to the amount one person
could theoretically receive on top of one benefit. Usually, the widow's
benefit is paid in full with any additional benefit being paid as invalidity
pension. As invalidity pension is not taxable, it is advantageous to apply
for the full invalidity pension, with widow's benefit merely topping it
up.[8]

Additions to benefits

Increases for dependants are covered below.

Invalidity allowance is treated as part of invalidity pension and similarly the age-related addition of SDA is treated as part of the basic
benefit. Invalidity allowance is reduced by an additional pension under

SERPS, [9] and guaranteed minimum pensions under occupational pension schemes.

The increase of retirement pension equivalent to invalidity allowance counts merely as part of the pension but it may be paid with a Category B retirement pension if you are receiving such a pension because it is payable at a higher rate than the Category A retirement pension you would otherwise have.[10] An age addition overlaps only with another age addition.[11]

Additional pensions under SERPS and graduated retirement benefit do not overlap with basic benefits. However, if two or more benefits would otherwise be payable with an additional pension and graduated retirement benefit, only the higher or highest total of additional pension and graduated retirement benefit payable in addition to one of the basic benefits is due.[12]

There are exceptions to this rule for Category B retirement pensioners whose own contribution records would entitle them to Category A retirement pensions and for widows who receive IVB (see p104).

Benefits for people with disabilities

DLA care component and attendance allowance overlap with constant attendance allowance.[13] Otherwise attendance allowance, disablement benefit, REA and retirement allowance do not overlap with any of the other benefits described in this *Guide*. You may therefore receive, say, invalidity pension, both components of DLA, disablement benefit and REA all at once.

Increases in respect of adult dependants

Only one person may receive an increase of benefit in respect of the same dependant, except when one of the claimants receives an increase because the dependant is a woman employed by her/him to look after a child. Equally, you may only receive one increase in respect of an adult dependant. If, apart from those rules, more than one increase would be payable, only the higher or highest total is paid.[14]

An increase for an adult dependant also overlaps with any basic benefit payable to that dependant. If the increase is less than the basic benefit payable to the dependant, the increase will not be paid. If the increase is greater than the basic benefit, it is paid at a rate equal to the difference between the two rates of benefit.[15]

Benefits in respect of children and for child dependants

Only one person may receive child benefit or an increase for a child dependant for the same child (see p192 and 205).

The basic rate of child benefit does not overlap with any other benefit but if you receive the extra £1.95 per week payable for the eldest child, any other benefit or increase paid for the same child will be reduced by £1.20.[16]

You cannot get **one parent benefit** if, for the same child, you get child's special allowance (see p198), industrial death benefit for children (see p199) or an increase in widow's benefit, disablement benefit, ICA or a retirement pension.[17] Increases in IVB, SDA, UB or sickness benefit will be reduced by the same amount of any one parent benefit that is paid for the same child.[18]

All increases for children and child's special allowance overlap with guardian's allowance and industrial death benefit for children.[19]

5. CALCULATING EARNINGS

These rules apply whenever earnings have to be calculated for social security purposes.[1]

The important figure is your earnings *before* tax but after the deduction of national insurance contributions and certain other expenses.

All items provided by your employer count as earnings except:[2]

- meals provided by your employer at your place of work;
- accommodation in which you are required to live as a condition of employment;
- food or produce provided for your normal needs;
- luncheon vouchers up to a maximum of 15 pence per day;
- a Christmas bonus.

Payments from an occupational pension count as 'earnings' for the earnings rules for increases for dependants (see p209).

The following expenses can be deducted from your earnings:[3]

- national insurance contributions;
- trade union subscriptions;
- fares to and from work;
- the cost of making reasonable provision for looking after another member of your household (for example, childminding fees);
- overalls and the cost of cleaning them;

- tools and equipment including, in the case of the self-employed, the cost of business premises other than your home;
- any other reasonable expense.

The basic principle is that any expense incurred because of your work is deductible.

It is *your* responsibility to report any earnings over an earnings limit in a given week to the local Benefits Agency office. Note that these rules are different from the rules governing the calculation of earnings for the purposes of IS and other means-tested benefits.

6. CHRISTMAS BONUS

A Christmas bonus of £10 is payable to those receiving one or more of the qualifying benefits in respect of at least part of the 'relevant week' (even if the benefit is paid later).[1] The 'relevant week' is usually the week beginning with the first Monday in December.

The qualifying benefits are:

- invalidity benefit
- severe disablement allowance
- invalid care allowance
- widowed mother's allowance
- widow's pension
- retirement pension
- disability living allowance
- attendance allowance
- disablement benefit (but only if unemployability supplement or constant attendance allowance is payable)
- industrial death benefit for widows or widowers
- war disablement pension
- war widow's pension
- income support (but only if you reach pensionable age before the end of the 'relevant week').

You may also claim an **extra bonus** for your husband or wife (or someone who you live with as husband or wife) if:[2]

- you are both over pensionable age at the end of the 'relevant week'; *and*
- s/he has not received a bonus in her/his own right; *and*
- you are entitled, or may be treated as entitled, to an increase of benefit in respect of her/him.

You are treated as entitled to a benefit if you are not receiving it because some other payment is being made from public funds. Similarly, you are treated as entitled to an increase in respect of your wife if the reason for it not being paid is either that some other payment is being made from public funds or that she earns too much.[3] The bonus is tax free and has no effect on other benefits. A claim is not necessary in most cases, but if you have not obtained it within a year, your right is lost.[4]

7. RECOVERY OF BENEFITS FROM COMPENSATION PAYMENTS

The general rule

The general rule is that damages are awarded by courts to compensate for loss so that if, as the result of the defendant's action, a plaintiff has had to claim benefit, the amount of damages to be awarded is reduced by the amount of benefit received by the plaintiff.

Thus, in a wrongful or unfair dismissal case, the claim for loss of earnings is reduced by the amount of UB received.[1] The Secretary of State is able to recover an equivalent sum from the employer if it is an unfair dismissal case dealt with in an industrial tribunal[2] (see p30), but *not* if there is a settlement, or it is a wrongful dismissal case dealt with by a court.

Personal injury cases

These rules apply to the victims of an accident or injury suffered on or after 1 January 1989 or to a person who first claimed benefit in respect of a disease on or after that date. They apply to out of court settlements as well as to payments ordered by the courts. A compensator may not make a payment (unless it is 'exempt' – see p264) to the victim of the accident, injury or disease before obtaining a 'certificate of total benefit' from the Secretary of State. The compensator must deduct from the payment the amount required by the 'certificate of total benefit' and must then provide the victim with a **certificate of deduction**. The 'certificate of total benefit' should require the deduction of the amount of 'relevant benefits' paid, or likely to be paid, during the 'relevant period' to the victim in respect of the accident, injury or disease.[3]

'**Relevant benefits**' are UB, sickness benefit, IVB, SDA, DLA (both components), attendance allowance, industrial injuries benefits, IS, family credit (FC) and statutory sick pay (SSP).[4] The '**relevant period**' is the period of five years from the date of any accident or injury or from the date the victim first claimed a 'relevant benefit' in respect of the disease, unless the compensator makes a final payment before the end of that period, in which case the 'relevant period' ends when the payment is made.[5]

'**Exempt payments**' are any payments under £2,500 and also any made in a Fatal Accident Act case or by criminal courts. Payments made under the Vaccine Damage Act 1979 (see Appendix One), the National Health Service industrial injury scheme and redundancy payments are also exempt, as are payments from certain trusts and insurance companies.[6]

The Secretary of State may review a 'certificate of total benefit' if satisfied that it was issued in ignorance of, or was based on a mistake as to, a material fact or if there was an error in its preparation, eg, a miscalculation.[7] The compensator and the victim (or intended recipient) can both appeal against the certificate but not until the payment has been made. Appeals are heard by social security appeal tribunals (SSATs) (see p303) but questions as to whether a person suffered a particular injury, sickness or disease, or for what period, are referred to a medical appeal tribunal (see p311) instead. Further appeals lie to a commissioner in the usual way (see p313).[8] You should appeal if deduction has been made of benefits you would have been receiving even if the accident or disease had not occurred.

Details of the procedures to be followed and other advice can be obtained from: Compensation Recovery Unit, Department of Social Security, Reyrolle Building, Hebburn, Tyne and Wear NE31 1XB (Tel: 091-489 2266). An excellent guide to the procedures called *Deduction from Compensation* is available free from the DSS leaflets unit (see Appendix Five).

Old cases

Different rules apply to the victim of an accident or injury suffered before 1 January 1989.

Most social security benefits, including attendance allowance and mobility allowance (a benefit which was replaced by DLA in 1992), reduce the amount of damages payable by the person who caused the injuries leading to the payment of the benefits.[9] However, there are two major exceptions:

• In a personal injury case, only half of any sickness benefit, IVB, SDA or disablement benefit is taken into account when assessing loss of earnings for the five years after an accident or onset of a disease or disablement.[10] After that five-year period, those benefits are ignored entirely.[11]

- In a fatal accident case, any widow's benefit, death benefit or other benefit resulting from the death is ignored.[12]

8. DEDUCTIONS FROM BENEFIT

Overpayments of non-means-tested benefits

If any of the benefits covered in this *Guide* are overpaid and the overpayment is recoverable (see p295), deductions are usually made from future payments of benefit. It can also be recovered by deductions from or by stopping any of the other benefits covered in this guide except SSP or statutory maternity pay (SMP).[1] The only exceptions are that child benefit or guardian's allowance cannot have deductions made from them except to recover an overpayment of the same benefit.[2] Deductions can also be made from IS or FC but there are limits to the rate at which deductions can be made from IS (see CPAG's *National Welfare Benefits Handbook*).

Overpayment of means-tested benefits

Overpayments of IS and FC which are recoverable can also be recovered from any of the benefits covered in this *Guide*, except SSP, SMP, child benefit, guardian's allowance or attendance allowance for a child.[3] So can overpayments of housing benefit (HB) or council tax benefit (CTB), but only if the overpayment was due to a misrepresentation or failure to disclose.[4] (The circumstances in which those two benefits can be recovered by other methods are quite wide.) Overpayments of those two benefits are recovered from social security benefits only when a local authority is unable to recover them from HB or CTB.

Social fund loans

These are recoverable from any of the benefits covered in this guide, except SSP, SMP, widow's payment, DLA, attendance allowance, child benefit, guardian's allowance or child's special allowance.[5]

9. CRIMINAL OFFENCES

When dealing with the DSS you must not:

- make any statement or representation which you know to be false; *or*
- provide documents or information which you know to be false; *or*

- knowingly cause or allow anyone else to provide documents or information which you know to be false.[1]

If you do so you are guilty of a criminal offence and can be fined up to £5,295 and/or imprisoned for up to three months. In addition, you may have to repay any overpaid benefit (see p295). It does not make any difference whether it is you or someone else that is actually claiming benefit – eg, an employer who gave false reasons for having dismissed a former employee would be committing an offence (and s/he might also have to repay the Benefits Agency any benefit overpaid as a result – see p295). Neither does it matter if you were not successful in being paid benefit. **Simply giving false information is a crime.** These offences can be tried only in a magistrates' court (in Scotland, a Sheriffs' Court), and the prosecution must be commenced within 12 months of the commission of the offence or within three months of sufficient evidence coming to light, whichever is later.[2]

To prove that you have made a statement or representation that you knew to be false, the prosecution must show that you knew both that you were making the statement and that it was false. It is usual for the prosecution to rely on your signing the statement on the girocheque or order book to the effect that you are entitled to the money and have reported all relevant changes of circumstances. You must sign that statement when cashing the girocheque or order. It is a defence if you believed that you were entitled to the money and had reported everything necessary. You are guilty only if you are dishonest.[3] On the other hand, it is not necessary for the prosecution to show that you intended to defraud the DSS rather than someone else. If you knew the statement was false, it does not matter why you made it.[4]

For more serious frauds, the prosecution usually brings charges of deception under section 15 of the Theft Act 1968, which carry very much heavier penalties.

Because the signing of each girocheque or order may be a separate offence, the prosecution usually brings charges in relation to just two or three weeks.

For a deliberate and prolonged fraud, such as claiming UB while working full-time, a sentence of imprisonment may be considered even for a person with no previous convictions. However, it has been emphasised that such offences are non-violent, non-sexual or non-frightening crimes so that custodial sentences are by no means inevitable.[5]

A court may order compensation to be paid in addition to or instead of any sentence imposed on a convicted defendant. If this is for a sum less than the overpayment, the Benefits Agency may still recover the rest from you (see p295).

If you are charged with an offence of this nature you should apply for legal aid and see a solicitor, even if you are thinking of pleading guilty.

Fraud in relation to contributions attracts the same penalties as the fraudulent claiming of benefits.[6] Again, more serious offences may be charged under the Theft Acts.

Non-payment of Class 1 or Class 2 contributions within the time limits renders a person liable to a fine of up to £1,000.[7] Failure to comply with other contribution regulations may also lead to a fine of £1,000, but in this case there may be a further £40 fine for each day the contravention continues.[8]

The Secretary of State may appoint inspectors to investigate possible fraud, and it is an offence wilfully to delay or obstruct an inspector in the exercise of her/his powers or to refuse or neglect to answer any questions or to furnish any information or to produce any document when required to do so under the Social Security Administration Act 1992. Again, the maximum penalty is £500, and there can be a further daily penalty of £40 for refusing to answer questions or produce documents.[9] However, you are not required to answer any questions or give any evidence which might incriminate you or your spouse.[10]

10. EQUAL TREATMENT FOR MEN AND WOMEN

As discussed in Chapter 13, entitlement to social security benefits is not governed by British law alone. There are also Regulations and Directives made by the European Community (EC) which apply directly in all countries in the Community – and, in some cases, throughout the European Economic Area (EEA) (see p247).

In particular, there are a number of Directives which are designed to ensure that (subject to limited exceptions which are kept under review) social security benefits, occupational pensions, pay and other benefits from employment are received on an equal basis by both men and women.

British courts (including adjudication officers, SSATs and social security commissioners) are obliged to apply European law as well as domestic British law and although British law has been amended to take these Directives into account, the European rules override the British rules where the two still conflict.[1] Cases which involve points of European law will usually be referred to the European Court of Justice (ECJ) in Luxembourg, unless there has already been a ruling of that Court which directly covers the issue.

There has been a vast amount of case law in the ECJ and national courts on the anti-discrimination provisions of EC law and a book the length of this *Guide* could not begin to cover the subject comprehensively. What follows is an outline of the general principles and a discussion of what these mean in practical terms for people claiming non-means-tested benefits. If you think there is a chance that you may benefit from the principle of equal treatment, there is no substitute for getting proper advice on the particular circumstances of your claim. See p329 for the names and addresses of organisations which may be able to help you with this.

For present purposes, the most important Directive is the *Council Directive of 19th December 1978 on the progressive implementation of the principle of equal treatment for men and women in matters of social security*.[2] This Directive, which became binding on all member states on 22 December 1984, has *direct effect*. This means that individual citizens of the EEA countries can rely on it to claim benefits from their governments on a non-discriminatory basis even if those governments have not introduced national legislation putting the Directive into operation or if they have implemented it only in part.

The 'Principle of Equal Treatment' which is established by the Directive is that:

> There shall be **no discrimination whatsoever** on ground of sex either directly, or indirectly by reference in particular to marital or family status . . . [3]

Discrimination simply means treating one person less favourably than another. *Indirect* discrimination occurs when a rule appears to be neutral but in practice can be complied with by fewer members of one sex than the other and that rule cannot be justified for reasons other than discrimination based on sex. It will often be necessary to rely on statistical evidence to prove indirect discrimination.

If the principle of equal treatment applies to you, then your claim for benefit should be decided on the rules which would have applied if you were a member of the opposite sex if those rules would be more favourable.[4]

However, this broad general principle is subject to a number of limitations and to exceptions (known as 'derogations'). In practice this means that you have to ask three questions before you can know whether the principle of equal treatment applies in your case:

- **Is the benefit you are claiming (or your liability to pay contributions) covered by the Directive?** Only schemes for benefits which cover certain risks (see p269) are subject to the principle of equal treatment. This is sometimes referred to as the **material scope** (or scope *rationae materiae*) of the Directive;
- **Does the Directive apply to you?** You are only entitled to benefit from

the principle of equal treatment if you are a member of the *working population* (see below). This is sometimes referred to as the **personal scope** (or scope *rationae personae*) of the Directive;

- **Does the Directive include a derogation which applies in your case?** If so, member states are allowed to discriminate against you even if you are within both the personal and material scope of the Directive.

The material scope of the Directive

The Directive applies to schemes for *state benefits* which are designed to protect against the following risks:[5]

- sickness
- invalidity
- old age
- accidents at work and occupational diseases
- unemployment

This means that all the benefits discussed in Chapters 1 to 11 of this *Guide* (except for maternity benefits and widows' benefits – which are beyond the scope of the Directive[6] – and category B and C retirement pensions – which are the subject of derogations (see p270)) are covered by the Directive.

The Directive also applies to means-tested benefits (referred to as *social assistance*) to the extent that they are intended to supplement or replace the schemes referred to above.[7] For a discussion of what this means in the context of the means-tested benefits available in Great Britain see CPAG's *Ethnic Minorities Benefits Handbook*.

The fact that the Directive applies only to state schemes means that other schemes (such as occupational pensions schemes) are beyond its scope. These are, however, covered by a later Directive[8] which is in similar terms.

The personal scope of the Directive

The Directive applies to you if you are a member of the **working population**. If you are not a member of the working population then you cannot use the Directive to stop the government discriminating against you even if the benefit which you are claiming is within the material scope of the Directive.

The working population is defined as being: [9]

- workers (ie, people in employment);
- the self-employed;

- people seeking employment;
- workers and self-employed people whose jobs have been interrupted by illness, accident or involuntary unemployment;
- workers and self-employed people who have retired or become unable to work because of invalidity.

In practical terms this means that to be covered by the Directive you must have been either working or actively looking for work when you became affected by one of the risks set out on p269. So, for example, the Directive will not apply to you if:

- you have been so ill or disabled since before you reached the age of 16 that you have never been able to contemplate working or looking for work; *or*
- you stopped working for a reason which is not included in the list of risks on p269 (eg, because you were pregnant) and before you began to look for work again you became too ill to work.

It is not, however, necessary for the risks to be suffered by you personally. In one case, a woman who gave up work to look after her severely disabled mother was held to be a member of the working population because her work had been interrupted by invalidity, even though it was the invalidity of her mother and not her own personal invalidity.[10]

Exceptions to the principle of equal treatment

The Directive permits member states to adopt or continue discriminatory rules on certain aspects of entitlement to benefits even if they are within its material scope.

The types of discriminatory rule which may be lawful are:[11]

- rules which set a different age for men and women to become entitled to retirement pensions. This derogation also covers rules which deal with the *possible consequences* for other benefits of having a differential pensionable age;
- rules which allow people who have looked after children to claim retirement pensions and other benefits on advantageous terms. In Britain, this derogation would seem to permit the rules about Home Responsibilities Protection (see p229) which are probably indirectly discriminatory against men;
- rules which allow wives to derive entitlement to old-age pensions and incapacity benefits on the basis of their husbands' contributions or periods of insurance. This permits the British rules on Category B and C retirement pensions which discriminate directly against men;
- rules which cover increases for a dependent wife of incapacity benefits,

retirement pensions and industrial injuries benefits. The UK Government argues that this allows the discrimination in the different rules for dependency increases in Category A and C retirement pensions (see p204)

- rules which allow special treatment for people who before 22 December 1984 have opted 'not to acquire rights or incur obligations under a statutory scheme'. This is intended to cover the British rules on the married woman's reduced national insurance contribution (see p219).

The derogations should not be regarded as a *carte blanche* to discriminate. As part of the progressive implementation of the principle of equal treatment, EEA states are supposed to keep these discriminatory rules under review to ensure that they are still justified in the light of social developments,[12] and to notify the European Commission of the measures that they have taken to do so.[13]

Perhaps more importantly, the ECJ has repeatedly held that the elimination of discrimination based on sex is a fundamental EC right which it has a duty to protect. It therefore scrutinises the validity of rules which rely on the derogations very carefully to ensure that the principle of *proportionality* is observed.[14] This means that any derogation from the individual rights granted by the Directive will be narrowly interpreted so that it remains within the limits of what is appropriate and necessary for achieving the aim which the derogation was intended to permit.

Because of this, it does not follow that a discriminatory rule is valid just because it has one of the effects allowed by the derogations. In each case it is for the government of the member state which made the rule to establish that the discriminatory means which it has adopted are an appropriate way of achieving the ends permitted by the derogation.

The effect of the principle of equal treatment on British social security benefits

The principle of equal treatment has had a significant impact on claimants' entitlement to non-means-tested benefits. Even before the Directive came into force, many discriminatory rules about entitlement to benefit were abolished in order to comply with Britain's community obligations. Since December 1984, the Directive has been used by the ECJ to extend entitlement for many women by overruling many discriminatory laws which still remained.

For example:

- In 1986, the ECJ struck down a rule which meant that ICA (see p158) was not paid to married or cohabiting women who were living with or

- maintained by their partners, even though it would have been paid to married men who met the other conditions of entitlement and who lived with or were maintained by their wives.[15]
- In 1987, a transitional rule which perpetuated the discriminatory effects of a benefit which had been abolished (non-contributory invalidity pension (NCIP)) and which meant that it was more difficult for women than men to establish entitlement to SDA was held to be unlawful.[16] Four years later this was extended to cover women who had not even claimed NCIP because they knew they would not have qualified under the discriminatory rules.[17]
- In 1993, the ECJ held that it was unlawful discrimination to deny ICA and SDA to women aged 60 or over when those benefits would be paid to men up to the age of 65.[18] This is the *Thomas* decision referred to p273.

Currently, the most important issue for British social security law is the scope of the derogation for 'the possible consequences' for other benefits of different retirement ages.[19]

This affects:

- women with incomplete contribution records who are or were receiving IVB immediately before their 60th birthday and whose benefit has been reduced to the level at which their retirement pension would have been paid if they had claimed it. Such women (together with those referred to in the next paragraph) are sometimes referred to as '*Graham* lookalikes' after the *Graham* case (see p273)
- women who become incapable for work aged between 54 and 59 and who are therefore refused invalidity allowance which would be payable if they were male (see p78);
- women claiming UB or sickness benefit whose contribution record does not entitle them to a full Category A retirement pension (see pp43 and 65);
- men with full contribution records aged between 60 and 64 who are claiming UB or sickness benefit (see p43); *and*
- some men aged between 60 and 64, who are claiming UB and have dependent children or are claiming sickness benefit and have dependent adults or children (see p43)
- women aged between 65 and 70 who have been refused reduced earnings allowance (REA) (see p179).

It is clear that not just any connection between a rule and pensionable age will be sufficient for the derogation to apply. To take a far-fetched example, a country could not (say) pay UB to women aged over 20 while making men wait until they were 25 and then justify the discrimination against men by claiming that the qualifying age was pensionable age less 40 years. The question is how close the link must be before it is covered by the derogation.

This question has recently been considered by the ECJ in the *Thomas* case and the *Equal Opportunities Commission* (EOC) case[20] which concerned the liability of men to pay primary Class 1 national insurance contributions for five years longer than women (see p229). The combined effect of the judgments in these cases is that a national rule only counts as a 'possible consequence' of the setting of different pensionable ages if it is objectively linked to the difference of pensionable age and is 'necessary to guarantee the consistency and the financial equilibrium' of the social security system.

Applying this test, it was held in *Thomas* that non-contributory benefits such as ICA and SDA could not be withdrawn at different ages for men and women because it was not necessary to do this to maintain the equilibrium of the system. However, the *EOC* case decided that the rules requiring that men pay contributions for five more years than women to get the same basic pension and that working men aged between 60 and 64 must continue to pay contributions even though working women of the same age do not were covered by the derogation. It was held that the whole purpose of the derogation was to allow discrimination on a temporary basis so that the benefits system could be moved smoothly towards an equal pensionable age without financial disruption. As the financial equilibrium of the system was based on men contributing for five years longer than women, it would be contrary to the objective of the derogation to exclude from it discrimination concerning contribution periods.

The question is therefore whether the rules which link contributory earnings replacement benefits to pensionable age are more like the similar rules for non-contributory benefits which were struck down in *Thomas* or the rules on contributions which were upheld in *EOC*. In the case of IVB, a commissioner has held in the case of *Graham*[21] that the discrimination between men and women aged between 60 and 65 and the refusal of invalidity allowance to women who became ill between the ages of 55 and 59 is not covered by the derogation and is therefore unlawful. The DSS has appealed this decision to the Court of Appeal which referred the case to the ECJ in January 1994.

Realistically, it will probably be at least 18 months before the ECJ gives its decision. If you think you may be affected by it (and remember this is likely to include people who are claiming UB and sickness benefit and REA as well as IVB) you should take advice (see p329). The general position for *Graham* lookalikes is as follows:

- if you already have an appeal in the system, you are likely to find that you win at every stage on the basis of the commissioner's decision in *Graham*. The DSS will eventually appeal your case all the way to the Court of Appeal, where it will be put to one side while the decision of the ECJ in *Graham* is awaited. It is likely that payment of the increased benefit will be suspended in the meantime.
- if you have turned 60 (or asked for a review of the decision to reduce your IVB on your 60th birthday) since the commissioner's decision in *Graham*, you will probably find that the adjudication officer will decide in your favour but that the Secretary of State will suspend *payment* of the increased benefit (see p295) until the decision of the ECJ is known.

In either case, the Secretary of State has a discretion whether or not to suspend payment and will not do so if you can convince your local office that this would cause you *exceptional* hardship. If you think you are in this category you should write to your local office explaining the position. It may be wise to take advice first (see p329).

Above all, it is important *not* to claim your retirement pension while you are waiting. If you do so, you risk not getting any arrears of benefit even if Mrs Graham wins her case. Some DSS offices are telling women over 60 on IVB either that they have no choice but to retire or that it will make no financial difference for them either way. That is not correct and if you have been misled in this way you should immediately complain to the customer service manager at your local office (see p276). This will mean that you and the DSS have a record of what you say has happened if it should be necessary to make a claim for compensation later on. *Graham* lookalikes who have claimed their retirement pensions (whether by accident or because of incorrect advice) should immediately de-retire (see p116) unless they are now aged 70 or over. If you are now aged between 65 and 69, the DSS may say that you are not allowed to do this. You should argue that a rule which allows men aged between 65 and 69 to de-retire but not women is itself discriminatory and contrary to the Directive.

PART FOUR

Administration and appeals

CHAPTER FIFTEEN

Administration

This chapter covers:

1. Claims (see below)
2. Decisions (p283)
3. Reviews (p288)
4. Payments (p294)
5. Recovery of overpayments (p295)
6. Complaints (p301)

1. CLAIMS

The Benefits Agency

The benefits covered in this *Guide* (and also the main means-tested benefits) are administered by part of the DSS called the Benefits Agency. Most benefits are dealt with at your local Benefits Agency office. However, there are exceptions. For example, if you live in certain parts of London, your claim will be processed by special Benefits Agency offices in Glasgow (although you should still claim at your local office) and all claims for certain benefits are processed centrally. For example, child benefit is administered in Washington, Tyne and Wear – see p193. Unemployment benefit is administered by the Employment Service, part of the Department of Employment, on behalf of the DSS – claims are dealt with at local unemployment benefit offices and payments are made from a central computer.

All enquiries about social security benefits should first be made at the appropriate local office, which you will find listed under 'S' in the telephone directory.

Every Benefits Agency office has a 'customer service manager' whom you can contact if you are unhappy about the service you are receiving and cannot resolve the problem with the reception supervisor. Benefits Agency leaflet BAL1 (*Have Your Say*) contains a form for you to write to the customer service manager but you do not have to use it if you prefer to write your own letter, or speak to her/him in person. If you are still dissatisfied after the customer service manager has looked into your case, you should write to either the district manager or to the Chief Executive of the Benefits Agency, Mr Michael Bichard, Benefits Agency, 286 Euston Road, London NW1 3DN, marking your letter for his personal attention.

As part of the Government's 'Citizen's Charter' initiative, the Benefits Agency has produced a 'customer charter'. This sets out standards of service which cover matters such as the prompt and accurate payment of your benefits. There are specific targets set for processing your claim – eg, in the case of sickness benefit, 65 per cent of claims should be processed within 10 working days, and 95 per cent within 30 working days. You can get a copy of the customer charter from your local office or from the customer service branch of the Benefits Agency at the address above. If you have to complain, it may help you if you can show that the Benefits Agency has failed to meet its published standards in your case.

Whenever you write to the Benefits Agency, you should be sure to quote your national insurance number and, if you are not writing to the office which is handling your claim, the name and address of that office.

Making a claim

A claim must be made for almost all benefits. You become entitled to benefit only when you submit a claim. This is the case even if you satisfy all the other conditions,[1] although in some instances, claims can be backdated (see pp281-283). (The only exceptions to this rule are retirement allowance and certain retirement pensions which do not have to be claimed if you are already receiving certain other retirement pensions or widows' benefits.[2])

Claims for benefit should normally be made on the appropriate DSS form. However, the Secretary of State *may* decide to treat any letter or other written communication as being a valid claim.[3]

Example

You were claiming sickness benefit and wrote to the Benefits Agency office to say that your husband had died. You were unaware that you could claim a widow's payment. Two years later, you find out about widow's payment. You can ask the Secretary of State to treat your letter as being a claim for widow's benefit. Write to your local Benefits Agency office arguing that you should have been given proper advice two years ago.

Because the decision is formally made by the Secretary of State (see p286), you cannot appeal. However, the Secretary of State only decides the question whether the manner of a claim was sufficient (eg, whether your letter gave enough information to make it obvious that you were entitled to a benefit). Whether a claim has been made (eg, if the Benefits Agency has no record of your letter and suggests that you never wrote it) and, if so, when it was received by the Benefits Agency, are questions to be decided by an adjudication officer (AO), so you can appeal to a tribunal.[4]

A claim for unemployment benefit must be made *in person* at the unemployment benefit office, unless the Secretary of State directs you otherwise.[5]

A claim form is generally found at the back of the DSS leaflet describing each benefit. Personal interviews are rarely required, but medical examinations may be. Since backdating is possible only to a limited extent, you should claim as soon as you think that you *might* be entitled to a benefit, even if it will take you some time to collect all the information required by the form. Very occasionally, it may be in your interests to wait for the next calendar year to claim on the basis of a better record of national insurance contributions (see p232).

You can amend your claim form by writing to the local office and, if this is received before a decision is made, the Secretary of State can treat the claim as amended from the date it was initially made.[6] A claim form submitted without a proper signature or certification may be treated in a similar way, provided you correct this within a month of the form being returned to you.[7]

If the claimant is a child or is otherwise unable to act on her/his own behalf, another person may apply in writing to be appointed to take all the necessary steps in relation to a claim, unless a court has already appointed someone else.[8] Even if you could act on your own behalf, there is nothing to prevent your asking someone else to act for you (except in the case of a claim for unemployment benefit[9]) provided that you inform the Benefits Agency in writing. However, you must still take reasonable steps to make sure that time limits are kept to.[10]

The Secretary of State may require you to provide documentation and evidence relevant to the claim and you can be asked for an interview if one is reasonably required.[11] You may be able to claim travelling expenses for this.[12] However, personal interviews (other than for unemployment benefit) are relatively rare and most claims for social security benefits are administered by post. Once completed, the claim should be referred forthwith to the AO (see p283) for decision.[13] If you do not provide the evidence asked for by the Secretary of State, or you do not attend an interview, your claim still has to be referred to an AO who is not entitled to withhold a determination even if you have not complied with the Secretary of State's request.[14] The AO must make a decision on the available evidence, as must a tribunal if you appeal. Obviously an AO or tribunal is unlikely to decide in your favour if you fail to provide evidence which would be available to you if your claim were justified.

Even if the Secretary of State does not ask for further documents, you should make sure that the AO has all the evidence that might be relevant. If you were sacked and there is a dispute over whether you lost your job through misconduct, you might ask your former workmates to write statements for you to send to the AO to back up your version of events.

Until the claim is passed to the AO to decide, there is no decision on it against which you can appeal. See p283 for suggestions as to what to do if you think there is unreasonable delay in processing your claim or an unreasonable demand for further information or evidence.

Interchange of claims

If you have claimed the wrong benefit but are in fact entitled to another benefit, your original claim can be treated as a claim for the right benefit.

Unless your claim was made between 6 April 1987 and 10 April 1988 (in which case the decision should be made by an AO and there is a right of appeal[15]), the decision on this point is taken by the Secretary of State (see p286). He does not have to accept a claim for one benefit as a claim for another but will usually decide in your favour if the Benefits Agency should have realised from your claim that you had made a mistake.

Not all benefit claims are interchangeable. A claim for unemployment benefit may be treated as a claim for any incapacity benefit (ie, sickness benefit, invalidity benefit or severe disablement allowance), maternity allowance or invalid care allowance (ICA). A claim for invalidity benefit (IVB) may be treated as a claim for any other incapacity benefit or maternity allowance but not for unemployment benefit (UB). A claim for maternity allowance may be treated as a claim for any incapacity benefit. A claim for widow's benefit may be treated as a claim for retirement pension and vice versa. A claim for income support may be treated as a claim for invalid care allowance but not as a claim for other benefits.[16]

In the case of claims for children, a claim for child benefit may be treated as a claim for one parent benefit, guardian's allowance, an increase of other benefits for the child or even maternity allowance for the period since the child's birth and vice versa. A claim for guardian's allowance may also be treated as a claim for an increase of another benefit for the child if you are not entitled to guardian's allowance.[17]

If a person claims a benefit (other than child benefit) but is not entitled to it, the claim may be treated as a claim by someone else for an increase in his/her benefit for the person who originally claimed. If a person claims an increase of benefit for a child or adult dependant but is not entitled to it, the claim may be treated as a claim by someone else who is entitled.[18]

Time limits for claims

Benefits may be claimed up to three months before you actually become entitled to them, except for maternity allowance (which may be claimed no earlier than 14 weeks before the expected date of confinement), retirement pension (which may be claimed up to four months in advance), and attendance allowance.[19]

Once you have made your initial claim, benefit is awarded for an indefinite period, except for disability living allowance (DLA) (see p152) and UB which is usually awarded for a fortnight at a time.[20] An award is reviewed if your circumstances change or if you cease to satisfy the conditions for entitlement.

There are strict time limits for claiming benefits. These may be extended for 'good cause' in the case of some benefits only (see pp281-283). Otherwise a benefit must be claimed within a specified period after the day for which the claim is made.

The specified periods are:[21]

Unemployment benefit (UB)	This must be claimed on the very day for which the claim is made unless you have been told to claim on another particular day.[22] In practice, after your first claim, you will usually be told to claim fortnightly.
Sickness benefit, invalidity benefit (IVB) and severe disablement allowance (SDA):	
• on the first claim ever made by a claimant	1 month
• on any other initial claim	6 days
• on any continuation claim	10 days
Industrial injuries benefits	3 months
Child benefit, guardian's allowance and any increase of benefit for a dependant	6 months
Retirement pensions, widows' benefits, maternity allowance and invalid care allowance (ICA)	12 months

Disability living allowance (DLA)
and attendance allowance:

- on any initial claim   The very day for which benefit is
                                       claimed[23]

- on any continuation claim   6 months[24]

The time limits for UB, sickness benefit and IVB and for SDA may be increased to one month if the Secretary of State certifies that to do so would be consistent with the proper administration of the legislation.[25]

The time limits for widows' benefits may be extended in some cases (see p103).

Failing to claim within the time limit does not usually mean that you do not receive any benefit at all for the period of your claim; but benefit will be backdated only to a limited extent. So, if you claim industrial injuries benefits five months after becoming entitled to them and you have no good cause for the delay, you will receive three months' arrears only. That is because your claim will have been in time for the last three months. The exceptions to this are disablement benefit for occupational deafness (prescribed disease A10) or occupational asthma (prescribed disease D7) where missing the time limits may mean that you lose your right to benefit altogether (see p178).

'Good cause' for a late claim

If you claim outside the time limit, you will still be entitled to arrears of some benefits if you can show that there has been 'good cause' for not claiming throughout the period of the delay.[26] However, this applies only to UB, sickness benefit, IVB, SDA and industrial injuries benefits.

Even if you have 'good cause' for a late claim, you will still not receive any benefit other than industrial injuries benefits due more than 12 months before the date of your claim.[27] It may be possible to argue that a claim for one benefit may be treated as a claim for another, or that any written document may be treated as a claim (see pp279 and 277).

It is not always easy to show good cause for a late claim. Ill health can amount to good cause in some circumstances. If you are a hospital in-patient, you are assumed to have good cause for not claiming sickness or IVB or SDA until either 13 weeks after your admission or three weeks after your discharge, whichever date comes sooner.[28] In other cases, ill health, whether physical or mental, may also amount to good cause.[29]

Claimants frequently say that they did not know that they could claim. AOs usually reply that ignorance is no excuse. That is an oversimplification of the law. It has been held that good cause means 'some fact which, having regard to all the circumstances (including the claimant's state of health and the information which he had received and that which he might have obtained), would probably have caused a reasonable person of his age and experience to act (or fail to act) as the claimant did'.[30] So, while there is a general duty to find out your rights, your age and experience are taken into account when deciding whether you have acted reasonably. If you claim late because you were ignorant of your rights, the first thing you need to explain is why.[31] You are expected to make enquiries by looking at the relevant DSS leaflets[32] or asking the DSS,[33] a solicitor[34] or a citizens' advice bureau.[35] Merely relying upon the advice of friends,[36] or even a doctor,[37] is not enough.

If you have made enquiries, you will have good cause for a late claim if you were misinformed, or insufficiently informed of your rights, or were accidentally misled.[38] The enquiries need not necessarily have been in connection with that particular claim and people have succeeded where they have simply misunderstood the system. So, a person who had once made enquiries about the rights of the self-employed to UB and who thought the answers applied equally to sickness benefit succeeded in showing good cause.[39] People who know that certain benefits depend upon contributions paid while working, and who leave work not realising that they are covered for benefit by their contributions for up to two years afterwards (due to the rules relating to periods of interruption of employment), have also succeeded.[40] While language difficulties, illiteracy and unfamiliarity with technical documents do not in themselves amount to good cause for not claiming, they obviously increase the likelihood of confusion and are important matters to be taken into consideration.[41]

If you have made no enquiries at all it is more difficult to show good cause. You must show that your ignorance was due to a mistaken belief 'reasonably held', so you must explain exactly how you came to be under the wrong impression.[42] The general rule is that you cannot be expected to claim something if you have no reason to suspect you have a right to claim it. Being unaware that you have an industrial disease is good cause,[43] but if you know you have the disease and you suspect it was caused at work, you are expected to enquire whether it is a prescribed industrial disease. You are likely to be excused ignorance of detailed changes in the law which give you new rights.[44]

If a person has been *formally* appointed by a court or the Secretary of State to act on your behalf, the question is whether the appointee had good cause for any late claim – not whether you have had.[45] If someone is *informally* acting on your behalf, the question is whether you have good cause and you must show that the delegation of the claim was reasonable and that reasonable supervision was exercised.[46]

The good cause must continue up to the date of claim. Although the odd day may be overlooked, a substantial break in the good cause for not claiming will result in only the later period being taken into account.[47]

If you are prevented from receiving benefit because your claim was more than 12 months late due to an error on the part of the DSS, it may still be possible to persuade the DSS to meet its moral obligation and make an *ex gratia* payment to you even though it is not strictly obliged to do so. The intervention of an MP or the Ombudsman (see p301) may help in these circumstances.

2. DECISIONS

It is important to know who is making the decision on any particular question in your case because this determines how you can challenge it. There are three separate bodies who may be responsible for making initial decisions.

The adjudication officer

The AO makes most initial decisions on claims for social security benefits.[1] The exceptions to this general rule are:

- decisions which have to be taken by the Secretary of State (see p286);
- disablement questions in relation to SDA and disablement benefit, which are referred to adjudicating medical authorities (see p287).
- forfeiture questions (if you have killed your husband), which are decided by a social security commissioner (see p315).

AOs are civil servants in either the Benefits Agency or, in relation to UB, the Employment Service of the Department of Employment. A chief adjudication officer is appointed to give them advice and keep the adjudication system under review.[2] A decision should be taken on your claim within 14 days of receiving your papers so far as practicable.[3] Sometimes the decision will take longer than this. In the interim, you may be able to claim income support if you have inadequate resources. The amount of any income support paid to you may be deducted from arrears of social security benefits which you subsequently receive.[4]

If you need to contact the AO, you can write to her/ him at the local office.

Delay in making decisions is a relatively common problem. To remedy this, you can quote the statutory time limit of 14 days and the service targets in the Benefits Agency Customers' Charter (see p277). You can also threaten to complain to the customer service manager or the Chief Executive of the Benefits Agency (see p277) or threaten a complaint to the Ombudsman (see p301), or to write to the Chief Adjudication Officer (at the address in Appendix Four see p350). In an extreme case it might be possible to make an application for judicial review, but you would need to see a solicitor (see p330). In one case, where there had been a four month delay in deciding an UB claim, a decision was made within 24 hours of the claimant being granted legal aid for judicial review!

It is not possible to sue an AO for negligence in the way s/he decides your claim.[5] If the decision is wrong, the only thing you can do is appeal against it. But the position is different if you are given *wrong advice* by an employee of the Benefits Agency (see p302).

There is a special procedure for the 'diagnosis' and 'recrudescence' questions for industrial diseases (see p285).

In all other cases, the AO may decide the case for you, or against you, or may decide to refer it to a social security appeal tribunal (SSAT)(see p303).[6] It is uncommon to refer cases to a tribunal unless an appeal is already pending on the claim, but it is a procedure which is sometimes used when the evidence is contradictory – eg, a dispute between a claimant and his/her former employers over the circumstances of a dismissal.

If you are not happy with the AO's decision on your case, you may appeal to an SSAT (see p303). Alternatively, the decision may be reviewed (see p288).

The 'anti-test-case' rules

The AO must make decisions in accordance with the law, including commissioners' decisions (see p326). However, there are rules which say that some decisions should be ignored when AOs are considering claims for periods before the decision was given. This is intended to prevent claimants from taking advantage of test cases brought against the DSS, but it goes rather wider.

If a commissioner or court has recently held that a tribunal (or, in limited circumstances explained on p286, an AO) in a totally different case has made an error of law, the AO must decide any part of your claim which relates to the period *before* the decision of the commissioner or court as if that tribunal decision 'had been found by the commissioner or court in question *not* to have been erroneous in point of law'.[7] That appears to mean that the AO in your case must make exactly the same error as the tribunal had made. However, such an interpretation could lead to absurd results. Unless it is in your favour, you should argue instead that the effect of this provision is simply that the decision of the commissioner or court should not be taken into account by the AO. This would limit the effect of the provision to situations where a commissioner or court overrules a previous binding decision because, in other cases, the AO would be free to, and so likely to, reach the same result as the commissioner or court anyway.[8]

Note that this applies *only* if the claim or request for review post-dates the test-case decision and only to that part of your claim which relates to a period before that decision. Also, it means that the decision of the commissioner or court has to be disregarded for that period only if the tribunal has been held to have been wrong; not if it has been upheld.

This rule applies if the High Court (in Scotland, the Court of Session) has found an AO to have been wrong on an application for judicial review, but not in cases where a commissioner or court has disagreed with an AO but has agreed with a *tribunal* which allowed a claimant's appeal.

The rules may not apply where a claimant has *successfully* appealed to the Court of Appeal against an adverse decision of a commissioner. This is because they only apply if a decision of an 'adjudicating authority' has been held to be erroneous and commissioners are not included in the definition of 'adjudicating authority'.[9] A recent commissioner's decision[10] throws some doubt on this argument but this has been appealed to the Court of Appeal. That appeal is expected to be heard very shortly after this *Guide* goes to press. CPAG's *Welfare Rights Bulletin* will report the decision of the Court and give details if there is to be a further appeal.

If there is an *unsuccessful* appeal from a commissioner to the Court of Appeal (in Scotland, the Court of Session) in another case, it is unclear whether the tribunal's error has to be applied to the whole period before the commissioner's decision. If the error is helpful to you, you should argue that the relevant date is the date of the court's decision because that decision replaces the commissioner's decision. If the error is unhelpful to you, you should argue that the relevant date is the date of the commissioner's decision because that decision is not quashed by the court and so is left standing. The latter argument is the better one, but it is worth trying the other if it is more helpful, particularly if the court has reached the same result as the commissioner for totally different reasons.

It is important to note that these provisions apply *only* when an AO is considering a new claim or a review on the ground of error of law. They do not apply to reviews on other grounds or if you are given leave to make a late appeal (see p318).

Industrial disease cases

The 'diagnosis' and 'recrudescence' questions for industrial diseases (see pp168 and 170) are decided by a special procedure.

First, the AO must obtain a medical report, unless a suitable one is already available.[11] Then the case may either be decided by the AO or referred to a medical board (see p287) for its decision.[12] These references are much more common than those to tribunals – particularly in industrial disease cases (where there must always be a reference if a disablement question (see p168) arises[13]).

If the case is decided by an AO, you may appeal to a medical board. The appeal must be in writing and must be given to the local office within three months.[14] The time may be extended by the chairperson of the medical board if there are special reasons.[15] See p287 for the procedure before medical boards. Alternatively, the decision may be reviewed (see p288).

The Secretary of State

The legislation specifies that some matters are to be decided by the Secretary of State. In practice, they are taken by specially authorised officials who are called Secretary of State's representatives. A Secretary of State's decision cannot be appealed to a tribunal.

A large number of matters – many of them procedural but others dealing with substantive matters such as whether benefit is to be paid while a person is abroad – are decided entirely at the Secretary of State's discretion. You can always ask the Secretary of State to reconsider the decision by writing to your local office giving reasons.[16] There is no other remedy against an unsatisfactory decision other than an application to the High Court for judicial review, which will rarely be possible.

However, certain matters are dealt with by a special procedure.[17] These are to do with contributions and a person's employment; eg, whether a person is an 'employed earner' for the purposes of paying contributions or entitlement to industrial injuries benefits, or satisfies the contribution conditions for a benefit or the conditions for receipt of home responsibility protection. Also included are questions concerning the calculation of earnings factors and certain questions concerning occupational pensions and personal pension schemes. Decisions on these matters may be taken first by the AO if it appears that they are not in dispute. You are notified of the decision and the reasons for it and invited to reply if dissatisfied.[18] On receipt of your reply, the AO certifies that the matter is for determination by the Secretary of State and you are invited to apply for a formal decision.[19]

The Contributions Agency will investigate the facts and reach a provisional decision. If you are not happy with this, the question is then determined by an oral hearing before someone appointed by the Secretary of State, generally a DSS solicitor.[20] The decision is given in writing.[21] You may appeal to the High Court (in Scotland the Court of

Session) and can apply for a statement giving the grounds of the decision, which will enable you to decide whether or not you want to do this.[22] Alternatively, you may ask for a review of the decision (see p291).

Adjudicating medical authority

An adjudicating medical authority is a doctor, known as an **adjudicating medical practitioner**, or a **medical board** which consists of two or more doctors. Cases involving some prescribed diseases (B6, C15, C17, C18, C22(b), D1, D2, D3, D7, D8, D9 or D10 – see Appendix Three) are determined by specially qualified medical boards.[23]

The questions dealt with by adjudicating medical authorities are:

- the 'diagnosis' and 'recrudescence' questions relating to industrial diseases where medical boards hear appeals and references from AOs (see pp168 and 170);
- the 'disablement questions' relating to SDA and disablement benefit (see pp84 and 171) which are referred to adjudicating medical authorities for their initial decision. These questions are usually dealt with by a single adjudicating medical practitioner. If it is an industrial disease case or if the Secretary of State so directs, the questions are referred to a medical board;[24]
- an application for a review of any decision on the above questions. This is referred to a medical board for its initial decision.[25]

The adjudicating medical authorities do not hold hearings in the same way as tribunals. You have no right of representation before them although, with your consent, the presence of anyone 'likely to assist them' to make the decision can be allowed.[26] The doctor or board is there to give you a medical examination and is not concerned with other aspects of your case. The doctor will probably take a statement of your condition from you, so make sure you are clear in your mind about what your symptoms are. This is particularly important if your condition is fluctuating or if you want to describe an aspect of your condition that the doctor will not be able to see for her/himself. One way of making sure that you give the doctor all the relevant information is to write it down before you go so that you can just hand it to the doctor when you attend the examination (remembering to keep a copy for yourself). However, you should still talk to the doctor about your symptoms because that makes it easier for any uncertainties to be cleared up.

The decision will be sent to you in writing.[27] You may appeal against a decision of an adjudicating medical authority to a medical appeal tribunal (see p308).

3. REVIEWS

Any decision affecting entitlement to benefit may be reviewed if certain conditions are met. Following the review, the decision may be revised either to increase, decrease or take away your entitlement to benefit. This enables decisions to be altered to correct mistakes or to take account of new circumstances without appeals being necessary. (Reviews and appeals are compared on p293.)

Reviews can be considered if you ask for one (in writing to your local Benefits Agency office) or because an AO or the Secretary of State feels that one is needed. A review may be considered at any time. In some cases decisions are reviewed several years after they were originally made.

Reviews of decisions on DLA or attendance allowance are considered on p154.

Review by an adjudication officer

An AO may review any decision of an AO (except in the case of the 'diagnosis' or 'recrudescence' questions for industrial diseases), or of a SSAT or commissioner. Reviews usually arise if new information comes to the attention of the AO or because there is a change in the law. A decision may be reviewed only if:[1]

- it was given in ignorance of, or was based on a mistake as to, a material fact; *or*
- there has been any relevant change of circumstances; *or*
- the original decision must be changed to take account of a new decision of the Secretary of State or the adjudicating medical authorities (eg, to increase the amount of disablement benefit after a new assessment of disablement by a medical board); *or*
- the original decision was made by an AO (not a tribunal or commissioner) and was wrong in law;
- in the case of an advance award of benefit, that the claimant no longer satisfies the requirements for entitlement to the benefit.

It is open to an AO to review a case on the ground of, say, ignorance of a material fact, but then decide not to revise the decision because the 'new' fact would not have affected it.

'Ignorance of, or mistake as to, a material fact'

If a decision is reviewed on this ground, any revision will take effect from the beginning of the period covered by the original decision. If it is in your favour, you will receive arrears (but see p290 for the limits). If it is not in your favour there may have been an overpayment so the AO will decide whether or not you should pay it back (see p295). You would then want to consider whether the AO really had the power to review the decision.

It is only ignorance of, or a mistake about, a primary (or specific) fact which justifies a review.[2] This means that an AO does not have the power to review a decision on this ground merely because a doctor has expressed a different view about your capacity for work. A doctor's opinion is not itself a primary fact; it is a conclusion drawn by the doctor from a number of primary facts.

Example

You are a plumber claiming reduced earnings allowance. The doctor examines you and records his findings, including the results of his examination of your ability to bend your legs at the knees. He decides that you are permanently incapable of performing your regular occupation. You are awarded benefit. A second doctor then decides that you are not incapable of performing your regular occupation. That alone does not permit the AO to review the original decision on the ground of ignorance or mistake. However, the AO could do so if there was evidence that you had been misleading the first doctor so that there had been a mistake by him as to the extent of your disability or, if the first AO had been under a misapprehension as to the nature of your regular occupation.

It is often difficult to draw the line between medical opinion and primary fact and it is not often that AOs review decisions based on medical evidence on the ground of ignorance or mistake.

A different medical opinion may allow an AO to review a decision on the ground that the requirements for entitlement to the benefit are no longer satisfied (see below) but such a review will have effect only from the date of the review and will not be retrospective.

'Relevant change of circumstances'

Reviews on this ground take effect from the date of the change.

Again, a difference of medical opinion does not necessarily mean that there has been a change of circumstances[3] but an AO can review a decision on the ground that the requirements for entitlement to the benefit are no longer satisfied (see below).

'Requirements for entitlement ... are not satisfied'

This power to review decisions is entirely separate from the power to review on grounds of ignorance or mistake of a material fact or change of circumstances.[4] It applies where benefit is awarded in advance. Most

290 Administration and appeals 15: Administration

awards of benefit are indefinite, ie, they do not state on what day they end. The AO can take away benefit by reviewing the award but, once an award has been made, the burden of proving that the requirements for entitlement are no longer satisfied rests on the AO.[5]

A review on this ground takes effect from the date of the AO's decision (or the next pay day). This is because the AO is terminating an award and has no power to do that retrospectively.

Error of law

An AO can review a decision based on an error of law made by her/himself or by another AO but cannot correct such an error on the part of a tribunal.[6] S/he must appeal or ask for the decision to be set aside in the same way as a claimant.

The 'anti-test-case' rules affect these reviews in the same way as they affect decisions on new claims (see p284). So, if a commissioner or court in another case has held that a tribunal (or an AO) has made an error of law in that case, the AO reviewing your case on the ground of error of law must decide your case as though the decision of the tribunal (etc) 'had been found . . . not to have been erroneous in point of law' if the request for a review post-dates the test case and to the extent that the review covers a period before the date of the decision of the commissioner or court.[7] See pp284-285 for further discussion of the problems caused by this provision.

One possible effect is that if a commissioner or court decides that a tribunal made an error and that error would assist you, you should ask the AO to review the original decision awarding you benefit and to apply that error for the whole period before the date of the commissioner's or court's decision. CPAG will try and publicise suitable cases. The amount of arrears you receive may be limited to 12 months' (see below) but may nevertheless be a useful windfall.

Although these rules affect reviews, they do not apply to appeals (see Chapter 16). So, if you hear of a test case which might benefit you, you should appeal (asking permission for a late appeal if necessary – see p318) and only ask for a review if permission to appeal late is refused.

Arrears of benefit

If the review results in an award of benefit, or an increase in the amount of benefit to be paid, there will be only a limited backdating of benefit for the period before the date when you applied for the review or, if you did not apply, before the AO decided upon the review.

Unless you had 'good cause' for not applying earlier for the review, the arrears will be limited as follows:[8]

- no arrears of UB and maternity allowance will be paid;
- only two weeks' arrears of sickness benefit, IVB or SDA will be paid;
- only three months' arrears of widows' benefits, invalid care allowance, guardian's allowance or retirement pension will be paid;
- only a maximum of 12 months' arrears of child benefit will be paid.

'Good cause' in this context is the same as for late claims (see pp281-283).

If you did have 'good cause' for not applying earlier for the review, you will be entitled to a maximum of 12 months' arrears[9] unless *either*:

- the review is based on evidence which was before the adjudicating authority (ie, AO, SSAT or commissioner) at the time of the original decision but which was not taken into account; *or*
- the original decision was made by an SSAT or by a commissioner and the review is based on a document which was in the possession of the officer of the DSS or Department of Employment who made a submission to the adjudicating authority but was not included in that submission; *or*
- the review is based on evidence which did not exist at the time of the original decision but which was produced to the DSS, Department of Employment or to the adjudicating authority as soon as practicable after it became available to the claimant; *or*
- the original decision was made by an AO and the review is for error of law because s/he overlooked or misinterpreted an Act of Parliament, Regulations or a decision of a commissioner or a court.

In these cases arrears will be paid either from the date of claim or the date upon which the new evidence was made available.[10]

Appeal

You may appeal to a SSAT against a decision of an AO to review or not to review an earlier decision (see p303).[11]

Review by the Secretary of State

Questions which are determined at the discretion of the Secretary of State may be reconsidered by him at any time on any ground.[12]

On other questions (ie, those decided by the special procedure described on p286), the Secretary of State may review a decision only if:[13]

- new facts have been brought to his notice;
- the original decision was given in ignorance of, or based on a mistake as to, a material fact;
- the original decision was wrong in law.

Review by a medical board

A medical board may review a decision of:

- an AO on the 'diagnosis' and 'recrudescence' questions for industrial diseases (see pp168-170);
- an adjudicating medical practitioner;
- a medical board;
- a medical appeal tribunal.

The grounds upon which a decision may be reviewed depend upon the type of benefit under consideration and the body which made the original decision.

Any decision may be reviewed if the medical board is satisfied that it was given in ignorance of, or was based on a mistake as to, a material fact.[14] The test is the same as for an AO (see p288) but the limitations are more important here because there is no alternative basis of review on the ground that the requirements of entitlement are no longer satisfied. Furthermore, there is another important limitation; the decision may be reviewed only if there is 'fresh evidence'.[15] That means evidence that could not reasonably have been obtained and produced to the body making the first decision.[16]

Any decision concerning the disablement questions for SDA or disablement benefit may be made on the ground of unforeseen aggravation of your disability.[17] That implies a change of circumstances leading to an increase in your disablement. A change of circumstances leading to an improvement in your condition cannot be grounds for a review but, of course, when your current period of assessment comes to an end, any further assessment will be based upon your improved condition. If you wish to apply for a review of a decision of a medical appeal tribunal (but not an adjudicating medical practitioner or medical board) on the ground of unforeseen aggravation, you must first apply to the tribunal for leave.[18] Write to your local Benefits Agency office.

Any decision of a medical board may be reviewed on the ground that it was wrong in law.[19] (An adjudicating medical practitioner can review a decision of another adjudicating medical practitioner on the same ground.)

'Relevant change of circumstances'

A difference of medical opinion does not necessarily mean that there has been a change of circumstances.[20] The burden of proving a change of circumstances rests on the medical board. It will be possible to show a change only if the new medical board has found different 'primary' facts upon which to base their opinion when compared with the original medical board's primary findings of fact, noted in their report of the examination.

Arrears of benefit

If a medical board reviews a decision, it will be necessary for the AO to review her/his decision about the amount of benefit you are to receive. Any increase of disablement benefit or reduced earnings allowance will be paid from the date of your application for the review 'or from such earlier date as appears . . . to be reasonable in the circumstances'.[21] In the case of a review on the grounds of unforeseen aggravation, the amount of arrears will be limited to the period of the new assessment which will not begin more than three months before the date of the application for review.[22]

Appeal

You may appeal to a medical appeal tribunal (see p308) against a decision of a medical board to review or not to review a decision.[23]

Reviews and appeals

Reviews and appeals are both ways of challenging decisions and in cases where it is suggested that the original decision was made in ignorance of, or was based on a mistake as to, a material fact, either method may be used. Indeed, if you appeal, your appeal will often be treated as an application for a review and a decision may be reviewed before it ever reaches a tribunal. However, there are occasions when it is necessary to choose your method of challenge with care.

The main advantages of applying for a review are that it is simpler than appealing and you receive a decision more quickly. You also get two bites at the cherry because, if your application is turned down, you can always appeal against that decision.

However, there is a major disadvantage in applying for a review in some cases because you may not be paid all the arrears due to you even if you are successful. In considering whether or not to ask for a review, you have to take into account all the factors that might lead to arrears of benefit being limited. These include the length of time since the original decision, the type of benefit, whether or not you have 'good cause' for the delay in asking for the review, whether the original decision was simply an administrative error on the part of the Benefits Agency, whether the 'anti-test-case' rules apply to you and so on (see pp284 and 290). **If you think there is a risk that you will not obtain all the arrears, you should appeal instead of asking for a review.**

There is not usually any risk attached to an appeal. The only problem is that you have to obtain leave from the tribunal chairperson if you wish to appeal against a decision more than three months after it has been made (see p318). If you have a good reason for the delay, you will usually be given leave to appeal (but see p319). In theory there is a risk that you might lose arrears of benefit by delaying an application for a review while making an unsuccessful application for leave to appeal. However, you can then ask for your application for leave to appeal to be treated as an application for a review and the Benefits Agency will usually agree to do this.

4. PAYMENTS

Method of payment

Benefit is paid by girocheque or order book. Payment is made at nominated post offices. UB is payable fortnightly in arrears. Sickness benefit, IVB, SDA and maternity benefit are payable weekly in arrears. Child benefit is usually paid at four-weekly intervals, although there are circumstances in which you can have it paid weekly (see p294). Other benefits are payable weekly in advance.[1]

Alternatively you can choose to be paid some benefits by direct credit transfer into a bank account either four-weekly or quarterly in arrears. An overpayment of benefit due to the credit transfer arrangement itself is recoverable by the Benefits Agency, but not when the Secretary of State confirms that it would be inappropriate, or where it is not materially due to the credit transfer arrangement itself (unless you have misrepresented or failed to disclose a material fact – see p295.[2]

If the claim is for a child or any other person unable to act for her/ himself, or if a person has died since the claim was originally made, another person may be appointed to receive the benefit and take any necessary actions on the claim.[3] Benefit may also be paid to a third party if you are entitled to an increase of benefit on condition that payments are made to someone and you do not make those payments, or if the benefit is payable together with income support and you are in debt.[4]

For rules preventing the duplication of payments, see p288.

Interim payment

An interim payment may be made, usually when a reference, review, application or appeal is pending, but also when it is impractical either for the claimant to claim the benefit or for the Benefits Agency to pay it.[5] Interim payments are very rare in practice.

Any interim payment is offset against or deducted from the eventual award of benefit.[6] If no benefit is eventually awarded on the claim or the amount is less than the interim payment, the balance of the interim payment is treated as an overpayment.[7]

Suspension of payment

When a review is being considered, or when an appeal or reference by the Secretary of State or an AO is awaiting consideration by a medical appeal tribunal or a commissioner, the payment of benefits may be suspended. If you win an appeal to an SSAT, payment may be suspended pending an appeal to the commissioner provided that you are given written notice within 30 days from when the AO was told of the tribunal's decision that an application for leave to appeal has been made.[8] The standard Benefits Agency letter saying that it is 'considering' an appeal is *not* sufficient.

Benefit may also be suspended if a question of law arises on your claim and the same question is being appealed to the commissioner or a court in a different case, or if it is to be considered by the High Court on an application for judicial review.[9]

5. RECOVERY OF OVERPAYMENTS

You have to pay back an overpayment 'in respect of a benefit' *only* if it was due to *either*:[1]

- a misrepresentation as to a material fact; *or*
- a failure to disclose a material fact.

The misrepresentation or failure to disclose may be entirely innocent but the Secretary of State is still entitled to recover the overpayment.

The overpayment may be recovered either from the claimant or from whoever made the misrepresentation or failed to disclose the material fact.[2] If it is to be recovered from that other person s/he has an independent right of appeal against any decision that there has been an overpayment or that it is recoverable.[3] The method of recovery is explained below.

A payment is only recoverable when the decision awarding the benefit has been revised on either a review or an appeal and an AO, SSAT or commissioner has ruled that the payment is recoverable.[4] Even if you accept that there has been an overpayment, you still have a separate right of appeal against the decision that you should repay it. The burden of proving that any overpayment was due to a misrepresentation or failure to disclose rests on the AO.[5]

Misrepresentation

Any positive statement by you is a representation, and if it turns out to be wrong it is a misrepresentation. Thus, if you are asked 'are there any changes in your circumstances?' and you answer 'No' and it is later discovered that, unknown to you, your spouse's earnings have increased, there will have been a misrepresentation by you. But if you had answered 'Not to my knowledge', there would have been no misrepresentation.[6]

Furthermore, a written representation may be qualified by an oral one so that, if you fill in a form incorrectly but explain the situation to an officer when handing the form in, the explanation has to be taken into account when deciding whether what is stated on the form amounts to a misrepresentation. If you say you have no income on the form but, when handing it in, ask whether you should have mentioned your occupational pension, you should be treated as having mentioned the occupational pension on the form.[7]

The Court of Appeal has recently held[8] that the DSS can rely on the statement you sign on each order from your order book in order to recover an overpayment on the ground of misrepresentation. This says:

> I declare that I have read and understood all the instructions in this Order Book, that I have correctly reported any facts which would affect the amount of any payment and that I am entitled to the above sum. I acknowledge receipt of the above sum.

This is disadvantageous for claimants because it means that overpayments which do not result from the positive action of the claimant will be recoverable on the basis of misrepresentation even if they would not be recoverable on the basis of failure to disclose (because, say, you could not have known of the relevant fact – see p297).

The Court of Appeal's decision is binding on SSATs and commissioners for the moment but there are good reasons for thinking that it may be incorrect. The judges were not unanimous and if – as is the effect of the majority decision – all failures to disclose are in practice automatically misrepresentations as well, it is difficult to see why the legislation treats the two as separate categories.

In addition, a misrepresentation must be as to a *material* fact – ie, one which relates to a condition of entitlement to or disqualification from benefit or to the amount of benefit. The *reporting* of changes in circumstance to the DSS is not a condition of entitlement to any benefit although the *changes themselves* may affect those conditions. For this reason, it is arguable that (as the dissenting judge in the Court of Appeal put it) the declaration in the order book 'does not purport to make any statement or representation as to the material facts themselves as distinct from the fact of their disclosure'.

Similarly, it is strongly arguable that the part of the declaration which reads 'I am entitled to the above sum', is also not a representation as to a material *fact* but a representation of *law* because it is a *conclusion* based on the facts of the case.[9]

There is not going to be an appeal to the House of Lords against the decision of the Court of Appeal but CPAG hopes to find another claimant to take a test case to challenge the decision. If the DSS seeks to recover an overpayment which would otherwise be irrecoverable simply on the basis of your having signed the order book, you should take advice and ask your adviser to contact CPAG's solicitor.

On some claim forms for benefit the declaration says:

As far as I know, the information on this form is true and complete.

Such a declaration cannot be relied on by the DSS in the same way as the declaration in the order book because it is qualified by the words 'as far as I know'. Only an unqualified misrepresentation or a failure to disclose facts which are known to the claimant will lead to the overpayment being recoverable.[10]

Failure to disclose

You cannot be said to have 'failed to disclose' a fact that you did not know about unless there is some reason why you should have been aware of it.[11] Nor can you be said to have failed to disclose something unless you were *either* asked to disclose it *or* you should have realised that it was relevant and so had to be disclosed.[12]

An AO can often point to warnings and instructions at the back of an order book that you should have read.[13] On the other hand, the AO ought not to rely on warnings on forms you were asked to sign without having a proper chance to read.[14]

It has been said that there is a failure to disclose only if disclosure 'was reasonably to be expected'.[15] On the other hand, the legislation makes it quite clear that an innocent failure to disclose will nonetheless make any overpayment recoverable.[16] Difficulties may arise if a person is mentally ill or 'vague'. If you are, or have been, aware of a fact (such as that your spouse has received an increase in her/his occupational pension) and have been told to report that fact to the Benefits Agency (perhaps through the notes in an order book), then if you do not tell the Benefits Agency about the increase and benefit is overpaid as a result, that overpayment will inevitably be recoverable. Even if you did not read the notes in the order book, the AO can say that you ought to have done so or to have had someone else read them to you. But your mental state would be relevant in deciding whether you ever knew your spouse had an increase in the pension.[17] It would also be relevant in deciding whether you ought to have realised the significance of the occupational pension increase if you had been aware of the increase but had not been specifically told to report it.

Disclosure does not have to be in writing and it does not have to be made by the claimant personally. But it does have to be made to the right part of the Benefits Agency and you cannot assume that mentioning a fact to the Child Benefit Centre means that the local office will hear about it and adjust any other benefit. On the other hand, you cannot be expected to understand exactly how the Benefits Agency works so that making a disclosure to the office where your claim is being handled and making specific reference to your claim will be enough because you can then reasonably expect the person receiving the information to pass it on to the right person.[18]

Once a disclosure has been made *to the right person*, any continued overpayment due to the Benefits Agency not acting on it will not be recoverable. However, if you do not make the disclosure to the right person but make it to someone else in the reasonable expectation that it will be passed on, you will have satisfied the duty to disclose only for a while. The duty to disclose is then a continuous one and if it later becomes obvious to you that the information has not filtered through to the right person, you should disclose the facts again; if you fail to do so there will be a further recoverable overpayment.[19] It is unclear whether this applies only if you actually realise that you are being overpaid or whether it is enough that you should have realised. You should argue that since the Benefits Agency also ought to have realised that you were being overpaid – and since the legislation does not require the recovery of an overpayment in a case where you have disclosed everything to the right person even if you should have realised later that you are being overpaid – only actual knowledge that you are being overpaid gives rise to a further duty to disclose in a case where you expected the information to be passed on.

If it is suggested that an overpayment is recoverable because someone other than the claimant failed to make a disclosure, it is extremely important for the AO to establish that disclosure was reasonably to be expected from that person.

Recovery 'at common law'

There has been an increasing number of cases in which the DSS is claiming to be entitled to recover overpayments of benefit not under the rules in the Social Security Acts but relying instead on what it claims are its rights under the *common law*.

At common law it is possible to reclaim money through the courts from someone to whom you have paid it as a result of a mistake of *fact*. If the DSS does retain its common law rights then it is entitled to use this procedure to recover overpayments even where there has been no misrepresentation or failure to disclose and indeed even if the overpayment was entirely caused by its own mistake.

Although there has yet to be a decision, two points are strongly arguable. The first is that the rules about overpayments in the Social Security Acts have replaced the common law as far as overpayments of benefit are concerned. The second is that those Acts say that the question whether there has been an overpayment is one which should be made by an AO (and is therefore subject to an appeal by an SSAT) – on this basis, a court would have no jurisdiction to decide the point. If the DSS threatens to use the common law in your case you should get advice from a solicitor immediately. Tactically the best course may be to apply for judicial review of the decision to proceed in this way. Alternatively, you may simply wish to defend the action in the County Court. There are a number of defences to this type of court action which would not be available to you if the DSS had used the Social Security Act procedure.

The amount to be recovered

The amount of benefit to be recovered is only that sum arising from the misrepresentation or failure to disclose a material fact. Also deducted from the amount to be recovered is the amount of any other social security benefit (including income support) which would have been payable had you not received the overpayment.[20]

Overpayments made before 6 April 1987

Before 6 April 1987, overpayments were not recoverable unless a claimant had failed to use due care and diligence to avoid overpayment. In most cases, overpayments recoverable under the present law would have been recoverable under the old test too, but in some cases the results would have been different. The old law tended to be more favourable to claimants, although sometimes it worked the other way round.

The Court of Appeal has ruled that the new test applies even if the overpayment was made before 6 April 1987. CPAG takes the view that this decision was wrong.[21] However, it was not appealed to the House of Lords because the Secretary of State undertook not to ask the claimant to repay the overpayment even though she had lost her case. CPAG now has another case [22] which raises the same point and which will be heard by the House of Lords shortly after this *Guide* goes to press. The *Welfare*

Rights Bulletin will report the outcome of this appeal as soon as it is known.

If the appeal might be relevant to you, you should try and delay any tribunal hearing on your case (although make sure you lodge your appeal in time). If the tribunal hears your case, ask for leave to appeal to the commissioner, saying that you are awaiting the outcome of CPAG's case.

The method of recovery

Whether or not the Secretary of State is entitled to recover benefit from either the claimant or someone else is decided by the AO, with the usual rights of appeal. However, if it is decided that he is *entitled* to recover the benefit, it is still up to the Secretary of State to decide whether or not he *will* do so.[23] He does not always do so and may be persuaded that it would be unduly harsh in a particular case.

Benefit may be recovered by stopping payment of any of the benefits covered in this *Guide* or equivalent benefits payable under EC legislation or the legislation of Northern Ireland or any income support or family credit, although there are limits to the extent by which income support may be reduced.[24]

Otherwise, any benefit may be recovered by enforcement proceedings in the County Courts in England and Wales or the Sheriffs' Courts in Scotland.[25] Once the decision of the AO, SSAT or commissioner is produced, the court has to enforce it unless you persuade the court to delay enforcement ('grant a stay of execution') while you appeal against the relevant decision.

Criminal proceedings

Sometimes the DSS commences criminal proceedings (see p265) at the same time as attempting to recover overpaid benefits. There is no general rule as to which proceedings should be determined first. If you are in this position, it is open to you to request either the tribunal or the magistrates' court to adjourn while the other body decides the issue. It is generally better for the tribunal to deal with any appeal before any criminal trial because tribunals have a better understanding of social security law than courts and also because they tend to be more sympathetic to claimants' confusion about the social security system (although that is not always the case). Also, any conviction by a court carries great weight in a tribunal whereas the fact that you were unsuccessful in your appeal would probably not be mentioned in any criminal court.

An acquittal on the criminal charge does not prevent the Benefits Agency recovering the overpayment.[26] Nor will conviction on the criminal charge necessarily prevent you from showing that an overpayment is not recoverable, or even that you have an entitlement to the benefit.[27] The right of the Benefits Agency to reclaim money paid to you is independent of the powers of the court to fine you or to order compensation.

6. COMPLAINTS

The Benefits Agency will sometimes pay compensation if you can show that you have lost out through its error or delay and the loss cannot be made good by an appeal or review. For instance, if you failed to claim guardian's allowance because you were misled by the Benefits Agency, you could not have the benefit backdated for more than six months. Even when you can get arrears on a review, you still receive them at the original rates with no interest to make up for the effects of inflation.

The Benefits Agency

You should first complain to the customer service manager of the local office. If that does not work, write to the district manager. If you are still dissatisfied, try writing for the personal attention of Michael Bichard, Chief Executive, Benefits Agency, 286 Euston Road, London NW1 3DN. If you are still unsuccessful, you can try the Ombudsman.

The Ombudsman

The Ombudsman (technically known as the Parliamentary Commissioner for Administration) investigates complaints about civil service administration and publishes reports on them. A report in your favour by the Ombudsman may help to persuade the Benefits Agency to pay compensation. You cannot contact the Ombudsman direct but must apply through a Member of Parliament.

Compensation

This obviously varies from case to case but there is a general rule which applies in cases where benefit has been delayed due to an error by the DSS.[1]

If the total delay in making payment is six months or more beyond the Benefits Agency Customers' Charter targets (or one year if that is less) and at least some of it was due to DSS error, compensation is paid in the form of interest. However, the interest is payable only from the end of the six months (or one year) period. In calculating that date, any time your case was in the hands of any appeal tribunal is ignored as is any period of three months or more due to excessive delay on your part. This formula has been agreed with the Ombudsman.

There are special arrangements for people who suffered excessive delays when DLA was first introduced in April 1992. If:[2]

- you claimed DLA, attendance allowance or mobility allowance (a benefit which was abolished in April 1992) on or after 3 February 1992; *and*
- you suffered a delay in payment of more than 8 months; *and*
- you were finally paid benefit before 1 April 1993

you should already have received a compensation payment of £10 for each additional month of delay after the expiry of the eight-month period. If you qualify but have not received your payment, you should write to the office of the DSS which dealt with your claim.

In some cases there may be a legal obligation to pay compensation which can be enforced against the DSS in the courts if necessary. Although you cannot sue an AO if s/he negligently decides your claim wrongly and you lose out as a result, the situation is probably different if you are given wrong advice about your entitlement to benefit. This is because the DSS holds itself out (in its leaflets and in the public statements of some ministers) as being a competent source of advice on social security and, as a result, a court is likely to say that it must take reasonable care to get that advice right. So, for example, if you ask about your entitlement to a retirement pension and are told that you have not paid enough contributions and it subsequently turns out that you could have topped up your contributions and become entitled, you should see a solicitor or a law centre (see p330) if the DSS refuses to pay you full arrears. In practice such claims for compensation are almost always settled without need for a court hearing.

CHAPTER SIXTEEN

Appeals

This chapter covers:
1. Social security appeal tribunals (see below)
2. Medical appeal tribunals (p308)
3. Disability appeal tribunals (p311)
4. Social security commissioners (p313)
5. Late appeals (p318)
6. How to prepare an appeal (p323)

If you are dissatisfied with a decision of an adjudication officer (AO) or an adjudicating medical authority (including a medical board), you can appeal to an independent tribunal (although it is sometimes worth applying for a review instead – see p288). If you are claiming disability living allowance (DLA) (see pp127 and 134), or attendance allowance (see p142), appeals on a question about your disability will be heard by disability appeal tribunals (DATs).

Appeals from AOs are heard by social security appeal tribunals (SSATs). Appeals from adjudicating medical authorities are heard by medical appeal tribunals (MATs).

If you are dissatisfied with the decision of a tribunal, you can appeal to a social security commissioner if a point of law is involved.

I. SOCIAL SECURITY APPEAL TRIBUNALS

The tribunal

SSATs are independent of the DSS. There is a President of Social Security, Medical and DATs and he has overall responsibility for them.[1] They are grouped together into regions, each of which has a regional chairperson who is responsible for the administration of the tribunals in his region.[2] The names and addresses of the President and regional chairpersons are given in Appendix Four (p350).

Each region has a panel of chairpersons and a panel of lay members for SSATs. The chairpersons are always lawyers.[3] The lay members are required to have knowledge or experience of conditions in their area and to be representative of people living in it.[4] If you want to be a member, write to the regional chairperson.

The tribunals' administration is dealt with by clerks who are civil servants assigned to the tribunals by the President.[5] They are based at the offices of the regional chairpersons. In practice, there are 'indoor clerks' who stay in the office and 'outdoor clerks' who travel to the various towns and cities where tribunals sit. They have purely administrative duties and do not take part in making any of the tribunals' decisions.

A tribunal may hear up to about a dozen cases a day. For each hearing, there should be a lawyer chairperson and two lay members. Decisions are made by a majority vote so the lay members can, and often do, out-vote the chairperson.[6] If only the chairperson and one other member are present, the tribunal can still hear your case provided that you agree, but the chairperson then has a second vote.[7]

If practical, at least one of the members of the tribunal should be the same sex as the claimant.[8]

Very occasionally, a tribunal may sit with an expert assessor to advise it on the evidence. The expert is not a member of the tribunal and the tribunal still has to make its own decision.[9]

How to appeal

SSATs hear appeals from AOs on all matters except for certain questions concerning DLA, attendance allowance, and industrial accidents and diseases (see pp157 and 285).[10] They also hear appeals from the Secretary of State concerning the recovery of benefits from compensation payments (see p263).[11]

To appeal, you can either complete an appeal form provided by the Benefits Agency or you can simply write a letter. In either case, you should try to make sure it gets to your local Benefits Agency office within three months of the date of your being sent notice of the AO's decision against which you are appealing. If your appeal is outside the three-month time limit, a chairperson may still allow it to go ahead but only if there are 'special reasons' (see p318).

Your letter of appeal should contain your reasons for appealing and make it clear which decision you are appealing against. If you are unsure of your position, you can always send in a short letter of just two or three lines, to keep within the time limit, and follow it up with more details (or withdraw it) later. The AO or chairperson can ask for more details.[12] In any case, it is a good idea to give as much detail as possible in your letter of appeal. Include any documents which are relevant, such as medical reports. Such detail may lead the AO to review the decision in your favour (see p288), in which case it would not be necessary to attend a hearing. If not, your letter and documents will be included in the papers sent to the tribunal members and read by them before the hearing.

When your letter of appeal is received, the AO prepares a written submission, explaining the reasons for her/his decision. Your letter of appeal and accompanying documents, the AO's submission and any documents such as your claim form, medical certificates or employer's statements which the AO considers relevant, are all sent to the tribunal clerk. Copies of this bundle of papers are then sent to the members of the tribunal and to you. If there are any more documents you would like the tribunal to see, send them to the clerk if there is time before the hearing. Otherwise, you can produce them for the tribunal on the day.

For advice on how to prepare a case and where to find advice or representation, see pp323-330.

If an AO has decided that you are entitled to statutory sick pay (SSP) or statutory maternity pay (SMP), your employer has the same right of appeal to a tribunal as you.[13]

A tribunal chairperson may dispose of the appeal without a hearing if s/he is satisfied that the tribunal has no power to hear the case (eg, if you are trying to appeal against a Secretary of State's decision on a contribution question and should have appealed to the High Court – see p286).[14] This does not allow a chairperson to dispose of an appeal merely because s/he thinks it looks hopeless.

Your appeal lapses if in the meantime an AO reviews the decision you are appealing against and you get everything you would have got had your appeal been successful.[15] If the review only gives you part of what you are appealing for, your appeal will still be heard.

Cases referred by the adjudication officer

Sometimes – particularly where there is a dispute about the facts between a claimant and, say, an employer in a case of dismissal due to alleged misconduct – the AO does not make any decision at all but simply refers the case to a tribunal.[16] In such cases, the procedure is the same as it is on an appeal except that the bundle of papers does not include a letter of appeal from you.

The hearing

Together with the bundle of papers you will also be sent a form to return saying whether or not you intend to attend the hearing and also whether you want to abandon the appeal. It is vital that you complete and return this form in good time. You will then be told when and where the hearing will take place. You will be given 10 days' notice.[17] If you want to put off the appeal to another day, ask for an adjournment and explain why. It is for the chairperson or the tribunal to decide whether your request should be granted. One adjournment is usually accepted (although this cannot be guaranteed) but you need good reasons for more than one.

If you do not attend and you have not asked for an adjournment or your request is not accepted, the tribunal will hear your case in your absence. **You are much more likely to succeed if you attend the hearing**.

If you are disabled, check that there is proper access to the building where the hearing will take place and that facilities are suitable. If the premises are not suitable, ask for the hearing to be held elsewhere.

When you arrive for your hearing, you should be directed to a waiting room or area. The tribunal clerk will meet you there and will ask whether you have any representative or witnesses. The clerk will also take details of your travel expenses and loss of earnings and those of any witnesses. You are usually paid in cash there and then but sometimes expenses are paid later by girocheque.

When the tribunal is ready to hear your case, you are taken into its room with the presenting officer. The presenting officer is usually an AO but not the one who made the decision in your case. S/he is there to represent the AO.

The three members of the tribunal sit on one side of a large table. The clerk sits at a separate table to one side. You are shown where to sit. Usually you and the presenting officer both sit directly opposite the tribunal.

The proceedings are open to the public, but it is very rare for anyone to attend unless they are either involved in the case or are civil servants or tribunal members undergoing training. Of course, the right of the public to watch does mean that you can watch the case before yours to see what happens. If intimate personal or financial matters are involved in your case, you can ask the tribunal to exclude any members of the public.[18]

There are no strict rules of procedure. Usually the chairperson starts by introducing the members of the tribunal and everyone else who is present. The presenting officer then summarises the AO's written submission and you are asked to explain your reasons for disagreeing with it. You can call any witnesses and ask questions of any witnesses called by the presenting officer. Usually the presenting officer does not say very much and the tribunal members ask questions. The chairperson takes a note of the evidence and arguments.

When both you and the presenting officer have put your cases, everyone except the tribunal and its clerk leaves the room and the tribunal members discuss the evidence and law and reach a decision.

Your case may be adjourned unfinished to be heard on another day because, for instance, more evidence is wanted or there is insufficient time. If this happens, the new tribunal hearing your case must rehear your case from the beginning unless it has the same three members as before or you agree to it being heard by two members of the previous tribunal without the third.[19]

The decision

The tribunal decides by a majority. If there are only two members of the tribunal, the chairperson has a second vote (see p304).[20] The chairperson has the duty of writing up the decision, including the findings of fact and the reasons for the decision.[21]

Usually, you are asked to wait while the tribunal makes its decision so that you can be told the result of your appeal straight away. If you are unsuccessful, you can immediately ask the chairperson for leave to appeal to a commissioner (see p313).[22] However, unless there has been a dispute about the law (as opposed to the facts) during the course of the hearing, it is usually better to wait until you receive the written decision.

The written decision is sent to you a couple of weeks later with a note about your right of appeal to a commissioner [23] (see p313).

In certain circumstances, a decision of an SSAT may be reviewed by an AO (see p288).

Correcting and setting aside decisions

The tribunal may correct an accidental error in its written decision.[24]

A tribunal may also set aside a decision of its own or of another SSAT if a relevant document went astray or any party to the proceedings or a representative was absent. It may also do so if 'the interests of justice so require' because of any other procedural irregularity.[25]

These provisions are most relevant to tribunals, but also apply to other adjudicating authorities.

If you make an application to have a decision set aside, it must be in writing to the local office of the Benefits Agency or the office of the tribunal or other body giving the decision within three months of your being given notice of the decision. A late application may be accepted if there are 'special reasons' (see p318).[26] This procedure is not often used but can be helpful where something has gone wrong or a case was decided in your unavoidable absence and you now wish to give evidence.[27] If you are able to use it, it can also be very much quicker than an appeal to the commissioners.

2. MEDICAL APPEAL TRIBUNALS

The tribunal

MATs are also independent of the DSS. They are organised by the same President and regional chairpersons as SSATs (see p303) and again, their clerks are based in the offices of the regional chairpersons.

Each tribunal consists of a lawyer chairperson and two consultants. Neither is necessarily an expert in the field of medicine relevant to your case. The tribunal cannot proceed if any member is absent.[1]

How to appeal

MATs hear all appeals by claimants against decisions of adjudicating medical authorities, including medical boards (see p287).[2] They also answer some questions arising in appeals from the Secretary of State concerning the recovery of benefits from compensation payments (see p263).[3]

To appeal, you must write to your local Benefits Agency office within three months of being notified of the decision of the adjudicating medical authority. A chairperson may allow a late appeal if there are 'special reasons' (see p318).[4] As with appeals to SSATs, it is a good idea to give as much detail as possible when appealing. If you obtain an independent medical report, send that to the tribunal clerk before the hearing, if possible. Before the hearing, you will be sent a bundle of documents containing the Secretary of State's submission and the records of all the medical examinations you have had in connection with the claim (or previous claims for the same benefit).

See pp323-330 for advice about preparing a case and finding advice or representation.

Any benefit payable by virtue of the adjudicating medical authority's decision may be suspended until the appeal is heard.[5] This may include the payment of reduced earnings allowance.

A tribunal chairperson may dispose of the appeal without a hearing if s/he is satisfied that the tribunal has no power to hear the case (eg, if you are trying to appeal against an AO's decision and have appealed to the wrong tribunal).[6] This does not allow a chairperson to dispose of an appeal merely because s/he thinks it looks hopeless.

References on behalf of the Secretary of State

If the Secretary of State considers that a decision of an adjudicating medical authority is wrong, s/he can ask the AO to refer the case to a

MAT.[7] Such a reference is rather like a claimant's appeal and is usually made because the Secretary of State considers that the adjudicating medical authority was too generous. However, it can be because the award is thought to be too low, or because it is believed that the adjudicating medical authority made an error of law. The procedure on a reference is the same as on an appeal and again, any benefit payable by virtue of the adjudicating medical authority's decision is usually suspended until the hearing.

The hearing

The arrangements for the hearing are similar to those for SSATs (see p305) but hearings take place only where there are facilities for the doctors to examine claimants. Where a claimant is very ill, the tribunal will sometimes go to the claimant's home.

When you go into the tribunal's room, the chairperson introduces the members of the tribunal. Usually the doctors will be ask you questions first, then, if it is your appeal, the chairperson usually asks you to present your case first. The Secretary of State's representative is usually asked to go first if it is a reference. It is very rare for a Secretary of State's representative to say much. They usually rely on the written submission.

If you think there are mistakes in the tribunal papers, point them out. It is important to explain how the injury (if any) occurred and your subsequent treatment. Where the extent of your disablement is at issue, it is also necessary to convey to the tribunal how your disability affects you at work or in your daily life at home. You should be completely straightforward with the tribunal, neither diminishing nor exaggerating your symptoms. If you feel better on some days than others, explain in what ways and give them an idea as to whether they are seeing you on a 'good' day or a 'bad' one.

The tribunal members tend to ask a lot of questions. After the main hearing, the medical members often examine you in a separate room in the absence of everyone else, including the chairperson and your representative, although you can have someone with you as a chaperone or to help you if you need assistance undressing. When you are examined, make sure you tell the members of the tribunal if you are in pain or suffering discomfort. It is also a good idea to give the tribunal a full list of any medicines you are taking.

After the hearing and any examination, the tribunal members discuss the evidence and the law by themselves.

The decision

The tribunal decides by a majority.[8]

You may be asked to wait while the tribunal reaches its decision. You are then told the result but, should you wish to appeal, you have to wait for the written decision before applying for leave to appeal.[9]

The written decision must contain a statement of the reasons for the decision and record all relevant findings of fact.[10] Until recently claimants often encountered problems with MATs giving wholly inadequate – or sometimes no – reasons for refusing an appeal. In particular, these decisions often failed to state clearly why the tribunal was disagreeing with the medical evidence put forward on behalf of the claimant or with the doctors whose views had formed the basis of previous awards of benefit.

This failure made it very difficult to appeal further and claimants who did so often found that the commissioners were prepared to uphold uninformative MAT decisions on the basis that, as MATs are expert tribunals, their members were allowed to decide on the basis of their professional experience and judgement and were not expected to do more by way of explanation than simply announce the conclusion which had been reached.

However, a recent decision of the Court of Appeal[11] makes it clear that this is no longer acceptable. The Court set out the following guidelines:

- the decision should record the medical question or questions which the tribunal has to answer so the parties can be sure what issues have been addressed;
- the tribunal should record the findings of any medical examination. These may be sufficient on their own to explain why the tribunal has reached its decision:
- where the clinical findings do not point to an obvious diagnosis, the tribunal should explain briefly why it has reached one diagnosis rather than another. This is particularly important where the tribunal's diagnosis differs from a reasoned diagnosis of another doctor who has examined the claimant;
- questions of *causation* can cause particular difficulties. Sometimes it will be enough for the tribunal to say that it is not satisfied that the claimant's condition was caused by the industrial accident or by working in the prescribed occupation in question. However, where the claimant has previously been receiving benefit and the effect of the tribunal's decision will be that s/he will not receive it in the future, fairness demands that s/he should be given a brief explanation of where the break in the chain of causation has been found.

Following the Court's decision, a commissioner has decided[12] that the need for consistency between earlier and later decisions affecting the same claimant means that it is not restricted to those situations where causation is in issue. In all cases where a MAT differs from an earlier decision, it must – at least – be possible to infer the explanation for the difference.

The tribunal's decision is sent to you with a note of your right of appeal on a point of law to a social security commissioner (see p313).[13]

The rules for correcting and setting aside decisions are the same as for SSATs (see p307).

In certain circumstances, a decision of a MAT may be reviewed by a medical board (see p292).

3. DISABILITY APPEAL TRIBUNALS

The tribunal

DATs hear appeals about questions concerning DLA, attendance allowance and also disability working allowance (DWA) (which is covered in CPAG's *National Welfare Benefits Handbook*).

Like SSATs and MATs, DATs are independent of the Benefits Agency and are organised by the same President and regional chairpersons. There is a national disability appeal tribunal office in Nottingham.

DATs have three members: a lawyer chairperson, a doctor and someone drawn from a panel made up of people experienced in dealing with the needs of people with disabilities, either in a professional or voluntary capacity, or because they themselves have a disability.[1] People who receive invalidity benefit or severe disablement allowance are still treated as incapable of work if they serve on the tribunal for no more than one day a week.[2]

No one may act as a tribunal member on a case where they would be affected by the outcome or in which they have already been involved in some capacity.[3] This means that your own doctor cannot be the medical member.

The tribunal cannot proceed if any one of the three members is absent.[4]

The jurisdiction of the disability appeal tribunal

DATs hear appeals about the disability conditions referred to in Chapter 7, including matters concerning the period during which the claimant satisfies those conditions and the rate at which the relevant allowance is payable.

Very occasionally a tribunal also deals with a non-disability question relating to DLA or attendance allowance.[5]

A tribunal chairperson may refer the claimant to a doctor for a medical examination and report where s/he thinks that the appeal cannot properly be decided unless such an examination and report take place.[6]

Some people appealing to the tribunal may be appealing about not being awarded one component of DLA when they are already in receipt of the other. Or they may be appealing against the rate of one component while they are quite satisfied with the rate they receive of the other. In these circumstances, the tribunal need not consider the component which is not the subject of the appeal, although it can if it so wishes.

If a person has been awarded a component of DLA for life, a tribunal should not consider the rate of that component, or the length of time for which it has been awarded, unless either the appeal is expressly about one of those questions, or 'information is available to the tribunal which gives it reasonable grounds for believing that entitlement to the component, or entitlement to it at the rate awarded or for that period, ought not to continue'.[7]

These provisions may raise some problems for claimants and their advisers – eg, a case where someone has a serious accident and is awarded the higher rate mobility component because of walking difficulties, but is only awarded the lower rate care component. That person may then challenge the decision on the care component by an appeal. Where the mobility component is awarded for life, a DAT may not remove it unless it becomes clear to the tribunal that there is no entitlement to it at that rate, or at all, or for such a period. In the course of its deliberations, the tribunal will, typically, consider medical evidence and discuss the claimant's disabilities. It is precisely this process which might point to information which could threaten the existing mobility component award. This problem is more acute if the award of the mobility component is for a limited period only. In this case, a tribunal is entitled to reconsider the mobility component award, although it may choose not to do so.

The hearing

The procedure at a DAT hearing is similar to that at an SSAT.

The adjudication officer who made the decision which is the subject of the appeal is represented by a presenting officer.

The tribunal holds an oral hearing of the case. The independent tribunal system tries to ensure that there are sufficient accessible tribunal venues to enable claimants to get into the buildings where their cases will be heard. Nevertheless, there are some people appealing who are unable to get to a hearing. It is, therefore, not unusual for hearings to be held in a claimant's home.

The tribunal listens to claimants and asks questions about their disability, examines medical reports, medical evidence and other evidence relevant to the case. However, there is no physical examination of the claimant, nor any 'walking test' for the mobility component.[8]

The decision

If the tribunal is unable to come to a unanimous decision, it makes a majority decision. This is almost always announced after the hearing and is in any event sent in writing to the claimant and any representative. The written decision should include findings on all questions of fact material to the decision, and give reasons for the decision. It is sent out with a note explaining the further right of appeal to a social security commissioner on a point of law.[9]

4. SOCIAL SECURITY COMMISSIONERS

Social security commissioners are professional judges of the same standing as circuit judges who sit in the crown court and county courts. Indeed, some commissioners do also sit in those courts.

Commissioners hear appeals from SSATs, MATs and DATs. In all cases, you can only appeal to a commissioner on a point of law.[1]

Point of law

A commissioner allows an appeal only if the tribunal has made an error of law. An error of law has been made if the tribunal:[2]

- has made a decision based on a mistake as to what the relevant law is; *or*
- has failed to give an adequate statement of the reasons for its decision and the findings of fact on which it is based; *or*
- has made a decision based on a finding of fact for which there is no evidence; *or*
- has made a decision which no tribunal, acting judicially and applying the relevant law, could reasonably have made on the basis of their findings of fact; *or*
- has broken its obligations to act fairly (sometimes called the rules of 'natural justice').

The most common error of law is a breach of the requirement to give adequate reasons for the decision.

314 Administration and appeals 16: Appeals

> The obligation to give reasons for the decision . . . imports a requirement to do more than only to state the conclusion . . . the minimum requirement must at least be that the claimant looking at the decision should be able to discern on the face of it the reasons why . . . evidence has failed to satisfy the authority.[3]

On the other hand, when looking at a decision it is often quite clear what is meant, even if it is not expressly stated, and in such a case there will be no error of law.[4] A tribunal needs to record findings of fact only on matters in dispute, but it should remember that points may arise by implication and these should also be dealt with.[5]

A tribunal is under a duty to employ a fair procedure when hearing your appeal. In particular, the rules of 'natural justice' mean you must be allowed to present your case properly and that the tribunal must consider what you say without bias. But 'natural justice' does not mean that there is an error of law if the tribunal reaches a decision which seems unfair or anomalous. On the contrary, the tribunal has to apply the regulations, however unfair the result may be to you.

How to appeal

You must first obtain permission (known as 'leave') to appeal.[6] This procedure is designed to weed out hopeless cases. It means that you have to show that there has *possibly* been an error of law and that you have the beginnings of a case.

If you wish to appeal from an SSAT or DAT, you should first apply to the chairperson of the tribunal.[7] You may do this either orally, at the end of the hearing when you are told the decision, or by writing to the clerk of the tribunal within three months of being sent the decision of the tribunal. If the application is made in writing, it will almost invariably be considered without any further hearing, usually – but not always – by the chairperson who originally heard your case.[8]

If the chairperson refuses leave to appeal, do not be discouraged. You may make a fresh application for leave to appeal direct to a commissioner within six weeks of being sent the decision refusing you leave.[9]

The addresses of the offices of the commissioners are set out in Appendix Four (see p350). The commissioners will often give leave to appeal even though the chairperson has refused to do so.

If you wish to appeal from a decision of a MAT, the rules are the same except that there is no right to make an oral application at the end of the hearing.[10]

In all cases, if you miss any time limit, you may still apply for leave to appeal but any application must then be made direct to a commissioner who will give you leave only if there are 'special reasons' (see p318).[11]

If you are given leave to appeal by the chairperson, you have six weeks in which to send in notice of the appeal itself.[12] You are sent a form on which to do this. The time may, again, be extended for 'special reasons'. If your application for leave was considered by a commissioner, you will be told that your notice of application for leave has been treated as a notice of appeal. There is no need to send in another form or letter.[13]

If a commissioner refuses you leave to appeal there is no further appeal against that decision. The only course open to you is to apply to the High Court (the Court of Session in Scotland) for a judicial review of the commissioner's decision. It is vital that before you take this step you obtain expert legal advice and apply for legal aid. If you do not do so, you may end up paying the DSS's legal costs if you lose. The time limits for applying to the Court are very short so you should act without delay as soon as you receive the commissioner's decision.

AOs and the Secretary of State have the same rights of appeal as you. So too does your union or an 'association which exists to promote the interest and welfare of its members'.[14] Your employer may appeal against a decision concerning SSP or SMP.[15] The procedure is always the same. If an AO or the Secretary of State appeals, your benefit may be suspended (see p295).

If the decision against which you have appealed is reviewed and revised so as to give you everything you are appealing for, your appeal lapses.[16] If you are dissatisfied with the review decision, you must launch a new appeal against that review decision. If you miss the time limit for the new appeal because you thought your original appeal was still effective, then this might amount to a 'special reason' for you to be allowed to appeal late.

References in forfeiture cases

Apart from appeals, commissioners decide all cases concerning the forfeiture rule (see p102) and if any question of forfeiture arises, the AO or Secretary of State must refer the question to the commissioner.[17] References are dealt with in the same way as appeals.

The written procedure

At this level, all AOs' cases are taken over by AOs at Central Adjudication Services (see Appendix Four, p350). A bundle of documents is prepared by the commissioners' office which then sends copies to each party, and the AO and/or Secretary of State are directed to make a submission in response to the appeal within a time limit of 30 days. This is often late. If you have not heard anything from the commissioners' office after a month, write to them and ask what is happening.

Once the submission of the AO or Secretary of State has been received, you will be given 30 days in which to reply (although the commissioner may extend the time limit). If you have nothing to add and do not want to reply at any stage, tell the commissioners' office. A commissioner has the power to strike out an appeal that appears to have been abandoned, although you can apply for it to be reinstated.[18]

When the commissioner has all the written submissions, s/he decides whether or not there should be an oral hearing of the appeal. If you ask for an oral hearing, the commissioner will hold one unless s/he feels that the case can properly be dealt with without one.[19] It is not usual for a commissioner to refuse a claimant's request for an oral hearing unless s/he is going to decide the case in the claimant's favour. Occasionally, the commissioner decides to hold an oral hearing even if you have not asked for one.

If there is no oral hearing, the commissioner reaches a decision on the basis of written submissions and other documents.

Because of the length of time you have to wait before your case is dealt with, you should consider making a fresh claim for benefit. This is particularly important in attendance allowance or DLA cases because there is no power to backdate a claim and if your appeal is unsuccessful you will get no benefit at all, even if your condition has deteriorated while you have been waiting.

The hearing

If the commissioner decides to hold an oral hearing, the appeal is heard either at the commissioners' offices in London or Edinburgh or at the law courts in Cardiff, Leeds or Liverpool. You are told the date in good time and your fares are paid in advance if you want to attend. At least half a day is set aside for each case.

Usually, one commissioner hears your case but, if there is a question of 'law of special difficulty', the hearing may be before a tribunal of three commissioners.[20] The procedure is still the same.

The hearing is a little more formal than those before SSATs, DATs or MATs but the commissioner will still be concerned to try and make sure that you say everything you want. Commissioners usually intervene a lot and ask questions so you need to be prepared to argue your case without a script. A full set of commissioners' decisions and the 'Blue Volumes' (see p325) are available for your use. The AO or Secretary of State is usually represented by a lawyer, so you should consider trying to obtain representation as well (see p329). The commissioner may exclude members of the public if intimate personal or financial circumstances or matters of public security are involved.[21] This is not usually necessary because it is rare for anyone not involved in the case to attend.

The decision

The decision is always given in writing[22] – often at some length.

After a successful appeal against a decision of an SSAT or DAT, the case is usually sent back to a differently constituted tribunal with directions about how to reconsider the case.[23] However, if the commissioner feels that the record of the decision of the original tribunal contains all the material facts, or s/he feels that it is 'expedient' to make findings on any extra factual issues necessary to the decisions, s/he will make the final decision.[24] It is unusual for a commissioner not to send a case back to a tribunal if there is a dispute about facts not determined by the original tribunal, unless all the evidence points in one direction.[25]

After a successful appeal against a decision of a MAT, the case is always sent back to a tribunal (which is usually differently constituted).

A commissioner may correct or set aside a decision in the same way as a tribunal (see p307).[26]

In certain circumstances, an AO may review a commissioner's decision (see p288).

Decisions of commissioners establish precedents and so may affect many cases other than your own (see p326).

Appeals from social security commissioners

You may appeal against a decision of a commissioner to the Court of Appeal (in Scotland, the Court of Session). Again, the appeal can only be based on a point of law and you must first obtain leave to appeal.[27]

Although the staff of the Court of Appeal do their best to be helpful, the procedure in the Court is strict, formal and far less flexible than the procedure before a tribunal or a commissioner. The Chief Adjudication Officer or Secretary of State will certainly be represented by a barrister at the hearing. You should therefore obtain legal advice and apply for legal aid before appealing. If you are unable to get help and have to represent yourself, the procedure is as follows.

The application for leave to appeal must first be made to a commissioner, in writing within three months of the date when you were sent the commissioner's decision. The commissioner may extend the time limit for 'special reasons' (see p318).[28] If you do not apply to the commissioner within the time limit and the commissioner refuses to extend it, the Court of Appeal (or Court of Session) cannot hear your appeal and you can only proceed by applying to the High Court (in

318 Administration and appeals 16: Appeals

Scotland, the Court of Session) for judicial review of the refusal to extend the time allowed for the appeal (see p321).[29]

Applications to a commissioner for leave to appeal are almost invariably considered without an oral hearing. If the commissioner refuses to give you leave to appeal (for reasons other than being outside the time limit), you can apply to the court for leave.[30] If your appeal is to the Court of Appeal, your notice of application should be lodged with the Civil Appeals Office within six weeks of notification of the commissioner's refusal being sent to you.[31] The court may extend the time but you must explain the reasons for your delay and file a sworn statement (called an 'affidavit') in support of an application for an extension of time.[32]

Generally, the Court of Appeal will first consider your application without an oral hearing. If leave is refused, you may renew your application in open court within seven days. Similarly, if leave is granted, the Chief Adjudication Officer or the Secretary of State has seven days in which to ask for an oral hearing.[33]

If leave to appeal was granted by a commissioner, you must serve a notice of appeal on the relevant parties within six weeks of being sent notification of the commissioner's grant of leave.[34] If leave was granted by the Court of Appeal, the notice of appeal must be served within the same six-week period or within seven days of the grant of leave, whichever is later (unless your notice of application for leave was lodged outside the six week time limit, in which case a time limit for lodging the notice of appeal should be contained in the Court's order).[35] The solicitor to the DSS will accept service at New Court, 48 Carey Street, London WC2A 2LS on behalf of the Chief Adjudication Officer or the Secretary of State.

You cannot appeal to the Court of Appeal against a decision of a commissioner refusing you leave to appeal *to* a commissioner (against a decision of a tribunal), but you can apply to the High Court for judicial review of such a decision.[36]

If the Court of Appeal refuses you leave to appeal after an oral hearing, you cannot appeal further, nor apply for a judicial review.

The procedures in Scotland are similar.

The Chief Adjudication Officer or the Secretary of State has the same rights of appeal as you.

5. LATE APPEALS[1]

An appeal against a decision of an AO must be received by the DSS within three months of the date on which the letter notifying you of the decision was posted.[2] However this time limit '*may* be extended for *special reasons*' by the chair of the tribunal or board to which the appeal is to be made.[3]

The power to extend time limits where there are 'special reasons' is found in a number of areas of social security adjudication. In particular, the 'special reasons' test also applies when commissioners are considering whether or not to grant leave to appeal out of time both *from* a decision of a tribunal and *to* the Court of Appeal.

There is no right to appeal against a refusal of a tribunal chair or a commissioner to allow a late appeal[4] (although a chair may[5] – but does not have to [6] – reconsider the decision if s/he is given new reasons). It is possible for a claimant who is refused a late appeal to make an application to the High Court for judicial review. But such an application is a lengthy and (unless you are entitled to legal aid with no contribution) expensive process and you are fairly unlikely to win not least because it is rare for reasons to be given for a refusal to extend time.

It is therefore important that if you have to ask for a late appeal you should give full and detailed reasons why the tribunal chair should grant your request first time round. You should not assume that permission will be granted as a matter of course or that you will get a second bite of the cherry if it is initially refused. Recent experience suggests that the *pro forma* late appeal requests which some advice agencies have used as part of benefit take-up campaigns will not usually be successful.

So, what counts as a 'special reason'? The brief answer seems to be potentially anything, as long as it is special enough! In particular, special reasons do not have to relate to why the appeal was late [7] (although they may do so). The decision whether or not to allow an extension of time must be made bearing in mind the merits of the appeal and the conse-quences for the claimant (and the DSS). In a case concerning immigration law,[8] the Court of Appeal has said that a similarly worded rule:

> gives . . . a discretion to do what is just and right. It should be liberally interpreted . . . so as not to let an appellant suffer unfairly.

In other words, what may or may not be a special reason cannot be defined in advance. It depends on the circumstances of each case and the tribunal chair or commissioner has to make his or her decision on an individual, case by case basis.

There are two particular problems for people who are asking for a late appeal in order to get around the anti-test-case rules (see p284). The first is that the Benefits Agency may simply treat the request for a late appeal as if it were a request for a review, carry out a review and then refuse to revise the original decision because of the anti-test-case rules. This is wrong. The DSS cannot use a review to stop you appealing unless the outcome of the review is the same as if your appeal had been entirely successful.[9] *Insist* that your request for a late appeal is passed to the tribunal chair for a decision. If the Benefits Agency still will not do so, send a copy yourself to the regional chair and the president (at the addresses in Appendix Four) and make a formal complaint to the customer services manager at your local office. If that does not do the trick follow the complaints procedure on p301 or ask a solicitor to threaten the DSS solicitor with judicial review.

The second problem arises because of a commissioner's decision (in an appeal brought by a Mrs White) which seems to say that the fact that there has been a decision in a test case which establishes that an earlier decision against a claimant was incorrect cannot *by itself* amount to a special reason.[10]

It may be that all the commissioner meant to say was that there were no special reasons in that particular case (although if so, it is hard to see why the decision has been reported). If not, then the *White* decision is probably wrong[11] and certainly open to misinterpretation.

A general rule that a favourable decision in a test case can never be a special reason for a late appeal would be wrong because of the principles – established by the Court of Appeal and the decisions of other commissioners – that one cannot say in advance what is and is not a special reason and that the discretion whether or not to allow a late appeal should be exercised individually in each case and liberally in favour of the applicant. Suppose, to take an extreme example, that the decision in the test case is given on the very last day for appealing and you submit an application for a late appeal the following day. It is difficult to see why the test-case decision should not count on its own as a special reason; the appeal is only one day late and the DSS would scarcely be prejudiced should it be allowed to go ahead.

In addition, the House of Lords has held since the *White* case that a court decision which overrules a view of the law which was previously accepted can amount to a 'special circumstance' which entitles litigants to re-open legal issues which have been decided against them.[12]

It may be that a commissioner or a tribunal chair feels that it would be harmful to good administration for a lot of old appeals which were previously closed to be re-opened many years later as a result of a test case. If so, then s/he still has a discretion to refuse to extend time – s/he does not *have* to allow a late appeal just because there are special reasons. The fact that it is desirable for people to be able to rely on decisions being final after the time for appeal has expired and the convenience of the DSS are not reasons for deciding *in advance* that test-case decisions can never be special reasons.

Perhaps more importantly, the *White* decision is open to being misinterpreted to mean that there can never be special reasons in 'anti-test-case rule' appeals. However, the commissioner did not say that – only that the fact of the test-case decision was not a special reason *by itself*.

So, if there are other reasons why a late appeal should be granted (see below for examples) these should be emphasised. In particular, such appeals will often involve large sums of money and (given the test case) a 'clear error' in the decision which is being appealed against. Both of these have been accepted as special reasons in other contexts (usually when it is the DSS which wishes to appeal late rather than the claimant!).

The High Court will probably hear an application for judicial review (*R v SSAT ex parte Taylor Young*[13]) challenging the commissioner's decision in *White* shortly after this *Guide* goes to press. Meanwhile, *White* is binding on tribunal chairs. If you are refused a late appeal and suspect that the chair or commissioner may have been influenced by the *White* decision you should (at least if there is a substantial amount of money at stake in your appeal) see a solicitor and apply for legal aid to ask the High Court for a judicial review. Do this immediately. Do not wait until the decision in the *Taylor Young* case is known because you only have a maximum of three months to make your application to the court. If the chair or commissioner has not given reasons for the refusal, your solicitor should write and ask them for an explanation and (if there are further reasons why an extension should be granted) to reconsider their original decision. If they still refuse, do not be deterred. In practice, it will be difficult for them to avoid justifying the refusal once leave to apply for judicial review has been obtained from the court unless they want to lose the case.[14]

So what should a tribunal chair or commissioner take into account when deciding whether or not to grant leave for a late appeal? As explained above, there are no hard and fast rules but the following are obviously relevant:

- **the length of the delay**. The less delay there has been the easier it will be to justify it but even a short delay may be too long unless there is either a good reason for it or some other factor which outweighs it. In one case in the 1960s,[15] a tribunal of commissioners said that it would not have extended time for appealing by as little as seven days if it had not been supported by the DSS. A commissioner or chair nowadays would probably be rather more generous than this but the general principle holds good – time limits are meant to be observed. Having said that, there have been cases where leave has been granted five years[16] and even 20 years[17] out of time.
- **the reasons for delay**. Where possible, explaining the delay is an important part of any application for a late appeal. Do not be worried if some or all of the delay is your fault – almost any explanation is

better than none at all. The worst situation is where you have known of the time limit but simply ignored it, but even then it may be possible to say something favourable. For example, things may have been difficult at home or perhaps you were confused by the rules or just assumed that the Benefits Agency were the experts and had got it right.

If the appeal is late because the claimant was ill, there will probably be special reasons. Applications based on illness should be supported by medical evidence if at all possible. There may also be special reasons if an appeal is late:
– because of a reasonable mistake in calculating the time limit; *or*
– because for some reason you did not receive the decision or you posted your appeal in time but the letter went astray in the post; *or*
– because of a mistake by your advisers. It should not make any difference that you might be able to sue your advisers for negligence. Professional advisers are not normally negligent and if yours does make an error then that is *special* to your case. [18]

If a claimant was given wrong advice or otherwise misled by the DSS, that is also relevant. Many claimants are discouraged from appealing by the contents of the DSS leaflets at the time the decision to refuse benefit was made and, in some cases, by AOs who advise them incorrectly that any appeal would be doomed to failure. This seems to have been particularly prevalent in the cases of people who stand to benefit from the *Cottingham* and *Geary* decision [19] (on occupational pensions and the earnings rule for increases for adult dependants – see p209). Similarly, claimants who stand to benefit from the decision of the Court of Appeal in *Pearse* [20] (that receipt of Graduated Retirement Benefit prior to 5 August 1992 did not prevent a claimant from receiving an increment as a result of deferring his/her pension – see p115) should point out that the DSS failed to implement an earlier decision of a commissioner to the same effect. If you have been badly advised by the DSS and lose money because you are refused a late appeal you should consider claiming compensation (see p301).
• **the merits of the appeal**. This has been discussed above. The more likely an appeal is to succeed, the greater the injustice in refusing to allow an extension of time. A strong case is particularly useful if there has been a very long delay and leave will usually be granted where there has been a 'clear error' which will have long-term continuing effects unless corrected. [20]
• **the amount of money at stake**. The long-term effects of the grant or refusal of leave to appeal are also relevant here. Even if there has been no clear error, leave may be granted if there is a lot of money at stake. [22] The reported decisions in this area often involve the DSS appealing late against tribunal decisions which would cost them

thousands of pounds unless corrected. You should argue that the same principles should apply for claimants – particularly if the reason you are appealing is to get around the 'anti-test-case rules'.

Above all, you should stress reasons which are personal to you. Rightly or wrongly, leave is sometimes refused because the reasons given are *general* ones – ie, ones which apply in a large number of cases – rather than *special* ones which apply to the individual claimant.

6. HOW TO PREPARE AN APPEAL

Appeals are taken on all sorts of issues so the advice given here can only be fairly general.

Cases may concern disputes of fact or disputes about the law or both. You usually need to think about both the facts and the law because they are connected. The law tells you which facts are relevant and the facts tell you which bits of the law you need to consider.

Establishing the facts

You are likely to know more than anyone else about the facts of your case. Your key task is to pass your knowledge (and the knowledge of others who know something about the facts) on to the tribunal.

Tribunals decide cases on the evidence presented to them. The evidence may consist of oral evidence (what they are actually told during the hearing) and written evidence (contained in statements and other documents shown to them). What you yourself say during the hearing is perfectly good evidence.[1] It does not have to be backed up by any other evidence. On the other hand, a tribunal is not bound to believe you or to accept your opinion on, say, a medical matter. It is therefore a good idea to obtain additional evidence, if possible, of those facts likely to be in dispute.

When you appeal, you are likely to have some idea of the main areas in dispute. However, it is vital that you study the AO's or Secretary of State's submission when it arrives. That tells you which bits of your case are not disputed. You then know which facts are not agreed and so what you have to prove. Any evidence you collect must deal with the matters really in dispute.

For example, in a case where you have to prove that you are incapable of work, the AO may well accept that you are not fully fit and that you have, say, difficulty in bending down. S/he may simply be saying that this does not prevent you from working at some suitable employment. In this instance, a medical report which says that you are disabled and cannot bend down would not be a great deal of help to you because it does not answer the AO's point. You need evidence which shows either that you are more disabled than the AO believes, or that the type of employment suggested by the AO would involve bending down or is unsuitable for some other reason. Such evidence might come from a number of sources. You can try and obtain a more detailed medical report. You can tell the tribunal yourself about the effect of your disabilities. You can also ask someone working in the relevant employment to say what the work really involves.

Evidence given orally by people who actually attend the hearing is always best. That is why it is so important for you to be there. It enables a tribunal to assess the reliability of the person giving the evidence and also enables the witness to answer any questions. But it is not always possible to persuade people to attend hearings although expenses are paid not only for travel costs but also for loss of earnings up to £38.50 (for over four hours) together with a small subsistence allowance. The next best evidence is a detailed signed written statement. This may be more persuasive if it is a sworn statement (called an 'affidavit'). A solicitor may be able to help you with this at no charge under the 'Green Form' scheme (see p330) if you are on income support or have a very low income.

Medical evidence is almost invariably in the form of written reports. As already mentioned, it is essential that they deal with the points in dispute if that is possible. Sometimes, a doctor does not really know much about the effect of a disability on a person's everyday life, in which case your evidence or that of a friend or relation may well be of more use. However, where a medical report is required, there are two ways of obtaining one apart from simply writing to the doctor yourself. Either a solicitor can obtain one for you (see p58); or the tribunal (or an AO) can refer you for an examination and obtain a report if the medical issue in your case is one of 'special difficulty'.[2] If the lack of a report is causing you difficulties at a tribunal hearing, you could remind the tribunal of this power to obtain one itself.

If you do obtain statements or reports, you should send copies to the tribunal clerk in advance if there is time. The clerk will send a further copy to the AO or the Secretary of State who might then decide to support your appeal.

If you are appealing to a commissioner, remember that commissioners have only very limited powers to deal with questions of fact. However, if you have new evidence, it might enable you to apply for a review (see p288) of the tribunal's decision and you can do that while the appeal is pending. Reviews are usually quicker than appeals but you may receive a lower amount of arrears (see pp290 and 293).

Checking the law

It is not usual for there to be a major dispute about the law. Do not worry if you do not have the time or resources to follow all the advice given here. The vast majority of cases involve parts of the law which tribunals are likely to know well.

However, the Benefits Agency does not always get the law right and you might well want to emphasise a point that the AO or Secretary of State has overlooked. Also, if you know what the law says, you will know what facts you have to prove.

The primary sources of social security law are **statute law** and **case law** (decided by commissioners and the courts). As explained below, it is fairly easy to find both sorts of law once you know what you are looking for. The notes in this *Guide* are intended to point you in the right direction. You should also look carefully at the submission of the AO or Secretary of State, as that refers to the statute law and case law which s/he thinks is relevant. There are also a number of books which can help by explaining the law and referring you to relevant legislation and cases (see Appendix Five – p352).

Statute law

There are a number of important Acts of Parliament. The one which sets out the basic rules is the Social Security Contributions and Benefits Act 1992. The Act sets out the main framework and empowers the Secretary of State to make regulations covering the details. These regulations are laid before Parliament as 'statutory instruments'. Appendix Six (see p355) contains a list of Acts and regulations.

They can be purchased individually from HMSO bookshops. However, both Acts and regulations are amended from time to time and this can lead to difficulties when you are trying to discover the current state of the law or chase up a reference. It is therefore much easier to refer to the looseleaf book, *The Law Relating to Social Security* (unless your case is a very old one and the law has changed since the relevant time). This is in ten volumes known as the 'Blue Volumes' or the 'Blue Book'. It is published by HMSO and is kept up to date with regular supplements. Most large reference libraries have a copy. In addition, your local Benefits Agency office has a copy which you are allowed to look at.

Less unwieldy is a single volume, published annually, which contains all the most important Acts and regulations with comprehensive notes explaining them. This is *Non-Means-Tested Benefits – The Legislation* edited by Bonner *et al* (see p352).

Case law

When a commissioner or a court decides a question of principle, the decision sets a precedent. An AO, adjudicating medical authority, SSAT, MAT or DAT deciding a similar case must follow that precedent.[3] The vast majority of relevant cases on social security law are commissioners' decisions.

All commissioners' decisions have file numbers. One example is CU/255/1984. The last numbers indicate the year in which the appeal was lodged. The second letter indicates the type of benefit involved in the decision. Each year, the most important cases are chosen by the Chief Commissioner to be reported. These are given a new number – eg, CU/255/1984 became R(U) 3/86. Again, the second letter denotes the type of benefit. The last numbers indicate the year in which the case was decided. All reported cases since 1951 begin with an 'R'. There used to be an intermediate category of 'numbered' cases with references such as CG 2/70; reported cases before 1951 have such references. An extra 'S' or 'W' after a 'C' denotes a Scottish or Welsh case, as in CWG 3/78. In all cases, the type of benefit is indicated as follows:

A   attendance allowance
CR   compensation recovery
F   family allowance (now child benefit)
FC   family credit
FIS   family income supplement
G   general (all benefits not covered in other categories)
I   industrial injuries benefits
IS   income support
M   mobility allowance
P   retirement pensions
S   sickness and invalidity benefit and severe disablement
        allowance
SB   supplementary benefit
SMP   statutory maternity pay
SSP   statutory sick pay
U   unemployment benefit

Individual reported decisions may be purchased from HMSO book-shops, as may bound volumes, although all the early ones are out of print. However, each local Benefits Agency office has a set which you are allowed to look at. If a commissioner's decision is challenged in the courts, the decision of the court is usually reported as an appendix in the series of reported commissioners' decisions.

Unreported decisions may be obtained from the offices of the commissioners (see p313) for £1 each. If one is to be used at a tribunal hearing by an AO or the Secretary of State, a copy should be supplied to you. Similarly, if you wish to use one, you should supply copies to everyone, preferably by sending one to the tribunal clerk in advance of the hearing. Unreported decisions must be followed by appeal tribunals in the same way as reported ones. [4]

It is worth checking the decisions relied on by AOs and the Secretary of State. Sometimes, they rely on part of a decision only and fail to mention another part which is more favourable to you. To find other cases relevant to your own, you can use the notes in this guide or any of the books listed in Appendix Five (see p352). A particularly useful publication is *Neligan's Social Security Case Law: A Digest of Commissioners' Decisions*, published by HMSO in two volumes. This sets out summaries of decisions under subject headings. Again, your local Benefits Agency office has a copy which you may look at and your local reference library probably has one too.

Case law appears less precise than statute law and frequently cases seem to contradict each other. Very often there are small differences in the facts of the cases which justify the different results. You need to find cases where the facts are similar to yours. If cases appear to be against you, look at the facts of those cases and see whether any differences justify a different decision in your case. This is known as 'distinguishing' cases. One distinction may simply be that what seemed reasonable in the 1950s does not seem fair in the 1990s. [5] It should also be remembered that most old cases were decided when there was a right of appeal to commissioners on questions of fact as well as law so tribunals may not necessarily be erring in law if they take a different view from the commissioner's.

Where there is an irreconcilable conflict between cases, a tribunal has to choose which decision to follow. It *normally* follows a reported decision in preference to an unreported one, and *must* follow a decision of a tribunal of commissioners (see p316) in preference to a decision of a single commissioner. [6] Decisions of the House of Lords, the Court of Appeal or of the High Court on an application for judicial review (or, in Scotland, the Court of Session) take precedence over all commissioners' decisions. [7]

Commissioners have more freedom and do not have to follow the decision of another single commissioner if satisfied that the earlier decision was wrong. [8] However, a single commissioner must follow a decision of a tribunal of commissioners (see p316) although, if s/he thinks it may be wrong, s/he can ask the Chief Commissioner to appoint another tribunal to reconsider the point. A tribunal of commissioners does not have to follow the decision of another tribunal but will usually do so. [9]

Debates in Parliament

The House of Lords has recently decided[10] that, where the law is ambig-
uous, the courts – which will include SSATs and the commissioners – can
look at statements made to Parliament by ministers when the law was
first made. It may therefore be worth checking the House of Commons
and House of Lords official reports (known as *Hansard*) to see what was
said in Parliament when the rules which apply to your case were first
introduced.

Hansard can be difficult to find. The House of Commons Public Information Office publishes a book called 'PHIL' (Parliamentary Holdings in
Libraries in Britain and Ireland) which will tell you the nearest library in
which you can find *Hansard*. Unfortunately PHIL costs £10 but your
local library may have a copy even if it does not have *Hansard* as well. If
you live in the London area there is another alternative as the House of
Commons Public Information Office also publishes a leaflet called
'APRILL' (Access to Parliamentary Resources and Information in London Libraries). This leaflet – which is free – has similar information to
PHIL but only covers London. It was a predecessor to PHIL. There are
only a few copies left and no definite plans for it to be reprinted. If you
need a copy of APRILL or want more detailed help, ring the Public
Information Office on 071-219 4272.

Hansard can also be a confusing publication. To begin with, you need
the volumes which deal with parliamentary debates and written answers
rather than those covering the proceedings of standing committees. Then
each volume has two sets of numbering – one for parliamentary debates
and one for written answers. There are two columns on each page, each
of which has a separate number, so, for example, a single volume may
have two columns numbered 609. The best way of finding what you
want is to use the comprehensive index which is updated fortnightly.
Again, references in the index are to column numbers and those relating
to Written Answers are prefixed by the letter 'W'. The ones you may need
for your appeal are the ones which relate to parliamentary debates and
have no prefixes.

Presenting your case

Each case is different and hearings are informal so there is no set pattern
for presenting cases.

As already suggested, it is a good idea to send in a detailed submission
and any medical reports before the hearing. Some claimants like to use a
written submission at the hearing and to read directly from it. However,
tribunals usually ask questions so it is necessary to be able to talk about
your case without the script.

The tribunal will decide whether you or the presenting officer speaks first. It is helpful to make it clear at the beginning of the hearing which bits of the AO's or Secretary of State's submissions are in dispute. In most cases, much of those submissions are agreed and it is only a small, but vital, part which is not. It is, then, usually best to tell the tribunal about the facts first and to call any witnesses before turning to legal arguments.

It is the tribunal's job to help you to say everything you want by putting you at your ease and asking the right questions. If you forget to say something when it is your turn to speak, do not hesitate to add it at the end of the hearing.

Advice and representation

There are a number of agencies which can advise you about social security matters and can help you prepare cases for tribunal hearings. Some can also represent you at hearings if you feel that someone else can put your case better than you can yourself.

Most areas have a citizens' advice bureau. The nearest one to you should be in the telephone directory, but you can also obtain its address from the National Association of Citizens' Advice Bureaux, Myddleton House, 115/123 Pentonville Road, London N1 9LZ (tel: 071-833 2181). If there are more specialist advice agencies in your area, the citizens' advice bureau or your local library or town hall will be able to tell you and every Benefits Agency office also has a list of advisers.

Many local authorities have good welfare rights advisers. Ask your town hall.

If you have been a member of a union, the union may be able to help you, particularly in industrial injuries cases.

Different groups of claimants have different sorts of problems. If you are unemployed, you could contact your local centre for the unemployed.

A list of such centres can be obtained from the Trades Union Congress, Great Russell Street, London WC1B 3LS (tel: 071-636 4030). If you are disabled, you may be able to get help from the Disability Alliance, First Floor East, Universal House, 88-94 Wentworth Street, London E1 7SA (tel: 071-247 8776), or Network for the Handicapped, 16 Princeton Street, London WC1R 4BB (tel: 071-831 8031) or the Disablement Income Group, Millmead Business Centre, Millmead Road, London N17 9QU (tel: 081-801 8013). Pensioners can obtain advice from Age Concern, Astral House, 1268 London Road, London SW16 4ER (tel: 081-679 8000).

Many of these agencies will provide free representation or can put you in touch with a tribunal representation unit. However, it is easier to find free representation in large cities than in the country.

Advice from lawyers is not always easy to find either. Network for the Handicapped employs one and so do some unions. Many citizens' advice bureaux have evening sessions when you can obtain free legal advice, but their non-lawyer advisers are often better at dealing with social security problems. On the other hand, a citizens' advice bureau will be able to tell you whether any solicitors in its area handle social security cases as part of their ordinary work.

Legal aid does not cover representation before tribunals or even the commissioners. However, if you are on income support or have a very low income, the 'Green Form' scheme (in Scotland, the 'Pink Form' scheme) of free legal advice and assistance may cover not only advice but also preparatory work for a hearing, such as obtaining medical reports and writing submissions. Using it, a solicitor can obtain counsel's advice on a difficult point. If you have a solicitor acting for you in an industrial injury claim against your employer, s/he may have medical and other reports and evidence which you can use for your benefit claim.

If you are not eligible for 'Green' (or 'Pink') Form advice and assistance, or you want to be represented by a lawyer at hearing, you are likely to have to pay. If your claim is worth hundreds of pounds, it may be a worthwhile investment. But, remember that many non-lawyer advisers know more about social security law than most lawyers and their advice is usually free.

Legal aid is available for cases in the Court of Appeal, the High Court and the Court of Session and you should certainly obtain legal advice and representation. The legal aid authorities have, in the past, taken the view that an application to a commissioner for leave to appeal to the Court of Appeal cannot be covered by legal aid. However, it is arguable that such an application is a step 'preliminary to' proceedings in the Court of Appeal and is thus work for which legal aid is available.[11] You should always consult a solicitor if you are taking a social security case to a court rather than to a tribunal or a commissioner.

Miscellaneous benefits for the disabled

This appendix covers various schemes providing money for those disabled by particular causes and it also very briefly deals with the Department of Employment's services for the disabled.

It does *not* cover forms of assistance provided by local authority social services departments, the National Health Service or district health authorities.

If you want to know more about rights, benefits and services for the disabled, obtain the *Disability Rights Handbook* (19th edn, 1994-95, £8.95 post-free) published by the Disability Alliance of which CPAG is a member organisation. You can obtain this from CPAG Ltd, 1-5 Bath St, London EC1V 9PY. Also very helpful is *Disability or Health Problems: A Guide to Employment Services and Schemes*, published by Youthaid and available from them at 409 Brixton Road, London SW9 7DG price £5 post-free.

I. WAR PENSIONS

There are a number of different schemes providing benefits for those disabled, or for the dependants of those killed, in the First World War and in all conflicts since 3 September 1939. The most important schemes are those covering members of the Armed Forces, but there are others covering auxiliary personnel, civil defence volunteers, merchant mariners and also ordinary civilians. Many of the benefits are similar to those provided under the industrial injuries scheme but there are important differences.

Scope of the schemes

This varies from scheme to scheme but, generally, servicemen and servicewomen are covered if their disablement arises out of their service even if not due to the conflict itself, whereas civilians are covered only if their disablement is due to a 'war injury'.

Disablement benefit

The basic disablement benefit is assessed in the same way as for industrial injuries benefits (see p163). For those at least 20 per cent disabled it is paid at the same rate as industrial disablement benefit (£93.20 a week for someone assessed as 100 per cent disabled), although there are small additional components for those above the rank of ordinary seaman, private or aircraftsman (or their equivalents).

If the assessment is below 20 per cent, a lump-sum gratuity is paid even if the assessment is less than 14 per cent.

A claimant's assessment can be increased if her/his disability worsens at any time.

Increases of disablement benefit

Unemployability allowance is like invalidity benefit and includes equivalent increases for dependants and invalidity allowances.

Allowance for lowered standard of occupation is similar to reduced earnings allowance paid under the industrial injuries scheme (see p179). The most important difference is that it is limited so that the total of the basic disablement pension and the reduced earnings allowance cannot exceed £98.90 a week. Otherwise the maximum is £37.28 a week.

Constant attendance allowance is again like that paid under the industrial injuries scheme (see p177) except that it is payable if the assessment of disablement is 80 per cent or 90 per cent as well as 100 per cent.

Exceptionally severe disablement allowance is payable only to those receiving constant attendance allowance – again, as in the industrial injuries scheme (see p178).

Severe disablement occupational allowance is paid at the rate of £18.70 a week to those entitled to constant attendance allowance at more than the lower rate but who are nonetheless ordinarily employed in gainful employment.

Comforts allowance is payable to those receiving constant attendance allowance and who *either* receive unemployability allowance *or* who are assessed as 100 per cent disabled. The rate is either £16 or £8 a week.

Mobility supplement is payable to those who have amputations of both legs or who satisfy conditions similar (but not identical) to those for the mobility component of disability living allowance (see p127). The rate is £35.55 a week.

Age allowance is payable to those aged over 65 who are assessed as at least 40 per cent disabled. The rates are £6.60 a week (40 or 50 per cent), £10.20 a week (60 or 70 per cent), £14.55 a week (70 or 80 per cent) and £20.40 a week (90 or 100 per cent).

Other allowances are made for clothing for those with artificial limbs and for the education and maintenance of dependants.

Awards in respect of death

Widows may be paid a pension at a rate depending on her age and her husband's rank. A private's widow aged over 80 may receive £99.10 a week. A widow under 65 with a child receives £74.70 *plus* £15.10 for each child (except the first for whom only £13.90 is payable) *plus* up to £28.25 rent allowance a week. Those widows whose husbands were in the Armed Forces on or after 1 January 1973 receive a further earnings-related pension under the service pensions scheme.

Widowers may be paid up to £74.70 a week. A widower must have been incapable of self-support when his wife died if he is to be entitled to the benefit.

An unmarried dependant who was living as the spouse of the deceased and caring for a child of the deceased may receive up to £72.65 a week. Again a rent allowance of up to £28.25 is also payable.

Orphan's pension is payable at the rate of £15.50 a week for the first child and £16.70 a week for each other child under 16. An adult incapable of self-support may be paid up to £57.60 a week.

Decisions

Claims should be made to The Controller, Central Office (War Pensions), DSS, Norcross, Blackpool FY5 3TA.

Decisions are taken by the Secretary of State who has a great deal of discretion. If there is a dispute as to whether disablement or death was due to service or a war injury (as the case may be) since 3 September 1939, or as to the extent of disablement, the claimant may appeal to the Pension Appeal Tribunal. There is a further right of appeal to the High Court (in Scotland, the Court of Session).

Further information

The DSS publish a number of leaflets about war pensions. There are also local war pensions committees in each area which may be able to assist with claims. The Royal British Legion also provides experienced advice and representation.

2. CRIMINAL INJURIES COMPENSATION

Criminal injuries compensation is payable if you suffer personal injury directly resulting from a crime of violence or from trying to stop someone committing a crime or from trying to apprehend a suspected criminal. A dependant of someone killed in those circumstances may also make a claim.

The compensation

This is paid as a tax-free lump sum. From April 1994, compensation will no longer be based on what would be received if the claimant were to sue in the courts. Instead there will be 25 bands of compensation varying between £1,000 and £250,000 and injuries are defined in advance as falling in one of these bands. This means that people with the same injury will get the same compensation even if their needs are different (eg, they have lost earnings or have dependants to support).

Disqualification

Payments are not made if the award would be less than £1,000. Nor are they made for *road traffic accidents* except deliberate runnings down.

Payments may also be withheld or reduced if the claimant did not make sure the police were notified or did not co-operate with them.

More controversially, payments may be withheld or reduced if the claimant's conduct connected with the injury, or past convictions or conduct, make it appropriate that an award should not be made.

Decisions

Claims should be sent to the Criminal Injuries Compensation Authority, Tay House, 300 Bath Street, Glasgow G2 4JR (tel: 041-331 2726).

Decisions are made by the Board. It consists of senior lawyers. The first assessment is made by a single member. If a claimant is dissatisfied (or if the single member decides to refer the case) a hearing is held before three members of the Board. There is a right of appeal on a point of law to the High Court (in Scotland, the Court of Session).

Further information

The Authority publishes quite a full guide with a separate leaflet giving examples of the amounts that might be claimed for different sorts of injuries. Legal advice may be a good idea in these cases. A claimant can obtain advice and assistance (but not representation) under the Green Form scheme (in Scotland, the Pink Form scheme).

3. VACCINE DAMAGE PAYMENTS

These are payable if a person is now over two years old and is assessed as at least 80 per cent disabled (see pp171-4) as a result of vaccination for diphtheria, tetanus, whooping cough, polio, measles, rubella (German measles), tuberculosis or smallpox. Except in the case of polio or rubella, the vaccination must have been carried out when the person was under 18.

The payment

A lump sum of £30,000 tax free.

Decisions

Claims should be made to the Vaccine Damage Payments Unit, DSS, North Fylde Central Offices, Norcross, Blackpool FY5 3TA within six years of the vaccination.

The Secretary of State makes the initial decision. An appeal may be made to the Vaccine Damage Tribunal which is a medical appeal tribunal (see p308) under a different name. A decision of the tribunal can be challenged on a point of law in the High Court (in Scotland, the Court of Session).

4. THE PNEUMOCONIOSIS ETC. (WORKERS' COMPENSATION) ACT 1979

This provides for lump-sum payments to those disabled, and the dependants of those who have died while disabled, as the result of pneumoconiosis, byssinosis or diffuse mesothelioma incurred through employment. The Act allows payments if no action for damages has been brought before the courts or settled and none can be now because the employer has ceased to carry on business. Actions dismissed on technical grounds do not count as having been brought. The claimant must be entitled to disablement benefit (or an equivalent payment under schemes for those employed before 5 July 1948). If the disabled person has died, either s/he must have been receiving disablement benefit (or an equivalent) when s/he died or death benefit or widow's benefit must be payable as a result of the disease.

The compensation

Lump sums of up to £47,890 for disabled claimants and £21,740 in the event of death are awarded. The precise amount in any case depends upon the age and the extent of disablement of the claimant or the deceased.

Decisions

Claims should be made to the Department of Employment, HS1, Level 2, Caxton House, Tothill Street, London SW1H 9NF (tel: 071-273 5248) within 12 months of the claimant first becoming entitled to disablement benefit (or an equivalent) or within 12 months of the disabled person's death. The time limit may be extended if it is 'appropriate, having regard to the circumstances of the case'. Decisions are made by the Secretary of State in the same way as for contributions (see p286) and there is the same right of appeal to the High Court (in Scotland, the Court of Session). A guide for claimants is obtainable from the Department of Employment at the above address.

5. DEPARTMENT OF EMPLOYMENT SERVICES

Assessment, training and sheltered employment

The disablement resettlement officer at your local JobCentre may be able to help you obtain further education or training or simply work experience if you are finding it difficult to obtain employment. In particular, s/he can give you advice about Employment Rehabilitation Centres which assess your employment potential through talking to you and giving you written and practical exercises. Two of the centres run residential courses and lodgings can be arranged near the others if they are too far away for you to travel to them daily. These courses provide both assessment and rehabilitation following an injury, disease or illness (either physical or mental). Training allowances and travel expenses are usually paid and your benefits are unaffected during the assessment.

The disablement resettlement officer can also advise you about the availability of sheltered employment.

Access to work programme

From April 1994 the new 'Access to Work' programme will replace the previous schemes for help with special aids to employment, adaptations to premises and equipment, fares to work and the personal reader service schemes. The new programme is intended to be more flexible than the old schemes. You should ask for details at the JobCentre if you think you might benefit.

Help for employers

The Employment Service publishes pamphlets for employers with guidance about employing disabled people and, in particular, those suffering from blindness or visual impairment, deafness or hearing impairment, epilepsy, haemophilia, mental handicap, mental illness or multiple sclerosis.

An employer can be paid £45 a week for up to six weeks (or up to three months in exceptional circumstances) towards your wages during a trial period to see whether you can manage the job. There are also grants under the Pathway Employment Service run by MENCAP for those who offer trial periods or training for mentally handicapped people. The JobCentre can provide details.

Prescribed degrees of disablement

1. SCHEDULE 2 TO THE SOCIAL SECURITY (GENERAL BENEFIT) REGULATIONS 1982

Description of injury	Degree of disablement %
1 Loss of both hands or amputation at higher sites	100
2 Loss of a hand and a foot	100
3 Double amputation through leg or thigh, or amputation through leg or thigh on one side and loss of other foot	100
4 Loss of sight to such an extent as to render the claimant unable to perform any work for which eyesight is essential	100
5 Very severe facial disfiguration	100
6 Absolute deafness	100
7 Forequarter or hindquarter amputation	100
Amputation cases – upper limbs (either arm)	
8 Amputation through shoulder joint	90
9 Amputation below shoulder with stump less than 20.5 cms from tip of acromion	80
10 Amputation from 20.5 cms from tip of acromion to less than 11.5 cms below tip of olecranon	70
11 Loss of a hand or of the thumb and 4 fingers of 1 hand or amputation from 11.5 cms below tip of olecranon	60
12 Loss of thumb	30
13 Loss of thumb and its metacarpal bone	40
14 Loss of 4 fingers of 1 hand	50
15 Loss of 3 fingers of 1 hand	30
16 Loss of 2 fingers of 1 hand	20
17 Loss of terminal phalanx of thumb	20

Description of injury	Degree of disablement %
Amputation cases – lower limbs	
18 Amputation of both feet resulting in end-bearing stumps	90
19 Amputation through both feet proximal to the metatarso-phalangeal joint	80
20 Loss of all toes of both feet through the metatarso-phalangeal joint	40
21 Loss of all toes of both feet proximal to the proximal inter-phalangeal joint	30
22 Loss of all toes of both feet distal to the proximal inter-phalangeal joint	20
23 Amputation at hip	90
24 Amputation below hip with stump not exceeding 13 cms in length measured from tip of great trochanter	80
25 Amputation below hip and above knee with stump exceeding 13 cms in length measured from tip of great trochanter, or at knee not resulting in end-bearing stump	70
26 Amputation at knee resulting in end-bearing stump or below knee with stump not exceeding 9 cms	60
27 Amputation below knee with stump exceeding 9 cms but not exceeding 13 cms	50
28 Amputation below knee with stump exceeding 13 cms	40

Description of injury	Degree of disablement %	Description of injury	Degree of disablement %
Amputation cases – lower limbs (*cont.*)		43 2 phalanges	6
29 Amputation of 1 foot resulting in end-bearing stump	30	44 1 phalanx	5
		45 Guillotine amputation of tip without loss of bone	2
30 Amputation through 1 foot proximal to the metatarso-phalangeal joint	30	**Loss of toes of right or left foot:**	
		Great toe:	
31 Loss of all toes of 1 foot through the metatarso-phalangeal joint	20	46 Through metatarso-phalangeal joint	14
		47 Part, with some loss of bone	3
Other injuries		Any other toe:	
32 Loss of 1 eye, without complications, the other being normal	40	48 Through metatarso-phalangeal joint	3
		49 Part, with some loss of bone	1
33 Loss of vision of 1 eye, without complications or disfigurement of the eyeball, the other being normal	30	2 toes of 1 foot, excluding great toe:	
		50 Through metatarso-phalangeal joint	5
Loss of fingers of right or left hand		51 Part, with some loss of bone	2
Index finger:		3 toes of 1 foot, excluding great toe:	
34 Whole	14	52 Through metatarso-phalangeal joint	6
35 2 phalanges	11	53 Part, with some loss of bone	3
36 1 phalanx	9		
37 Guillotine amputation of tip without loss of bone	5	4 toes of 1 foot, excluding great toe:	
Middle finger:		54 Through metatarso-phalangeal joint	9
38 Whole	12	55 Part, with some loss of bone	3
39 2 phalanges	9		
40 1 phalanx	7		
41 Guillotine amputation of tip without loss of bone	4		
Ring or little finger:			
42 Whole	7		

The degree of disablement due to occupational deafness is assessed using tables and a formula to be found in regulation 34 of and Schedule 3 to the Social Security (Industrial Injuries) (Prescribed Diseases) Regulations 1985 as amended.

Prescribed industrial diseases

Part I of Schedule I to the Social Security (Industrial Injuries) (Prescribed Diseases) Regulations 1985 as amended

Prescribed disease or injury	*Occupation*
A Conditions due to physical agents	**Any occupation involving:**
A1 Inflammation, ulceration or malignant disease of the skin or subcutaneous tissues or of the bones, or blood dyscrasia, or cataract, due to electro-magnetic radiations (other than radiant heat), or to ionising particles	Exposure to electro-magnetic radiations (other than radiant heat) or to ionising particles.
A2 Heat cataract	Frequent or prolonged exposure to rays from molten or red-hot material.
A3 Dysbarism, including decompression sickness, barotrauma and osteonecrosis	Subjection to compressed or rarified air or other respirable gases or gaseous mixtures.
A4 Cramp of the hand or forearm due to repetitive movements	Prolonged periods of handwriting, typing or other repetitive movements of the fingers, hand or arm.
A5 Subcutaneous cellulitis of the hand (Beat hand)	Manual labour causing severe or prolonged friction or pressure on the hand.
A6 Bursitis or subcutaneous cellulitis arising at or about the knee due to severe or prolonged external friction or pressure at or about the knee (Beat knee)	Manual labour causing severe or prolonged external friction or pressure at or about the knee
A7 Bursitis or subcutaneous cellulitis arising ator about the elbow due to severe or prolonged external friction or pressure at or about the elbow (Beat elbow)	Manual labour causing severe or prolonged external friction or pressure at or about the elbow
A8 Traumatic inflammation of the tendons of the hand or forearm, or of the associated tendon sheaths	Manual labour, or frequent or repeated movements of the hand or wrist.
A9 Miner's nystagmus	Work in or about a mine.
A10 Sensorineural hearing loss amounting to at least 50dB in each ear, being the average of hearing losses at 1, 2 and 3 kHz frequencies, and being due in the case of at least one ear to occupational noise (occupational deafness)	(*a*) The use of powered (but not hand-powered) grinding tools on cast metal (other than weld metal) or on billets or blooms in the metal-producing industry, or work wholly or mainly in the immediate vicinity of those tools whilst

| *Prescribed disease or injury* | *Occupation* |

they are being so used; *or*

(*b*) the use of pneumatic percussive tools on metal, or work wholly or mainly in the immediate vicinity of those tools whilst they are being used; *or*

(*c*) the use of pneumatic percussive tools for drilling rock in quarries or underground or in mining coal, or work wholly or mainly in the immediate vicinity of those tools whilst they are being used; *or*

(*d*) work wholly or mainly in the immediate vicinity of plant (excluding power press plant) engaged in the forging (including drop-stamping) of metal by means of closed or open dies or drop hammers; *or*

(*e*) work in textile manufacturing where the work is undertaken wholly or mainly in rooms or sheds in which there are machines engaged in weaving manufactured or natural (including mineral) fibres or in the high speed false twisting of fibres; *or*

(*f*) the use of, or work wholly or mainly in the immediate vicinity of, machines engaged in cutting, shaping or cleaning metal nails; *or*

(*g*) the use of, or work wholly or mainly in the immediate vicinity of, plasma spray guns engaged in the deposition of metal; *or*

(*h*) the use of, or work wholly or mainly in the immediate vicinity of, any of the following machines engaged in the working of wood or material composed partly of wood, that is to say: multi-cutter moulding machines, planing machines, automatic or semi-automatic lathes, multiple cross-cut machines, automatic shaping machines, double-end tenoning machines, vertical spindle moulding machines (including high-speed routing machines), edge banding machines, bandsawing machines with a blade width of not less than 75 mm and circular sawing machines in the operation of which the blade is moved towards the material being cut; *or*

(*i*) the use of chain saws in forestry.

A11 Episodic blanching, occurring throughout the year, affecting the middle or proximal phalanges or in the case of a thumb the proximal phalanx, of:

(*a*) The use of hand-held chain saws in forestry; *or*

(*b*) the use of hand-held rotary tools in grinding or in the sanding or polishing of

Prescribed disease or injury	*Occupation*
(a) in the case of a person with 5 fingers (including thumb) on one hand, any 3 of those fingers; or	metal, or the holding of material being ground, or metal being sanded or polished by rotary tools; or
(b) in the case of a person with only 4 such fingers, any 2 of those fingers; or	(c) the use of hand-held percussive metal-working tools, or the holding of metal being worked upon by percussive tools, in riveting, caulking, chipping, hammering, fettling or swaging; or
(c) in the case of a person with less than 4 such fingers, any one of those fingers, or, as the case may be, the one remaining finger (Vibration White Finger)	(d) the use of hand-held powered percussive drills or hand-held powered percussive hammers in mining, quarrying, demolition, or on roads or footpaths, including road construction; or
	(e) the holding of material being worked upon by pounding machines in shoe manufacture.
A12 Carpal tunnel syndrome	The use of hand-held vibrating tools
B Conditions due to biological agents	
B1 Anthrax	Contact with animals infected with anthrax or the handling (including the loading or unloading or transport) of animal products or residues.
B2 Glanders	Contact with equine animals or their carcases
B3 Infection by leptospira	(a) Work in places which are, or are liable to be, infested by rats, field mice or voles, or other small mammals; or
	(b) work at dog kennels or the care or handling of dogs; or
	(c) contact with bovine animals or pigs or their meat products
B4 Ankylostomiasis	Work in or about a mine
B5 Tuberculosis	Contact with a source of tuberculous infection
B6 Extrinsic allergic alveolitis (including farmer's lung)	Exposure to moulds or fungal spores or heterologous proteins by reason of employment in:
	(a) agriculture, horticulture, forestry, cultivation of edible fungi or malt-working; or
	(b) loading or unloading or handling in storage mouldy vegetable matter or edible fungi; or
	(c) caring for or handling birds; or
	(d) handling bagasse
B7 Infection by organisms of the genus brucella	Contact with:
	(a) animals infected by brucella, or their carcases or parts thereof, or their untreated products; or
	(b) laboratory specimens or vaccines of, or containing, brucella

Prescribed disease or injury	*Occupation*
B8 Viral hepatitis	Close and frequent contact with: (*a*) human blood or human blood products; *or* (*b*) a source or viral hepatitis infection by reason of employment in the medical treatment or nursing of a person or persons suffering from viral hepatitis, or in a service ancillary to such treatment or nursing
B9 Infection by *Streptococcus suis*	Contact with pigs infected by *Streptococcus suis*, or with the carcases, products or residues of pigs so infected
B10 (a) Avian chlamydiosis	Contact with birds infected with chlamydia psittaci, or with the remains or untreated products of such birds
B10 (b) Ovine chlamydiosis	Contact with sheep infected with chlamydia psittaci, or with the remains or untreated products of such sheep
B11 Q fever	Contact with animals, their remains or their untreated products
B12 Orf	Contact with sheep, goats or with the carcases of sheep or goats
B13 Hydatidosis	Contact with dogs

C Conditions due to chemical agents

C1 Poisoning by lead or a compound of lead	The use or handling of, or exposure to the fumes, dust or vapour of, lead or a compound of lead, or a substance containing lead
C2 Poisoning by manganese or a compound of manganese	The use or handling of, or exposure to the fumes, dust or vapour of, manganese or a compound of manganese, or a substance containing manganese
C3 Poisoning by phosphorus or an inorganic compound of phosphorus or poisoning due to the anti-cholinesterase or pseudo anti-cholinesterase action of organic phosphorus compounds	The use or handling of, or exposure to the fumes, dust or vapour of, phosphorus or a compound of phosphorus, or a substance containing phosphorus
C4 Poisoning by arsenic or a compound of arsenic	The use or handling of, or exposure to the fumes, dust or vapour of, arsenic or a compound of arsenic, or a substance containing arsenic
C5 Poisoning by mercury or a compound of mercury	The use or handling of, or exposure to the fumes, dust or vapour of, mercury or a compound of mercury, or a substance containing mercury
C6 Poisoning by carbon bisulphide	The use or handling of, or exposure to the fumes or vapour of, carbon bisulphide, or a substance containing carbon bisulphide

Prescribed disease or injury	*Occupation*
C7 Poisoning by benzene or a homologue of benzene	The use or handling of, or exposure to the fumes of, or vapour containing benzene or any of its homologues
C8 Poisoning by a nitro- or amino- or chloro-derivative of benzene or of a homologue of benzene, or poisoning by nitrochlorbenzene	The use or handling of, or exposure to the fumes of, or vapour containing, a nitro- or amino- or chloro-derivative of benzene, or of a homologue of benzene, or nitrochlorbenzene
C9 Poisoning by dinitrophenol or a homologue of dinitrophenol or by substituted dinitrophenols or by the salts of such substances	The use or handling of, or exposure to the fumes of, or vapour containing, dinitrophenol or a homologue or substituted dinitrophenols or the salts of such substances
C10 Poisoning by tetrachloroethane	The use or handling of, or exposure to the fumes of, or vapour containing, tetrachloroethane
C11 Poisoning by diethylene dioxide (dioxan)	The use or handling of, or exposure to the fumes of, or vapour containing, diethylene dioxide (dioxan)
C12 Poisoning by methyl bromide	The use or handling of, or exposure to the fumes of, or vapour containing methyl bromide
C13 Poisoning by chlorinated naphthalene	The use or handling of, or exposure to the fumes of, or dust or vapour containing, chlorinated naphthalene
C14 Poisoning by nickel carbonyl	Exposure to nickel carbonyl gas
C15 Poisoning by oxides of nitrogen	Exposure to oxides of nitrogen
C16 Poisoning by gonioma kamassi (African boxwood)	The manipulation of gonioma kamassi or any process in or incidental to the manufacture of articles therefrom
C17 Poisoning by beryllium or a compound of beryllium	The use or handling of, or exposure to the fumes, dust or vapour of, beryllium or a compound of beryllium, or a substance containing beryllium
C18 Poisoning by cadmium	Exposure to cadmium dust or fumes
C19 Poisoning by acrylamide monomer	The use or handling of, or exposure to, acrylamide monomer
C20 Dystrophy of the cornea (including ulceration of the corneal surface) of the eye	(*a*) The use or handling of, or exposure to, arsenic, tar, pitch, bitumen, mineral oil (including paraffin), soot or any compound, product or residue of any of these substances, except quinone or hydroquinone; *or* (*b*) exposure to quinone or hydroquinone during their manufacture
C21 (*a*) Localised new growth of the skin, papillomatous or keratotic (*b*) squamous-celled carcinoma of the skin	The use or handing of, or exposure to, arsenic, tar, pitch, bitumen, mineral oil (including paraffin), soot or any compound, product or residue of any of

Prescribed disease or injury	Occupation
	these substances, except quinone or hydroquinone
C22 (a) Carcinoma of the mucous membrane of the nose or associated air sinuses (b) primary carcinoma of a bronchus or of a lung	Work in a factory where nickel is produced by decomposition of a gaseous nickel compound which necessitates working in or about a building or buildings where that process or any other industrial process ancillary or incidental thereto is carried on
C23 Primary neoplasm (including papilloma, carcinoma-in-situ and invasive carcinoma) of the epithelial lining of the urinary tract (renal pelvis, ureter, bladder and urethra)	(a) Work in a building in which any of the following substances is produced for commercial purposes: (i) alpha-naphthylamine, beta-naphthylamine or methylene-bis-orthochloroaniline; (ii) diphenyl substituted by at least one nitro or primary amino group or by at least one nitro and primary (including benzidine); (iii) any of the substances mentioned in sub-paragraph (ii) above if further ring substituted by halogeno, methyl or methoxy groups, but not by other groups; (iv) the salts of any of the substances mentioned in sub-paragraphs (i) to (iii); (v) auramine or magenta; or (b) the use or handling of any of the substances mentioned in sub-paragraph (a) (i) to (iv), or work in such a process in which any such substance is used, handled or liberated; or (c) the maintenance or cleaning of any plant or machinery used in any such process as is mentioned in sub-paragraph (b), or the cleaning of clothing used in any such building as is mentioned in sub-paragraph (a) if such clothing is cleansed within the works of which the building forms a part or in a laundry maintained and used solely in connection with such works or (d) exposure to coal tar pitch volatiles produced in aluminium smelting involving the Soderberg process (that is to say the method of producing aluminium by electrolysis in which the anode consists of a paste of petroleum coke and mineral oil which is baked in situ).
C24 (a) Angiosarcoma of the liver (b) Osteolysis of the terminal phalanges of the fingers	(a) Work in or about machinery or apparatus used for the polymerization of vinyl chloride monomer, a process which, for the purposes of this provision,

Prescribed disease or injury	*Occupation*
(c) Non-cirrhotic portal fibrosis	comprises all operations up to and including the drying of the slurry produced by the polymerization and the packaging of the dried product; *or* (b) work in a building or structure in which any part of that process takes place
C25 Occupational vitiligo	The use or handling of, or exposure to, para-tertiary-butylphenol, para-tertiary-butylcatechol, para-amyl-phenol, hydroquinone or the monobenzyl or monobutyl ether of hydroquinone
C26 Damage to the liver or kidneys due to exposure to carbon tetrachloride	The use of or handling of, or exposure to the fumes of, or vapour containing carbon tetrachloride
C27 Damage to the liver or kidneys due to exposure to trichlormethane (chloroform)	The use of or handling of, or exposure to the fumes of, or vapour containing trichloromethane (chloroform)
C28 Central nervous system dysfunction and associated gastro-intestinal disorders due to exposure to chloromethane (methyl chloride)	The use of or handling of, or exposure to the fumes of, or vapour containing chloromethane (methyl chloride)
C29 Peripheral neuropathy due to exposure to n-hexane or methyl n-butyl ketone	The use of or handling of, or exposure to the fumes of, or vapour containing, n-hexane or methyl n-butyl ketone

D Miscellaneous conditions

D1 Pneumoconiosis	[*Occupations specified in reg 2(b) of, and Part II of Schedule 1 to, the Social Security (Industrial Injuries) (Prescribed Diseases) Regulations 1985 which are too numerous to set out here. They are all occupations involving exposure to dust, such as mining, quarrying, sand blasting, grinding, making china or earthenware, boiler-sealing and other work involving the use of stone, asbestos, etc.*]
D2 Byssinosis	Work in any room where any process up to and including the weaving process is performed in a factory in which the spinning or manipulation of raw or waste cotton or of flax, or the weaving of cotton or flax, is carried on
D3 Diffuse mesothelioma (primary neoplasm of the mesothelium of the pleura or of the pericardium or of the peritoneum)	(a) The working or handling of asbestos or any admixture of asbestos; *or* (b) the manufacture or repair of asbestos textiles or other articles containing or composed of asbestos; *or* (c) the cleaning of any machinery or plant used in any of the foregoing operations and of any chambers, fixtures

Prescribed disease or injury	*Occupation*
	and appliances for the collection of asbestos dust; *or* (*d*) substantial exposure to the dust arising from any of the foregoing operations
D4 Inflammation or ulceration of the mucous membrane of the upper respiratory passages or mouth produced by dust, liquid or vapour	Exposure to dust, liquid or vapour
D5 Non-infective dermatitis of external origin (including chrome ulceration of the skin but excluding dermatitis due to ionising particles or electro-magnetic radiations other than radiant heat)	Exposure to dust, liquid or vapour or any other external agent capable of irritating the skin (including friction or heat but excluding ionising particles or electromagnetic radiations other than radiant heat)
D6 Carcinoma of the nasal cavity or associated air sinuses (nasal carcinoma)	(*a*) Attendance for work in or about a building where wooden goods are manufactured or repaired; *or* (*b*) attendance for work in a building used for the manufacture of footwear or components of footwear made wholly or partly of leather or fibre board; *or* (*c*) attendance for work at a place used wholly or mainly for the repair of footwear made wholly or partly of leather or fibre board
D7 Asthma which is due to exposure to any of the following agents: (*a*) isocyanates (*b*) platinum salts (*c*) fumes or dusts arising from the manufacture, transport or use of hardening agents (including epoxy resin curing agents) based on phthalic anhydride, tetrachlorophthalic anhydride, trimellitic anhydride or triethylenetetramine (*d*) fumes arising from the use of rosin as a soldering flux (*e*) proteolytic enzymes (*f*) animals including insects and other anthropods used for the purposes of research or education or in laboratories (*g*) dusts arising from the sowing, cultivation, harvesting, drying, handling, milling, transport or storage of barley, oats, rye, wheat or maize, or the handling, milling, transport or storage of meal or flour made therefrom (*h*) antibiotics (*i*) cimetidine (*j*) wood dust	Exposure to any of the agents set out in column 1 of this paragraph

Prescribed disease or injury	*Occupation*

(*k*) ispaghula
(*l*) castor bean dust
(*m*) ipecacuanha
(*n*) azodice-bonamide
(*o*) animals including insects and other arthropods or their larval forms, used for the purposes of pest control or fruit cultivation, or the larval forms of animals used for the purposes of research, education or in laboratories;
(*p*) glutaraldehyde;
(*q*) persulphate salts or henna;
(*r*) crustaceans or fish or products arising from these in the food processing industry;
(*s*) reactive dyes;
(*t*) soya bean;
(*u*) tea dust;
(*v*) green coffee bean dust;
(*w*) fumes from stainless steel welding;
(*x*) any other sensitising agent
(occupational asthma)

D8 Primary carcinoma of the lung where there is accompanying evidence of one or both of the following:
(*a*) asbestosis;
(*b*) bilateral diffuse pleural thickening

(*a*) The working or handling of asbestos; or any admixture of asbestos; *or*
(*b*) the manufacture or repair of asbestos textiles or other articles containing or composed of asbestos; *or*
(*c*) the cleaning of any machinery or plant used in any of the foregoing operations and of any chambers, fixtures and applicances for the collection of asbestos dust; *or*
(*d*) substantial exposure to the dust arising from any of the foregoing operations

D9 Bilateral diffuse pleural thickening

(*a*) the working or handling of asbestos or any admixture of asbestos; *or*
(*b*) the manufacture or repair of asbestos textile or other articles containing or composed of asbestos; *or*
(*c*) the cleaning of any machinery or plant used in any of the foregoing operations and of any chambers, fixtures and applicances for the collection of asbestos dust; *or*
(*d*) substantial exposure to the dust arising from any of the foregoing operations

D10 Primary carcinoma of the lung

(*a*) work underground in a tin mine; *or*
(*b*) exposure to bis(chloromethyl) ether produced during the manufacture of chloromethyl methyl ether; *or*

Prescribed disease or injury	*Occupation*
	(*c*) exposure to zinc chromate, calcium chromate or strontium chromate in their pure forms.
D11 Primary carcinoma of the lung where there is accompanying evidence of silicosis	Exposure to silica dust in the course of – (*a*) the manufacture of glass or pottery; (*b*) tunnellling in or quarrying sandstone or granite; (*c*) mining metal ores; (*d*) slate quarrying or the manufacture of artefacts from slate; (*e*) mining clay; (*f*) using silicous materials as abrasives; (*g*) cutting stone; (*h*) stone masonry; *or* (*i*) work in a foundry
D12 Except in the circumstances specified in regulation 2(d), (*a*) chronic bronchitis; *or* (*b*) emphysema; *or* (*c*) both where there is accompanying evidence of – (*i*) coal dust retention demonstrated by a chest radiograph to at least the level of Category 1 in the International Labour Office's publication *The Classification of Radiographs of Pneumoconioses*, Revised Edition 1980, 8th Impression 1992 published at Geneva; and (*ii*) a forced expiratory volume in one second at least one litre below the mean value predicted in accordance with *Lung Function: Assessment and Application in Medicine*, by JE Cotes, 4th Edition 1979 published at Oxford by Blackwell Scientific Publications Limited (ISBN 0-63200033-3) for a person of the claimant's age, height and sex, measured from the position of maximum inspiration with the claimant making maximum effort.	Exposure to coal dust by reason of working underground in a coal mine for a period of, or periods amounting in the aggregate to, at least 20 years (whether before or after 5th July 1948).

Social security adjudication

I. THE CHIEF ADJUDICATION OFFICER

Mr E Hazelwood, Central Adjudication Services,
Room GE30 Quarry House, Quarry Hill, Leeds LS2 7UA, tel: 0532
324000

2. SOCIAL SECURITY APPEAL TRIBUNALS, DISABILITY APPEAL TRIBUNALS AND MEDICAL APPEAL TRIBUNALS

The President

His Honour Judge Thorpe, City Centre House, 39-45 Finsbury Square,
London EC2A 1UU, tel: 071-814 6500

The Regional Chairpersons

Midlands
Mr I G Harrison, Albion House, 5-13 Canal Street, Nottingham NG1
7EG, tel: 0602-472869

North Eastern
Mr J W Tinnion, York House, York Place, Leeds LS1 2ED, tel:
0532-451246

North Western
Mr R S Sim, 36 Dale Street, Liverpool L2 5UZ, tel: 051-236 4334

Scotland
Ms L T Parker, Wellington House, 134-136 Wellington Street, Glasgow
G2 2XL, tel: 041-353 1441

South Eastern
Mr R G Smithson, Whittington House, 19-30 Alfred Place, London
WC1E 7LW, tel: 071-580 3941

Wales and South Western
Mr C B Stephens, Oxford House, Hills Street, Cardiff CF1 2DR, tel:
0222-378071

3. SOCIAL SECURITY COMMISSIONERS

England and Wales   Harp House, 83 Farringdon Street, London
EC4A 4DH, tel: 071-353 5145

Scotland   23 Melville Street, Edinburgh EH3 7PW, tel:
031-225 2201

Northern Ireland   Lancashire House, 5 Linenhall Street, Belfast BT2
8AA, tel: 0232 332344

Cases are also heard in the Law Courts in Cardiff, Leeds and Liverpool
but administration in all English and Welsh cases is dealt with in London.

Books, leaflets and periodicals

Many of the books listed here will be in your main public library – the official publications probably being in the reference section.

You can get books published by HMSO from the six HMSO Bookshops but also from many others. Alternatively, they may be ordered by post, telephone or fax from HMSO Books, PO Box 276, London SW8 5DT (tel: 071-873 9090, fax: 071-873 8463). Enquiries should be addressed to PC51D, HMSO Books, 51 Nine Elms Lane, London SW8 5DR (tel: 071-873 0011).

I. TEXTBOOKS

The Law of Social Security by AI Ogus and EM Barendt (Butterworths, 3rd Edition, 1988) (4th edition 1994 in preparation). This is the standard textbook on social security law.

Compensation for Industrial Injury by R Lewis (Professional Books, 1987). This is an excellent and detailed study of industrial injuries benefits.

Claim in Time by M Partington (Legal Action Group, 2nd edition, 1989). This is a detailed study of the rules for claiming benefits and, in particular, what amounts to 'good cause' for a late claim. It is available, price £8.50 including postage and packing, from Legal Action Group, 242 Pentonville Road, London N1 9UN.

Tolley's National Insurance Contributions 1993-94 (Tolley Publishing Company), a dry but more useful book on contributions.

2. CASE LAW AND LEGISLATION

Social Security Case Law – Digest of Commissioners' Decisions by D Neligan (HMSO, looseleaf in two volumes). This consists of summaries of Commissioners' decisions grouped together by subject.

The Law Relating to Social Security (HMSO, looseleaf in ten volumes). This consists of *all* the legislation but without any comment.

Non-Means Tested Benefits: The Legislation by D Bonner, I Hooker and R White (Sweet & Maxwell, 1994). This contains the most useful legislation with a detailed commentary. The 1994 edition will be available from July, price £29.95, post-free from CPAG Ltd, 1-5 Bath Street, London EC1V 9PY (for CPAG members). A supplement will be similarly available from December, price £7.50. If you order both the main work and the supplement from CPAG before 31 May, the total cost is £36 (£37.45 post-May).

Medical and Disability Appeal Tribunals: The Legislation by Mark Rowland (former editor of this *Guide*) 2nd edition (Sweet & Maxwell, 1993/4). This contains the rules on the new disability benefits, DATs and MATs with a detailed commentary on the law. It will be available in June 1994, price £29.95 post-free from CPAG Ltd at the above address (for CPAG members).

3. OFFICIAL GUIDANCE

Adjudication Officers' Guide (HMSO, looseleaf in ten volumes).
Industrial Injuries Handbook for Adjudicating Medical Authorities (HMSO, looseleaf).
Handbook for Delegated Medical Practitioners (HMSO, 1988).
Notes on the Diagnosis of Prescribed Diseases (except pneumoconiosis and related occupational diseases and occupational deafness) (HMSO, 1991).

4. TRIBUNAL HANDBOOKS

Social Security Appeal Tribunals: A Guide to Procedure (HMSO, 2nd edition, 1988).
Medical Appeal Tribunals: A Guide to Procedure (HMSO, 1987).

5. LEAFLETS

There are innumerable leaflets published by the DSS which cover particular benefits or particular groups of claimants or contributors. They have been greatly improved in recent years and contain quite detailed information. The bigger ones are really 48-page booklets. They are free from your local DSS office or from DSS Information Division, Leaflets Unit, Block 4, Government Buildings, Honeypot Lane, Stanmore, Middlesex HA7 1AY.

6. PERIODICALS

The *Welfare Rights Bulletin* is published every two months by CPAG for welfare rights advisers. It covers developments in social security law and so updates this *Guide* between editions. The annual subscription is £15 but it is sent automatically to CPAG Rights and Comprehensive members.

Articles on social security are also to be found in *Legal Action* (Legal Action Group, monthly) and the *Journal of Social Welfare Law* (Sweet & Maxwell, bi-monthly).

Legislation

This list of legislation is not exhaustive. Only those statutes and statutory instruments to which reference is made in this *Guide* are included. It is anticipated that most readers who wish to look up the legislation will do so either in *The Law Relating to Social Security* (the 'Blue Volumes') or in *Non-Means-Tested Benefits – The Legislation* (see p352) where it is all set out in amended form. For that reason, legislation which simply amends earlier legislation is not listed here.

The abbreviations used in the notes in this *Guide* are not officially recognised, so it is better to use the proper title of legislation when writing letters.

I. ABBREVIATIONS USED IN THE NOTES

Acts of Parliament

ECA 1972	European Communities Act 1972
EP(C)A 1978	Employment Protection (Consolidation) Act 1978
FA 1982	Forfeiture Act 1982
ICTA 1988	Income and Corporation Taxes Act 1988
LAA 1988	Legal Aid Act 1988
PSA 1993	Pension Schemes Act 1993
MCA 1863	Matrimonial Causes Act 1973
NIA 1965	National Insurance Act 1965
CA 1973	Matrimonial Causes Act 1973
SB(D)A 1992	Still-Birth (Definition) Act 1992
SSA 1975	Social Security Act 1975
SSA 1979	Social Security Act 1979
SSA 1985	Social Security Act 1985
SSA 1986	Social Security Act 1986
SSA 1990	Social Security Act 1990
SSA 1993	Social Security Act 1993
SSAA 1992	Social Security Administration Act 1992
SSCBA 1992	Social Security Contributions and Benefits Act 1992
SSPA 1975	Social Security Pensions Act 1975

Regulations

Each set of regulations has a statutory instrument (SI) number and a date. You ask for them by giving their date and number.

CB Regs	The Child Benefit (General) Regulations 1976 No. 965
CB(Amdt) Regs	The Child Benefit (General) Amendment Regulations 1987 No. 35
CB(RPA) Regs	The Child Benefit (Residence and Persons Abroad) Regulations 1976 No. 963
CB&SS(FAR) Regs	The Child Benefit and Social Security (Fixing and Adjustment of Rates) Regulations 1976 No. 1267
CB&SS (Misc Amdt) Regs 1993	The Child Benefit and Social Security (Miscellaneous Amendment) Regulations 1993 No. 965
CTB Regs	The Council Tax Benefit (General) Regulations 1992 No. 1814
DWA Regs	The Disability Working Allowance (General) Regulations 1991 No. 2887
EP(RUB&SB) Regs	The Employment Protection (Recoupment of Unemployment Benefit and Supplementary Benefit) Regulations 1977 No. 674
EP(VL)O 1992	The Employment Protection (Variation of Limits) Order 1992 No. 312
FC Regs	Family Credit (General) Regulations 1987 No. 1973
HB Regs	The Housing Benefit (General) Regulations 1987 No. 1971
IS Regs	The Income Support (General) Regulations 1987 No. 1967
IT(E) No 13 Regs	The Income Tax (Employment) (No. 13) Regulations 1982 No. 66
MA(VSB) Regs	The Mobility Allowance (Vehicle Scheme Beneficiaries) Regulations 1977 No. 1229
NHS(GMPS) Regs	The National Health Service (General Medical and Pharmaceutical Services) Regulations 1974 No. 160
SF(RDB) Regs	The Social Fund (Recovery by Deductions from Benefits) Regulations 1988 No. 35
SFM&FE Regs	The Social Fund Maternity and Funeral Expenses (General) Regulations 1987 No. 481
SMP Regs	The Statutory Maternity Pay (General) Regulations 1986 No. 1960
SMP(ME) Regs	The Statutory Maternity Pay (Medical Evidence) Regulations 1987 No. 235
SS(AA) Regs	The Social Security (Attendance Allowance) Regulations 1991 No. 2740
SS(AB) Regs	The Social Security (Airmen's Benefits) Regulations 1975 No. 494

	The Social Security (Adjudication) Regulations 1986
SS(Adj) Regs	No. 2218
SS(C1CCP)O	The Social Security (Class 1 Contributions – Contracted-out Percentages) Order 1992 No. 795
SS(C&P) Regs	The Social Security (Claims and Payments) Regulations 1987 No. 1968
SS(CatE) Regs	The Social Security (Categorisation of Earners) Regulations 1978 No. 1689
SS(CE) Regs	The Social Security (Computation of Earnings) Regulations 1978 No. 1698
SS(Con) Regs	The Social Security (Contributions) Regulations 1979 No. 591
SS(Con) Amdt 4 Regs	The Social Security (Contributions) Amendment (No. 4) Regulations 1992 No. 668
SS(Cr) Regs	The Social Security (Credits) Regulations 1975 No. 556
SS(DLA) Regs	The Social Security (Disability Living Allowance) Regulations 1991 No. 2890
SS(EEEIIP) Regs	The Social Security (Employed Earners' Employment for Industrial Injuries Purposes) Regulations 1975 No. 467
SS(EF) Regs	The Social Security (Earnings Factor) Regulations 1979 No. 676
SS(GA) Regs	The Social Security (Guardian's Allowance) Regulations 1975 No. 515
SS(GB) Regs	The Social Security (General Benefits) Regs 1982 No. 1408
SS(GRB) No. 2 Regs	The Social Security (Graduated Retirement Benefit) (No. 2) Regulations 1978 No. 393
SS(HI) Regs	The Social Security (Hospital In-Patients) Regulations 1975 No. 555
SS(ICA) Regs	The Social Security (Invalid Care Allowance) Regulations 1976 No. 409
SS(IDLA) Regs	The Social Security (Introduction of Disability Living Allowance) Regulations 1991 No. 2891
SS(II&D)MP Regs	The Social Security (Industrial Injuries and Diseases) Miscellaneous Provisions Regulations 1986 No. 1561
SS(IIPD) Regs	The Social Security (Industrial Injuries) (Prescribed Diseases) Regulations 1985 No. 967
SS(IIPD) Amdt No. 2 Regs	The Social Security (Industrial Injuries) (Prescribed Diseases) Amendment (No. 2) Regulations 1993 No. 1985
SS(IIRE) Regs	The Social Security (Industrial Injuries) (Regular Employment) Regulations 1990 No. 256
SS(IoM)O	The Social Security (Isle of Man) Order 1977 No. 2150

SS(IoM)O	The Social Security (Isle of Man) Order 1977 No. 2150
SS(J&G)O	The Social Security (Jersey and Guernsey) Order 1992 No. 1735
SS(MA) Regs	The Social Security (Maternity Allowance) Regulations 1987 No. 416
SS(MAP) Regs	The Social Security (Maximum Additional Pension) Regulations 1978 No. 949
SS(MB) Regs	The Social Security (Mariners' Benefits) Regulations 1975 No. 529
SS(ME) Regs	The Social Security (Medical Evidence) Regulations 1976 No. 615
SS(NIRA) Regs	The Social Security (Northern Ireland Reciprocal Arrangements) Regulations 1976 No. 1003
SS(OB) Regs	The Social Security (Overlapping Benefits) Regulations 1979 No. 597
SS(PAOR) Regs	The Social Security (Payments on Account, Overpayments and Recovery) Regulations 1988 No. 664
SS(R) Regs	The Social Security (Recoupment) Regulations 1990 No. 322
SS(SDA) Regs	The Social Security (Severe Disablement Allowance) Regulations 1984 No. 1303
SS(SDA) Amdt Regs	The Social Security (Severe Disablement Allowance) Amendment Regulations 1992 No. 704
SS(STB)(T) Regs	The Social Security (Short-Term Benefits) (Transitional) Regulations 1974 No. 2192
SS(US&IB) Regs	The Social Security (Unemployment, Sickness and Invalidity Benefit) Regulations 1983 No. 1598
SS(US&IB) Amdt Regs	The Social Security (Unemployment, Sickness and Invalidity Benefit) Amendment Regulations 1992 No. 2913
SS(WB&RP)Regs	The Social Security (Widow's Benefit and Retirement Pensions) Regulations 1979 No. 642
SS(WB&RP) Amdt Regs 87	The Social Security (Widow's Benefit and Retirement Pension) Amendment Regulations 1987 No. 1854
SS(WB&RP) Amdt Regs 92	The Social Security (Widow's Benefit and Retirement Pensions) Amendment Regulations 1992 No. 1695
SS(WBRP&OB)(T) Regs	The Social Security (Widow's Benefit, Retirement Pensions and Other Benefits) (Transitional) Regulations 1979 No. 643
SS(W&WIP) Regs	The Social Security (Widow's and Widower's

	Invalidity Pensions) Regulations 1978 No. 529
SSA86(Comm 5)O	The Social Security Act 1986 (Commencement No. 5) Order 1987 No. 354
SSB(ACUICC) Regs	The Social Security Benefits (Amendments Consequential upon the Introduction of Community Care) Regulations 1992 No. 3147
SSB(Dep) Regs	The Social Security Benefit (Dependency) Regulations 1977 No. 343
SSB(Dep) Amdt Regs 1987	The Social Security Benefit (Dependency) Amendment Regulations 1987 No. 355
SSB (Dep) Amdt Regs 1992	The Social Security Benefits (Dependency) Amendment Regulations 1992 No. 3041
SSB(MF) Regs	The Social Security (Benefit) (Members of the Forces) Regulations 1975 No. 493
SSB(MW&WSP) Regs	The Social Security (Benefit) (Married Women and Widows' Special Provisions) Regulations 1974 No. 2010
SSB(PA) Regs	The Social Security Benefit (Persons Abroad) Regulations 1975 No. 563
SSB(PA) Amdt Regs 1994	The Social Security Benefit (Persons Abroad) Amendment Regulations 1994 No. 268
SSB(PRT) Regs	The Social Security Benefit (Persons Residing Together) Regulations 1977 No. 956
SSBU(No 2)O 1991	The Social Security Benefits Up-rating (No. 2) Order 1991 No 2910
SSBUO 1993	The Social Security Benefits Up-rating Order 1993 No. 349
SSCP Regs	The Social Security Commissioners Procedure Regulations 1987 No. 214
SSFA(PM) Regs	The Social Security and Family Allowances (Polygamous Marriages) Regulations 1975 No. 561
SSP Regs	The Statutory Sick Pay (General) Regulations 1982 No. 894
SSP(HR&MA) Regs	The Social Security Pensions (Home Responsibilities and Miscellaneous Amendments) Regulations 1978 No. 508
SSP(MAPA) Regs	The Statutory Sick Pay (Mariners, Airmen and Persons Abroad) Regulations 1982 No. 1349
SSREFO	The Social Security Revaluation of Earnings Factor Order 1993 No. 1159

Notes

References such as CS/50/1950 and R(U) 2/80 are references to Commissioners' decisions. See pp325-7 for an explanation.

Decisions of courts are referred to by the names of the parties and there follows a reference to the volume and page of a series of law reports unless the case is unreported or reported only in *The Times* newspaper. *Clear v Smith* [1981] WLR 399(DC) is to be found reported in volume 1 of the Weekly Law Reports at p399 and it was a decision of the Divisional Court. The abbreviations used inthese notes are in general use and are as follows:

AC	Appeal Cases
All ER	All England Reports
CMLR	Common Market Law Reports
Crim App R(S)	Criminal Appeal Reports (Sentencing)
ECR	European Court Reports
FLR	Family Law Reports
ICSR	Industrial Cases Reports
QB	Queen's Bench
WLR	Weekly Law Reports

(DC), (CA), (HL) and (ECJ) indicate decisions of the Divisional Court, Court of Appeal, House of Lords and European Court of Justice respectively.

References such as s14(1) SSA 1975 and reg 3 SS(C&P) Regs are references to legislation. A list of the titles of the legislation with a key to these abbreviations will be found in Appendix Six on p355. Other abbreviations are:

Art	Article
Dir	Directive
O	Order
para	paragraph
r	rule
reg	regulation
RSC	Rules of the Supreme Court
s	section
ss	sections
Sch	Schedule

Chapter 2: Unemployment benefit
(pp8-46)

1. Conditions of entitlement
1. ss25 and 57(1) SSCBA 1992

2. Payment
1. s25(4)-(6) and Sch 4 para 1 SSCBA 1992
2. s25(7) SSCBA 1992
3. Reg 24(1) SS(C&P) Regs

4. s25(3) SSCBA 1992
5. s26(1) SSCBA 1992
6. s26(2) and (3) SSCBA 1992
7. s122(1) SSCBA 1992
8. s26(2)(a) and (b) SSCBA 1992
9. s26(3) SSCBA 1992; reg 6A SS(US&IB) Regs
10. Reg 6A(2)(a)-(c) SS(US&IB) Regs
11. Reg 6A(2)(d) SS(US&IB) Regs
12. Reg 6A(3) SS(US&IB) Regs
13. s26(5) SSCBA 1992
14. R(U) 7/86 disapproving R(U) 6/83
15. Reg 16 SS(US&IB) Regs

3. How to claim
1. Reg 19(1) and Sch 4 para 1 SS(C&P) Regs
2. Reg 19(1) and Sch 5 para 1 SS(C&P) Regs
3. Reg 8 SS(C&P) Regs

4. Availability for work
1. s57(1)(a)(i) SSCBA 1992
2. R(U) 1/82; *Ali v Chief Adjudication Officer* (CA) reported as an appendix to R(U) 1/85
3. s57(1)(a)(i) SSCBA 1992
4. R(U) 44/53
5. Reg 7B(1) SS(US&IB) Regs
6. Reg 7B(2) SS(US&IB) Regs
7. Reg 7B(4)(c), (5) and (6) SS(US&IB) Regs
8. Reg 7B(6) SS(US&IB) Regs
9. Reg 7B(4)(b) SS(US&IB) Regs
10. Reg 7B(4)(a) SS(US&IB) Regs
11. Reg 12 SS(US&IB) Regs
12. Reg 1(2) SS(US&IB) Regs – 'voluntary body' & 'volunteer'
13. Reg 9(a) SS(US&IB) Regs
14. Reg 9(b) SS(US&IB) Regs
15. Reg 10 SS(US&IB) Regs
16. Reg 11 SS(US&IB) Regs
17. Reg 7(1)(i) SS(US&IB) Regs
18. Reg 12A(1), (2) and (3)(b) SS(US&IB) Regs
19. Reg 12A(1), (2) and (3)(a) SS(US&IB) Regs
20. Reg 12D(2) SS(US&IB) Regs
21. R(U) 4/66
22. Reg 19, Sch 4 para 1 and Sch 5 para 1 SS(C&P) Regs

5. Actively seeking employment
1. s57(1)(a)(i) SSCBA 1992
2. Reg 12B(1) SS(US&IB) Regs
3. Reg 12B(3) SS(US&IB) Regs
4. Reg 12B(4) SS(US&IB) Regs
5. Reg 12B(4)(a) SS(US&IB) Regs
6. Reg 12B(4)(b) SS(US&IB) Regs
7. Reg 12B(4)(c) SS(US&IB) Regs
8. Reg 12B(4)(d) SS(US&IB) Regs
9. Reg 12B(2) SS(US&IB) Regs
10. Reg 12B(2) SS(US&IB) Regs
11. Reg 12D(1)(a) SS(US&IB) Regs
12. Reg 12D(1)(b) SS(US&IB) Regs
13. Reg 12D(3) SS(US&IB) Regs
14. Reg 12D(1) SS(US&IB) Regs
15. Reg 12D(2)(a) SS(US&IB) Regs
16. Reg 12D(2)(c) SS(US&IB) Regs as amended by reg 2 SS(US&IB) Amdt Regs
17. Reg 12D(2)(b) SS(US&IB) Regs
18. Reg 12D(1)(d) SS(US&IB) Regs
19. Reg 12D(1)(e) SS(US&IB) Regs
20. Reg 12D(1)(f) SS(US&IB) Regs
21. Reg 12C(1)(a) SS(US&IB) Regs
22. Reg 12C(2) and (3) SS(US&IB) Regs
23. Reg 12C(1)(b) SS(US&IB) Regs
24. Reg 12C(4) SS(US&IB) Regs
25. Reg 37(1)(a) SS(C&P) Regs
26. Reg 22 IS Regs

6. Special rules if you work part-time
1. Sch 8 IS Regs
2. s124(1)(c) SSCBA 1992; reg 5 IS Regs
3. Reg 7(1)(o) SS(US&IB) Regs
4. Reg 7(1)(g) SS(US&IB) Regs
5. Reg 3(3) SS(CE) Regs
6. s57(1)(b) SSCBA 1992
7. Reg 7(1)(e) and (2) SS(US&IB) Regs
8. s57(1)(b) SSCBA 1992
9. Reg 19(3)(e) SS(US&IB) Regs
10. Reg 19(3)(a) SS(US&IB) Regs
11. Reg 19(3)(b) SS(US&IB) Regs
12. s57(1)(b), (c) and (e) SSCBA 1992
13. s57(1)(e) SSCBA 1992; reg 19(2) SS(US&IB) Regs

14. Reg 19(6) SS(US&IB) Regs
15. s122 SSCBA 1992
16. Reg 7(1)(e) SS(US&IB) Regs; EP
    (VL)O 1992
17. R(U) 30/53
18. CU/518/1949; *Chief Adjudication
    Officer v Brunt* [1988] AC 711 (HL)
    also reported as R(U) 9/88
19. R(U) 14/59; R(U) 14/60
20. Reg 7(1)(e) SS(US&IB) Regs
21. Reg 7(1)(h) SS(US&IB) Regs
22. See for example R(U) 2/87
23. R(U) 7/63

7. Payments from your previous job
1. Reg 7(1)(k)(iii)-(v) SS(US&IB) Regs
2. Reg 9 EP(RUB&SB) Regs
3. Reg 7(1)(k) SS(US&IB) Regs
4. R(U) 4/82
5. Reg 7(1)(k) SS(US&IB) Regs
6. R(U) 6/85
7. R(U) 5/74
8. Reg 7(1)(d) SS(US&IB) Regs
9. R(U)4/92
10. Reg 7(6) SS(US&IB) Regs
11. R(U)5/92
12. Reg 7(5) SS(US&IB) Regs
13. Reg 7(6) SS(US&IB) Regs
14. s99 EP(C)A 1978
15. Reg 7(5)(b) SS(US&IB) Regs
16. Reg 7(5)(c) and (6) SS(US&IB) Regs;
    EP(VL)O 1992
17. s30(4) SSCBA 1992
18. s30(1) SSCBA 1992; reg 24
    SS(US&IB)Regs; R(U) 8/83
19. s122(1) SSCBA 1992 'payments by way
    of occupational or personal pension'
20. CP/7/1987
21. Reg 25 SS(US&IB) Regs

8. Disqualifications
1. s28(1)(a) SSCBA 1992
2. s28(1)(e) SSCBA 1992
3. R(U) 2/77, para 1
4. R(U) 8/57, para 6
5. R(U) 10/52
6. R(U) 10/53
7. R(U) 26/56
8. CU/190/1950

9. s26(6) SSCBA 1992
10. s28(1)(a) SSCBA 1992
11. s28(1)(e) SSCBA 1992
12. Reg 22 IS Regs
13. R(U) 2/54; R(U) 7/74
14. s28(4) SSCBA 1992; R(U) 3/91
15. *Crewe v Social Security
    Commissioner* [1982] 1 WLR 1209
    (CA) also reported as an appendix to
    R(U) 3/81; R(U) 20/64(T); R(U)
    4/87
16. R(U) 14/52
17. *Crewe v Social Security
    Commissioner*, supra
18. R(U) 4/87
19. R(U) 19/52
20. R(U) 6/53
21. R(U) 13/52
22. R(U) 19/52
23. R(U) 2/90
24. R(U) 4/87, para 9
25. R(U) 14/52
26. R(U) 15/53
27. R(U) 18/57
28. R(U) 13/52
29. R(U) 27/59 30 s29 SSCBA 1992; reg
    12G SS(US&IB) Regs
31. Reg 12G(2)(a) SS(US&IB) Regs
32. R(U)1/92
33. Reg 12G(2)(b) SS(US&IB) Regs
34. s28(1)(b) and (f) SSCBA 1992
35. s28(6)(a) SSCBA 1992
36. s28(1)(c) and (g) SSCBA 1992
37. s28(1)(d) SSCBA 1992
38. Reg 12E(2)(a) SS(US&IB) Regs
39. Reg 12E(2)(b) SS(US&IB) Regs
40. Reg 12E(2)(c) SS(US&IB) Regs
41. Reg 12E(2)(d) SS(US&IB) Regs
42. Reg 12E(4)(b) SS(US&IB) Regs
43. Reg 12E(2)(e) SS(US&IB) Regs
44. Reg 12E(4)(a) SS(US&IB) Regs
45. Reg 12H SS(US&IB) Regs
46. Reg 12E(5) SS(US&IB) Regs
47. Reg 12E(6) SS(US&IB) Regs
48. Reg 12E(7)(a) SS(US&IB) Regs
49. Reg 12E(7)(b) and (8) SS(US&IB)
    Regs
50. s27(1)(b) SSCBA 1992
51. s27(1)(a) SSCBA 1992

52. s27(3)(a) SSCBA 1992
53. R(U) 23/64; R(U) 24/57; R(U) 4/62; R(U) 1/70
54. *Presho v Insurance Officer* [1984] AC 310 (also reported as an appendix to R(U)1/84)
55. s27(2)(a) SSCBA 1992; R(U) 6/74
56. s27(2)(b) SSCBA 1992
57. s27(2)(c) SSCBA 1992

9. Special rules for people over pensionable age
1. s25(2)(b) and (c) SSCBA 1992
2. s25(5) SSCBA 1992; reg 6 SS(WB&RP) Regs

10. Special rules for students
1. Reg 7(1)(m) and (3) SS(US&IB) Regs

11. Other benefits
1. Reg 22 IS Regs
2. s126 SSCBA 1992

12. Tax
1. s617 ICTA 1988
2. Reg 14 IT(E) No 13 Regs

Chapter 3: Benefits for people incapable of work (pp47-87)

1. Incapacity for work
1. ss57(1)(a)(ii) and 68(11)(c)(i) SSCBA 1992; reg 7 SS(SDA) Regs
2. Reg 3 SS(US&IB) Regs; reg 7 SS(SDA) Regs
3. R(S) 7/60; R(S) 2/78
4. CS/320/1950
5. s58(1) SSCBA 1992; reg 7A SS(SDA) Regs as amended
6. Reg 3(3) SS(US&IB) Regs; *Hunt and Merriman v Insurance Officer* (CA) reported as R(S) 3/86; CSS/5/1987
7. R(S) 6/86
8. s58(2) SSCBA 1992; reg 8A SS(SDA) Regs as amended
9. Reg 3(4) and (5) SS(US&IB) Regs
10. CS/8/1979; CS/42/1987

11. CS/35/1987
12. CS/42/1987
13. Reg 7(1)(f) SS(US&IB) Regs as amended
14. Reg 2(1) SS(ME) Regs
15. Reg 5 SS(ME) Regs
16. Sch 1 para 31 NHS(GMPS) Regs

2. 'Invalidity cut-off' – disputes about your capacity for work
1. Reg 17 SS(C&P) Regs; R(S)1/92
2. R(S)3/90, R(S)1/92
3. ss 33(7) & 68(10) SSCBA 1992
4. AOG Vol 6. para 53548
5. R(S)6/85
6. AOG Vol 6. para 53548
7. R(S)11/51
8. s.53 SSAA 1992; R(S)3/84
9. R(S)1/88
10. R(I) 13/75
11. s.57 SSCBA 1992

3. Statutory sick pay
1. ss152-5 and Schs 11 and 12 SSCBA 1992
2. s163(1) SSCBA 1992; reg 16 SSP Regs
3. s151(2) SSCBA 1992
4. Reg 4 SSP Regs
5. Reg 16(2) SSP Regs
6. s153(3) and Sch 11 para 2 SSCBA 1992
7. *Secretary of State for Social Security v Thomas, The Times*, 22 August 1990 (CA); *Barber v Guardian Royal Exchange Assurance Group* 1991 2 WLR 72 (ECJ)
8. Reg 3 SSP Regs
9. R(SSP) 1/86
10. Reg 10 SSP(MAPA) Regs
11. s152(2) SSCBA 1992
12. s152(5) SSCBA 1992
13. s152(3) SSCBA 1992; reg 2A SSP Regs as amended
14. s153(2) SSCBA 1992; reg 3(3) SSP Regs
15. Art 10 reg 1408/71 EEC
16. Reg 2A SSP Regs as amended
17. Reg 3A SSP Regs as amended

18. s154(3) SSCBA 1992
19. Reg 5(2) and (3) SSP Regs as amended
20. R(SSP) 1/85
21. Reg 7(4)(a) SSP Regs
22. Reg 7(4)(b) SSP Regs
23. Reg 7(5) SSP Regs
24. Reg 7(1)(a) SSP Regs
25. Reg 7(1)(b) SSP Regs
26. Reg 7(3) SSP Regs
27. s156(3) SSCBA 1992
28. s157 SSCBA 1992
29. s163(2) SSCBA 1992; reg 19 SSP Regs
30. CSSP/2/1984; CSSP/3/1984
31. Reg 17(3) SSP Regs
32. s157(3) SSCBA 1992
33. s155(1) SSCBA 1992
34. s155(4) SSCBA 1992
35. Sch 12 para 1 SSCBA 1992
36. Sch 12 para 3 SSCBA 1992
37. s4(1) SSCBA 1992
38. s14(3) SSAA 1992
39. s14(1) SSAA 1992
40. Reg 16(1) SSP Regs
41. Reg 22(1) SS(Adj) Regs
42. ss20(3) and 22(1)(a) SSAA 1992
43. Reg 22(3) SS(Adj) Regs
44. Reg 9A SSP Regs as amended
45. Regs 9 and 22 SSP Regs

4. Sickness benefit
1. ss31 and 57 SSCBA 1992; reg 19 SS(C&P) Regs
2. Sch 4 SSCBA 1992
3. Reg 24 SS(C&P) Regs
4. Reg 5 SS(ME) Regs as amended
5. s31(2), (6) and (7) SSCBA 1992
6. Reg 17 SS(US&IB) Regs
7. R(S) 2/53
8. R(S) 9/51

5. Invalidity benefit
1. s33 SSCBA 1992
2. ss33(3), (4) and (5), 44(4) and Sch 4 SSCBA 1992
3. s34 SSCBA 1992
4. CS/27/1991
5. s47(1) SSCBA 1992

6. Sch 12 para 1 SSCBA 1992
7. Sch 12 para 1 SSCBA 1992
8. Reg 7A(3) and (4) SS(US&IB) Regs
9. Reg 7A(1)(c)(i) SS(US&IB) Regs
10. Reg 7A(5) SS(US&IB) Regs
11. Reg 8A SS(US&IB) Regs as amended
12. s33(1)(b) SSCBA 1992
13. s33(4) and (5) SSCBA 1992
14. s102 SSCBA 1992; reg 31 SS(US&IB) Regs as amended
15. CS/27/1991
16. s40 SSCBA 1992
17. s41 SSCBA 1992
18. ss40(7) and 41(7) SSCBA 1992; reg 3 SS(W&WIP) Regs

6. Severe disablement allowance
1. ss68 and 69 SSCBA 1992
2. Sch 4 SSCBA 1992
3. Sch 2 Part I IS Regs
4. CS/27/1991
5. s68(5) SSCBA 1992
6. Reg 7(2) SS(SDA) Regs
7. Regs 4 and 5 SS(SDA) Regs
8. *Thomas and others v Chief Adjudication Officer*, ECJ Case No. C328/91
9. Reg 8 SS(SDA) Regs; CS/20/1986
10. R(S) 2/87
11. Reg 7(3) SS(SDA) Regs
12. s68(13) and Sch 6 SSCBA 1992
13. Reg 10 SS(SDA) Regs
14. s36 SSA 1975 as originally enacted
15. *Insurance Officer v McCaffrey* [1984] 1 WLR 1353 (HL)
16. *Clarke v Chief Adjudication Officer* [1987] ECR 2865 (ECJ)
17. Reg 20 SS(SDA) Regs
18. *Johnson v Chief Adjudication Officer* (Case C31/90 ECJ 11 July 1991); CS/111/1989
19. *Johnson v Chief Adjudication Officer (No. 2)* (Case C410/92 ECJ)
20. Reg 19(1) and Sch 4 para 2 SS(C&P) Regs
21. Reg 6 SS(SDA) Regs
22. Reg 9 SS(SDA) Regs

Chapter 4: Maternity pay and benefits
(pp88-96)

I. Statutory maternity pay

1. s164 SSCBA 1992
2. s164(2)(a) SSCBA 1992
3. s171(1) SSCBA 1992
4. s166(1) SSCBA 1992
5. s166(2) and (4) SSCBA 1992
6. s166(8) SSCBA 1992
7. s166(2) SSCBA 1992
8. s166(5) SSCBA 1992
9. Reg 6 SMP Regs as amended
10. s4(1)(a)(ii) SSCBA 1992
11. Sch 2, para 27 FC Regs; Sch 3, para 27 DWA Regs
12. Sch 13 para 1 SSCBA 1992
13. Sch 13 para 2 SSCBA 1992
14. Reg 27 SMP Regs
15. s165(1) SSCBA 1992
16. s165(2) and (3) SSCBA 1992
17. Reg 2(1) SMP Regs
18. Reg 2(2) SMP Regs
19. s171(1) SSCBA 1992
20. s165(6) SSCBA 1992; reg 8(2) SMP Regs
21. Reg 8(1) SMP Regs
22. s171(1) SSCBA 1992; reg 17 SMP Regs
23. s171(1) SSCBA 1992
24. s164(6) and (7) SSCBA 1992
25. s164(8) SSCBA 1992; reg 3 SMP Regs
26. Reg 9 SMP Regs
27. s57(2) SSCBA 1992
28. s164(4) SSCBA 1992
29. Reg 22(3) SMP Regs; reg 2 SMP(ME) Regs
30. s164(4)(b) SSCBA 1992
31. s15(1)(b) SSAA 1992; reg 24 SMP Regs
32. Regs 25 and 32 SMP Regs
33. Regs 22(4) and 23(3) SMP Regs
34. s15(2) SSAA 1992
35. Reg 7 SMP Regs
36. s164(2)(b) SSCBA 1992
37. Reg 21 SMP Regs
38. Reg 20 SMP Regs
39. s164(2)(a) SSCBA 1992
40. Reg 11(1) SMP Regs
41. Reg 13 SMP Regs
42. Reg 14 SMP Regs
43. Regs 2(3) and 23(2) SMP Regs
44. s171(1) SSCBA 1992; s2 SB(D)A 1992

2. Maternity allowance

1. s35 SSCBA 1992
2. Reg 2(1)(a) SS(MA) Regs
3. s35(1) and Sch 4 para 4 SSCBA 1992
4. Reg 8(1) & Sch 1, para 9 IS Regs
5. s35(1)(d) SSCBA 1992
6. s57(2) SSCBA 1992
7. s35(2) SSCBA 1992
8. Reg 2(3) SS(ME) Regs
9. Reg 14 SS(C&P) Regs

Chapter 5: Widows' benefits
(pp97-111)

I. Introduction

1. R(G)1/71
2. R(G)5/83
3. R(G) 1/80
4. ss37(3) and 38(2) SSCBA 1992
5. R(G) 1/53
6. R(G) 3/81
7. R(G) 3/71
8. R(G) 2/64
9. Robson v Supplementary Benefits Commission (1982) 3 FLR 232 (QBD)
10. CI/142/1949; R(I) 14/51
11. Sch 7 para 20 SSCBA 1992
12. Sch 7 para 21 SSCBA 1992
13. s4(1) FA 1982
14. s5 FA 1982; R(G) 1/90
15. s4(1C) FA 1982 as amended
16. R(G) 2/90
17. s4(1E) FA 1982 as amended
18. Reg 28(2) SSCP Regs
19. s617 ICTA 1988
20. Reg 3 SS(OB) Regs
21. Reg 40 IS Regs
22. Reg 8 and Sch 1 para 13 IS Regs
23. Reg 17(1)(d), Sch 2 paras 8 and 15(1) IS Regs; reg 2(4)(a) and (5)(a)(ii) CB&SS(FAR) Regs

24. Reg 9(2)(d) SFM&FE Regs as amended
25. s3 SSAA 1992

2. Widow's payment
1. s36 SSCBA 1992
2. Sch 4 SSCBA 1992
3. s36(2) SSCBA 1992

3. Widowed mother's allowance
1. ss37 and 60(2) and (3) SSCBA 1992; reg 16 SS(WB&RP) Regs
2. ss39, 44, 45, 46(2) and Sch 4 SSCBA 1992
3. s37(3) SSCBA 1992
4. s37(2) SSCBA 1992
5. Reg 16(2) SS(WB&RP) Regs

4. Widow's pension
1. ss38 and 60(2) and (3) SSCBA 1992
2. ss39, 44, 45, 46(2) and Sch 4 SSCBA 1992
3. s39(4) and (5) SSCBA 1992
4. s39(6) SSCBA 1992
5. s38(2) SSCBA 1992

5. Industrial death benefit for widows
1. s106 and Sch 7 para 15(1) SSCBA 1992; reg 23 SS(GB) Regs
2. Sch 7 para 15(4) SSCBA 1992
3. Sch 4 para 10 and Sch 7 para 16(2) SSCBA 1992; reg 24 SS(GB) Regs
4. Sch 7 para 16(3) SSCBA 1992
5. Sch 7 paras 15(2) and (3) SSCBA 1992

6. Special rules for polygamous and invalid marriages
1. *Hyde v Hyde* (1866)
2. Reg 1(2) SSFA(PM) Regs
3. Reg 1(4) SSFA(PM) Regs; s6 IA 1978
4. Reg 2 SSFA(PM) Regs
5. R(S) 2/92
6. s11(3) MCA 1973
7. R(G)2/63
8. R(G)1/73

Chapter 6: Retirement pensions (pp112-125)

1. Introduction
1. s78(1), (2) and (7)-(9) SSCBA 1992; regs 9, 11 and 12 SS(WB&RP) Regs
2. s122(1) SSCBA 1992
3. Reg 19 and Sch 4 SS(C&P) Regs
4. Reg 15 SS(C&P) Regs
5. Sch 5 paras 1 and 2 SSCBA 1992
6. Sch 2 SS(GRB) No 2 Regs
7. Sch 5 para 2(5) SSCBA 1992
8. Sch 5 para 4 SSCBA 1992
9. s28(4) SSA 1975 as originally enacted
10. Reg 4(1)(b)(i) SS(WB&RP) Regs
11. Reg 4(1)(a) SS(WB&RP) Regs
12. Reg 4(1)(b)(ii) SS(WB&RP) Regs
13. *Chief Adjudication Officer v Pearse, The Times*, 18 June 1992
14. Reg 2(3) SS(WB&RP) Regs
15. s54 SSCBA 1992; reg 2(3) SS(WB&RP) Regs
16. Reg 2(1) SS(WB&RP) Regs
17. Reg 2(2)(a) SS(WB&RP) Regs
18. s53(4) SSCBA 1992; reg 2(2)(b) SS(WB&RP) Regs
19. s617 ICTA 1988
20. Reg 40 and Sch 2 paras 9 and 10 IS Regs

2. Category A retirement pension
1. s44(1) SSCBA 1992
2. ss44(4) and 45 SSCBA 1992
3. ss34(3) and 47(1) SSCBA 1992
4. s47(2) SSCBA 1992
5. Reg 3 SS(C&P) Regs
6. s48 SSCBA 1992; reg 8 SS(WB&RP)Regs
7. Reg 8(2) and (3) SS(WB&RP) Regs
8. Reg 8(2) and (4) SS(WB&RP) Regs
9. Sch 1 SS(WB&RP) Regs
10. s48(3) SSCBA 1992
11. s48(2) SSCBA 1992
12. Sch 7 SSA 1975 as preserved by Sch 1 para 20 SSA 1979
13. s48 SSCBA 1992; reg 8(1)(a) SS(WB&RP) Regs
14. s48 SSCBA 1992; reg 8(1)(c) SS(WB&RP) Regs

15. s48(2) SSCBA 1992
16. s52 SSCBA 1992

3. Category B retirement pension for a married woman
1. s49(1), (2) and (3) SSCBA 1992
2. s50(1)(a)(i) and Sch 4 SSCBA 1992

4. Category B retirement pension for a widow
1. ss49(4), 60(2) and (3) SSCBA 1992
2. s49(5)(a) SSCBA 1992; reg 7 SS(WB&RP) Regs
3. s49(5)(a) SSCBA 1992
4. ss44, 45, 50(1)(a)(ii), (3) and (4) SSCBA 1992
5. ss38, 39(4), 49(5) and 50(1)(c) SSCBA 1992
6. Reg 7 SS(WB&RP) Regs
7. s49(7) SSCBA 1992

5. Category B retirement pension for a widower
1. s51 SSCBA 1992
2. ss44, 45 and 51(2) SSCBA 1992
3. s51(4) SSCBA 1992

6. Category D retirement pension
1. s78(3) SSCBA 1992; reg 10 SS(WB&RP) Regs
2. s78(6) and Sch 4 para 7 SSCBA 1992
3. Reg 3(b) SS(C&P) Regs

7. Graduated retirement benefit
1. s36 NIA 1965 as kept in force by Sch 1 SS(GRB) No 2 Regs; Art 7(1) SSBU(No 2)O 1991
2. Reg 17(1)(h) & (3) SS(WB&RP) Regs
3. Reg 3(c) SS(C&P) Regs
4. s37 NIA 1965 as kept in force by Sch 1 SS(GRB) No 2 Regs
5. s36(4) NIA 1965 as kept in force by Sch 1 SS(GRB) No 2 Regs

8. Future changes
1. *Equality in State Pension Age –* HMSO Cm2420

Chapter 7: Benefits for severely disabled people (pp126-157)

2. DLA mobility component
1. s73 SSCBA 1992
2. s73(1)(d) SSCBA 1992
3. Reg 4 SS(DLA) Regs
4. s73(4) SSCBA 1992
5. Reg 3(1)(a) SS(DLA) Regs
6. Reg 12(1)(a) SS(DLA) Regs
7. Reg 12(4) SS(DLA) Regs
8. R(M) 2/89
9. CM/208/1989
10. CM/47/1986
11. R(M) 1/83
12. R(M) 1/81
13. R(M) 3/78
14. CM/23/1985
15. R(M) 3/78
16. Reg 12(1)(b) SS(DLA) Regs
17. Reg 12(2) SS(DLA) Regs
18. Reg 12(3) SS(DLA) Regs
19. Sch 2 SS(GB) Regs
20. Reg 34(2) SS(IIPD) Regs as amended
21. s73(3) SSCBA 1992; Reg 12(6) SS(DLA) Regs
22. R(M)3/86
23. CM/5/1986
24. s73(12) SSCBA 1992
25. Reg 42 SS(C&P) Regs
26. Reg 42(4) SS(C&P) Regs
27. Reg 6 MA(VSB) Regs

3. DLA care component
1. s72 SSCBA 1992
2. Reg 4 SS(DLA) Regs
3. s72(6) SSCBA 1992
4. s75 SSCBA 1992; Reg 3 SS(DLA) Regs
5. R(A) 2/92
6. R(A) 3/86
7. R(A) 3/89
8. R(A) 5/90
9. R(A) 1/73
10. *R v National Insurance Commissioner ex parte Secretary of State for Social Services* [1974] 1WLR 1290 (DC), also reported as an appendix to R(A) 4/74

11. R(A) 1/78
12. R(A) 3/74
13. R(A) 2/75
14. CA/86/1987
15. Reg 7 SS(DLA) Regs
16. s72(5) SSCBA 1992
17. s66(2) SSCBA 1992
18. s66(2)(b) SSCBA 1992
19. s72(6)(a) SSCBA 1992
20. House of Lords debates, *Hansard*, 7 March 1991, col 1554
21. s72(1) SSCBA 1992
22. *R v National Insurance Commissioner ex parte Secretary of State for Social Services* [1981] 1 WLR 1017 (CA), also reported as an appendix to R(A)2/80
23. R(A) 1/87
24. R(A) 1/91
25. *R v Social Security Commissioner ex parte Butler* (unreported), February 1984
26. House of Lords debates, *Hansard*, 25 March 1991, col 884
27. R(A) 3/78
28. R(A) 1/83
29. R(A) 2/89
30. CA/15/1979 approved in R(A) 1/83
31. CA/33/1984
32. R(A) 2/75
33. *Moran v Secretary of State for Social Services* reported as an appendix to R(A) 1/88
34. R(A) 5/81
35. R(A) 2/91
36. R(A) 3/92

4. Attendance allowance
1. s64 SSCBA 1992
2. Sch 4 SSA 1975 as amended
3. Reg 5 SS(AA) Regs
4. s66(1) SSCBA 1992

5. Matters common to DLA and attendance allowance
1. s617 ICTA 1988
2. Regs 8, 9 and 10 SS(DLA) Regs; regs 6,7 and 8 SS(AA) Regs
3. Reg 10 SS(DLA) Regs; reg 8 (SS)AA Regs

4. R(S) 4/84; CS/249/1989
5. Reg 6(2) SS(AA) Regs; reg 8(2) SS(DLA) Regs
6. Reg 10(6) and (7) SS(DLA) Regs; reg 8(4) and (5) SS(AA) Regs
7. Reg 10 SS(DLA) Regs; reg 8 (SS)AA Regs
8. Reg 9(1) SS(DLA) Regs; regs 7(1) SS(AA) Regs
9. Reg 9(6) SS(DLA) Regs; regs 7(5) SS(AA) Regs
10. Regs 7(4)(z)(a) and 8(4)(z)(a) SSB(ACUICC) Regs
11. Regs 7(4)(a) and 8(4)(a) SSB(ACUICC) Regs
12. Reg 10(8) SS(DLA) Regs; regs 8(6) SS(AA) Regs
13. Reg 9(1)(A) SS(DLA) Regs
14. Reg 9(2)(a) and (2A) SS(DLA) Regs
15. Reg 9(2)(b) and (2A) SS(DLA) Regs
16. Reg 9(2)(c) SS(DLA) Regs
17. Reg 10(9) SS(DLA) Regs; Reg 8(7) SS(AA) Regs
18. Reg 10(8) SS(DLA) Regs; Reg 8(6) SS(AA) Regs
19. Reg 9(1)(c) SS(DLA) Regs; Reg 7(1)(c) SS(AA) Regs
20. Reg 9(4) (a) and (b) SS(DLA) Regs; Reg 7(3)(a) SS(AA) Regs
21. Reg 9(5) SS(DLA) Regs; Reg 7(4) SS(AA) Regs
22. Adjudication Officers' Guide memo 7/17
23. s21(3) SSAA 1992
24. Reg 6(8) SS(C&P) Regs
25. s1(3) SSAA 1992
26. Regs 6 and 11 SS(DLA) Regs; reg 3 SS(AA) Regs
27. Reg 16(1) SS(DLA) Regs
28. s54(2) SSAA 1992
29. s54(1) SSAA 1992
30. s54(6) SSAA 1992
31. s71(3) SSCBA 1992
32. Reg 11 SS(DLA) Regs
33. Reg 13 SS(DLA) Regs
34. Reg 43 SS(C&P) Regs
35. s30(1) SSAA 1992
36. Reg 26A SS(Adj) Regs
37. s30(2) SSAA 1992

38. s33(1) SSAA 1992
39. ss32(2) and (3) SSAA 1992
40. ss32(4) SSAA 1992
41. Reg 65 SS(Adj) Regs
42. Reg 64A SS(Adj) Regs

Chapter 8: Invalid care
allowance
(pp 158-162)

1. s70 SSCBA 1992
2. Reg 19(2) and (6) SS (C&P) Regs
3. Sch 1 SS (C&P) Regs
4. R(A) 3/81
5. Sch 4 SSCBA 1992
6. s617 ICTA 1988
7. Reg 10 SS(OB) Regs
8. Reg 8 and Sch 1 para 4(a) IS Regs
9. Reg 8 and Sch 1 para 4(b) IS Regs
10. Sch 2 para 14 ZA IS Regs and HB Regs; Sch 1 para 16 CTB Regs
11. Reg 40 IS Regs; Reg 33 HB Regs; Reg 24 CTB Regs
12. Sch 2 paras 13(2)(a)(iii) and (b) and 14ZA IS Regs and HB Regs; Sch 1 paras 14(2)(a)(iii) and (b) and 16 CTB Regs
13. Reg 4(1) SS(ICA) Regs
14. CG/6/1990
15. R(G) 3/91
16. Reg 4(1A) SS(ICA) Regs
17. Reg 4(2) SS(ICA) Regs
18. Reg 8 SS(ICA) Regs
19. Reg 5 SS(ICA) Regs
20. s70(5) SSCBA 1992; Reg 10 SS(ICA) Regs
21. Dir 79/7 EEC; *Secretary of State for Social Security v Thomas et al*, Case C – 328/91 ECJ 1993
22. Reg 11 SS(ICA) Regs

Chapter 9: Industrial injuries
benefits
(pp163-187)

2. Industrial accidents and diseases
1. CI/257/1949; CI/159/1950

2. R(I) 22/59
3. R(I) 1/76
4. R(I) 8/81
5. R(I) 1/82
6. R(I) 7/56
7. s94(1) SSCBA 1992
8. *Fenton v Thorley* [1903] AC 443 (HL)
9. *Jones v Secretary of State for Social Services* [1972] AC 944 (HL), also reported as an appendix to R(I) 3/69
10. *Trim Joint District School Board of Management v Kelly* [1914] AC 667 (HL)
11. *Roberts v Dorothea Slate Quarries Co. Ltd* [1948] 2 All ER 201 (HL)
12. R(I) 24/54; R(I) 43/55
13. R(I) 43/61; R(I) 4/62
14. R(I) 18/54
15. CI/159/1950
16. *Moore v Manchester Liners Ltd* [1910] AC 498 at p500 (HL)
17. *R v National Insurance Commissioner ex parte East* [1976] ICR 206 (DC), also reported as an appendix to R(I) 16/75
18. R(I) 1/59
19. *R v Industrial Injuries Commissioner ex parte AEU* [1966] 2 QB 31 (CA), also reported as an appendix to R(I) 4/66
20. R(I) 10/81
21. *R v National Insurance Commissioner ex parte Reed* (DC), also reported as an appendix to R(I) 7/80
22. s94(3) SSCBA 1992
23. *R v Industrial Injuries Commissioner ex parte AEU* [1966] 2 QB 31 (CA), also reported as an appendix to R(I) 4/66
24. R(I) 46/53
25. R(I) 17/63
26. *R v Industrial Injuries Commissioner ex parte AEU* [1966] 2 QB 31 (CA), also reported as an appendix to R(I) 4/66
27. s98 SSCBA 1992
28. s99 SSCBA 1992
29. R(I)1/88

30. R(I) 12/75
31. R(I) 4/70
32. *Nancollas v Insurance Officer* [1985] 1 All ER 833 (CA), also reported as an appendix to R(I) 7/85
33. *Smith v Stages* [1989] 2 WLR 529 (HL)
34. R(I) 1/91
35. *Nancollas v Insurance Officer* [1985] 1 All ER 833 (CA), also reported as an appendix to R(I) 7/85
36. R(I) 6/82
37. R(I) 12/52
38. s101 SSCBA 1992
39. s100 SSCBA 1992
40. R(I) 6/63
41. ss108(1) and 109(1) SSCBA 1992; reg 2 SS(IIPD) Regs
42. Reg 3 SS(IIPD) Regs
43. R(I) 3/90
44. CI/202/1990
45. Regs 2(c) and 25 SS(IIPD) Regs
46. Reg 36 SS(IIPD) Regs
47. Reg 4 SS(IIPD) Regs
48. Reg 6(2)(c) SS(IIPD) Regs
49. Reg 7 SS(IIPD) Regs
50. s45(1)(a) and (b) SSCBA 1992
51. *Jones v Secretary of State for Social Services* [1972] AC 944 at p1009 (HL), also reported as an appendix to R(I) 3/69
52. s60(3) SSAA 1992
53. s103(2) and (3) SSCBA 1992; regs 15A and 15B SS(IIPD) Regs as amended
54. s103(3) SSCBA 1992
55. Sch 2 SS(GB) Regs; Sch 3 SS(IIPD) Regs
56. Reg 11(6) SS(GB) Regs
57. Sch 6 para 1 SSCBA 1992
58. Reg 11(8) SS(GB) Regs
59. Reg 11(3) SS(GB) Regs
60. Reg 11(7) SS(GB) Regs
61. Reg 11(4) SS(GB) Regs
62. Reg 11(5) SS(GB) Regs
63. R(I) 1/91
64. Reg 21 SS(IIPD) Regs
65. Reg 22 SS(IIPD) Regs
66. Reg 2(d) SS(IIPD) Regs
67. Sch 6 para 6 SSCBA 1992
68. Sch 6 para 7 SSCBA 1992
69. s45(3) SSAA 1992
70. Reg 29(a) SS(IIPD) Regs
71. Reg 29(b) and 34(b) SS(IIPD) Regs
72. ss94(1) and 108(1) SSCBA 1992
73. s2(1) SSCBA 1992
74. Reg 10(6)(c) SSB(PA) Regs as amended
75. Regs 2,4 and 6 SS(EEEIIP) Regs
76. Reg 3 SS(EEEIIP) Regs

3. Disablement benefit

1. Sch 4 SSCBA 1992
2. s103(1) and Sch 7 para 9(1) SSCBA 1992
3. Reg 20(1) SS(IIPD) Regs
4. Sch 7 para 9(1)(a) SSCBA 1992; regs 12 and 14 SS(II&D)MP Regs
5. Sch 7 para 9(1) and (2) SSCBA 1992; reg 14 SS(GB) Regs
6. Regs 7 (5) and (6) SS(II&D)MP Regs
7. s617 ICTA 1988
8. s104 SSCBA 1992
9. Reg 20 SS(GB) Regs
10. Sch 4 SSCBA 1992; Reg 19(b) SS(GB) Regs
11. Sch 4 SSCBA 1992; Reg 19(a) SS(GB) Regs
12. s105 SSCBA 1992
13. Sch 7 para 1 SSCBA 1992; reg 11 SS(II&D)MP Regs; SSA86(Comm 5)O
14. Sch 7 para 10(1) SSCBA 1992; SSA86(Comm 5)O
15. Reg 19 and Sch 4 SS(C&P) Regs
16. Sch 6 para 4(3) SSA 1990
17. Reg 9 SS(IIPD) Amdt (No 2) Regs 1993
18. s47(1) SSAA 1992; reg 29 (1)(a) SS(Adj) Regs
19. s47(4) SSAA 1992; reg 29 (1)(a) SS(Adj) Regs
20. s47(6) SSAA 1992
21. s47(7) SSAA 1992
22. Reg 48 SS(Adj) Regs
23. Reg 68 SS(Adj) Regs
24. s47(9) SSAA 1992
25. Reg 40 SS(GB) Regs

4. Reduced earnings allowance
1. Sch 7 paras 11 and 12(1),(2) and (7) SSCBA 1992
2. Reg 23(a) SS(IIPD) Regs
3. Reg 40 SS(GB) Regs; R(I) 2/86
4. Reg 17 SS(GB) Regs
5. Reg 23(b) SS(IIPD) Regs
6. *R v National Insurance Commissioner ex parte Mellors* [1971] 2 QB 401 (CA); also reported as an appendix to R(I) 7/69
7. R(I) 28/51
8. R(I) 65/54
9. CI/80/1949
10. Reg 2 SS(II&D)MP Regs
11. Reg 17 SS(IIPD) Regs
12. *R v Deputy Industrial Injuries Commissioner ex parte Humphreys* [1966] 2 QB 1 (CA), also reported as an appendix to R(I) 2/66
13. R(I) 22/61
14. Sch 7 Part IV paras 11(4)-(7) SSCBA 1992
15. R(I) 3/83
16. Reg 2 SS(IIRE) Regs
17. CS/27/91
18. Sch 7 para 11(10) SSCBA 1992
19. Sch 7 para 11(14) SSCBA 1992
20. R(I) 8/67
21. Sch 7 para 11(10) SSCBA 1992
22. Sch 7 para 11(10) SSCBA 1992
23. Sch 7 para 11(11) SSCBA 1992
24. Sch 7 para 12(6) SS CBA 1992
25. R(G) 4/68

5. Retirement allowance
1. Sch 7 para 13 SSCBA 1992
2. Sch 7 para 13(4) SSCBA 1992

6. Industrial death benefit
1. Sch 7 paras 14(1) and 17 SSCBA 1992
2. Sch 7 para 17 SSCBA 1992

Chapter 10: Benefits for children *(pp188-200)*

1. Child benefit
1. ss141 and 146 SSCBA 1992

2. Reg 2(1) CB&SS(FAR) Regs as amended
3. s142(1) SSCBA 1992
4. s142(2) SSCBA 1992; R(P) 1/93
5. Reg 5 CB Regs as amended
6. R(F) 1/93
7. Reg 6(1) CB Regs
8. Regs 1(2) and 7A CB Regs as amended
9. Regs 7B and 7C CB Regs
10. Reg 7(4) CB Regs as amended
11. Reg 7D(1) CB Regs as amended
12. Reg 7D(2) CB Regs as amended
13. Reg 7D(1)(e) CB Regs as amended
14. Sch 9 para 1(c) SSCBA 1992; reg 16(5)(a),(c)(e),(h) CB Regs
15. Sch 9 para 1(b) SSCBA 1992; reg 16(5)(b) CB Regs
16. Sch 9 para 1(c) SSCBA 1992; reg 16(5)(f) & (g) CB Regs
17. Reg 16(6)(a) CB Regs
18. Reg 16(6)(b) and (7) CB Regs
19. s147(1) SSCBA 1992
20. R(F) 3/85
21. R(F) 1/81
22. Reg 16(8),(9) and (10) CB Regs; reg 8 CB(Amdt) Regs
23. Sch 9 para 3 SSCBA 1992
24. Reg 10 CB Regs
25. Regs 1(2), 7(3) and 7D(1)(b) CB Regs as amended
26. Sch 9 para 5 SSCBA 1992; reg 7C CB Regs as amended
27. Reg 7B CB Regs
28. Sch 9 para 1(1)(a) SSCBA 1992; reg 16 CB Regs
29. R(F) 2/81
30. R(F) 2/79
31. s143(2) SSCBA 1992
32. s143(3)(a) SSCBA 1992
33. s143(3)(b) and (c) SSCBA 1992; reg 4 CB Regs
34. s143(4) SSCBA 1992
35. s143(1)(b) SSCBA 1992
36. R(U) 14/62
37. R(U) 3/66
38. Reg 2(3) CB Regs
39. Reg 2(1) CB Regs
40. s13(1) SSAA 1992
41. Sch 10 para 1(2) SSCBA 1992

42. Sch 10 SSCBA 1992
43. s147(3) SSCBA 1992
44. Reg 14 CB Regs
45. *Grove v Insurance Officer* reported as an appendix to R(F) 4/85
46. Reg 11(1)(a) CB Regs
47. R(F) 3/81
48. Reg 11(1)(b) CB Regs
49. Reg 11(2) CB Regs
50. Reg 11(1) CB Regs; R(F) 4/85
51. R(F) 4/85
52. R(F) 3/81
53. Reg 11(3) CB Regs
54. Reg 19(6)(a) SS(C&P) Regs
55. Sch 10 para 1(2) SSCBA 1992
56. Reg 13 SS(C&P) Regs
57. Reg 7 SS(C&P) Regs
58. Reg 23(1)(b) SS(C&P) Regs
59. Sch 8 para 1(a) SS(C&P) Regs
60. Sch 8 paras 1(b), 3 and 4 SS(C&P) Regs
61. Sch 8 para 2(a) SS(C&P) Regs
62. Sch 8 para 2(b) SS(C&P) Regs
63. Reg 23(3) SS(C&P) Regs
64. s144(2) and Sch 9 para 4 SSCBA 1992; reg 9(1) CB Regs
65. s146(3)(a) SSCBA 1992
66. s617 ICTA 1988
67. Reg 40 IS Regs

2. One parent benefit
1. Reg 2(2) and (2A) CB&SS(FAR) Regs; R(F) 4/85
2. Reg 2(2) CB&SS(FAR) Regs as amended
3. s617 ICTA 1988
4. Reg 40 IS Regs
5. Reg 2(4)(a) and (5) CB&SS(FAR) Regs
6. Reg 8 SS(OB) Regs

3. Guardian's allowance
1. s77 SSCBA 1992
2. Sch 4 SSCBA 1992
3. s617 ICTA 1988
4. Reg 40 IS Regs
5. Sch2 para 50 FC Regs; Sch 3 para 48 DWA Regs; Sch4 para 5 HB Regs; Sch 4 para 49 CTB Regs

6. Reg 7(4) SS(OB) Regs
7. Reg 2(4) CB&SS (Misc Amdt) Regs 1993
8. Reg 19(6)(a) SS(C&P) Regs
9. s77(2) SSCBA 1992
10. R(G) 11/52
11. R(G) 6/52
12. Reg 2 SS(GA) Regs
13. CWG/3/1978
14. s77(10) and (11) SSCBA 1992
15. Reg 3 SS(GA) Regs
16. s77(10) SSCBA 1992; reg 4 SS(GA) Regs
17. Reg 5 SS(GA) Regs

4. Child's special allowance
1. s56(6) SSCBA 1992
2. ss56(1) and (2), 80(6) and 81 SSCBA 1992
3. Sch 4 SSCBA 1992

5. Industrial death benefit for children
1. Sch 7 paras 14(1) and 18 SSCBA 1992; reg 32 SS(GB) Regs
2. *Insurance Officer v McCaffrey* [1984] 1 WLR 1353 (HL); Sch 7 para 15(1) SSCBA 1992
3. Reg 33 SS(GB) Regs
4. Sch 4 Part V, para 12 SSCBA 1992

Chapter 11: Increases for dependants
(pp201-211)

2. Extra money for your wife
1. ss23, 82 and 83 SSCBA 1992; regs 8, 12 and Sch 2 SSB(Dep) Regs
2. Reg 19(6) SS(C&P) Regs
3. Sch 4 SSCBA 1992; SSBUO 1993

3. Extra money for your husband
1. ss23 and 84 SSCBA 1992
2. R(P) 3/88
3. *Thomas and others v Chief Adjudication Officer* ECJ Case No. C328/91; *R v Secretary of State for Social Security ex parte Equal*

Opportunities Commission ECJ Case
No. C9/91

4. Extra money if you are not married

1. s82(4) SSCBA 1992; reg 10 and Sch 2
   SSB(Dep) Regs as amended
2. Reg 19(6) SS(C&P) Regs
3. Reg 10(2)(f) SSB(Dep) Regs as
   amended
4. Sch 4 SSCBA 1992; SSBUO 1993

5. Extra money for your children

1. ss80 and 81 SSCBA 1992
2. Reg 19(6) SS(C&P) Regs
3. Sch 4 SSCBA 1992; SSBUO 1993
4. Reg 4A SS(C&P) Regs

6. Residence and maintenance

1. Reg 2(4) SSB(PRT) Regs
2. Reg 2(2) SSB(PRT) Regs
3. R(S) 3/74
4. R(U) 3/66
5. Reg 3 SSB(Dep) Regs
6. R(U) 25/58
7. R(S) 3/74
8. R(U) 14/62
9. R(S) 1/59
10. Reg 3 SSB(Dep) Amdt Regs 1987
11. R(I) 20/60; R(S) 12/83
12. R(S) 2/85
13. Reg 2 SSB(Dep) Regs
14. CS/130/1987
15. Reg 2(1) SSB(Dep) Regs
16. Reg 2(2) SSB(Dep) Regs
17. Reg 2(2)(i) and (ii) SSB(Dep) Regs

7. The earnings rules

1. Regs 8(2) and 12 SSB(Dep) Regs
2. R(P) 4/93
3. Reg 8(6) SSB(Dep) Regs as amended
   by SSB(Dep) Amdt Regs 1987 and
   preserved by Reg 4 SSB (Dep) Amdt
   Regs 1992; s45(3) SSA 1975 (as it
   existed immediately prior to its repeal
   by s29(2) and Sch 6 SSA 1985)
4. ss82 and 83(2)(b) SSCBA 1992; regs
   8(4) and 12 and Sch 2 para 7
   SSB(Dep) Regs

5. s92 and Sch 7 para 8 SSCBA 1992
6. *Cottingham and Geary v Secretary of
   State* (CA), [1993] Pensions Law
   Reports 79; see also CP/7/1987
7. s80(4) SSCBA 1992; Sch 3 para 2B
   SSB(Dep) Regs as amended

8. Trade disputes

1. s91 SSCBA 1992
2. CS 252/91

9. Tax

1. s617 ICTA 1988

Chapter 12: Contributions and earnings-related pensions
(pp214-239)

1. Introduction

1. s1(1) SSCBA 1992; s162 SSAA 1992
2. s1(2) SSCBA 1992
3. s21(1) and (2) SSCBA 1992
4. s2(1)(a) SSCBA 1992 5 s2(1)(b)
   SSCBA 1992
6. *Ready Mixed Concrete South East
   Ltd v Ministry of Pensions and
   National Insurance* [1968] 2 QB 497
   (QBD); *Global Plant v Secretary of
   State for Health and Social Security*
   1971 3 All ER 385 (QBD)
7. Sch 1 paras 1-5 SS(CatE) Regs
8. Sch 1 para 6 SS(CatE) Regs
9. Sch 1 paras 7-12 SS(CatE) Regs
10. s21(5)(d) SSCBA 1992
11. s5(1) SSCBA 1992
12. Sch 1 SS(EF) Regs as amended
13. s17(1)(b) SSAA 1992; and see
    generally *Secretary of State v Scully,
    The Independent*, 22 June 1992 and
    Casenote WRB 109 (August 1992),
    p10

2. Payment of contributions

1. ss 6(1)(a) and 13(1) SSCBA 1992; reg
   60 SS(Con) Regs
2. s6(2) SSCBA 1992; reg 58 SS(Con)
   Regs

3. s2(1)(a) SSCBA 1992
4. Reg 119(1)(a) SS(Con) Regs
5. Reg 119(2) SS(Con) Regs
6. Reg 119(3) SS(Con) Regs
7. Reg 120 SS(Con) Regs
8. Reg 120(2)(b) SS(Con) Regs
9. s2(1)(b) SSCBA 1992; reg 119(1)(d) SS(Con) Regs
10. Reg 119(1)(c) SS(Con) Regs
11. Regs 121 and 122 SS(Con) Regs
12. Reg 123A SS(Con) Regs
13. Regs 119(1)(e), 120(2)(b), 121 and 122 SS(Con) Regs
14. Reg 58(b) SS(Con) Regs
15. Reg 100 SS(Con) Regs
16. s22(4) SSCBA 1992; regs 5(2), 7(3), 7A(2)(b), 8(2)(b) and 9(6) SS(Cr) Regs as amended
17. Reg 103 SS(Con) Regs
18. Reg 101(1) SS(Con) Regs as amended
19. ss 6 and 7 SSCBA 1992
20. Regs 8(2) and 8A(2) SS(Con) Regs
21. s8(1) and (2) SSCBA 1992
22. s27 SSPA 1975 as amended (not consolidated); para 2(a) SS(CICCP)O
23. s3 SSA 1986 (not consolidated)
24. s3 SSPA 1975 as amended (not consolidated); reg 104 SS(Con) Regs
25. Regs 89 and 115 SS(Con) Regs as amended
26. Regs 10, 11, 12, 12A and 17 SS(Con) Regs as amended
27. s9(2), (3) and (4) SSCBA 1992
28. s27(2) SSPA 1975 (not consolidated); para 2(b) SS(CICCP)O
29. Sch 1 para 3 SSCBA 1992
30. s1(2) SSCBA 1992
31. s11 SSCBA 1992
32. s11(5) SSCBA 1992
33. Reg 25 SS(Con) Regs
34. Reg 26 SS(Con) Regs
35. s11(1) SSCBA 1992 as amended
36. Regs 98 and 123A-F SS(Con) Regs; reg 2 SS(Con) Amdt 4 Regs; reg 13B SSB(PA) Regs as amended
37. Reg 17 SS(Con) Regs as amended
38. Reg 26A SS(Con) Regs as amended
39. s13 SSCBA 1992
40. s14 SSCBA 1992
41. Reg 34 SS(Con) Regs
42. s13(1) SSCBA 1992 as amended
43. s15(1) and (3) SSCBA 1992
44. Regs 62-66 SS(Con) Regs as amended
45. Reg 67 SS(Con) Regs as amended
46. s114 SSAA 1992
47. Reg 39 SS(Con) Regs
48. Reg 54(2) SS(Con) Regs
49. Reg 38 SS(Con) Regs
50. Reg 27(3)(b) SS(Con) Regs as amended
51. Reg 38(5) and (6) SS(Con) Regs as amended
52. Reg 43 SS(Con) Regs

3. Credits and home responsibilities protection

1. Reg 3 SS(Cr) Regs as amended
2. Regs 5(2), 7(3), 7A(2)(b), 8(2)(b), 9B(3) and 9C(3) SS(Cr) Regs as amended
3. Reg 9(1) SS(Cr) Regs as amended
4. Reg 9(9) SS(Cr) Regs as amended
5. Reg 7A SS(Cr) Regs as amended
6. Reg 4 SS(Cr) Regs
7. Reg 8 SS(Cr) Regs
8. Reg 7 SS(Cr) Regs
9. Reg 9C SS(Cr) Regs as amended
10. Reg 9B SS(Cr) Regs as amended
11. Reg 3(1)(b) SSB(MW&WSP) Regs
12. Reg 3(1)(a) SSB(MW&WSP) Regs
13. *Equal Opportunities Commission v Secretary of State for Social Security*, ECJ Case No C9/91, reported at 1992 3 CMLR 233
14. Reg 9A SS(Cr) Regs as amended
15. Reg 7B SS(Cr) Regs
16. Reg 2(2) SSP(HR&MA) Regs as amended
17. Reg 2(4) SSP(HR&MA) Regs
18. Sch 3 para 5(7) SSCBA 1992
19. Sch 3 para 5(7)(a) SSCBA 1992

4. Contribution conditions for benefit

1. s21 and Sch 3 paras 1 and 2 SSCBA 1992
2. s21(1) and (2) SSCBA 1992
3. s21(6) SSCBA 1992
4. Sch 3 paras 1(6) and 2(6) SSCBA 1992

5. Reg 3(1) SSB(MW&WSP) Regs as amended
6. Reg 15 SS(STB)(T) Regs
7. s21 and Sch 3 paras 1 and 2 SSCBA 1992
8. Reg 7(1)(b) and (c) SS(US&IB) Regs
9. CS/174/1949; R(U) 13/80
10. Sch 3 para 3 SSCBA 1992
11. Sch 3 para 4 SSCBA 1992
12. Sch 3 para 7 SSCBA 1992
13. Reg 13(1) SS(STB)(T) Regs
14. Sch 3 para 5 SSCBA 1992
15. Sch 3 para 5(8) SSCBA 1992
16. Reg 6 SS(WBRP&OB)(T) Regs
17. Sch 3 para 5 SSCBA 1992
18. Sch 3 para 5(8) SSCBA 1992
19. Reg 7(7) SS(WBRP&OB)(T) Regs 20 Sch 3 para 5(5) SSCBA 1992
21. Reg 7(7) SS(WBRP&OB)(T) Regs
22. Reg 6 SS(WB&RP) Regs
23. s60(4)-(6) SSCBA 1992; regs 13 and 14 SSB(Dep) Regs as amended; reg 6(2) SS(WB&RP) Regs

5. The State Earnings Related Pension Scheme (SERPS)

1. s54 SSCBA 1992
2. s27 SSPA 1975 as amended; [s41 PSA 1993]
3. s29 SSPA 1975 as amended; [s46 PSA 1993]
4. s15 SSA 1986; [s160 PSA 1993]
5. ss1 and 2 SSA 1986; [s7 PSA 1993]
6. s3(1)(a) SSA 1986; [ss43(1) & 45(1) PSA 1993]
7. s3(1)(aa) SSA 1986 inserted by s1(a) SSA 1993; [s45(2) PSA 1993]
8. s4 SSA 1986
9. ss18 and 19 SSA 1986
10. ss33, 44 and 45 SSCBA 1992
11. ss50 and 51 SSCBA 1992
12. Art 2 SSREFO
13. s45(1) SSCBA 1992
14. Art 4(3) SSBU(No 2)O 1991

Chapter 13: Residence conditions and going abroad
(pp240-250)

2. Residence and presence conditions

1. Reg 3(1) SS(SDA) Regs; regs 2 and 3 SS(SDA) Amdt Regs
2. Reg 3(3) SS(SDA) Regs
3. Reg 2(1) SS(AA) Regs; reg 2(1) SS(DLA) Regs; reg 9(1) SS(ICA) Regs
4. Reg 2(4) SS(DLA) Regs
5. Reg 2(5) SS(DLA) Regs
6. Reg 2(2)(d) & (e) SS(AA) Regs; reg 2(2)(d) & (e) SS(DLA) Regs
7. Reg 9(2) SS(ICA) Regs
8. Reg 10 SS(WB&RP) Regs
9. s146(2)(a) SSCBA 1992
10. Reg 2(2) CB(RPA) Regs
11. Reg 2(3) CB(RPA) Regs
12. s146(3)(a) SSCBA 1992
13. Reg 4 CB(RPA) Regs as amended
14. s146(2)(b) and (3)(b) SSCBA 1992
15. Regs 3 and 5 CB(RPA) Regs
16. Reg 5(2)(b) CB(RPA) Regs
17. Reg 5(2)(d)(i) CB(RPA) Regs
18. Reg 5(2)(d)(ii) CB(RPA) Regs
19. Reg 3(2)(b) CB(RPA) Regs
20. Reg 6(1) SS(GA) Regs as amended
21. R(S) 1/66
22. R(S) 1/66
23. Reg 2(2) SS(AA) Regs; Reg 2(2) SS(DLA) Regs; Reg 6(2) SS(GA)Regs; Reg 9(3) SS(ICA) Regs; Reg 3(2) SS(SDA) Regs
24. Reg 11 SSB(PA) Regs as amended
25. R(P) 1/78
26. R(G) 2/51
27. CG/204/1949
28. R(P) 1/78
29. R(G) 2/51

3. Absence from Great Britain

1. ss113(1)(a) and 146 SSCBA 1992
2. Reg 2 SS(AB) Regs; reg 4 SS(MB) Regs; reg 4 SSB(MF) Regs; reg 11 SSB(PA) Regs
3. Reg 2 SSB(PA) Regs as amended

4. *R v Social Security Commissioner ex parte Akbar*, *The Times*, 6 November 1991 disapproving R(S) 1/85; *Chief Adjudication Officer v Ahmed* (CA), 16.3.94
5. Reg 3 SSB(PA) Amdt. Regs 1994
6. Reg 2(IB)(a) SSB(PA) Regs as amended
7. Reg 2(IB)(b) SSB(PA) Regs as amended
8. Reg 4 SSB(PA) Regs as amended
9. Reg 6 SSB(PA) Regs
10. Reg 4(2A) SSB(PA) Regs as amended
11. Regs 10, 10A and 10B SSB(PA) Regs as amended;
12. Regs 2-5 CB(RPA) Regs
13. Reg 9(3) SSB(PA) Regs as amended
14. Reg 9(4) SSB(PA) Regs
15. Reg 9(5) SSB(PA) Regs as amended
16. Reg 10C SSB(PA) Regs as amended
17. Reg 13 SSB(PA) Regs
18. Reg 13A SSB(PA) Regs

4. Northern Ireland, The Isle of Man and the Channel Islands

1. Reg 2 and Sch 1 SS(NIRA) Regs; Art 2 and Sch 1 SS(IoM)O
2. Sch 1 SS(J&G)O
3. Reg 12(1) SSB(PA) Regs

5. The European Community and the European Economic Area

1. Art 6 Reg 1408/71 EEC; R(U) 4/84
2. Art 2 Reg 1408/71 EEC; *Walsh v National Insurance Officer* 1980 ECR 1639 (ECJ); R(G) 3/83
3. Reg 1247/92 EEC
4. *Pinna* [1986] ECR 66 (ECJ)
5. *Ten Holder v Nieue Algemene Bedrijfsvereniging* [1986] ECR 1821 (ECJ)
6. *Petroni v Office National des Pensions pour Travailleurs Salaries* [1975] ECR 1149 (ECJ)
7. *Coppola v Insurance Officer* [1983] ECR 43 (ECJ); R(S) 13/83
8. CS/102/1977 reported as *re an Italian claimant* [1978] 2 CMLR 331
9. Art 10 Reg 1408/71 EEC
10. Art 69 Reg 1408/71 EEC
11. R(U) 5/78

Chapter 14: Other general provisions *(pp251-274)*

1. Periods of interruption of employment

1. s57(1)(d)(i) SSCBA 1992
2. s57(1)(d)(ii) SSCBA 1992
3. Reg 15 SS(US&IB) Regs
4. s57(1)(a)(i) SSCBA 1992; regs 7 and 7B SS(US&IB) Regs
5. Regs 7(1)(f) and 13(2)(a) SS(US&IB) Regs
6. Reg 13(2)(b) SS(US&IB) Regs; Sch 1 para 14 IS Regs
7. Reg 14 SS(US&IB) Regs
8. s57(1)(a)(ii) SSCBA 1992; reg 7(1)(c) and (f) SS(US&IB) Regs
9. s57(2) SSCBA 1992
10. Reg 5(1)(a) SS(US&IB) Regs
11. Reg 5(1)(b) SS(US&IB) Regs
12. Reg 5(2) and (3) SS(US&IB) Regs
13. s57(1)(e) SSCBA 1992
14. Reg 4(1) SS(US&IB) Regs
15. Reg 4(3) SS(US&IB) Regs
16. s57(1)(d) SSCBA 1992
17. ss33(7) and 68(10) SSCBA 1992

2. Hospital in-patients

1. Reg 17(4) SS(HI) Regs; reg 6(2) SS(AA) Regs; reg 10(5) SS(DLA) Regs
2. Reg 2(3) SS(HI) Regs
3. Reg 5 SS(HI) Regs as amended
4. Regs 6 and 7 SS(HI) Regs as amended
5. Reg 16 SS(HI) Regs
6. Regs 8 and 10(1) and (2) SS(DLA) Regs
7. Regs 6 and 8(1) SS(AA) Regs
8. Reg 21 SS(GB) Regs
9. Sch 7 para 10 SSCBA 1992
10. Reg 11 SS(HI) Regs
11. Reg 13 SS(HI) Regs

3. People in legal custody

1. s113(1)(b) and Sch 9 para 1(a) SSCBA 1992
2. Reg 2(2) and (8) SS(GB) Regs
3. R(S) 1/71
4. Reg 2(6) and (7) SS(GB) Regs

5. Reg 2(3) SS(GB) Regs
6. Reg 2(2) and (8) SS(GB) Regs
7. CS/541/1950
8. Reg 10(2)(d) and Sch 2 para 7(b)(ii) SSB(Dep) Regs as amended
9. s113(1)(b) SSCBA 1992 – Child benefit is not a 'benefit under Parts II to V' of that Act and is therefore outside the scope of the disqualification.
10. Reg 2(5) SS(GB) Regs
11. Sch 9 para 1(a) SSCBA 1992; reg 16(6) CB Regs
12. Reg 16(2) CB Regs

4. Overlapping benefits
1. Reg 4(5) SS(OB) Regs
2. Reg 6 SS(OB) Regs
3. Reg 6 SS(OB) Regs
4. s43(1) SSCBA 1992
5. ss52(2) and 53(2) SSCBA 1992
6. ss16(1), (2) and (6) SSCBA 1992; reg 2 SS(MAP) Regs as amended
7. Reg 3(2) SS(OB) Regs
8. Reg 3(3) SS(OB) Regs
9. s34(4) SSCBA 1992
10. s50(2) SSCBA 1992
11. Reg 4(3) SS(OB) Regs
12. Reg 4(4) SS(OB) Regs
13. Reg 6 SS(OB) Regs
14. Reg 9 SS(OB) Regs
15. Reg 10 SS(OB) Regs
16. Reg 8 SS(OB) Regs
17. Reg 2(4)(a) and (5) CB&SS(FAR) Regs
18. Reg 8 SS(OB) Regs
19. Reg 7 SS(OB) Regs

5. Calculating earnings
1. Reg 2 SS(CE) Regs
2. Reg 3 SS(CE) Regs
3. Reg 4 SS(CE) Regs

6. Christmas bonus
1. ss148, 149 and 150 SSCBA 1992
2. s148(2) SSCBA 1992
3. s149(2) and (3) SSCBA 1992
4. Reg 38 SS(C&P) Regs

7. Recovery of benefits from compensation payments
1. *Nabi v British Leyland (UK) Ltd* [1980] 1 WLR 529 (CA)
2. Reg 9 EP(RUB&SB) Regs
3. s81 SSAA 1992
4. Reg 2 SS(R) Regs
5. s81(2) SSAA 1992
6. s81(3) SSAA 1992; regs 3 and 4 SS(R) Regs
7. s97 SSAA 1992
8. s98 SSAA 1992; reg 11 SS(R) Regs
9. *Hodgson v Trapp* [1989] AC 706 (HL)
10. s2(1) Law Reform (Personal Injuries) Act 1948 as amended
11. *Jackman v Corbett* [1988] QB 157 (CA)
12. s6 Fatal Accidents Act 1976

8. Deductions from benefit
1. Reg 15 SS(PAOR) Regs
2. Reg 16 SS(PAOR) Regs
3. Regs 15 and 16 SS(PAOR) Regs
4. Reg 105 HB Regs
5. s78(2) SSAA 1992; reg 3 SF(RDB) Regs

9. Criminal offences
1. s112 SSAA 1992
2. s116(2)(a) SSAA 1992
3. *Clear v Smith* 1981 1 WLR 399 (DC)
4. *Barrass v Reeve* 1981 1 WLR 408 (DC)
5. *Regina v Livingstone Stewart* 1987 9 Crim App R(S) 135 (CA)
6. s114(4) SSAA 1992
7. s114(1) SSAA 1992
8. s54(1) SSA 1986; reg 132 SS(Con) Regs as amended
9. s111 SSAA 1992
10. s110(7) SSAA 1992

10. Equal treatment for men and women
1. s2 ECA 1972
2. Directive 79/7/EEC (Official Journal of the European Communities (OJ) No.L 6, 10.1.79, p24)
3. Art 4(1) Directive 79/7/EEC

5. Art 3(1)(a) Directive 79/7/EEC
6. Art 3(2) Directive 79/7/EEC
7. Art 3(1)(b) Directive 79/7/EEC
8. Directive 86/378/EEC (OJ No. L225, 12.8.86, p40)
9. Art 2 Directive 79/7/EEC
10. *Drake v Chief Adjudication Officer* ECJ Case No. 150/85 11 Art 7(1) Directive 79/7/EEC
12. Art 7(2) Directive 79/7/EEC
13. Art 8(2) Directive 79/7/EEC
14. *Johnston v Chief Constable of the Royal Ulster Constabulary* (ECJ) (1986) ECR 723
15. *Drake v Chief Adjudication Officer,* ECJ Case No.150/85
16. *Clarke v Chief Adjudication Officer,* ECJ Case No. C384/85. Reported at (1987) 3 CMLR 277
17. *Johnson v Chief Adjudication Officer,* ECJ Case No. C31/90
18. *Thomas and others v Chief Adjudication Officer,* ECJ Case No. C328/91
20. *R v Secretary of State for Social Security ex parte Equal Opportunities Commission,* ECJ Case No. C9/91
21. CS/27/1991

Chapter 15: Administration
(pp276-302)

1. Claims
1. s1 SSAA 1992
2. Reg 3 SS(C&P) Regs as amended
3. Reg 4 SS(C&P) Regs
4. R(SB) 3/89
5. Reg 4(6) SS(C&P) Regs
6. Reg 5 SS(C&P) Regs
7. Reg 4(7) SS(C&P) Regs
8. Reg 33 SS(C&P) Regs
9. Reg 8(1) SS(C&P) Regs
10. R(P) 1/85
11. Reg 8(2) SS(C&P) Regs
12. s180 SSAA 1992
13. s20(1) SSAA 1992
14. R(SB) 29/83
15. R(S)9/93

16. Reg 9(1) and Sch 1 SS(C&P) Regs
17. Reg 9(2), (3) and (6) and Sch 1 SS(C&P) Regs
18. Reg 9(4) and (5) SS(C&P) Regs
19. Regs 13-15 and 39 SS(C&P) Regs
20. Reg 17 SS(C&P) Regs
21. Reg 19 and Sch 4 SS(C&P) Regs
22. Sch 5 para 1 SS(C&P) Regs
23. ss 65(4), (6) and 76 SSCBA 1992
24. Reg 4 SS(AA) Regs; reg 13(c)(i) SS(C&P) Regs
25. Reg 19(3) SS(C&P) Regs
26. Reg 19(2) SS(C&P) Regs
27. s1(2)(b) SSCBA 1992
28. Sch 3 para 2 SS(C&P) Regs
29. R(S) 10/59; R(S) 3/69; R(SB) 17/83
30. CS/371/1949
31. R(P) 1/79
32. R(I) 28/54
33. R(SB) 6/83
34. CS/50/1950
35. R(U) 9/74
36. R(U) 35/56
37. R(S) 5/56
38. R(S) 14/54; R(G) 4/68; R(U) 9/74
39. R(S) 14/54
40. R(S) 10/59; R(S) 11/59
41. R(S) 11/59; R(G) 1/75
42. R(SB) 6/83
43. R(I) 6/54
44. R(G) 2/74
45. CWG/6/1950
46. R(P) 1/85
47. Reg 19(2) SS(C&P) Regs

2. Decisions
1. s20 SSAA 1992
2. s38(1) SSAA 1992
3. s21(1) SSAA 1992
4. s74 SSAA 1992; regs 7-10 SS(PAOR) Regs
5. Jones v Department of Employment 1989 QB 1 (CA)
6. s21(2) SSAA 1992
7. s68 SSAA 1992
8. See Legal Action, October 1990, p21 for further discussion
9. ss68(4)(a) and 69(4)(a) SSAA 1992
10. CIS/787/1991

11. Regs 42 and 56 SS(Adj) Regs
12. Regs 43 and 57 SS(Adj) Regs
13. Reg 44 SS(Adj) Regs
14. Regs 45(2), 58(2) and Sch 2 SS(Adj) Regs
15. Reg 3(3) SS(Adj) Regs
16. Reg 19(2) SS(Adj) Regs
17. s17(1) SSAA 1992
18. Reg 21(1) SS(Adj) Regs
19. Reg 21(3) SS(Adj) Regs
20. s17(4) SSAA 1992; reg 15 SS(Adj) Regs
21. Reg 16(1) SS(Adj) Regs
22. s18(3) SSAA 1992; reg 16(2) SS(Adj) Regs
23. Regs 27 and 29(2) SS(Adj) Regs
24. s45 SSCBA 1992; reg 29(1) SS(Adj) Regs
25. Regs 29(1)(a), 50(1) and 62(1) SS(Adj) Regs
26. Reg 29(9) SS(Adj) Regs
27. Reg 30 SS(Adj) Regs

3. Reviews

1. s25(1), (2) and (3) SSAA 1992; reg 17(4) SS(C&P) Regs
2. R(M) 5/86
3. R(S) 6/78; R(M) 5/86
4. Reg 17(4) SS(C&P) Regs; R(S) 3/89
5. R(S) 3/89
6. s25(2) SSAA 1992
7. s69 SSAA 1992
8. Reg 65(1) SS(Adj) Regs
9. Reg 65(2) SS(Adj) Regs
10. Reg 64A SS(Adj) Regs
11. s28 SSAA 1992
12. Reg 19(2) SS(Adj) Regs
13. s19(1) SSAA 1992
14. s47(1) SSAA 1992; regs 29(1)(a), 50(1) and 62(1)(a) SS(Adj) Regs
15. Regs 50(1) and 67 SS(Adj) Regs
16. R(I) 16/57; R(P) 3/73
17. s47(4) SSAA 1992; reg 29(1)(a) SS(Adj) Regs
18. s47(7) SSAA 1992
19. s47(2) SSAA 1992; regs 29(1)(a) and 62(1)(c) SS(Adj) Regs
20. R(M) 5/86
21. Reg 66(1) SS(Adj) Regs
22. Reg 68 SS(Adj) Regs
23. s47(9) SSAA 1992; regs 29(1)(a), 50(3) and 62(4) SS(Adj) Regs

4. Payments

1. Regs 22 and 23 SS(C&P) Regs
2. Reg 21 SS(C&P) Regs; reg 12 SS(PAOR) Regs
3. Regs 30 and 33 SS(C&P) Regs
4. Regs 34 and 35 SS(C&P) Regs
5. Reg 2 SS(PAOR) Regs
6. Reg 3 SS(PAOR) Regs
7. Reg 4 SS(PAOR) Regs
8. Reg 37 SS(C&P) Regs
9. Reg 37A SS(C&P) Regs

5. Recovery of overpayments

1. s71 SSAA 1992
2. ss 71(3) and 155(1) SSAA 1992
3. s22(5) SSAA 1992
4. s71(5) SSAA 1992
5. R(SB) 34/83
6. R(SB) 9/85
7. R(SB) 18/85
8. *Jones v Chief Adjudication Officer* – CA 1 July 1993
9. CSB/790/1988
10. *Sharples v Chief Adjudication Officer* – CA 1 July 1993
11. R(SB) 54/83
12. R(SB) 21/82
13. R(G) 2/72
14. R(U) 6/70
15. R(SB) 21/82
16. s71(1) SSAA 1992
17. R(SB) 40/84
18. R(SB) 15/87
19. R(SB) 15/87
20. Reg 41 SS(PAOR) Regs
21. *Secretary of State for Social Security v Tunnicliffe, The Times*, 8 January 1991 (CA)
22. *Plewa v Chief Adjudication Officer*
23. R(SB) 44/83
24. s71(9) SSAA 1992; regs 16 and 17 SS(PAOR) Regs
25. s71(10) SSAA 1992
26. R(U) 7/75
27. R(S) 2/80

6. Complaints

1. DSS Press Release 93/81 – 4 May 1993
2. House of Commons Written Answers, *Hansard*, 4 May 1993 Col. 10

Chapter 16: Appeals
(pp303-330)

1. Social security appeal tribunals

1. S51(1) and Sch 2 paras 2 &5 SSAA 1992
2. s40 SSAA 1992
3. s41(5) SSAA 1992
4. s40(2) SSAA 1992
5. Sch 2 para 4 SSAA 1992
6. Reg 25(1) SS(Adj) Regs
7. Regs 24 (2) & 25(1) SS(Adj) Regs
8. s41(6) SSAA 1992
9. s56 SSAA 1992
10. s22 SSAA 1992
11. s98(7) SSAA 1992
12. Reg 3(5) & (6) SS(Adj) Regs
13. ss 22(1), (2) &(5) SSAA 1992
14. Reg 3(7) SS(Adj) Regs
15. s29 SSAA 1992
16. s21(2) SSAA 1992
17. Reg 4(2) SS(Adj) Regs
18. Reg 4(4) SS(Adj) Regs
19. Reg 24(3) SS(Adj) Regs
20. Reg 25(1) SS(Adj) Regs
21. Reg 25(2) SS(Adj) Regs
22. Reg 26(1)(a) SS(Adj) Regs
23. Reg 25(3) SS(Adj) Regs
24. Reg 10 SS(Adj) Regs
25. Reg 11 SS(Adj) Regs; R(S) 3/89, R(U) 3/89
26. Reg 3(3) & Sch 2 para 8 SS(Adj) Regs
27. R(S) 3/89, R(U) 3/89

2. Medical appeal tribunals

1. Reg 31(2) SS(Adj) Regs
2. s46(2) SSAA 1992; regs 46 & 60 SS(Adj) Regs
3. s98(5) SSAA 1992
4. Reg 3(3) & Sch 2 para 2 SS(Adj) Regs
5. Reg 37(1) SS(Adj) Regs
6. Reg 3(7) SS(Adj) Regs
7. s46(3) SSAA 1992; regs 46(2) and 60(2) SS(Adj) Regs
8. Reg 31(3) SS(Adj) Regs
9. Reg 32 SS(Adj) Regs
10. Reg 31(4) SS(Adj) Regs
11. *Kitchen & Evans v Secretary of State*, *The Times*, 14 September 1993
12. CM/140/92 (affirming CM/205/88)
13. Reg 31(5) SS(Adj) Regs

3. Disability appeal tribunals

1. s42(3) and (4) SSAA 1992
2. Reg 3 SS(US&IB) Regs as amended; Reg 9 SS(SDA) Regs as amended
3. Reg 26G SS(Adj) Regs
4. Reg 26E(2) SS(Adj) Regs
5. Reg 26C SS(Adj) Regs
6. s55(1) SSAA 1992; Reg 26F SS(Adj) Regs
7. s33 SSAA 1992
8. s55(2) SSAA 1992
9. Reg 26E(5) and (6) SS(Adj) Regs

4. Social security commissioners

1. ss23(1), 34(1) and 48(1) SSAA 1992
2. R(A) 1/72
3. R(A) 1/72
4. *Baron v Secretary of State for Social Services* (CA), reported as an appendix to R(M) 6/86
5. R(M) 1/83
6. ss23(9), 34(4) and 48(3) SSAA 1992
7. Reg 26(1) SS(Adj) Regs; reg 3(1) SSCP Regs
8. Regs 3(3), 26 and Sch 2 para 5 SS(Adj) Regs
9. Reg 3(1) and (3) SSCP Regs
10. Regs 3(3), 32 and Sch 2 para 6 SS(Adj) Regs; reg 3(1) and (3) SSCP Regs
11. Reg 3(2) and (5) SSCP Regs
12. Reg 7(1) SSCP Regs
13. Reg 5(2) SSCP Regs
14. ss23(3) and (4), 34(2) and (3) and 48(1)(d) and (2) SSAA 1992
15. s23(2) SSAA 1992
16. s29 SSAA 1992; R(P) 1/82
17. s4 FA 1982
18. Reg 27(3) and (4) SSCP Regs

19. Reg 15 SSCP Regs
20. s57(1) SSAA 1992
21. Reg 17(4) SSCP Regs
22. Reg 22(2) SSCP Regs
23. s23(7)(b) SSAA 1992
24. s23(7)(a) SSAA 1992
25. *Innes v Chief Adjudication Officer*, (unreported) (CA), 19 November 1986
26. Regs 24 and 25 SSCP Regs
27. ss 24 and 34(5) SSAA 1992
28. Regs 27(2) and 31(1) SSCP Regs
29. *White v Chief Adjudication Officer* [1986] 2 All ER 905 (CA), also reported as an appendix to R(S) 8/85
30. s24(2)(b) SSAA 1992
31. RSC 0.59 r.21(3)
32. RSC 0.3 r.5 and 0.59 r.14(2)
33. RSC 0.59 r.14(2), (2A) and (2B)
34. RSC 0.59 r.21(2)
35. RSC 0.59 r.4(3)
36. *Bland v Chief Supplementary Benefit Officer* [1983] 1 WLR 262 (CA), also reported as R(SB) 12/83

5. Late appeals

1. For a general discussion see Warren: 'Late Social Security Appeals' – *Legal Action*, February 1994, p13
2. Regs 1(3), 3(1) & Sch 2 SS(Adj) Regs
3. Reg 3(3) SS(Adj) Regs
4. R(SB)24/82; *White v Chief Adjudication Officer* (CA) reported as an appendix to R(S)8/85
5. CIS/93/92
6. Reg 3(4) SS(Adj) Regs
7. R(M) 1/87
8. *R v Home Secretary ex parte Mehta* applied to social security law by R(M)1/87 and R(I)5/91
9. s29 SSAA 1992
10. R(S)8/85
11. The subsequent application to the Court of Appeal reported as an appendix to the decision failed for procedural reasons. The Court did not say that the commissioner's decision was right but only that it had

no jurisdiction to entertain a further application for leave to appeal.
12. *Arnold v National Westminster Bank* [1991] All ER41
13. Crown Office Ref. CO/1834/93
14. See for example: *R v Civil Service Commission ex parte Cunningham* (CA) [1991] 4 All ER 310; *R v Home Secretary ex parte Doody* [1993] 3 WLR 154 and *R v Lambeth ex parte Walters*, *The Times* 6 October 1993
15. R(U) 6/68
16. R(S) 2/84
17. Unreported case referred to by Warren *op. cit*
18. But see R(U) 6/68
19. *Cottingham and Geary v Secretary of State*, (CA) [1993] Pension Law Reports 79; see also CP 7/87
20. *Chief Adjudication Officer v Pearse* – *The Times*, 18 June 1992.
21. R(M)1/87; R(I) 5/91
22. eg, R(M)1/87

6. How to prepare an appeal

1. R(I) 2/51; R(I) 33/85
2. s53 SSAA 1992
3. R(I) 12/75
4. R(SB) 22/86
5. *Nancollas v Insurance Officer* [1985] 1 All ER 833 (CA), also reported as an appendix to R(I) 7/85
6. R(I) 12/75
7. *Chief Supplementary Benefit Officer v Leary* reported as an appendix to R(SB) 6/85; see generally CS/140/1991
8. R(G) 3/62; R(U) 4/88
9. R(U) 4/88
10. *Pepper v Hart* [1992] 3 WLR 1032
11. ss 2(4)(a) and 15(1) LAA 1988

Index

abroad
 absence abroad and benefits 240-1,
  245-7
 – attendance allowance 246, 248
 – child benefit 246
 – disability living allowance 246, 248
 – disablement benefit 247
 – guardian's allowance 246
 – increases for dependants 247
 – invalid care allowance 246, 248
 – invalidity benefit 245-6
 – maternity allowance 245-6
 – reduced earnings allowance 247
 – retirement pension 246
 – severe disablement allowance 245-6
 – sickness benefit 245-6
 – statutory maternity pay 91
 – statutory sick pay 67, 68
 – widows' benefits 246
 Channel Islands 247
 contribution rules 217-9
 EC rules 241, 248-50
 Isle of Man 247
 Northern Ireland 247
 reciprocal agreements 241, 248, 250
 see also: residence/presence conditions
absence from home
 actively *seeking work* 22-3
 child benefit 191
 increases for dependants 206
 see also: abroad, holidays
Access to Work programme 337
accidents at work
 see: industrial accidents/diseases
accommodation rules
 attendance allowance/disability living
  allowance 144-9
actively seeking work 8, 20-5
 absence from home 22-3

 Actively Seeking Review 24
 Back to Work Plan 12
 checking if actively seeking work 24-5
 holidays while claiming 19-20
 steps to find work 20, 21
 treated as actively seeking work 22-3
 week defined 23-4
additional pension (SERPS)
 see: SERPS
adjudicating medical authority 287
adjudication officer
 cases referred to social security appeal
  tribunals 305
 decisions 283-4
 reviews 288-91
adoption
 child benefit 191, 192, 194
 guardian's allowance 197-8
advance claims 280
 child benefit 194
 retirement pension 113
advice
 incorrect advice
 – compensation 12, 302
 – good cause for a late claim 12, 282
 see also: complaints
age
 disability living allowance rules 127-8,
  135
 evidence of age 113-4
 limits for paying contributions 217
 pensionable age 113, 124, 239
age addition
 retirement pension 117, 120, 121, 122,
  123, 124
 severe disablement allowance 81, 82
agoraphobia 128, 132
annulment of marriage 110-11
 retirement pension 117-19

anti-test-case rules 284-5
  increases for dependants 210
  reviews/appeals 290, 319-21
appeal 303-30
  advice and representation 329-30
  attendance allowance/disability living
    allowance 157, 312
  choosing between an appeal or review
    293-4
  from commissioners 317-18
  late appeal 294, 304, 308, 314, 315,
    317-18, 318-23
  – anti-test-case rules 290, 319-21
  – special reasons 318-23
  legal aid 330
  preparing an appeal 323-8
  presenting a case 328-9
  Secretary of State's decisions 286-7
  statutory maternity pay 93
  statutory sick pay 72
  suspension of benefit 295
  see also: disability appeal tribunals,
    medical appeal tribunals, social
    security commissioners, social
    security appeal tribunals
appointee 86, 278, 294
  late claims 86, 156, 282
arrears
  following review 290-1, 293
  suspension of unemployment benefit
    24-5, 36
  see also: late claims
asthma, occupational
  claims 169, 178, 281
attendance allowance 126, 142-57
  absence abroad 246, 248
  accommodation rules 144-9
  – hospices 145
  – hospitals 145, 256
  – public/local funds 145-8
  amount 143
  appeals 157
  attention condition 143
  claims 149-52
  – administration 152
  – completing the claim form 149-51
  – renewal claims 151
  – terminally ill 151
  – time limit 281

  – transitional provisions 152
  decisions 149
  dialysis 143
  EC rules 248
  entitlement 143
  hospices 145
  hospital patients 145, 256
  imprisonment 257
  invalid care allowance 144
  means-tested benefits 144
  overlapping benefits 144, 260
  period of payment 152-3
  qualifying period 143
  residence/presence conditions 242
  respite care 148-9
  reviews 154-6
  supervision condition 143
  tax 144
  terminal illness 143, 151
attention condition 137, 139-41, 143
availability for work 8, 13-20
  as employed earner 13
  Back to Work Plan 12
  capable of work 13
  checking availability for work 15-19
  deemed availability for work 13, 14-15
  holidays while claiming 19-20
  part-time work 25-6
  permitted period 13-14
  questionnaire 15-18
  Restart interview 18-19
  restricting availability for work 13-14,
    16-17
  self-employment 13
  studying while unemployed 44
  voluntary work 15
autocredits 229, 239

backdated claims 278, 281
  see also: late claims
Back to Work Plan 12
behavioural problems
  disability living allowance 131-2
Benefits Agency administration 276
Benefits Agency Customers' Charter 283,
  301
Benefits Agency Medical Service (BAMS)
  examination 52, 53-6
  benefit stopped 56-61

BAMS examination (*cont.*)
  statutory sick pay 70, 72
Benefits Agency Overseas Branch 241
benefit year 231
birth certificates 113-4
blind/partially sighted
  disability living allowance 130-1, 132
boarding school
  child benefit 191
byssinosis 170, 335-6
  see also: industrial diseases

care, child in 190-1
carers
  credits 227
  home responsibilities protection 159,
    225, 227, 229-31, 234
**certificate of exemption for Class 2
  contributions** 222
change of circumstances 280
  review 289, 292-3
Channel Islands 247
charitable work while unemployed 15
chemotherapy 251
Chief Adjudication Officer 283, 350
Chief Executive Benefits Agency 301
child
  benefits for children 188-200
  definition 188-90
  disability living allowance 127-8, 135,
    138, 141, 142, 153
  increases of benefit
  – for carer of child 203-5, 208-10
  – for children 201, 205-6, 210
  industrial death benefit 199-200
  qualifying child for widowed mother's
    allowance 105-6
  see also: child benefit, one parent benefit
child benefit 188-195
  abroad 246
  absence from home 191
  – at school 191
  – in care 190-1
  – in custody 191
  – in hospital 191, 257
  adoption 191, 192, 194
  amount 188
  children for whom benefit not payable
    191

  claims and backdating 193-4, 279
  – time limit for claim 280
  definition of child 188-90
  entitlement 188
  – living with the claimant 191-2
  – maintaining the child 192
  extension period 189-90
  full-time education 189
  income support/family credit 195
  increase for dependant child 206
  one parent benefit 195-6
  overlapping benefit rules 195, 261
  parents from abroad 194
  payment 194
  priority between claimants 192-3
  residence/presence conditions 194-5,
    242-3
  tax 195
child's special allowance 196, 198-9, 257,
  261
Christmas bonus 262-3
chronic bronchitis for miners 178-9
claims 276-83
  advance claims 280
  amending a claim 278
  attendance allowance/disability
    allowance 149-52
  child benefit 193-4
  delaying a claim 12, 232, 254,
    278
  disablement benefit 178-9
  forms 277
  guardian's allowance 197
  interchange of claims 279-80
  invalid care allowance 158-9, 279
  invalidity benefit 279, 280, 281
  late claims 278, 281-3
  making a claim 277-9
  maternity allowance 96
  one parent benefit 196
  retirement pension 113, 117, 122,
    123
  severe disablement allowance 86, 280,
    281
  sickness benefit 74-5
  time limits for claims 280-1
  unemployment benefit 11-12
  – breaking a claim 10, 10-11
  widows' benefits 103-4

cohabitation
  increase of benefit for dependant
    looking after a child 203-5
  widows' benefits 98, 99-101, 104, 105,
    107, 109
commissioners
  see: social security commissioners
common law power of recovery 298-9
compensation 301-2
  delay in making a decision 283
  delay in making payments 301-2
  incorrect advice 12, 302
  recovery of benefits from compensation
    263-5
  treatment for unemployment benefit
    30-2
complaints 276-7, 301-2
  delayed decisions 283
  late appeal/review 320
compulsory holidays 25, 29-30
constant attendance allowance 177-8
  absence abroad 247
  hospital patients 256
  overlapping benefits 260
continuous employment for statutory
  maternity pay 93-4
contracting out of SERPS 220-1, 235-6
contributing to maintenance
  for child benefit 192
  for increases for dependants 207-8
contribution conditions 4
  insufficient contributions 235
  maternity allowance 232-3
  retirement pension 124, 233-4
  sickness benefit 226-7, 227-8, 231-2
  unemployment benefit 8, 226-7, 227-8,
    231-2
  widows 231-2
  - widowed mother's allowance 233
  - widow's payment 233
  - widow's pension 233-4
contributions 214-235
  abroad 217-9
  classes of contributions 214-5
  - Class 1 217-18, 220-2
  - Class 1A 222
  - Class 2 218, 222
  - Class 3 (voluntary) 218, 223
  - Class 4 218, 223-4

contracting out of SERPS 220-1, 235-6
contributory benefits 4
decisions 217
earnings factors 217
earnings limits 216
employed/self-employed earners 215
employer's liability for contributions
  221-2
equal treatment rules 217, 229
insufficient contributions 235
late payment 224-5
more than one job 221
non-payment 224-5, 267
overpayment of voluntary contributions
  223
paid before 1975 224
payment 217-25
personal pensions 221, 236
record of contributions 214, 217
reduced liability for married women
  and widows 219-20, 221, 222, 230
residence/presence rules 217-9
statutory maternity pay 89-90
statutory sick pay 70, 71
who does not have to pay contributions
  216
see also: contribution conditions,
  credits, home responsibilities
  protection
Contributions Agency 214
contributory benefits 4
correcting a decision of appeal tribunal
  307, 311
councillor
  effect of allowance on amount of
    benefit 74, 77, 82
  incapacity for work and therapeutic
    work 49
court action
  appeals from commissioners 317-18
  recovery of overpayments 298-9
Court of Appeal 317-18
Court of Session 317-18
credits 225, 226-9
  appealing refusal of incapacity benefits
    63-4
  autocredits 229, 239
  caring for an invalid 227
  disability working allowance 229

credits (*cont.*)
  incapacity for work 70, 74, 77, 159, 226-7
  jury service 228
  maternity pay period 90, 228
  men 60 and over 229
  remand prisoners 257
  starting credits 227
  training/education 227-8
  unemployed 45, 226-7
  widows 102, 228
criminal injuries compensation 334-5
criminal proceedings 265-7
  disqualification from unemployment benefit for misconduct 34, 35, 36
  non-payment of contributions 224
  overpayments 300-1
customer services manager 276-7, 301
  see also: complaints
custody
  see: imprisonment

damages
  see: compensation
day of incapacity 48, 252-3
day of unemployment 252
deafness, occupational 169, 170, 174
  claims 169, 178, 281
  disability living allowance 130-1
death
  presumption of death 98-9, 103, 104
  war pensions 333
  see also: industrial death benefit, widowers, widows, widows' benefits
decisions
  adjudicating medical authority 287
  adjudication officer 283-4
  – time limit and service targets for decisions 283-4
  anti-test-case rules 284-5
  contributions 217
  disability appeal tribunal 313
  medical appeal tribunals 310-11
  reported decisions 326
  Secretary of State 217, 286-7
  social security appeal tribunals 307
  social security commissioners 317
  unreported decisions 326-7
  war pensions 333

deductions from benefit 265
deemed actively seeking work 22-3
deemed availability for work 13, 14-15
deemed incapacity for work 48, 50
deferring retirement 113, 114-5
  de-retirement 116, 246
  future changes 124
  graduated retirement benefit 114-15, 124
  invalidity benefit 78, 79, 116, 117
  married women 115
  reduced earnings allowance 182-3
degrees of disablement 171-4, 338-9
delay
  in making decision 283-4
  in making payment 301-2
delaying a claim for benefit 12, 232, 254, 278
Department of Employment
  services for the disabled 336-7
dependants' increases
  see: increases for dependants
de-retirement 116, 246
diagnosis questions 285-6
dialysis 143, 251
diffuse mesothelioma 170, 335-6
  see also: industrial diseases
disability appeal tribunals 350, 311-13
  decision 313
  hearing procedure 312-13
  jurisdiction 311-12
  members treated as incapable of work 50
  tribunal membership 311
disability living allowance 126, 127-42
  absence abroad 246, 248
  accommodation rules 144-9
  – hospices 145
  – hospitals 145, 255-6
  – public/local funds 145-8
  age rules 127-8
  appeals 157
  – about one component only 312
  care component 134-42
  children 153
  claims 149-52
  – administration 152
  – completing the claim form 149-51
  – renewal claims 151

disability living allowance (*cont.*)
- terminally ill 151
- time limit 281
- transitional provisions 152
compensation for late payments 302
decisions 149
EC rules 248
imprisonment 257
income support and means-tested
    benefits 144
mobility component 127-34
overlapping benefits 144, 260
period of payment 152-3
residence/presence conditions 242
respite care 148-9
reviews 154-6, 312
tax 144
terminal illness 151
*see also: disability living allowance –
    care component, disability living
    allowance – mobility component*
**disability living allowance – care
    component** 134-42
age rules 135
amount 134-5
attention 137, 139-41
- bodily functions 139-40
- frequent attention 140
- limited attention 140
- night condition 140-1
- prolonged/repeated attention 140-1
children 138, 141, 142
cooking test 138-9
day defined 136-7
dialysis 137
disability conditions 136
entitlement 134
night defined 137
supervision 137, 141-2, 143
terminal illness 138
see also: disability living allowance
**disability living allowance – mobility
    component** 127-34
age rules 127-8
agoraphobia 128, 132
amount 127
amputees 130
behavioural difficulties 131-2
blind/deaf claimants 130-1, 132

children 127
dementia 132
directional mobility 132
enhanced facilities for locomotion 133
entitlement 127
higher rate 127, 128-32
invalid vehicles 133-4
lower rate 132
motability 134
overlapping benefits 144, 260
people with learning difficulties 132
residence/presence conditions 242
terminal illness 127, 133
unable to walk 128-30
- distance 129
- exertion 129-30
- out of doors 129
- personal circumstances 130
- physical disablement 128
- severe discomfort 129
see also: disability living allowance
disability working allowance
credits 229
extension of linking rule 56-7, 254
disablement benefit 175-9
absence abroad 247
amount 176-7
claims 178-9
- time limit 178, 280, 281
constant attendance allowance 177-8
degrees of disablement 338-9
disqualification 179
entitlement 175-6
exceptionally severe disablement
    allowance 178
hospital patients 256
hospital treatment allowance 178, 256
imprisonment 257
income support 177
loss of faculty 171
overlapping benefits 260
prescribed industrial diseases 168-70,
    340-9
reviews 179
tax 177
unemployability supplement 178,
    226-7, 259
unforeseen aggravation 179, 292
war pensions 332-3

discrimination
see: equal treatment rules
disqualification from benefit
disablement benefit 179
failing to attend medical examination
54, 76
forfeiture rule 102, 315
invalidity benefit 51-64, 80
severe disablement allowance 86
sickness benefit 76
unemployment benefit 33-42
– failing to attend a Restart interview
18, 33
– failing to take up a job/training place
39-41
– leaving job/training scheme
voluntarily 37-9
– misconduct 33-7, 179
– trade disputes 41-2
widows' benefits 99-101, 104, 105,
107, 109
divorce
retirement pension 117-19
widows' benefits 98
domicile 110

EC rules 248-50
exportability of benefits 241, 248, 249
residence/presence in EC 241, 245
see also: abroad, equal treatment rules
early retirement
credits 229
treatment of pension for unemployment
benefit 33
voluntary unemployment 37, 38
earnings
calculation of earnings 26-7, 261-2
factors 217
limits 216
payments from previous jobs 30-3
refusing employment because of poor
wages 40-1
restricting availability for work 16-17
statutory maternity pay 93
statutory sick pay 66, 70-1
therapeutic work 49, 49-50
see also: earnings rules
earnings replacement benefits 4-5
earnings rules 5

increases for dependants
– adults 74, 202, 204, 208-210
– children 205, 210
invalid care allowance 160
retirement pension 113
sickness benefit 77
unemployment benefit 26
– £2 rule 26-7
– £12 rule 27-8
widows' benefits 102
education
credits 227-8
full-time education
– child benefit 189
– severe disablement allowance 83
see also: students
emphysema for miners 178-9
employee
contributions 217-18, 220-2
definition of employed earner 215
– statutory maternity pay 91-2
– statutory sick pay 65-7
employer
liability for contributions 221-2
statutory maternity pay 91
– changing employer 91, 92
– more than one employer 89
statutory sick pay
– more than one employer 71
– non-payment by employer 72, 73
employment
continuous employment for statutory
maternity pay 93-4
failure to take up a job 39-41
gainful employment for invalid care
allowance 160
leaving job voluntarily 37-9
misconduct 33-7, 168, 179, 279
payments from previous jobs 30-3
schemes for the disabled 336-7
therapeutic work 49, 49-50
*see also: actively seeking work,
availability for work, earnings,
industrial accidents/diseases*
Employment Rehabilitation Centres 336
equal treatment rules 267-74
contributions 217, 229
exceptions to the rules 270-1, 272
graduated retirement benefit 124

equal treatment rules (*cont.*)
   increase for dependant looking after
      child 204-5
   increase for husband 203
   invalid care allowance 161-2, 271-2,
      272
   invalidity benefit 78, 79, 272, 273
   non-contributory invalidity pension 83,
      85, 272
   reduced earnings allowance 183
   retirement pension 113, 123
   severe disablement allowance 83, 85,
      272
   sickness benefit for people over
      pensionable age 75
   statutory sick pay 65
   unemployment benefit 43
error
   causing overpayment 299
   late claim caused by official error 283
error of law 290
   anti-test-case rules 284-5
   payment delays 301-2
European Economic Area
   see: EC rules
European Community
   see: EC rules
evidence 278, 279
   of age 113-4
   of incapacity for work 51, 57-60, 63
   of seeking work 21
   preparing an appeal 323-8
exceptional circumstances for late appeal
   see: special reasons
exceptionally severe disablement
   allowance 178
   absence abroad 247
ex gratia payments 283
extension period (child benefit) 189-90

failure
   to attend medical examination 54, 76
   to disclose 297-8
   to have suitable treatment 54, 76
   to take up employment/training 39-41
family fund test 207-8
fares
   to interview 278
   to tribunal 306

forfeiture rule 102, 315
foster child 191, 197
fraud 265-7
full extent normal rule 26, 27, 28-9
full-time education
   see: education
functional overlay 62
funeral expenses 103, 104

gay couples
   increase for dependant looking after a
      child 204
good cause
   failing to attend a Restart interview 18,
      33
   failing to take up job/training 39-41
   late appeals 318-23
   late claims 156, 280, 281-3
   – incorrect advice 12, 282
   late reviews 290-1
   leaving job/training scheme 37-9
   therapeutic work 49, 50
graduated retirement benefit 117, 124
   deferring retirement 114-15, 124
   overlapping benefits 260
guaranteed minimum pension 260
guardian's allowance 196-8
   absence abroad 246
   adoption 197-8
   amount 197
   claims 197, 279, 280
   hospital patients 257
   imprisonment 197, 198, 258
   income support 197
   one parent benefit 197
   overlapping benefits 197, 205, 261
   qualifying children 197-8
   residence/presence conditions 243
   tax 197

holidays
   invalid care allowance 160
   unemployment benefit 19-20
   – compulsory holidays 25, 29-30
home responsibilities protection 124-5,
   159, 223, 225, 227, 229-31, 234, 239
hospices
   attendance allowance/disability living
      allowance 145

hospital patients 254-7
  attendance allowance 145, 256
  child benefit 191, 257
  disability living allowance 145, 255-6
  disablement benefit 256
  guardian's allowance 257
  increases for dependants 206, 211, 256, 257
  invalid care allowance 160, 256
  invalidity benefit 255
  maternity allowance 256
  one parent benefit 257
  reduced earnings allowance 256
  retirement pensions 255
  severe disablement allowance 255
  sickness benefit 255
  widows' benefits 255
hospital treatment allowance 178, 256

ignorance of material fact 288-9, 292
imprisonment 257-8
  child benefit 191
  credits while on remand 257
  guardian's allowance 197, 198, 258
  increases for dependants 211, 257-8
  statutory maternity pay 91
  statutory sick pay 66-7
  see also: criminal proceedings
incapacity benefit 51-2, 86-7
incapacity for work 48-64
  day of incapacity 48, 252-3
  deemed incapacity 48
  – members of disability appeal tribunals 50
  disputes about incapacity 51-64
  – burden of proof 52
  – extent of incapacity 62
  – medical certificates/reports 57, 63
  – what work can be done 62-3
  – whether the work is reasonable 63
  future changes 86-7
  period of incapacity 48
  proving incapacity for work 48, 51
  review of capacity for work 51-64
  – appeal to social security appeal tribunal 61
  – benefit stopped immediately 60-61
  – Benefits Agency Medical Service examination 52, 53-6

  – certification 63
  – consideration of BAMS report by adjudication officer 56-61
  – credits and claiming other benefits while waiting for appeal 63-4
  – involving the GP 57-60
  – when review takes place 53
  therapeutic work 49, 49-50
  training for work 50-1
  working during period of incapacity 49-50
  see also: invalidity benefit, period of interruption of employment, sickness benefit, statutory sick pay
income support 3
  and other benefits
  – attendance allowance/disability living allowance 144
  – child benefit 195
  – disablement allowance 177
  – guardian's allowance 197
  – invalid care allowance 159, 279
  – invalidity benefit 78
  – maternity allowance 95
  – reduced earnings allowance 185
  – retirement allowance 186
  – retirement pension 116
  – severe disablement allowance 82
  – sickness benefit 74
  – statutory maternity pay 90
  – statutory sick pay 71
  – unemployment benefit 44-5
  – widows' benefits 103
increases for dependants 201-211
  absence abroad 247
  adults 201, 202
  – affected by occupational/personal pensions 32, 33, 209-10, 261
  – amount 202-3, 205
  – dependant looking after a child 203-5, 204-5
  – earnings rule 202, 204, 208-10
  – equal treatment rules 203, 204-5
  – husband 203
  – overlapping benefits 202, 204, 211, 260
  – residing with 206-7
  – trade disputes 210
  – wife 202-203

increases for dependants (*cont.*)
 children 201, 205-6
 – amount 206
 – claims 279
 – earnings rule 205, 210
 – entitlement 205-6
 – one parent benefit 196, 205,
 – overlapping benefit rules 205, 206,
  211, 261
 claims 280
 entitlement
 – contributing to maintenance 207-8
 – residing with 206-7
 hospital patients 206, 211, 256, 257
 imprisonment 211, 257-8
 tax 211
industrial accidents/diseases 129-30
 accidents 164-8
 – travelling to work 166-7
 causation 169-70
 diagnosis questions 285-6
 disablement questions 170-4
 – loss of faculty 171
 – percentage disablement 171-4
 – period of assessment 174-5
 entitlement to widows' benefits 97,
  108-9
 misconduct 168, 179
 onset 170
 personal injury 164
 Pneumoconiosis (Workers
  Compensation) Act 1979 335-6
 prescribed degrees of disablement
  171-4, 338-9
 prescribed industrial diseases 168-70,
  340-9
 recrudescence questions 170, 179,
  285-6
 retirement pension for widows 120-2
 widows' benefits 101
 see also: industrial injuries benefits
industrial death benefit 186-7, 259
 for children 199-200
 for widowers 187
 for widows 97, 108-9
industrial injuries benefits 163-87
 disablement benefit 175-9
 employees covered 175
 industrial death benefit 186-7

reduced earnings allowance 179-85
retirement allowance 186
time limits 280
see also: industrial accidents/diseases
ineligible period 32
interchange of claims 279-80
interim payments 294-5
interview 278
 unemployment benefit 12, 15-18
 – Restart interview 18-19
invalid care allowance 158-62
 abroad 246, 248
 amount 159
 claims and backdating 158-9, 279
 credits 159, 226-7
 earnings rule 160
 EC rules 248
 entitlement 158
 – full-time education 160-1
 – gainfully employed 160
 – regularly and substantially caring 160
 equal treatment rules 161-2, 271-2, 272
 holidays 160
 home responsibilities protection 159
 hospital stays 160, 256
 income support 159, 279
 increases for dependants 159, 201, 202,
  203, 204, 205, 206
 overlapping benefits 258
 people over pensionable age 161-2
 residence/presence conditions 242
 tax 159
invalid vehicles 133-4
invalidity benefit 76-81
 abroad 245-6
 additional pension from SERPS 77, 78
 amount
 – invalidity allowance 77-8
 – invalidity pension 77
 claims 279, 280, 281
 credits 77, 226-7
 disqualification 80
 entitlement 76-7
 equal treatment rules 78, 79, 272, 273
 future changes 86-7
 hospital patients 255
 imprisonment 257
 income support 78
 increases for dependants 77, 201

invalidity benefit (*cont.*)
  linking rule 78, 81, 254
  – for claiming unemployment benefit 9
  overlapping benefits 258, 259
  payment 79
  people over pensionable age 79, 83
  retirement pension 78, 79, 116, 117
  statutory maternity pay 90
  statutory sick pay 78-9
  tax 78
  widowers 80
  widows 79-80, 102-3, 107, 259
  see also: incapacity for work, period of
    interruption of employment
invalidity cut-off 51-64
  BAMS examination 52, 53-6
  BAMS report and decision by
    adjudication officer 56-61
  claiming income support 63
  signing on 13, 57, 63-4
Isle of Man 247

jobseekers allowance 45-6
judicial review 284, 286, 320, 321
jury service
  credits 227
just cause for leaving a job voluntarily
  37-8

kidney dialysis 143, 251

late appeals 294, 304, 308, 314, 315,
    317-18, 318-23
  anti-test-case rules 290, 319-21
  special reasons 318-23
late claims 278, 281-3
  Benefits Agency error 283
  child benefit 193-4
  good cause 281-3
  – incorrect advice 12, 282
  increases for dependants and
    occupational pensions 209-10
  made by appointee 86, 156, 282
  severe disablement allowance 85
  statutory sick pay 70
  time limits for claims 280-1
  unemployment benefit 12
  widows' benefits 103-4
late contributions 224-5

learning difficulties 132
leave to appeal
  from commissioners 317-18
  to commissioners 314-15
legal aid 330
lesbian couples
  increase for dependant looking after a
    child 204-5
linking rules 253-4
  breaking a claim for unemployment
    benefit 10, 10-11
  incapacity benefits 51, 56-7, 78, 81,
    82, 254
  period of incapacity 48
  statutory sick pay 68, 75
  see also: period of interruption of
    employment
local authority accommodation
  attendance allowance/disability living
    allowance 145-8
long-term benefits 5-6
loss of faculty 171

maintenance
  child benefit 192
  contributing to maintenance defined
    207-8
  guardian's allowance 196-7
  increase for child 207-8
married women
  deferring retirement pension 115
  reduced liability for contributions
    219-20, 221, 222, 230
  retirement pension 112, 119-20
maternity allowance 66, 92, 95-6, 279
  abroad 245-6
  contribution conditions 232-3
  credits 226-7
  hospital patients 256
  imprisonment 257
  increase of benefit for dependants 202
  overlapping benefits 258
  qualifying week 95
  time limit for claims 280
  see also: statutory maternity pay
maternity pay period 90-1
  credits 90, 228
  counting towards invalidity benefit 90
  exclusion from statutory sick pay 66

means-tested benefit 3
medical appeal tribunals 293, 308-11, 350
  decision and statement of reasons 310-11
  – correcting/setting aside a decision 311
  hearing procedure 309
  how to appeal 308
  – time limit for appeal 308
  references on behalf of Secretary of State 308-9
  tribunal membership 308
medical board 287, 292-3
medical certificates/reports 51, 63, 70, 74
  appeals/reviews of incapacity 57, 324
medical examinations
  Benefits Agency Medical Service 52, 53-6
  disqualification for failing to attend 54, 76
  statutory sick pay 70, 72
misconduct 33-7, 279
  appeals 35
  definition 34-5
  industrial accidents 168, 179
  period of disqualification 36-7
misrepresentation 296-7
  criminal proceedings 265-7
mistake
  as to a material fact 288-9, 292
  causing overpayment 299
mobility allowance 126, 152
motability 134
multiple births 94

national insurance contributions
  see: contributions
National Insurance Fund 4, 214
night work 27, 253
non-contributory benefits 4
non-contributory invalidity pension 82, 83, 85, 272
non-contributory retirement pension 112-13
non-contributory widows' benefits 97, 258
non-means-tested benefits 3
non-payment of contributions 224-5

normal idle day rule 26, 27-8
Northern Ireland 247
notice of appeal hearing 306, 315
notice, pay in lieu 31-2
nursing homes
  accommodation rules for attendance allowance/disability living allowance 145-8

occupational pensions 32-3
  contracting out of SERPS 220-1, 235-6
  guaranteed minimum pension 260
  increases for dependants 209-10, 261
  overlapping benefits 259-60
  treatment for unemployment benefit 32-3
occupational sick pay 64, 70
Ombudsman 301
one parent benefit 195-6, 197, 279
  hospital patients 257
  increase of benefit for dependant child 196, 205
  overlapping benefits 196, 261
  widowed mother's allowance 103
ordinarily resident 244-5
  see also: residence/presence conditions
overlapping benefit rules 5, 258-61
  additional pensions from SERPS 259, 259-60
  additions to benefits 259-60
  attendance allowance/disability living allowance 144, 260
  benefits for people with disabilities 260
  benefits for children 261
  child benefit 195, 261
  disablement benefit 260
  graduated retirement benefit 260
  guardian's allowance 197, 205, 261
  increases for dependants 202, 204, 205, 206, 211, 260, 261
  occupational pensions 259-60
  one parent benefit 196, 261
  personal benefits 258-9
  retirement benefit 258, 259, 260
  severe disablement allowance 258
  sickness benefit 74, 258
  statutory maternity pay 90
  unemployment benefit 45, 258
  widows' benefits 258, 259

overpayments 295-301
   amount to be recovered 299
   contributions 223
   criminal proceedings 300-301
   failure to disclose 297-8
   method of recovery 300
   misrepresentation 296-7
   overpayments before 6 April 1987
      299-30
   recovery at common law 298-9

parliamentary debates 328
part III accommodation
   attendance allowance/disability living
      allowance 146-8
part-time work
   unemployment benefit 25-30
   – normal employment pattern 28-9
patient
   see: hospital patient
payment in lieu of notice 31-2
payment of benefit 294-5
   child benefit 194
   deductions from benefit 265
   delays 301-2
   interim payments 294-5
   invalidity benefit 79
   maternity allowance 96
   method 294
   one parent benefit 196
   retirement pension 114
   sickness benefit 74
   statutory maternity pay 90-1
   statutory sick pay 71
   unemployment benefit 9-11
   widows' benefits 104
   see also: suspension of benefit
payments from previous employment
   effect on unemployment benefit 30-3
pensionable age 113, 239
   future changes 124
period of incapacity 48
   day of incapacity 252-3
   statutory sick pay 67-8
   see also: linking rules
period of interruption of employment 9,
   251-4
   breaking a claim for unemployment
      benefit 10, 10-11

   day of incapacity 252-3
   day of unemployment 252
   linking rules 253-4
   – for incapacity benefits 51, 56-7, 78,
      81, 82, 254
   – for unemployment benefit 9
   maternity allowance period 95
   night work 27, 253
   statutory sick pay 67-8, 71
   Sunday working 253
   waiting days for unemployment benefit
      9, 10
permitted period 13-14
personal injury
   recovery of benefit from compensation
      263-5
personal pensions 32-3, 221, 236
Pneumoconiosis 170, 174, 335-6
   see also: industrial diseases
point of law 313-14
polygamous marriages 98, 109-10
postal claims
   unemployment benefit 12
pregnancy
   credits 90, 228
   *see also: maternity allowance, statutory
      maternity pay*
premature birth 94
prescribed degrees of disablement 171-4,
   338-9
prescribed industrial diseases 168-70,
   340-9
presence tests
   see: residence/presence conditions
preserved rights 146
prison
   see: imprisonment
publicly funded accommodation
   attendance allowance/disability living
      allowance 145-8

qualifying day
   statutory sick pay 69
qualifying week
   maternity allowance 95
   statutory maternity pay 89

reasons for decision 313-14
   medical appeal tribunals 310-11

reciprocal agreements 241, 248, 250
recovery of overpayments
see: overpayments
recrudescence questions 170, 179, 285-6
reduced earnings allowance 5, 179-85
  absence abroad 247
  amount 184-5
  deferring retirement 182-3
  entitlement 180
  – continuing condition 181
  – employment of equivalent standard
   182
  – losing entitlement 182-3
  – permanent condition 180, 180-1
  – reduced earnings 180
  – regular occupation 181
  equal treatment rules 183
  giving up regular employment 182-3
  hospital patients 256
  imprisonment 257
  income support 185
  overlapping benefits 260
  tax 185
  withdrawal of reduced earnings
   allowance 185
**reduced liability for married women and
  widows** 219-20, 221, 222, 230
redundancy
  payments and unemployment benefit
   31-2
  voluntary 37
relevant day
  definition when taking steps to actively
   seek work 23
remarriage
  retirement pension 118-19, 122, 123
  widows' benefits 99, 105, 107, 109
residence/presence conditions 4, 240-1
  attendance allowance 242
  child benefit 194-5, 242-3
  contributions 217-19
  definitions
  – absent 244
  – ordinarily resident 244-5
  – present 244
  – resident 244-5
  disability living allowance 242
  EC rules 241, 245, 248-50
  guardian's allowance 243

  invalid care allowance 242
  retirement pension 242
  severe disablement allowance 241-2
  statutory sick pay 65
residential accommodation
  attendance allowance/disability living
   allowance 145-8
  child benefit 190, 191
residing together
  increases for dependants 206-7
  priority between child benefit claimants
   192, 193
  see also: cohabitation
respite care 148-9
Restart interview 18-19
retirement allowance 5, 186, 256, 257,
  260
retirement pensions 112-25
  absence abroad 246
  age addition 117, 120, 121, 122, 123,
   124
  annulment of marriage 117-19
  Category A pension (based on own
   contributions) 112, 116-19
  – amount 116-17
  – claims 117
  – divorced people 117-19
  – entitlement 116
  – widows/widowers 119
  Category B pension (married woman)
   112, 119-20
  Category B pension (widow) 120-2
  Category B pension (widower) 122-3
  Category C pension 112
  Category D pension 112, 123
  claims 113, 117, 122, 123
  – time limit 280
  contribution conditions 124, 233-4
  deferring pension 113, 114-15, 124
  – reduced earnings allowance 182-3
  – to keep invalidity benefit 78, 116
  de-retirement 116, 246
  divorce 117-19
  earnings rule 113
  equal treatment rules 113, 123
  future changes 124-5
  graduated retirement benefit 114-15,
   124
  hospital patients 255

retirement pensions (*cont.*)
  imprisonment 257
  income support 116
  increase of benefit for dependants
    201-3, 203, 204-5, 205, 206
  invalidity benefit 78, 79, 116, 117
  non-contributory retirement pension
    112-13
  overlapping benefits 258, 260
  – entitlement to more than one kind of
    pension 259
  payment 114
  pensionable age 113, 124, 239
  proving age 113-4
  reduced earnings allowance 182-3
  residence/presence conditions 242
  tax 116
  widowers 119, 122-3
  widows 99, 102, 107-8, 119, 120-2
reviews 288-94
  adjudication officer 288-91
  anti-test-case rules 290, 319
  arrears of benefit 290-1, 293
  attendance allowance/disability living
    allowance 154-6, 312
  choosing between an appeal or review
    293-4
  disablement benefit 179
  medical board 292-3
  Secretary of State 291
  suspension of benefit 295

Saturday working 17
school holidays 29-30
Secretary of State
  decisions 217, 286-7
  – appeals from 286-7
  references to medical appeal tribunal
    308-9
  review 291
self-certification 51, 70, 74
  see also: medical certificates/reports
self-employment
  actively seeking work 23
  availability for work 13
  contributions 218, 222, 223-4
  – self-employed earner 215
SERPS (additional pension) 6, 117, 235-8
  calculation 236-7

contracting out 220-1, 235-6
deferring retirement 114
future changes 125, 239
invalidity benefit 77, 78
overlapping benefits 259, 259-60
personal pensions 236
widows' benefits 103, 105, 106
service targets for decisions 283-4, 301-2
setting aside an appeal decision 307, 311
severe disablement allowance 81-6
  abroad 245-6
  amount 81-2
  calculating the 196 days 82-3
  claims 86, 280, 281
  disqualification 86
  entitlement 81
  – disablement assessed at 80 per cent 84
  – previous entitlement to non-
    contributory invalidity pension 82,
    83, 85, 272
  – under 20 when incapacity began 84
  equal treatment rules 83, 85, 272
  full-time education 83
  hospital patients 255
  imprisonment 257
  income support 82
  increase of benefit for dependants 201, 202
  overlapping benefits 258
  people over pensionable age 83
  residence/presence conditions 241-2
  tax 82
  unforeseen aggravation 292
  see also: incapacity for work, period of
    interruption of employment
share fishermen 222-3
sheltered employment for the disabled 336
short-term benefits 5-6
short-term contracts
  excluded from statutory sick pay 66
short-time working 25, 29
sickness benefit 47, 73-6
  abroad 245-6
  amount of payment 73-4
  – for people over pensionable age 74
  claims 74-5
  – time limit 280, 281
  contribution conditions 226-7, 227-8,
    231-2
  credits 74, 226-7

sickness benefit (*cont.*)
  disqualification 76
  employees 74-5
  entitlement 73
  equal treatment rules 75
  future changes 86-7
  hospital patients 255
  imprisonment 257
  income support 74
  increases for dependants 73-4, 74, 201,
    202
  linking rule for claiming unemployment
    benefit 9
  maternity benefits 92
  overlap with other benefits 74, 258
  payment 74
  people over pensionable age 74, 75, 83
  statutory sick pay 71, 74-5, 75
  tax 74
  *see also: incapacity for work, period of
    interruption of employment*
signing on 11, 12
  after a holiday 20
  protecting a contribution record 226
  refusal of incapacity benefits 13, 57,
    63-4
social security appeal tribunals 291,
    303-5, 350
  attending the hearing 306
  cases referred by the adjudication
    officer 305
  decisions 307
  hearing procedure 305-6
  how to appeal 304-5
  – time limit for appeals 304
  membership and administration 303-4
social security commissioners 313-18,
    351
  appeals from commissioners 317-18
  decision 317
  forfeiture cases 315
  hearing 316-17
  how to appeal 314-15
  – time limit for appeal 314, 315
  point of law 313-14
  procedure 315
special hardship allowance 177
special reasons for late appeal 318-23
starting credits 227

state earnings related pension scheme
  see: SERPS
statutory maternity pay 88-94
  abroad 91
  amount 89
  appeals 93
  continuous employment rule 93-4
  contributions 89-90
  disputes 93
  earnings condition 93
  employee defined 91-2
  employer 91
  – attempts to avoid liability 91
  – changing employer 91, 92
  – more than one employer 89
  – notification to employer 92
  – refuses to pay 93
  – restrictions imposed by employer 91
  entitlement 88-9
  imprisonment 91
  invalidity benefit 90
  means-tested benefits 90
  multiple births 94
  overlap with other benefits 90
  payment 90-1
  period of entitlement 90-1
  premature births 94
  qualifying week 89
  returning to work 89, 91
  sickness benefit 92
  stillbirths 94
  tax 89-90
  trade disputes 93-4
  written statement of entitlement 93
  see also: maternity allowance
statutory sick pay 47, 64-73
  abroad 67, 68
  amount 70-1
  appeals 72
  claiming other benefits 71
  contributions 70, 71
  credits 70, 226
  disputes 72-3
  during maternity allowance period 95
  employer
  – attempts to avoid liability 72
  – more than one employer 71
  – non-payment by employer 72, 73
  – notification of sickness 69-70

statutory sick pay (*cont.*)
  entitlement 65-7
  equal treatment rules 65
  imprisonment 66-7
  income support 71
  invalidity benefit 78-9
  late claims 70
  linking rules 68, 75
  maximum entitlement 71
  medical examinations 70, 72
  occupational sick pay 64, 70
  payment 71
  people over pensionable age 65
  period of entitlement 68
  period of incapacity 67-8
  pregnancy 66, 95
  qualifying day 69
  residence/presence test for employers 65
  short-term contracts 66
  sickness benefit 71, 74-5, 75
  tax 71
  time limit for referrals to adjudication officer/Secretary of State 73
  trade disputes 67
  waiting days 71
  written statement of entitlement 72
  see also: incapacity for work
stillbirths 94
strikes
  see: trade disputes
striking out an appeal 316
students
  credits 227-8
  invalid care allowance 160
  unemployment benefit 44
  see also: education
Sunday working 27, 28, 253
supervision condition 137, 141-2, 143
suspension of benefit
  during appeal/review 295
  industrial death benefit for widows 109
  remand prisoners 257
  unemployment benefit 24-5, 36
  widowed mother's allowance 105, 121
  widow's pension 107, 121

tax
  attendance allowance/disability living allowance 144

child benefit 195
disablement benefit 177
guardian's allowance 197
increases for dependants 211
invalid care allowance 159
invalidity benefit 78
maternity allowance 95
one parent benefit 196
reduced earnings allowance 185
retirement allowance 186
retirement pension 116
severe disablement allowance 82
sickness benefit 74
statutory maternity pay 89-90
statutory sick pay 71
unemployment benefit 45
widows' benefits 102
terminal illness
  attendance allowance/disability living allowance 143, 151
  deferring retirement pension 115
  residence/presence conditions 242
therapeutic work 49, 49-50
time limit
  appeals 304, 308, 314, 315
  - from commissioners 317-18
  claims 280-1
  - late claims 278, 281-3
  decisions 283-4
  referral of statutory sick pay disputes 73
  see also: late appeals
trade disputes
  disqualification from unemployment benefit 41-2
  increases for dependants 210
  statutory maternity pay 93-4
  statutory sick pay 67
training
  allowance reducing personal benefits 258
  credits 227-8
  failure to take up training place 39-41
  incapacity for work 50-1
  leaving training voluntarily 37-9
  schemes for the disabled 336
  treated as actively seeking work 22-3
travel
  expenses
  - to attend interview 278

travel *(cont.)*
- to attend tribunal 306
restricting availability for work 17
trial period 39
linking rules for incapacity benefits 51, 56-7, 78, 82, 254

unemployability supplement 178, 226-7, 259
unemployment benefit 8-46
actively seeking work 8, 20-5
amount 9
availability for work 8, 13-20
- capable of work 13
- checking availability for work 15-19
- part-time work 25-6
- permitted period 13-14
- restricting availability for work 13-14, 16-17
- self-employment 13
- treated as available for work 13, 14-15
breaking a claim 10, 10-11
claims 11-12
- following refusal of incapacity benefits 13, 57, 63-4
- time limit 280, 281
- treated as claim for incapacity benefits 279
compensation
- loss of job/in lieu of notice 31-2
- unfair dismissal 30-1
contribution conditions 8, 226-7, 227-8, 231-2
credits 45, 226-7
delaying a claim 12, 254
disqualification from benefit 18, 33-42
- failing to attend Restart interview 18, 33
- failure to take up job/training 39-41
- leaving job/training voluntarily 37-9
- misconduct 33-7, 179
- trade disputes 41-2
duration of payment 9-11
earnings rules 26
- £2 rule 26-7
EC rules 249-50
entitlement 8
equal treatment rules 43

full extent normal rule 26, 27, 28-29
holidays while claiming 19-20
- compulsory holidays 25, 29-30
income support 44-5
increases of benefit for dependants 201, 202
ineligible period 32
normal idle day rule 26, 27-8
occupational pensions 32-3
overlapping benefits 45, 258
part-time work 25-30
- normal employment pattern 28-9
payment 9-11
payments from previous employment 30-3
people over pensionable age 43-4
period of interruption of employment 8, 251-4
- breaking a claim 10, 10-11
- linking rule 9
permitted period 13-14
personal pension 32-3
proposed changes 45-6
requalifying for benefit 10
Restart interview 18-19
short-time working 25, 29
signing on 11, 12
students 44
tax 45
waiting days 9, 10
unfair dismissal 30-1
unforeseen aggravation 179, 292, 293

vaccine damage payments 335
voluntarily leaving employment 37-9
voluntary contributions 215, 218, 223, 225, 235
voluntary redundancy 37
voluntary work 15, 49
availability for work 15
contributions for volunteer development workers 218, 222-3

wages
see: earnings
waiting days
statutory sick pay 71
unemployment benefit 9, 10
see also: linking rule
war pensions 259, 331-4

week
definition
– actively seeking work 23-4
– normal idle day rule 28
– statutory maternity pay 89
widowed mother's allowance 97, 105-6
contribution conditions 233
increases for dependant children 201,
205, 206
one parent benefit 103
overlapping benefits 258, 259
see also: widows' benefits
widowers
deferred retirement pension 114
graduated retirement benefit 124
invalidity benefit 80
retirement pension 119, 122-3
widows
contribution conditions for benefits
231-2
credits 102, 228
deferring retirement pension 114
graduated retirement benefit 124
invalidity benefit 79-80, 259
reduced liability for contributions for
widows 219-20
retirement pension 99, 102, 107-8,
119, 120-2
widows' benefits 5, 97-111
absence abroad 246
additional pension 103, 105, 106
claims and backdating 103-4, 280,
281
– treated as claim for retirement
pension 279
cohabitation 98, 99-101, 104, 105,
107, 109
credited contributions 102, 228
definition of widow 98
disqualification 99-100, 104, 105, 107,
109

divorce 98
earnings 102
entitlement where industrial
accident/disease 97, 108-9
forfeiture rule 102, 315
hospital patients 255
imprisonment 257
income support 103
invalid marriages 110-11
invalidity benefit 79-80, 102-3, 107,
259
losing contact with husband 98-9
non-contributory widows' benefits 97,
258
overlapping benefits 258, 259
payment 104
polygamous marriages 98, 109-10
presumption of death 98-9, 103, 104
remarriage 99, 105, 107, 109
retirement pension 99, 102, 107-8,
119, 120-2
tax 102
see also: industrial death benefit,
widowed mother's allowance,
widow's payment, widow's pension
widow's payment 97, 104
absence abroad 246
contribution conditions 233
treatment as capital 103
see also: widows' benefits
widow's pension 97, 105, 106-8
absence abroad 246
additional pension 106
amount of benefit 106-7
contribution conditions 233-4
overlapping benefits 258, 259
retirement pension 107-8
see also: widows' benefits
work
see: employment
working life 233-4, 239

NATIONAL WELFARE BENEFITS HANDBOOK, 1994/95 edition

In April 1994 the benefit rates and regulations change again. The new Handbook is therefore completely revised and updated, telling you all you need to know about means-tested benefits and how to claim them. There is comprehensive coverage of **income support, housing benefit, the social fund, family credit, council tax benefit and disability working allowance,** and of the major changes affecting benefits this year. Coverage of the impact of **community care** and **child support** arrangements on benefits is revised and expanded in the light of the first year's practical experience of both schemes in operation. There are new tactical suggestions on how to deal with these and other issues, and practical information on benefits if you are unemployed, health and education benefits, and appeals.

£7.95 (£2.65 for individual benefit claimants — direct from CPAG)

RIGHTS GUIDE TO NON-MEANS-TESTED BENEFITS, 1994/95 edition

Fully revised and updated, this essential companion to the Handbook includes: unemployment benefit; expanded coverage of disputes about incapacity for work; revised information on disability benefits including disability living allowance; industrial injuries and diseases; statutory sick pay and statutory maternity pay; pensions and benefits for widows; the contributions system. The Rights Guide, the benefits Handbook and the Child Support Handbook are all fully indexed and cross-referenced to law, regulations and — where relevant — Commissioners' decisions.

£6.95 (£2.45 for individual benefit claimants — direct from CPAG)

CHILD SUPPORT HANDBOOK, 1994/95 edition

Already established as the most widely used guide to all aspects of the child support scheme, the 2nd edition is indispensable as it incorporates all that has been learnt from the first year of operation. All changes to the scheme are included (eg the February 1994 amendments) along with tactical suggestions based on practical experience. It gives full details on: who is affected and how to apply for maintenance; the powers of the Child Support Agency; the requirement to co-operate, exemptions and the benefit penalty; the formula for calculating maintenance; collection, enforcement and benefit deductions; shared care, second families, competing applications etc. All practical examples are updated to reflect recent changes to the formula. **Parents, welfare rights and legal advisers and social workers are amongst those who will have to use this new edition to get reliable and up-to-date information on the scheme.**

£6.95 (£2.45 for individual benefit claimants — direct from CPAG)

ALL THREE CPAG HANDBOOKS ARE AVAILABLE FROM APRIL — PLACE YOUR ORDER NOW AS COPIES ARE SENT ON A FIRST COME, FIRST SERVED BASIS.

Also, the CPAG/NACAB **Benefits Poster 1994/95** (A2 size, £2.50) gives you benefit rates at a glance.

Please send me:

_____ **National Welfare Benefits Handbook** @ £7.95 each   £ _____

_____ **Rights Guide to N.M.T. Benefits** @ £6.95 each   £ _____

_____ **Child Support Handbook** @ £6.95 each   £ _____

_____ Benefits Poster @ £2.50 each   £ _____

PRICES INCLUDE POSTAGE AND PACKING

I enclose a cheque/PO, payable to **CPAG Ltd** for —   Total: £ _____

Name _____

Address _____

_____

_____ Postcode _____

Return this form with your payment to CPAG Ltd, 1-5 Bath Street, London EC1V 9PY

Welfare Rights Bulletin

The *Bulletin* is essential reading for welfare rights advisers, lawyers and anyone else needing to keep up to date with social security issues. One of its unique roles is to provide a bi-monthly update to the National Welfare Benefits Handbook and Rights Guide, as well as to CPAG's Child Support Handbook and Ethnic Minorities' Benefits Handbook.

In 1994 the *Bulletin* expands in size — consolidating its position as the journal with the most detailed and comprehensive coverage of social security developments available.

Contents will include the fullest coverage of:
- the new incapacity benefit and job seekers allowance
- new regulations, guidance and procedure, with comment, analysis and practical advice
- Social Security Commissioners' decisions — these will appear sooner and in greater quantity than before
- Court decisions, including appeals to the European Court
- reports on benefit law and service delivery issues, eg National Audit Office, Parliamentary and advisory committees, ombudsmen
- news from welfare rights workers — campaigns, issues and tactics

There will also be expanded coverage of such issues as housing benefit, benefits for people with disabilities, people from abroad.

Like the **CPAG** benefit guides, the *Welfare Rights Bulletin* is the best value in the field — and compulsory reading for any adviser needing the very latest benefits information.

ISSN 0263 2098

£15.00 for a full year's subscription (6 issues)

Sent automatically to CPAG Rights and Comprehensive members, and Bulletin subscribers.